Fleeing Vesuvius

In memory of
Anne Behan 1959–2004
David O'Kelly 1946–2004
and
Will Howard 1951–2008

FLEEING VESUVIUS

OVERCOMING THE RISKS OF ECONOMIC AND ENVIRONMENTAL COLLAPSE

Edited by Richard Douthwaite *and* Gillian Fallon
Foreword by **RICHARD HEINBERG**

NEW SOCIETY PUBLISHERS

Cover design by Diane McIntosh.

Printed in Canada. First printing March 2011.

ISBN 978-0-86571-699-5   e ISBN 978-1-55092-476-3

Inquiries regarding requests to reprint all or part of *Fleeing Vesuvius*
should be addressed to New Society Publishers at the address below.

To order directly from the publishers, please call toll-free (North America)
1-800-567-6772, or order online at www.newsociety.com

Any other inquiries can be directed by mail to:
New Society Publishers
P.O. Box 189, Gabriola Island, BC V0R 1X0, Canada
(250) 247-9737

New Society Publishers' mission is to publish books that contribute in fundamental ways
to building an ecologically sustainable and just society, and to do so with the least possible
impact on the environment, in a manner that models this vision. We are committed
to doing this not just through education, but through action. Our printed, bound books
are printed on Forest Stewardship Council-certified acid-free paper that is **100% post-
consumer recycled** (100% old growth forest-free), processed chlorine free, and printed
with vegetable-based, low-VOC inks, with covers produced using FSC-certified stock. New
Society also works to reduce its carbon footprint, and purchases carbon offsets based on an
annual audit to ensure a carbon neutral footprint. For further information, or to browse
our full list of books and purchase securely, visit our website at: www.newsociety.com

Library and Archives Canada Cataloguing in Publication

Fleeing Vesuvius : overcoming the risks of economic and environmental collapse /
edited by Richard Douthwaite and Gillian Fallon ; foreword by Richard Heinberg.

Includes bibliographical references and index.

ISBN 978-0-86571-699-5

1. Sustainable development.   2. Sustainable living—Economic aspects.
I. Douthwaite, Richard   II. Fallon, Gillian

HC79.E5F64 2011   338.9'27   C2011-900096-2

NEW SOCIETY PUBLISHERS
www.newsociety.com

MIX
Paper from
responsible sources
FSC
www.fsc.org   FSC™ C016245

Contents

Part I: Energy Availability

Part II: Innovation in Business, Money and Finance

Part III: New Ways of Using the Land

Rather than bringing similar activities closer together to reap the benefits of scale and agglomeration, different activities should be situated beside each other to be more energy and carbon efficient.

Very few soils have a perfect balance of minerals. If the option of filling one's plate from all over the world disappears, human health will likely decline unless the missing minerals are applied to the soil while it is still possible to do so.

Ireland needs to implement new policies in order to get its land to absorb CO_2 rather than release it. Biochar could reduce nitrous oxide and methane emissions and build up the fertility and carbon content of the soil.

Part IV: Dealing with Climate Change

Any framework for dealing with the climate crisis should distribute the global carbon budget among the world's nations according to a transparent, equitable formula. To achieve this, global climate institutions will have to change.

Cap and Share is a fair, effective, cheap, empowering and simple way to reduce emissions from the burning of fossil fuels. It could form the basis of a wider global climate framework but how realistic is it to call for its introduction?

Decision-making at a global level is governed by a number of non-economic factors which need to be taken into account if the new systems required to deal effectively with climate change are to be introduced.

Part V: Changing the Way we Live

Now that the financial and political components of the present system have largely discredited themselves, a fluid situation exists that might allow more viable options to emerge.

We need to make an evolutionary leap in the way we do things if we are to make a controlled, planned transition to a post-industrial, low-carbon society. The Transition Towns movement provides a potential model.

Part VI: Changing the Way We Think

Part VII: Ideas for Action

Foreword

Richard Heinberg

"What a goldmine!" That was my first reaction upon digging into the contents of this book. Others might have said something more along the lines of, "Oh my God! I had no idea our predicament was this terrible! What a pit we are in!" My rather gleeful response was due to the fact that I happen to be in the midst of researching and writing a book exploring the evident fact that resource depletion, debt overhang, and climate change have brought about the end of world economic growth (as currently defined). When I drilled into *Fleeing Vesuvius,* I encountered a rich vein of thought very much attuned with my own, one that includes stimulating ideas and examples that were new and helpful to me.

While other readers may come to this book with backgrounds different from mine, I think they will nevertheless find just as much stimulation and help as I did.

The authors have applied themselves to an analysis of the most important and fateful economic transition in human history. They are among the People who are Paying Attention (PPA)—an almost completely unorganized demographic consisting of individuals who have the privilege to devote a substantial amount of time to following world political, economic, and environmental news, but who are not blinded by any fixed religious or political ideology. PPA probably number globally no more than a few million, and (if I may speak for them) have generally come to the conclusion that the world is facing a triple crisis:

1. The *depletion* of important resources including fossil fuels and minerals;
2. The proliferation of *environmental impacts, principally climate change* arising from both the extraction and use of resources (including the burning of fossil fuels) — leading to snowballing costs from both these impacts themselves and from efforts to avert them; and
3. *Financial disruptions* due to the inability of our existing monetary, banking, and investment systems to adjust to both resource scarcity and soaring environmental costs — and their inability (in the context of a shrinking economy) to service the enormous piles of government and private debt that have been generated over the past couple of decades.

While these three crises are converging on us, our leaders remain obsessed with one thing, and one thing only: the maintenance of economic expansion. For a variety of reasons, growth has become essential to the political well-being of modern societies. Yet our fixation on economic growth prevents our addressing any of the three crises: Governments refuse to curtail greenhouse gas emissions (and thus fossil fuel consumption) because doing so would reduce growth. They refuse to reduce their vulnerability to oil supply shocks because that would require them to proactively rein in oil use, thus threatening growth. And they refuse to explore fundamental changes to financial and monetary systems that would make their economies less susceptible to bubbles and crashes because…well, you can finish the sentence.

On the other hand, however, each of these three crises is threatening the continuation of growth. And not just threatening it; I for one would argue that, combined, they have effectively killed off growth once and for all: while we have seen some relative growth since 2008 (some months have seen increased economic activity as compared to others and some nations are still expanding as others swoon), over all the global economy is stalled and headed into a tailspin.

We can't address the problems that threaten economic growth because to do so would threaten economic growth.

A metaphor comes to mind: the spider monkey trap allegedly developed by tribes in South America, consisting of a staked container with a hole cut into it just wide enough for a monkey to insert its empty hand. The container is baited with banana or nuts. Monkey reaches for bait but cannot pull its fist through the hole while clutching its prize. Monkey is not smart enough to let go of bait and is thereby captured. Substitute "economic growth" for "bait" and "economic-environmental collapse" for "capture" and you have a fair picture of our human dilemma circa 2011.

The bitter irony is that we can't maintain continuous economic growth on a finite planet in any case. Resources are limited, and substitution and efficiency (economists' magic genies invoked to explain away the inevitable problems of depletion and pollution) are subject to the law of diminishing returns. But that hasn't stopped us from wishing for perpetual growth, believing in it, and trying to achieve it. Indeed, we are endeavoring to do the impossible so valiantly and single-mindedly that we are willing to wreck the only planet we have in the process. To hell with future generations! We must increase our GDP today!

To be fair, politicians are just attempting to do what the majority of their constituents demand that they do — produce more jobs and higher returns on investments. And this means growing the economy. The cognitive dissonance is unbearable: we *must* do something that is actually impossible to do. And so most of us simply give up and go quietly insane, or just stop paying attention.

The People Paying Attention are among the minority who eschew insanity as either a defense or a strategy.

Those among the PPA who happen to be writers or activists of one sort or another have been trying to explain all of this to policy makers for many years, mostly to no avail (one politician who does understand the dilemma is Eamon Ryan, the Irish MP who is a contributor to this book).

Sadly, efforts to address the triple crisis have been put off so long that today an easy escape from the monkey trap is no longer possible. (Warning: abrupt metaphor change immediately ahead!) The tectonic pressure is building and something has to give way. We have set ourselves up for an economic-environmental "correction" that will almost certainly be geological in scope and intensity. We could liken it to an earthquake or volcano of such force that it will likely destroy many of the basic structures of civilization on which we have come to depend.

This book is therefore something of a last warning. It outlines the triple crisis as clearly as can be done. Even more valuably, it points out things we still can do to help our society make the inevitable transition away from a fossil fuel-based, debt-based economy in such a way as to avert the worst of the impacts otherwise in store. And it suggests how to prepare ourselves for whatever seismic events are now unavoidable.

The editors are to be congratulated for assembling essays from contributors who are at the very forefront of efforts to understand and respond to the triple crisis. That's what makes this a goldmine. But (to burden a short Foreword with yet another metaphor) it is also an essential roadmap — an overview of the routes we can take to escape an eruption that has already begun.

Dig in to this goldmine. Refuse insanity or denial. Escape our monkey trap by letting go of the impossible dream of endlessly growing consumption. Follow the map; flee the volcano. And join with others who are paying attention: let's save as much of humanity and the natural world as we can.

— Richard Heinberg
Senior Fellow, Post Carbon Institute

Introduction: Where We Went Wrong

RICHARD DOUTHWAITE

This book grew out of a conference in 2009 called the "New Emergency." What emergency was that? Most people didn't think that there was an emergency then and they don't think there is one now. They know that the world is facing a lot of problems at present but they probably would not elevate any of them even to the status of a crisis, still less an emergency. The world has always had problems, they think, and it always will. Very few of them think that there's anything going on at present that requires Ireland to mobilize all its resources in the way that it did in response to the Old Emergency, the Second World War.

However, once you recognize that most of the worst problems the world faces have a common cause and that time is running out to solve them, you have an emergency. That's my position. I believe that the "development" path that the world has followed for the past three centuries has led to a dead end and that immediate action is required if humanity is to have any chance of getting on to a more sustainable path. Every day lost makes a satisfactory future less likely for billions of people, both born and yet-to-be-born, because our options are trickling away with our lifeblood, natural resources.

That's the emergency. We need to apply a tourniquet immediately to give us time to take more drastic action. But who is conscious of this? How many people really grasp the severity of the climate crisis? Or the fact that the production of conventional oil has almost certainly peaked and the amount of energy that is going to be available for the world to use is going to shrink rapidly? Or that energy and water shortages are going to curtail the world's food supply? What proportion of the general public is really worried about the rate at which species are being lost?

True, everyone knows that several countries have problems with debts or with their banking systems (or, like Ireland, with both), and that they, or people they know, are losing their jobs because of them, but they might not elevate these problems to the status of a crisis unless they live in Greece. They think that, in Ireland's case, these financial problems began when the housing bubble burst and that the burst was somehow linked to the credit crunch that began when worthless securities generated by the sub-prime mortgage fiasco in the US triggered what was, for a time, an international banking crisis. There's been almost no recognition that resource depletion was the underlying cause of that international banking crisis and there probably won't be for as long as the conventional wisdom is that the world economy is looking up and the crisis itself has come to an end.

Even at its height, the financial crisis was only an emergency for those responsible for handling it. A country faces an emergency if an enemy is mobilizing on its border to invade, or if its people are dying in thousands from a plague. A family faces an emergency if its house is on fire or if one of its members has been hit by a car and needs to be rushed to hospital. An emergency is a period in which everything else is ignored in favor of immediate action.

From time to time, the chronic problems that face the world erupt and cause a minor emergency such as that on the evening in September 2008 when the Irish banks told the government they might be unable to open the following day. When something like that happens, people stay up late, the eruption is dealt with and then life goes on until the next eruption occurs. Few of us think that anything radical has to be done. We assure each other that minor tinkering, like holding an inquiry, beefing up the regulatory system and limiting bankers' bonuses, will be enough to allow us to carry on living pretty much as we do now for the foreseeable future.

We are ignoring these eruptions in the way the inhabitants of Pompeii ignored the earthquakes which preceded the volcanic blast that destroyed them in 79 AD and which had been doing considerable damage for at least the previous sixteen years. Some of the earthquake-damaged houses were actually under repair at the time Vesuvius erupted, with piles of plaster and tools lying where the workers had left them. Rather than moving out, the Pompeiians wanted to carry on with life as usual. They had every reason to do so. The whole Bay of Naples area was booming and the holiday villas of the rich provided a lot of work. Interestingly, those who dropped everything and fled immediately when ash and pumice started raining down probably survived. However, many thought their best chance was to take shelter. They died when the avalanche of hot ash, pumice, rock fragments and volcanic gas began.

The common cause of all our crises today is our use of fossil fuel. Just as addictive drugs alter the metabolism of the human body in ways that create dependency and make it difficult to give them up, fossil fuels have profoundly altered the metabolism of economies and societies. As a result, the systems of production and distribution we have now, and the types of relationship we have with other people, including those within our own families, will be changed out of all recognition as the energy drug is withdrawn. The withdrawal period will be particularly painful in countries that fail to ensure that they have a decent supply of renewable energy methadone available to them. Cold turkey will mean that many people die. Thinking of Pompeii, if we leave it too late before we rush toward a new type of civilization, we will have to leave behind all our hi-tech, high-energy tools, and we may not survive without them.

Here are some of the ways in which fossil energy use has perverted our economies and our lives.

1. It has transformed manufacturing methods by displacing human labor.
2. It has transformed agricultural methods, replacing human labor, animal power and sunlight.
3. It has enabled the world population to grow to a level that may well be unsupportable without its use.
4. It has devalued human labor and led to widespread unemployment.
5. It has made the economy reliant on economic growth to avoid collapse.
6. It has enabled extremes of wealth and poverty to develop.
7. It has led to the development of industrial capitalism.
8. It has produced profits that had to be recycled. This led to the growth of the banking system and debt-based money.
9. By fueling powered transport, it has destroyed self-reliant local economies and the nature of local relationships.

Once fossil energy began to be used, these perversions were inevitable. About seven years ago, I wrote the concluding essay for *Before the Wells Run Dry*, a book about future energy supplies which emerged from a previous Feasta conference called Ireland's Transition to Renewable Energy. That conference was the forerunner for a lot of the thinking in Feasta that laid the foundations for the New Emergency event so I'm going to draw rather liberally on what I wrote in 2003. The essay asked where humanity had gone wrong. When did we take a path which, because "one path leads to another" in Robert Frost's phrase, inexorably led us to becoming totally dependent on a grotesquely unsustainable energy system?

I argued that the wrong turn was taken in England in the 16th Century as the population began to recover from the Black Death. The increased numbers — a rise from 1.6 million to 5.5 million in less than 200 years — naturally put greater pressure on resources and caused communities to have problems living within the limits imposed by their local environments. In 1631, Edmund Howes described how this had forced them to start to burn coal:

> Within man's memory it was held impossible to have any want of wood in England. But...such hath been the great expence of timber of navigation, with infinite increase of building houses, with great expence of wood for household furniture, casks and other vessels not to be numbered, and of carts, wagons and coaches, besides the extreme waste of wood in making iron, burning of bricks and tiles, that at this present, through the great consuming of wood as aforesaid, and the neglect of planting of woods, there is so great scarcity of wood throughout the whole kingdom that not only the City of London, all haven towns and in very many parts within the land, the inhabitants in general are constrained to make their fires of sea-coal or pit coal, even in the chambers of honourable personages and through necessity which is the mother of all arts, they have in late years devised the making of iron the making of all sorts of glass and the burning of bricks with sea-coal and pit-coal.[1]

That was it. The thin end of the wedge. The slippery slope. For the first time, humanity was starting to depend on a nonrenewable, and hence unsustainable, energy source for its comfort and livelihood. It was understandable that it did. Which of us would have worried about the long-term consequences of burning black stones collected from beaches in Northumberland, or which had been dug out of shallow holes in the ground?

I then pointed out that as the demand for coal increased, the easiest, shallowest mines were soon exhausted, and deeper and deeper pits had to be dug. This posed enormous problems since a shaft floods if it is sunk below the water table and a pump has to be installed to keep things reasonably dry.

The early pumps consisted of rags or buckets on continuous chains which were turned by horses or, if a stream was handy, a water wheel. However, the deeper a shaft went, the longer the chain had to be and the more friction the horse or the wheel had to overcome. As this placed a real limit on how deep a mine could go, mine-owners were keen to find other ways of powering their pumps. Around the time Edmund Howes was writing, coal-fired steam power began to be used for the first time for pumping water out of mines. In a somewhat incestuous way, coal energy was being used for mining coal.

The Transformation of Manufacturing Methods

The first steam engines just moved a piston back and forth, which was all that was required to work a cylinder-type pump. It was only during the following century that the piston was attached to a crank to turn a revolving shaft, an innovation in response to a demand for rotary power from cotton mills unable to find additional sites for their waterwheels. This was the type of engine, of course, that powered the industrial revolution and, in my view, led with an alarming inevitability to the problems we have today. It was steam power, in fact, which made the widespread use of machines possible and then, for competitive reasons, absolutely necessary.

The essence of industrialization is that it produces lower-cost goods by using capital equipment and external energy to replace the skilled, and thus relatively expensive, labor used in handcrafts. Since less labor is used per unit of output, unemployment develops unless sales expand. The mechanization of sock and lace production in the English midlands led to such widespread job losses that riots broke out in 1811 and 1812. Troops were sent to the area to stop the Luddites, as the bands of destitute working men were called, from breaking into the new factories and destroying the machines. Indeed, had the Napoleonic War not ended in 1815 allowing the factories to increase their sales in Europe and elsewhere, the disturbances might have become serious enough to kill off the industrial revolution. Without wider markets, firms using powered machinery would have either consumed themselves in a competitive frenzy, or seen their technologies banned as a result of popular unrest.

Eventually, however, British exports put most continental craft producers out of business and left the remainder with no alternative but to adopt more fossil energy-intensive methods too. A sales pyramid developed. The early participants in a sales pyramid get rich because they receive commission on the goods they sell to people whom they have persuaded to become dealers too; dealers who, in turn, can earn a commission from others they induce to join the pyramid as dealers later on, who themselves recruit and stock further dealers. And so it goes on, setting up a situation in which everyone in the pyramid can only fulfil their income aspirations if the pyramid does the impossible and expands indefinitely, eventually involving infinitely more people than there are in the world.

The fossil fuel-based production system became dominant by expanding on exactly the same lines. Just as British factories had needed to take over the markets previously served by craft-scale manufacturers in Europe to survive, industrial Europe had to oust artisanal producers elsewhere in the world, and the British sold them the machinery to do so.

Tariff barriers were maintained to allow the new continental industries to build themselves up until they could not only compete with their British rivals but had acquired export markets in which to sell themselves. It was the need for exclusive external markets to solve the problem of mass unemployment at home that led the European powers to scramble to assemble competing empires and eventually to confront each other in the First World War.

As each successive group of countries was forced to adopt mechanized production methods themselves in the hope of escaping poverty, so those who had mechanized earlier sold them the equipment. The pyramid this created grew and grew until it reached the point some years ago when there were no more markets supplied by craft producers to take over. This left firms in the pyramid with no–one to displace but each other, and since then, international competition has become so intense that only certain specialized types of manufacturing such as armaments, aerospace and pharmaceuticals thrive in high-wage countries, arguably because of the subsidies they receive through government contracts or patent protection.

How the Economy Came to Rely on Economic Growth to Avoid Collapse

The use of fossil energy not only displaced sustainable manufacturing methods, it also made the economy dependent on economic growth. In a stable, stationary economy, there is no net investment and no net saving. Everything produced in the course of a year either gets consumed or goes to replace things that have worn out. The return on capital is so low — somewhere between 2 and 3% — that it's only just worth using part of the sales income to maintain the buildings and equipment rather than the business owners spending it on themselves. In other words, the average rate of profit is just enough to balance the society's desire for income now against its desire for income in the future.

Suppose a new technology — steam power, perhaps — is introduced to this stable economy which enables much higher profits to be made in a particular business sector. The firms in the sector will race to adopt it because those that get it first will be able to cut prices a little and drive the laggards out of business. The would-be leaders won't be content to wait until they have saved up enough of the money they would normally have spent on maintaining the old equipment until they can afford the new type. No, they will want to borrow the money they need to get ahead. But where is the money they wish to borrow to come from, since their society has no net savings and no spare resources? The answer is that the money and resources can only come from those that would have been spent on maintaining capital equipment in other sectors. The output from the other sectors will therefore shrink, shortages will develop and prices will rise, putting up the return on the remaining capital until it reaches the rate that the sector with the new technology is able to offer.

The arrival of a new technology in one sector therefore increases the rate of return on capital in all sectors. Profits in excess of those needed to maintain production appear for the first time and workers get a reduced share of the amount the society produces. Moreover, the profits belong to the business owners. This creates a capitalist class with potential investment power. I say potential because what happens next depends on whether other innovations follow the first. If they don't, once the investment needs of the new technology are met, prices will fall and profits drop to the level set by people's time preference, the 2 or 3%. If, on the other hand, there is a stream of innovations, profits could grow to become a substantial part of national income.

This creates the problem noted by Major C. H. Douglas, the founder of the Social Credit movement, who realized that the wages paid to workers could not buy everything that they had produced and that if there was to be full employment, the profits firms produced had to be spent back into the system. It doesn't matter how it is spent, but people whose lifestyle is already satisfactory will probably either save it or use it for more investment. If they save it, someone else needs to borrow it and spend or invest it instead.

The situation in a typical country today is that just over 20% of its income needs to be invested back each year as, if it was all saved, 20% of the workforce would find themselves without jobs. But the people doing the investing demand a satisfactory return and only if economic growth takes place and incomes increase will they be able to get one. If the broad mass of investors fails to get a return one year, they will not invest the next. Unemployment will increase and prices will fall, pulling profits down with them. The amount available for investment will be reduced and the economy will move along a low-growth or no-growth path until another series of innovations comes along.

For the past 200 years, however, a flow of innovations has brought about rapid growth. Many of these innovations have involved the substitution of fossil energy for energy from human, animal and solar sources because, if a worker's efforts can be supplemented in this way, he or she can produce much, much more. An averagely fit man can apply about 75 watts to his work. If he is assisted by a one-horsepower motor, the sort you might find on a hobbyist's circular saw, he can apply ten times more power to the task and consequently work much faster. A positive feedback develops, with the greater productivity leading to higher profits and incomes and additional investment and energy use. The income gap between those using fossil energy and those who don't gets wider and wider. In 1960, the average income in high-fossil-energy-using countries was 30 times that in low-energy countries. By 2001 it was almost 90 times larger. Moreover, the 20% of the world living in high-energy, high-income countries enjoyed 80% of world income, investment and trade.

It is therefore reasonable to say that the use of fossil energy facilitated a greater division of income and wealth than was usual between worker and business owner in artisanal societies. It also led to industrial capitalism and the development of the banking system because, once some enterprise owners were making more profit than they needed to plow back into their own companies, a mechanism was required to take their savings and lend them out to people who did want to invest. A structure was also needed to handle the profit-sharing part of those investment funds—the limited liability company.

I need hardly say that, just as the use of fossil fuels drove people out of manufacturing, it also drove them off the land. The use of fertilizers, tractors and sprays made each farm worker much more productive so less labor was required. In 1790, at least 90% of the US labor force worked in agriculture. In the year 2000, less than 1.4% did while still producing enough to meet home and export demand. The average American farmer produced 12 times more an hour in 2000 than his predecessor did in 1950.[2] Again, these changes were irresistible. Food prices fell by about 90% in relation to average incomes between 1920 and 1990. This meant that farmers had to increase their output by at least 1,000% for their income to keep up with the rest of society. As this could only be done by using fossil energy and industrial sector inputs, their output had to increase further to pay for them.

In May 2005, however, this period of rapid income growth for some and the displacement and poverty for others came to an end when world oil production ceased to increase. Indeed world energy supplies, and the supplies of other commodities, had been struggling to keep up with growing demand for two years previously and their prices had begun to rise. In dollar terms, the price of oil had risen to five or six times its 2003 level by 2008, while there was, on average, a tenfold rise in the price of other commodities over the same period. To give two examples, the price of copper quadrupled between 2003 and 2006, while the lead price peaked in 2007 at eight times its 2003 value.

These price rises caused the international financial crisis, as I explain in a later chapter. They were a signal that we should stop doing our Pompeii-style repairs and move away from the present system by devoting all our resources to building a civilization on a different basis, just as we would in a military emergency.

This book is all about how such a new civilization might be built, the resources that might be available for the transition and how our attitudes will have to change to bring it about. Many of the perversions listed at the top of this article need to be undone. Some we can do for ourselves and our families. Some can only be achieved on a community scale. In other cases, national and/or international action is required. Suggestions for action are given in the final chapter.

The task is immense and, on a global level, our version of Vesuvius will probably overwhelm us while we are doing it. Only those countries and communities that have made a determined break with the past will have a chance of surviving at a comfortable level. The rest of us will find that the systems on which our lives and livelihoods depend are overwhelmed and break down entirely, never to recover, and that we have no alternative support systems upon which to fall back. We cannot expect to get any clearer warnings of impending disaster than the people of Pompeii received. There are already financial fires around the economic cone. If we are to survive we need to move out quickly. Now.

But which way are we to go? Is there a map? It would be a poor book about an emergency situation which did not provide one. So, for the final chapter, my co-editor and I asked the contributors to suggest actions which readers could take or support at four levels — personal, community, national and global. In general, it is only at the national and global levels that fairly firm suggestions can be made and these are exactly those over which our readers have least influence. There is, in fact, a continuum. Influence diminishes the more people are involved. Readers can do a lot to change their own behavior and probably have appreciable influence over their immediate families. They have less influence over what they could do, or try to get done, in their communities, and at a national and international level they have almost no influence at all.

There are two problems with this. One is that, at the personal level, circumstances vary so much that it is hard to find even broad general principles which apply to everyone. For example, should people spend their resources on cutting their household's energy use or would it be better to invest the money involved in a community renewable energy project? And the answer is...it all depends. There is no single right answer.

The other problem is that the key actions to ensure our survival can only be carried out at the national and international level. This is where the Pompeii analogy breaks down. The workmen who left their tools when the ash began to fall had somewhere they could run to with their families to be safe. People today don't. Nowhere on the planet will be left undamaged by the environmental and economic catastrophes that will occur if the nations of the world continue on their present path. So it's not just a question of some of us heeding the warning fires and running away, leaving the rest to their fate. We have to convince the majority of the world's population to come along too.

We should therefore adopt collective solutions wherever possible rather than personal ones. This does not mean that individual acts are unimportant, of course. Indeed, they often ease the way for everyone else. The more individuals who decide to cycle to work, for example, the better the collective provision that is likely to be made for them. Similarly, the more people who fit triple-glazed windows, the easier and cheaper such windows are likely to become for others to obtain. However, it would make no sense for you to buy your own single-house wind turbine unless you cannot get a connection to the electricity grid. Its cost would be high in relation to its output and the energy and materials used in its construction would have been more productive had they been used to make a bigger machine. Nor would you be able to regard yourself as a worthy eco-pioneer because your solution could never be adopted by everyone else. Power needs are better met collectively; and it was three neighboring families' battle to develop a collective supply that led to the development of the Danish wind energy industry.[3] The Transition Towns movement is potentially so important only because it has adopted a collective approach to energy, food and money supplies.

So Gill and I suggest that you should ask yourself three questions as you work your way through this book. The first is "What can I do myself?", the second "What can I do with other people?" and the third is "What can't I do anything about at all?" Each person will gather his or her individual set of answers because of their particular circumstances and we expect that they will find it interesting to compare them with those suggested by our authors in the final section.

Overall, we think you will find that this is an optimistic book because, although the world is facing huge problems, there are also a lot of potential solutions. Consequently, there's a lot that can be done. We hope that, by the time you have finished reading, you have found there are some things which you, personally, are in a better position than anyone else to do or to help others do.

Endnotes

1. Quoted by Richard G. Wilkinson, *Poverty and Progress* (Methuen, 1973), 115.
2. Keith O. Fuglie, James M. MacDonald and Eldon Ball, *Productivity Growth in U.S. Agriculture* (September 2007), downloadable at ers.usda.gov/publications/EB9 /eb9.pdf
3. See "How three families started a movement and created an industry" at feasta.org /documents/shortcircuit/index.html?sc5/windguilds.html or pp. 203–7 in my book *Short Circuit* (Green Books, 1996).

PART I

ENERGY AVAILABILITY

On The Cusp of Collapse: Complexity, Energy and the Globalized Economy

David Korowicz

The systems on which we rely for our financial transactions, food, fuel and livelihoods are so interdependent that they are better regarded as facets of a single global system. Maintaining and operating this global system requires a lot of energy and, because the fixed costs of operating it are high, it is only cost-effective if it is run at near full capacity. As a result, if its throughput falls because less energy is available, it does not contract in a gentle, controllable manner. Instead it is subject to catastrophic collapse.

Fragments from a Globalized Economy

- The eruption of the EyjafjallajÖkull volcano in Iceland led to the shutdown of three BMW production lines in Germany, the cancellation of surgery in Dublin, job losses in Kenya, air passengers stranded worldwide and dire warnings about the effects the dislocations would have on some already strained economies.
- During the fuel depot blockades in the UK in 2000, the supermarkets' just-in-time supply-chains broke down as shelves emptied and inventories vanished. Anxiety about the consequences rose to such an extent that the Home Secretary, Jack Straw, accused the blockading truckers of "threatening the lives of others and trying to put the whole of our economy and society at risk."
- The collapse of Lehman Brothers helped precipitate a brief freeze in the financing of world trade as banks became afraid to accept other banks' letters of credit.[1]

Just as we never consider the ground beneath our feet until we trip, these glimpses into the complex webs of interdependencies upon which modern life relies only come when part of that web fails. When the failure is corrected, the drama fades and all returns to normal. However, it is that normal which is most extraordinary of all.

Our daily lives are dependent upon the coherence of thousands of direct interactions, which are themselves dependent upon trillions more interactions between things, businesses, institutions and individuals across the world. Following just one track; each morning I have coffee near where I work. The woman who serves me need not know who picked the berries, who moulded the polymer for the coffee maker, how the municipal system delivered the water to the café, how the beans made their journey or who designed the mug. The captain of the ship that transported the beans would have had no knowledge of who provided the export credit insurance for the shipment, who made the steel for the hull, or the steps in the complex processes that allow him the use of satellite navigation. And the steel-maker need not have known who built the pumps for the iron-ore mine, or how the oxygen for the furnace was refined.

Every café has customers like me who can only buy coffee because we are exchanging our labors across the world in ways that are dependent upon the globalized infrastructure of IT systems, transport and banking. The systems and the myriad businesses upon which they depend are only viable because there are economies of scale. Our global infrastructure requires millions of users across the world, the ship needs to carry more than coffee beans, and my café needs more than a single customer. The viability of my morning coffee requires the interactive economic and productive efforts of the globalized economy.

Thinking this way enables us to see that the global economy, and thus our civilization, is a single system. This system's structure and dynamics are therefore central to understanding the implications of ecological constraints and, in particular for this analysis, peak oil.[2] Here are some of its principal features.

The Global Economy Is Self-Organizing

The usually seamless choreography of the global economy is self-organizing. The complexity of understanding, designing and managing such a system is far beyond our abilities. Self-organization can be a feature of all complex adaptive systems, as opposed to "just" complex systems such as a watch. Birds do not "agree" together that arrow shapes make good sense aerodynamically, and then work out who flies where. Each bird simply adapts to its local environment and path of least effort, with some innate sense of desire and hierarchy, and what emerges is a macro-structure without intentional design. Similarly, our global system emerges as a result of each person, company and institution, with their common and distinctive histories, playing their own part in their own niche, and interacting together through biological, cultural and structural channels.

The self-organization reminds us that governments do not control their own economies. Nor does civil society. The corporate or financial sectors do not control the economies within which they operate. That they can destroy the economy should not be taken as evidence that they can control it.

The Global Economy Has Growth-Dependent Dynamics

We have come to regard continued economic growth as normal, part of the natural order of things. Recessions are viewed as an aberration caused by human and institutional weakness, the resumption of economic growth being only a matter of time. However, in historical terms, economic growth is a recent phenomenon. Angus Maddison has estimated that Gross World Product (GWP) grew 0.32% per annum between 1500 and 1820; 0.94% (1820–1870); 2.12% (1870–1913); 1.82% (1913–1950); 4.9% (1950–1973); 3.17% (1973–2003), and 2.25% (1820–2003).[3]

We tend to see global economic growth in terms of change. We can observe it through increasing energy and resource flows, population, material wealth, complexity and, as a general proxy, GWP. This can be viewed from another angle. We could say that the globalizing growth economy has experienced a remarkably stable phase for the last 150 years. For example, it did not grow linearly by any percentage rate for any time, decline exponentially, oscillate periodically, or swing chaotically. What we see is a tendency to compound growth of a few percent per annum, with fluctuations around a very narrow band. At this growth rate, the system could evolve, unsurprisingly, at a rate to which we could adapt.

The sensitivity felt by governments and society in general to very small changes in GDP growth shows that our systems have adapted to a narrow range of variation. Moving outside that range can provoke major stresses. Of course small differences in aggregate exponential growth have major effects over time, but here we are concentrating upon the stability issue only.

The growth process itself has many push-pull drivers: in human behaviour; in population growth; in the need to maintain existing infrastructure and wealth against entropic decay; in the need to employ those displaced by technology; in the response to new problems; and in the need to service debt that forms the basis of our economic system.

The Global Economy Grows in Complexity

Complexity can be measured in several ways — as the number of connections between people and institutions, the intensity of hierarchical networks, the number of distinct products produced and the extent of the supply-chain networks required to produce them, the number of specialized occupations, the amount of effort required to manage systems, the amount of information available and the energy flows required to maintain them. By all these measures, economic growth has been associated with increasing complexity.[4]

As a species, we had to become problem solvers to meet our basic needs, deal with status anxiety and respond to the new challenges presented by a dynamic environment. The problem to be solved could be simple such as getting a bus or buying bread; or it could be complex, such as developing an economy's energy infrastructure. We tend to exploit the easiest and least costly solutions first. We pick the lowest hanging fruit or the easiest extractable oil first. As problems are solved new ones tend to require more effort and complex solutions.

A solution is framed within a network of constraints. One of the system constraints is set by the *operational fabric*, comprising the given conditions at any time and place which support system wide functionality. For modern developed economies this includes functioning markets, financing, monetary stability, operational supply-chains, transport, digital infrastructure, command and control, health services, research and development infrastructure, institutions of trust and socio-political stability. It is what we casually assume does and will exist, and which provides the structural foundation for any project we wish to develop. Our solutions are also limited by knowledge and culture, and by the available energetic, material, and economic resources available to us. The formation of solutions is also shaped by the interactions with the myriad other interacting agents such as people, businesses and institutions. These add to the dynamic complexity of the environment in which the solution is formed, and thus the growing complexity is likely to be reinforced as elements co-evolve together.

As a result, the process of economic growth and complexity has been self-reinforcing. The growth in the size of the networks of exchange, the operational fabric and economic efficiencies all provided a basis for further growth. Growing complexity provided the foundation for developing even more complex integration. In aggregate, as the operational fabric evolves in complexity it provides the basis to build more complex solutions.

The net benefits of increasing complexity are subject to declining marginal returns — in other words, the benefit of rising complexity is eventually outweighed by its cost. A major cost is environmental destruction and resource depletion. There is also the cost of complexity itself. We can see this in the costs of managing more complex systems, and the increasing cost of the research and development process.[5] When increased complexity begins to have a net cost, then responding to new problems arising by further increasing complexity may be no longer viable. An economy becomes locked into established processes and infrastructures, but can no longer respond to shocks or adapt to change. For the historian Joseph Tainter, this is the context in which earlier civilizations have collapsed.[6]

The Global Economy is Increasing Codependence and Integration

As the globalizing economy grows, increased population, wealth and integration opens up the possibility of greater economies of scale and more diverse productive niches. When new technologies and business models (solutions or sets of solutions) emerge, they co-adapt and co-evolve with what is already present. Their adoption and spread through wider networks depends on the efficiencies they provide in terms of lower costs and new market opportunities. One of the principal ways of gaining overall efficiency is by letting individual parts of the system share the costs of transactions by sharing common infrastructure platforms (information and transport networks, electric grid, water/sewage systems, financial systems), and integrating more. Thus there is a reinforcing trend of benefits for those who build the platform and the users of the platform, which grows as the number of users grows. In time, the scale of the system becomes a barrier to a diversity of alternative systems as the upfront cost and the embedded economies of scale become a greater barrier to new entrants, especially where there is a complex hub infrastructure. The lack of system diversity is not necessarily due to corporate monopolies. There is vigorous competition between mobile phone service providers but they share common information platforms and depend on electricity networks and the monetary system, both of which have little or no system diversity.

Our operational systems are integrated into the wider economy. Expensive infrastructure and continual need for replacement components mean that economies of scale and a large number of economically connected people are necessary to make them viable. For example, the resources required to maintain the IT infrastructure on which we rely for critical services demand that we also buy games consoles, send superfluous text messages and watch YouTube. In other words, our non-discretionary needs and the critical systems that support them are affordable because they are being cross-subsidized by discretionary spending, which itself depends on further economies of scale being generated by the globalized economy that provides us with our discretionary income in the first place.

From this perspective, asking about the resource requirements for individual products of the economy (a computer or my morning coffee, say) is akin to asking about the resource requirements for your finger; it only makes sense if the rest of the body is properly resourced.

Each new level of infrastructural complexity implies a new fixed cost in terms of energy flows and resources required for maintenance and operation, and an economy of scale that can support such flows. It also locks into place codependence amongst components of our critical infrastructure that integrate the operational fabric. For example, if our IT platform failed, so too would our financial, knowledge and energy systems. Similarly, if our financial system collapsed, it would not take long for our IT and supply-chains to collapse too. The UK-based Institute of Civil Engineers acknowledges that the complex relationships between codependent critical infrastructures are not understood.[7]

Finally, as new infrastructural platforms become established, legacy systems are left to shrink or decay. Thus, if suddenly we all were to lose the communications infrastructure introduced over the past ten years, we would not return to the system we had before that infrastructure was introduced. Instead, most of us would be left without any fallback communication system at all.

The Global Economy has Bounded Resilience

An isolated, poor and self-sufficient community is vulnerable to severe risk of a general failure of food production due to flooding or pestilence, say. Even comparatively rich France had 18 general famines in the eighteenth century and hundreds of local ones.[8] Without access to money, weak transport links, markets and communications, surplus production from elsewhere could not relieve local starvation. The growth in the interconnectedness, infrastructure and institutions of the globalizing economy meant local risks could be shared over wide networks, and this enhanced local resilience.

One of the great virtues of the global economy is that while factories may fail and links in a supply-chain break, the economy can quickly adapt by fulfilling its needs elsewhere or finding substitutes. This is a measure of the resilience within the globalized economy and is a natural feature of a delocalized and networked complex adaptive system. But it is true only within a certain context. There are common platforms or "hub infrastructure" that maintain the operation of the global economy and the operational fabric as a whole, and the collapse of such hubs is likely to induce systemic failure. Principal among these are the monetary and financial system, accessible energy flows, transport infrastructure, economies of scale and the integrated infrastructures of information technology and electricity.

Our Freedom to Change Can Be Limited by Lock-In

Lock-in can be defined broadly as an inability to deal with one problem by changing a sub-system in the economy without negatively modifying others upon which we depend. For example, our current just-in-time food system and agricultural practices are hugely risky. As the current economic crisis tightens, those involved in food production and distribution strive for further efficiencies and economies of scale as deflation drives their prices down. The lower prices help maintain welfare and social peace, and make it easier for consumers to service their debts, which in turn supports our battered banks, whose health must be preserved or the bond market might not show up at a government auction. As a result, it is very hard to do major surgery on our food systems if doing so required higher food prices, decreased productivity and gave a poor investment return.

However, the primary lock-in process is the growth economy itself. We are attempting to solve systemic ecological problems within systems that are themselves dependent upon increasing resource depletion and waste. We are embedded within economic and social systems whose operation we require for our immediate welfare. But those systems are too optimized, interconnected and complex to comprehend, control and manage in any systemic way that would allow a controlled contraction while still maintaining our welfare.

The problem of lock-in is part of the reason why there is no possibility of a managed degrowth.

The Global Economy's Adaption to Ecological Constraints Displaces and Magnifies Stresses

Peak oil is expected to be the first ecological constraint to impact significantly on the advanced infrastructure of the globalized economy. However, it is only one part of an increasingly integrated web of constraints including fresh-water shortages, biodiversity loss, soil erosion and reduced soil fertility, shortages of key minerals and climate change. As a result, it makes little sense to compartmentalize our focus as we do through the UN Framework Convention on Climate Change, for example. The interwoven nature of our predicament is clearly shown by the Green Revolution of the 1960s that supposedly "solved" the increasing pressure on food production from a growing population. Technology was marshalled to put food production onto a fossil-fuel platform, which allowed further population overshoot and thus a more general growth in resource and sink demands. The result is that even more people are more vulnerable as their increased welfare demands are dependent upon a less diverse and more fragile resource base. As limits tighten, we are responding to stress on one key resource (by, say, reducing greenhouse gas emissions or getting around fuel constraints by using biofuels) by placing stresses on other key resources that are themselves already under strain (food, water). That we have to do so demonstrates how little adaptive capacity we have left.

Our Local Needs Depend on the Global Economy

Our basic and discretionary needs are dependent on a globalized fabric of exchange. So too is our ability to exchange our labor for the means to pay those needs. The conditions that maintain our welfare are smeared over the globe.

We have adapted to the stability of globalizing growth over the decades. Our skills and knowledge have become ever more refined so as to contribute to the diverse niches within the global economy. The tools we interact with — computers and software, mobile phones, machines and payment systems — maintain our productivity. So too do the supply-chains that feed us, provide inputs to our production process and maintain the operation of the systems we depend upon. Our productivity also depends upon the global economy of scale, not just those reaped by our direct customers, but also the conditions that support their economic activity in the wider economy. We are all of us intertwined. For this reason we can say that there is no longer any wholly indigenous production.

Money and Credit Integrate the Global Economy

If one side of the global economy is goods and services, the other side is money and credit. Money has no intrinsic value; it is a piece of paper or charged capacitors in an integrated circuit. It represents not wealth, but a claim on wealth (money is not the house or food we can buy with it). Across the globe we exchange something intrinsically valuable for something intrinsically useless. This only works if we all play the game, governments mandate legal tender and monetary stability and trust are maintained. The hyper-inflation in Weimar Germany and in Zimbabwe until it adopted the US dollar shows what happens when trust is lost.

The Thermodynamics of the Global Economy

Like human beings and life on earth, economies require flows of energy through them to function and maintain their structure. If we do not maintain flows of energy (directly, or by maintenance and replacement) through systems we depend upon, they decay. Humans get their energy when they transform the concentrated energy stores in food into metabolizing, thinking and physical labor, and into the dispersed energy of heat and excreta. Our globalizing economy is no less energy constrained, but with one crucial difference. When humans reach maturity they stop growing and their energy intake stabilizes. Our economy has adapted to continual growth, and that means rising energy flows.

The self-organization and biodiversity of life on earth is maintained by the flows of low-entropy solar energy that irradiate our planet as it is transformed into high-entropy heat radiating into space. Our complex civilization was formed by the transformation of the living bio-sphere and the fossil reserves of ancient solar energy into useful work, and the entropy of waste heat energy, greenhouse gases and pollution that are the necessary consequences of the fact that no process is perfectly efficient.

The first law of thermodynamics tells us that energy cannot be created or destroyed. But energy can be transformed. The second law of thermodynamics tells us how it is transformed. All processes are winding down from a more concentrated and organized state to a more disorganized one, or from low to higher entropy. We see this when our cup of hot coffee cools to the room's ambient temperature, and when humans and their artifacts decay to dust. The second law defines the direction in which processes happen. In transforming energy from a low-entropy to a higher-entropy state, work can be done, but this process is never 100% efficient. Some heat will always be wasted and be unavailable for work. This work is what has built and maintains life on earth and our civilization.

So how is it that an island of locally concentrated and complex low-entropy civilization can form out of the universal tendency to disorder? The answer is that more and more concentrated energy has to flow through it so as to keep the local system further and further away from the disorder to which it tends. The evolution and emergence of complex structures maximizes the production of entropy in the universe (local system plus everywhere else) as a whole. Clearly, if growing and maintaining complexity costs energy, then energy supply is the master platform upon which all forms of complexity depends.[9]

The operational fabric evolves with new levels of complexity. As integration and codependency rise, and economies of scale become established, higher and higher fixed costs are required to maintain the operational fabric. That cost is in energy and resource flows. Furthermore, as the infrastructure, plant and machinery that are required to maintain economic production at each level expand, they are open to greater depreciation costs or, in thermodynamic terms, entropic decay.

The correlation between energy use and economic and social change should therefore come as no surprise. The major transitions in the evolution of human civilization, from hunter-gatherers through the agricultural and industrial revolutions, have been predicated on revolutions in the quality and quantity of energy sources used.

We can see this through an example. According to the 1911 Census of England and Wales, the three largest occupational groups were domestic service, agriculture and coal mining. By 2008, the three largest groups were sales personnel, middle managers and teachers.[10] What we can first notice is 100 years ago much of the work done in the economy was direct human labor. And much of that labor was associated directly with harnessing energy in the form of food or fossil fuels. Today, the largest groups have little to do with production, but are more focused upon the management of complexity directly, or indirectly through providing the knowledge base required by people living in a world of more specialized and diverse occupational roles.

What evolved in the intervening century was that human effort in direct energy production was replaced by fossil fuels. The energy content of a barrel of oil is equivalent to 12 years of adult labor at 40 hours a week. Even at $100 a barrel, oil is remarkably cheap compared with human labor! As fossil-fuel use increased, human effort in agriculture and energy extraction fell, as did the real price of food and fuel. These price falls freed up discretionary income, making people richer. And the freed-up workers could provide the more sophisticated skills required to build the complex modern economy which itself rested upon fossil-fuel inputs, other resources and innovation.

In energy terms a number of things happened. Firstly, we were accessing large, highly concentrated energy stores in growing quantities. Secondly, fossil fuels required little energy to extract and process; that is, the net energy remaining after the energy cost of obtaining the energy was very high. Thirdly, the fuels used were high quality, especially oil, which was concentrated and easy to transport at room temperature; or the fuels could be converted to provide very versatile electricity. Finally, our dependencies co-evolved with fossil-fuel growth, so our road networks, supply-chains, settlement patterns and consumer behavior, for example, became adaptive to particular energy vectors and the assumption of their future availability.

The growth and complexity of our civilization, of which the growing GWP is a primary economic indicator, is by necessity a thermodynamic system and thus subject to fundamental laws.

In neoclassical models of economic growth, energy is not considered a factor of production. It is assumed that energy is non-essential and will always substitute with capital. This assumption has been challenged by researchers who recognize that the laws of physics must apply to the economy and that substitution cannot continue indefinitely in a finite world. Such studies support a very close energy-growth relationship. They see rising energy flows as a necessary condition for economic growth, which they have demonstrated historically and in theory.[11,12,13] It has been noted that there has been some decoupling of GWP from total primary energy supply since

1979 but much of this perceived decoupling is removed when higher energy quality is allowed for.[14]

It is sometimes suggested that energy intensity (energy/unit GDP) is stabilizing, or declining a little in advanced economies, a sign to some that local decoupling can occur. This confuses what are local effects with the functioning of an increasingly integrated global economy. Advanced knowledge and service economies do not do as much of the energy-intensive raw materials production and manufacturing as before, but their economies are dependent upon the use of energy-intensive products manufactured elsewhere, and the prosperity of the manufacturers to whom they sell their services.

Peak Oil

The phenomenon of peaking—be it in oil, natural gas, minerals or even fishing—is an expression of the following dynamics. With a finite resource such as oil, we find in general that which is easiest to exploit is used first. As demand for oil increases, and knowledge and technology associated with exploration and exploitation progress, production can be ramped up. New and cheap oil encourages new oil-based products, markets and revenues, which in turn provide revenue for investments in production. For a while this is a self-reinforcing process but eventually the reinforcement is weakened because the energy, material and financial costs of finding and exploiting new production start to rise. These costs rise because, as time goes on, new fields become more costly to discover and exploit as they are found in smaller deposits, in deeper water and in more technically demanding geological conditions. In some cases, such as tar sands, the oil requires very advanced processing and high energy and water expenditures to be rendered useful. This process is another example of declining marginal returns.

The production from an individual well will peak and decline. Production from an entire oil field, a country and the whole world will rise and fall. Two-thirds of oil-producing countries have already passed their individual peaks. For example, the United States peaked in 1970 and the United Kingdom in 1999. The decline has continued in both cases. It should be noted that both countries are home to the world's best universities, most dynamic financial markets, most technologically able exploration and production companies, and stable, pro-business political environments. Nevertheless, in neither case has decline been halted.

As large old fields producing cheap oil decline, more and more effort must be made to maintain production with the discovery and production from smaller and more expensive fields. In financial terms, adding each new barrel of production (the marginal barrel) becomes more expensive. Sadad al-Huseini said in 2007 that the technical floor (the basic cost of producing oil) was about $70 per barrel on the margin, and that this would rise by $12 per annum (assuming demand was maintained by economic growth).[15] This rapid escalation in the marginal cost of producing oil is recent. In early 2002, the marginal cost of a barrel was $20.

It is sometimes argued that there is a huge amount of oil in deposits such as the Canadian tar sands. The questions this claim raises are "When will it be on-stream?", "At what rate can oil be made available?", "What is the net energy return?" and "Can society afford the cost of extraction?" If less available net energy from oil were to make us very much poorer, we could afford to pay even less. Eventually, production would no longer be viable as economies could no longer afford the marginal cost of a barrel. In a similar vein, our seas contain huge reserves of gold but it is so dispersed that the energetic and financial cost of refining it would far outweigh any benefits (Irish territorial waters contain about 30 tonnes).

Some Misconceptions Regarding Peak Oil
The Decline Curve Assumption

The now familiar image of a modeled global oil production curve showing a decline in production of 2–3% per annum (E_{Gross}), has led commentators to assume that this is what will be available in future to the global economy. Intuitively this might seem an almost manageable constraint. The assumption on which this curve is based, the *decline curve assumption*, is incorrect for three reasons. Firstly, it does not account for the increasing energy cost of extracting oil; the net energy (E_{Net}) available to society will decline at a faster rate than the modeled decline.

Secondly, oil exporters, for the moment at least, are growing consumers of oil, and will favor domestic consumption over exports. This will reduce the volume of internationally traded oil.

The third reason lies at the heart of why we must take a whole-systems approach to peak oil. The decline curve assumption assumes there is no strong feedback between declining production, the economy, and oil production. The modeled assumptions for the declining production, even ac-

Energy Supply Too Small to Permit Economic Growth

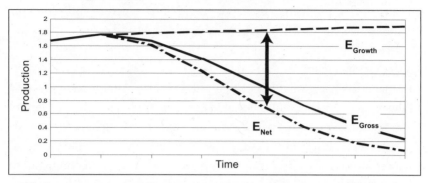

FIGURE 1. In this projection of a possible future, the steadily-increasing amount of energy required for economic growth to continue is shown by the line E_{Growth}. While the gross amount of energy that might be available is indicated by the line E_{Gross} and the net amount of energy after the energy required to deliver that energy has been deducted is marked E_{Net}. In theory, the gap between the energy available and the energy required for growth (E_{Gap}) grows smoothly and steadily as the graph shows but this ignores powerful feedbacks caused by the gap itself. As a result, the gap is likely to grow far more rapidly and erratically.

counting for declining net energy and producer consumption, assume a stable economy and infrastructure. In most of the modeling, the production curve (E_{Gross}) is derived from "proven reserves" or "proven plus probable" ones. "Proven" reserves imply we can afford to pay current real prices and deploy existing technology, while "proven plus probable" reserves are estimated on the basis of assumptions about the growth in technology and the idea that increasing wealth might allow us to pay higher prices more comfortably. In other words, at a minimum, the future production curve assumes that current technology and real prices would allow new oil to be brought on-stream to counter some of the effects of declining established production, without which the so-called natural decline rate could be greater than 7% per annum.[16]

A decline in oil production undermines economic production, thus reducing society's ability to pay for oil. A decline also, as we shall see, undermines the operational fabric, which in turn constrains the ability of society to produce, trade and use oil (and other energy carriers) in a reinforcing feedback loop. Energy flows through the economy are likely to be unpredictable, erratic and prone to sudden and severe collapse. The implication is that much of the oil (and other energy carriers) that are assumed to be available to the global economy will remain in the ground as the real purchasing power, productive demand, energy infrastructure and economic and financial systems will not be available to extract and use it.

Energy Independence

Another misconception is that the output from other energy sources — natural gas, coal, nuclear, and renewable energy — are largely independent of oil even though oil is part of the systemic fabric of the global economy. At the most direct level, oil is used to transport coal and re-supply the infrastructure of natural gas and coal. More broadly, while oil is predominantly a transport fuel, the demand for it is tied to production in the wider economy, which is dependent upon natural gas and coal. A forced reduction in oil use would reduce economic production, which would induce a system-wide reduction in electricity and heating demand. At a wider level, all energy sources interact to maintain the global economy. If there was a major failure in that economy, the continued production, processing, trade and distribution of all energy sources may be imperiled. There would only be energy source independence if there was perfect real-time substitutability and a real-time net energy surplus in one or more of the alternative sources.

We Can Fill the Gap

If the peak in global oil production is imminent, or occurs within the next decade, we have neither the time nor the resources to substitute for oil, or to invest in conservation and efficiency. This point has been made recently by the UK Energy Research Council[17] and many others.[18,19]

We can outline the general reasons as follows. It is not merely that we are replacing high-quality energy sources with lower-quality ones, such as tar sands and renewables. It is not that the costs of such alternatives are generally greater than established historical sources. Nor is it that the productive base for deploying alternative energy infrastructure is small, with limited ramp-up rates, or that it competes with food. Nor even that as the global credit crisis continues with further risks ahead, ramping-up financing will remain difficult while many countries struggle with ballooning deficits and pressing immediate concerns. The main point is that once the effects of peak oil become apparent, we will lose much of what we have called the operational fabric of our civilization. For example, any degradation and collapse of the operational fabric in the near future may mean that we already have in place a significant fraction of the renewable energy infrastructure that will ever be in place globally.

The Economics of Peak Oil

The thermodynamic foundations of the global economy are expressed through energy prices. Although the price of oil depends upon many things, supply and demand are the most basic. Speculation can be a major factor in setting prices too, but it may only have short-term effects and, if the world was awash with oil, there would be little incentive to speculate. On the supply side, the price paid for oil must be greater than the marginal cost of a barrel of oil, otherwise it's not worth producing. On the demand side, the price that users can afford to pay depends on the health of their economy, which can be undermined by high oil prices.

The *oscillating decline model* is an attempt to describe the effect of peak oil on an economy. In this model, constrained or declining oil production leads to an escalation in oil and food prices relative to available income, which feeds through to the whole economy. But economies cannot pay this price for a number of reasons. Firstly the price rises leave people with less money to spend on discretionary items, causing job losses and business closures amongst suppliers. Secondly, for a country that is a net importer of energy, the money sent abroad to pay for energy is lost to the economy unless it stimulates the export of goods of equivalent value (highly unlikely in this analysis).

The constricted growth leads to rising defaults on loans and to less international trade that would support the servicing of external debt. It would raise interest rates as the future economic outlook became more precarious. There would be a tendency to save against the increased risks of unemployment. The general effect would be deflationary as money supply dropped in relation to available goods and services. This would add to what are already huge deflationary pressures arising from the deleveraging of the hyper-credit expansion of the last two decades. The rising cost of debt servicing, on top of food and energy price rises, would further squeeze consumption. The oscillating decline model assumes such stresses are not great enough to cause a terminal systemic global banking failure or a major monetary collapse.

The decline in economic activity leads to a fall in purchasing power and a decline in all forms of energy demand and a fall in its price. Falling or volatile energy prices mean new production is less likely to be brought on stream. New energy investments in oil, renewable energy, natural gas or nuclear power, for example, become less competitive not just because energy prices are lower but also because existing energy infrastructure and supply has an overhang of spare capacity. Energy companies' reduced revenue and the bad credit conditions further constrain their ability to invest in new production.[20] The reduced revenue also means that the fixed costs of maintaining existing energy infrastructure (gas pipelines, the electric grid, refineries etc.) is a greater burden as a percentage of declining revenue.

If production falls significantly, companies lose the economies of scale they have been getting from their infrastructure. For example, once the revenue from natural gas sales becomes less than the fixed operating costs of production platforms and pipelines, then continuing to deliver gas becomes no longer viable. That means that loss of economies of scale can lead to an abrupt supply collapse and the withdrawal of supply, leading to a further reduction in production capability, and thus in economic production. This is yet another positive feedback loop.

These same conditions also constrain energy adaptation. For example, customers would find it more difficult to buy electric cars or invest in insulation, and governments to subsidize them. It would also be more difficult for the car manufacturers to ramp-up production and gain economies of scale (in addition to dealing with tight lithium supplies). In general, the tighter the economic and social constraints on an economy, the more likely it is that resources will be deployed to deal with current concerns rather than being invested in something that brings a future benefit. This expresses the generally observed increase in the social discount rate in times of growing stress.

In such an energy-constrained environment, one would also expect a rise in geopolitical risks. Bilateral arrangements between countries to secure oil and food would reduce the amount on the open market. It would also increase the inherent vulnerability to highly asymmetric price/supply shocks from state/non-state military action, extreme weather, or other "black swan" events.

When oil prices rise above the marginal cost of production and delivery, but can still be afforded despite the economy's decreased purchasing power, the energy for growth becomes available again. Of course local and national differences (in, for example, the degree of dependence on energy imports or the export of key production such as food) affect how regions fared in the recession and their general ability to pick up again. Even so, growth begins again, focusing maybe on more "sustainable" production and consumption.

However, the return of growth will not raise the purchasing power of the economy to its previous level because oil production will be limited by resource depletion; the lack of investment in production; the entropic decay of infrastructure and productive capacity; and the lower purchasing power which will reduce the price that the economy can afford to pay for its oil. The recovery will be cut short as rising oil, food and energy prices produce another recession.

The sequence of events in the oscillating decline model is therefore as follows: economic activity increases — energy prices rise — a recession occurs — energy prices fall — economic activity picks up again but to a lower bound set by declining oil production. As a result, the economy oscillates to a lower and lower level of activity.

There are good grounds for believing that this process has already begun. At least one authority links the record oil prices in 2007 to the pricking of the credit bubble.[21]

Collapse Dynamics

The oscillating decline model does not account properly for some of the embedded structures of the global economy which, while relatively obvious, have been obscured by the fact that they were adaptive in a growing economy. If oil production declines, and we cannot fill the gap between the energy required for growth and what can be produced, as we saw in the oscillating decline model, this limits the availability of other types of energy, then the global economy must continue to contract. In short, humanity is at, or has exceeded, the limits to growth.

Embedded structures that fail to contract in an orderly manner will break down. The structures that will break down include the monetary and financial system, critical infrastructure, global economies of scale, and food production. As argued earlier, these structures are deeply interdependent. As a result, they will reinforce each other's collapse. Their collapse undermines the whole operational fabric and the functioning of the global economy and all it supports.

It has been argued so far that our civilization is a single, complex adaptive system. Complex adaptive systems, and the sub-systems of which they are comprised, are a feature of open thermodynamic systems. And while they show great diversity, from markets to ecosystems to crowd behavior, their dynamic properties have common features. For most of the time complex adaptive systems are stable, but many of them have critical thresholds called tipping points, when the system shifts abruptly from one state to another. Tipping points have been studied in many systems including market crashes, abrupt climate change, fisheries collapse and asthma attacks. Despite the complexity and number of parameters within such systems, the meta-state of the system may often be dependent on just one or two key state variables.[22]

Recent research has indicated that as systems approach a tipping point they begin to share common behavioral features, irrespective of the particular type of system.[23] This unity between the dynamics of disparate systems gives us a formalism through which to describe the dynamic state of globalized civilization, via its proxy measure of Gross World Product (GWP) and its major state variable, energy flow.

Catastrophic bifurcation is the name given to a type of transition where once the tipping point has been passed, a series of positive feedbacks drives the system to a contrasting state. For example, as the climate warms, it increases methane emissions from the Arctic tundra, which drives further climate change, which leads to a further growth in emissions. This could trigger other tipping points such as a forest die-off in the Amazon Basin, itself driving further emissions. These positive feedbacks could mean that whatever humanity does would no longer matter as its impact would be swamped by the acceleration of much larger-scale processes.

Figure 2 shows how the system state responds to a change in conditions. The state of a system could represent the size of a fish population, or the level of biodiversity in a forest, while the conditions could represent nutrient loading or temperature (both effectively energy vectors). The continuous line represents a stable equilibrium; the dotted line an unstable one. In a stable equilibrium, the state of the system can be maintained once the condition is maintained. In figures A and B we see two different responses of a stable system under changing conditions. In the first, a given change in conditions has a proportional effect on the system state; in the latter, the state is highly sensitive to a change in conditions. In C and D the system is said to be close to a catastrophic bifurcation. In both of these cases there is an unstable region, where there is a range of system states that cannot be maintained. If a system state is in an unstable regime, it is dynamically driven to another available stable state. If one is close to a tipping point at a catastrophic bifurcation the slightest change in the condition can cause a collapse to a new state as in C, or a small perturbation can drive the system over the boundary as in D.

Small Changes Can Produce a Big Response

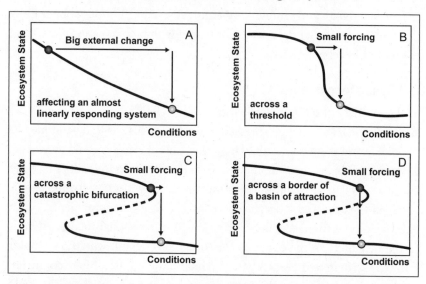

FIGURE 2. The state of a system responds to a change in conditions. The continuous line represents a stable equilibrium. In A a change in conditions drives an approximately linear response in the systems state, unlike B where a threshold is crossed and the relationship becomes very sensitive. The fold bifurcation (C, D) has three equilibria for the same condition, but the one represented by the dotted line is unstable. That means that there is a range of system states that are dynamically unstable to any condition. Source.[24]

The state of our civilization necessarily depends on the state of the global economy. I mentioned earlier that the global economy has been in a dynamic but stable state for 150 years or so, because it has had compound economic growth of about 3% per annum within a narrow band of fluctuation during that time. The state of the global economy is indicated by annual GWP growth of approximately 3%, and GWP is absolutely dependent upon rising energy flows.

To argue that civilization is on the cusp of a collapse, it is necessary to show that positive feedbacks exist which, once a tipping point has been passed, will drive the system rapidly toward another contrasting state. It is also necessary to demonstrate that the state of the global economy is driven through an unstable regime, where the strength of the feedback processes is greater than any stabilizing process. It acknowledges that there may be an early period of oscillating decline, but that once major structural components (international finance, techno-sphere) drop or "freeze" out, irreversible collapse must occur.

In the new post-collapse equilibrium state we would expect a collapse in material wealth and productivity, enforced localization/de-globalization, and collapse in the complexity as compared with before — an expression of the reduced energy flows.

Collapse Mechanisms

The Monetary and Financial System

As I write, fears are being expressed that a Greek sovereign default may be inevitable and that, as a result, the markets might refuse to lend to Ireland, Portugal and Spain, causing them to default as well. In Ireland, as in other countries, deflation is continuing as the money supply contracts, and people retrench their spending because of fears of future unemployment. As our debt burden becomes greater in relation to our national income, it adds to the instability in the eurozone. A contagious default would be a major blow to German and French banks, which have lent to all four countries. The economic historian Niall Ferguson argued that US fiscal deficits could lead at some point in time to a rapid collapse in the United States economy, noting "most imperial falls are associated with fiscal crisis".[25] Such a crisis would drag down every other economy, including those of China and Saudi Arabia.

These examples point to three things. One is that while money may not have any intrinsic value, it can nevertheless decide the fate of nations and empires. The second is that in an integrated globalized economy, a crisis in one region can become everybody's crisis. Finally, it emphasizes that the risks arising from huge indebtedness (and implied trade imbalances) are still with us, irrespective of resource constraints. The latter signifies the necessary irony that never before have we been so indebted, which is essentially an expression of our faith in future economic growth, just as that growth becomes impossible due to resource constraints.

Earlier I explained that the monetary and financial system was a hub infrastructure of the global economy, with no operational alternative. It is based upon credit, interest and fiat currencies. Credit underpins our monetary system, investment financing, government deficit financing, trade deficits, letters of credit, the bond market and corporate and personal debt. Credit, and the promise of future economic growth, supports our stock market, production, employment and much else besides. It is a primary institutional infrastructure of the global economy.

Over the whole of an economy, in order for debt to be repaid with interest, the money supply must increase year on year to replace the money lost to the economy when interest payments are made.* Money is injected into the economy when additional loans are taken out. Accordingly, the payment of interest requires an increasing level of debt, and eventually, the level of debt will become unsupportable unless incomes grow as well, either because the economy has grown or because there has been an inflation. If loan repayments including interest exceed the value of the new loans being taken out, the money supply contracts. If it does so, less business can be done, so firms fail and there is less purchasing power in the economy and increasing difficulties with servicing debts. This causes people to spend less, and investment borrowing to fall. In other words, a deflationary spiral develops. On the other hand, if debt, and thus the money supply, increases without a corresponding increase in GDP, money's purchasing power is reduced by inflation.

Increasing GDP requires increasing energy and material flows. With an energy contraction, the economy must contract. In a growing economy, debts can be paid off as they fall due, because borrowers are prepared to take out enough additional loans to cover the payment of the principal plus interest on old loans as they mature. In a permanently contracting economy, the shrinking income makes the payment of even the interest increasingly difficult as, with inadequate borrowing, the money supply declines. Another way of putting this is that reducing energy flows cannot maintain the economic production required to service debt. The value of the debt needs to be written down to a level appropriate to the new level of production. This write-down can be achieved by either mass defaults or by inflation. Consequently, if the economy is expected to shrink year after year, the number of people prepared to borrow or lend money in the conventional way will dry up, as no one will be confident that the borrowers will have enough income to make the interest payments.

---

* We are ignoring velocity of money for clarity, though it does not significantly change the main conclusion.

A bank's main assets are the loans on its books. If even a tenth of those loans cannot be repaid, that bank is wiped out because making good the losses would take more than its shareholders' capital and retained profits. Its depositors could not be repaid in full and its government or central bank would have to step in to make good the loss and allow the bank to continue to trade. If the bank's losses continued as incomes and asset values fell further, the government is likely to reach the end of its borrowing capacity. It would be open to the central bank to create money out of nothing to fill the hole in the bank's books, but it is likely to be reluctant to do so for fear that the new money would cause inflation.

Unlike previous monetary crises, one caused by declining incomes and asset values would be systemic and global. There would be no "outside" lender to provide rescue, or external hard currency to provide reserves for important imports. Nor could the system be "re-set" in the expectation of future growth, because those expectations would have little foundation.

As the deflationary pressures would continue as the crisis developed, the prices of oil, food, and debt servicing would rise in relation to people's falling incomes. There would be an increasing frequency of sovereign defaults, banking collapses and runs, declining production, panic buying and shattered public finances. In such a context, printing money (not necessarily by conventional quantitative easing) and currency reissues are likely to become necessary. Unless the money issue was tightly controlled, this could open the door to hyper-inflation. However, forecasting and control of money supply may be very difficult due to the intrinsic uncertainty of the monetary and economic environment. An additional inflation risk is that, if people began to have doubts over their bank deposits and future monetary stability, they may start spending on necessities and resilient assets, driving up the velocity of money and further increasing inflation.

Trust is the central principle underpinning the global monetary system and thus the trade networks upon which we rely. Governments can in theory print endless money, at almost no cost, to their hearts' content. That we trade it for our limited assets, or our finite labors, is a measure of the remarkable trust bequeathed to us through our experience of globalizing growth. The economist Paul Seabright argues that trust between unrelated humans outside our own tribal networks cannot be taken for granted.[26] Because trade is, in general, to all our benefit, we have developed institutions of trust and deterrence ('good standing', legal systems, the IMF, banking regulations, insurance against fraud, and the World Trade Organization, etc.) to reinforce cooperation and deter freeloaders. Trust builds compliance, which confers benefits, which in turn builds trust. But the reverse is also true. A breakdown in trust can cause defections from compliance, further reducing trust.

Because our governance and monetary policy is national (the Euro is likely to fail), but our basic needs are supplied globally, countries will be tempted to engage in predatory devaluations followed by inflations. This could occur even if governments were directly issuing debt-free money to citizens. Governments act firstly for their own citizens. In an evolving crisis, they are also likely to favor clear immediate benefits over uncertain future ones. Facing pressing immediate and projected national needs, the prospect of a continuing decline in the global productive base, and the risks of collapse in the operational fabric, governments are likely to face the following choice: maintain the value of your currency by limited issuance in the hope that it will in future be more acceptable to foreign traders, or "stealth" print money to make a grab for international assets and inputs before there is a major system failure. Furthermore, if currency crises are seen as inevitable, and hard asset barter or currency backing are likely to supersede it, then the breakup of countries' dedication to monetary stability becomes a matter of when, not if. In such a manner, the globalizing trust dynamics that evolved in the confidence in future growth begin to break down.

Remember, we only exchange something of intrinsic value for currency if we can assume that the money we get can be exchanged later on for something else of intrinsic value. In other words, we need to be able to assume that exchange rates will be stable and that inflation will be low in the period before we spend the money again. The instability of debt money, fiat currencies and competitive devaluations all remove the basis for this assumption. Money becomes very difficult to value in space (for foreign exchange and trade) and in time (for savings and investment). We can say that it becomes opaque.

Bank intermediation, credit and confidence in money holding its value are the foundations of the complex trade networks upon which we rely. The mismatch between our dependencies upon integrated global supply-chains, local and regional monetary systems, and nationalised economic policy, which has not been a problem up to now, will become so as the monetary crisis develops. A complete collapse in world trade is an extreme but not unlikely consequence.

Even if debts are written off or inflated away, a much higher proportion of everyone's reduced incomes will be absorbed by food and energy purchases. However, a country will only be able to import energy, food and inputs for its production processes by exporting something of equal value, because it will not be granted credit to run a trade deficit. The uncertainty about the value of money, and fears of future degradation of the operational fabric, is likely to mean that commodities such as gold, oil, grain and wood may be used as currency to settle accounts. However, this form of payment is ill suited to the complexity of global inputs.

Exports will collapse along with the level of production within a country, making it even more difficult to import energy or materials to increase production. As I explained earlier, modern economies produce almost nothing indigenously, as supply-chain breakdowns causing key production inputs to become unavailable become increasing likely. This will cause further production problems and make it likely that countries will remain trapped at a very low level of economic activity.

Moreover, because our supply-chains are so complex and globalized, local failures in monetary stability, lack of input or a failing operational fabric would propagate through supply-chain links and other national operational fabrics. In this way, localized failures quickly become globalized.

Food

Global food producers are already straining to meet rising demand against the stresses of soil degradation, water shortages, over-fishing and the burgeoning effects of climate change.[27] It is estimated that between seven and ten calories of fossil-fuel energy go into every one calorie of food energy we consume. It has been estimated that without nitrogen fertilizer, produced from natural gas, no more than 48% of today's population could be fed at the inadequate 1900 level.[28] No country is self-sufficient in food production today.

The fragility of the global food production system will be exposed by a decline in oil and other energy production. It is not just the more direct energy inputs, such as diesel, that would be affected, but fertilizers, pesticides, seeds, and spares for machinery and transport. The failing operational fabric may mean there is no electricity for refrigeration, for example.

It should be clear even from the above overview that a major financial collapse would not just cut actual food production, but could result in food left rotting in the fields, an inability to link surplus production with those in need, a lack of purchasing power and an inability to enact monetized food transactions.

Our critical reliance upon complex just-in-time supply-chain networks means there is little buffering to protect us from supply shocks. In the event of a shock, unless precautions are taken, it is likely that hunger could spread rapidly. Even in a country that could be food independent or a net exporter, it may take years to put new systems in place. In the interim, the risks are severe.

The Primacy of the Necessary and Reverse Economies of Scale

We mentioned that more and more of people's declining income will go on the most non-discretionary purchases, in particular food and energy. What does this mean for developed economies where most energy and a fair amount of food is imported, and which together employ only a few percent of a population? It means not only mass unemployment, but also a tiny amount of purchasing power chasing the declining availability of the necessities we depend upon. A similar position would exist in other countries. Imports and exports would drop rapidly. The unemployed, schooled and adapted to specialized and largely service roles in the globalized economy, would be quite at a loss for a considerable period.

In addition we would face reverse economies of scale. As the size, integration and complexity of the global economy has grown, our local well-being has become more and more dependent upon global economies of scale. Economies of scale work at every level — not just in the good you buy, but in all the components that went into making it, and so on. Similarly, all the hub infrastructures depend on globalized economies of scale. The lower unit prices have led to greater sales volumes and have also freed up discretionary income to be spent on other goods and services. Thus our purchasing power too is dependent upon economies of scale. The evolution of our economies and economic infrastructure has been predicated upon increasing economies of scale.

If the scaling-up process goes into reverse, reduced purchasing power, and the constriction in non-discretionary consumption, causes purchases to fall and unemployment to rise. Fewer goods and services are sold, which reduces economies of scale, which causes prices to rise, causing further falls in sales. The problem is particularly acute for very complex products and services with limited substitutability, and ones that have high operational costs.

For example, as fewer users can afford to replace mobile phones or computers, or use them less, the cost of the personal hardware and maintaining the network rises per user. Rising costs mean less discretionary use and so on. This is a serious matter for the operators because common IT platforms require a large number of users to keep costs per user low. In effect, the most discretionary use (say, Facebook, texting and Playstation) keeps down the cost for more important uses such as business operations, banking, the electricity grid and the emergency services. Remove the discretionary uses and the cost for businesses and critical services begins to escalate. Furthermore, large hub infrastructure has a fixed cost of operation and maintenance. Once income falls below the operating cost, the system will be switched off unless supported from outside. As government income is likely to fall greatly, this may not be possible.

Critical Infrastructure

We are deeply dependent on the grid, IT and communications, transport, water and sewage, and banking infrastructure. In general, these are amongst the most technologically complex and expensive products in our civilization. Their scale and capacity is determined by current and projected growth in economies, meaning they have high fixed costs. They are viable because there is purchasing power, economies of scale, open supply-chains and general monetary stability over the world. They both comprise and are dependent upon the operational fabric.

Because of their complexity and scale (implying high levels of entropic decay), this infrastructure requires continuous inputs for maintenance and repair. These inputs are often very complex, have limited lifetimes and require specialized components that depend upon very diverse and extensive supply-chains. For the various reasons discussed, substitutes and sub-components for missing inputs may not exist, causing critical infrastructure to break down. Or, the infrastructure provider or component suppliers may not be able to afford inputs due to loss of purchasing power in economies, loss of economies of scale or monetary collapse.

The tight coupling between different infrastructures magnifies the risk of a cascading failure in our critical infrastructure and thus a complete systemic failure in the operational fabric upon which our welfare depends. At the very least, a failing infrastructure feeds back into reduced economic activity and energy use, further undermining the ability to keep the infrastructure maintained.

Financial System Dynamics

Our knowledge and response to expectations of the future, shape that future. One area that is most sensitive to this is financial markets.

Money only has value because it can be exchanged for a real asset such as food, clothing or a train journey. As long as we share the confidence in monetary stability, we can save, trade and invest. It is a *virtual asset*, as it represents only a claim on something physically useful.[29] For most of us, bonds and equities are effectively virtual, as very few shareholders have any meaningful access to underlying physical assets; they are mediated by money. However, the current valuation of virtual assets towers over real productive assets on which their value is supposed to be based. A bond is valuable because we expect to be paid back with interest some years hence; paying 20 times earnings for shares in a company is a measure of confidence in the future growth of that company. Conversely, if a productive asset cannot be made to produce because of energy and resource constraints and the failing operational fabric, it loses its value. This implies that virtual wealth, including pension funds, insurance collateral and debt, will become worth much less than at present, or effectively evaporate.*

The widespread acknowledgment by market participants (and governments) that peak oil is upon us, coupled with an understanding of its consequences, is likely to crash the global financial system. Initially, just a few market participants will begin to question their faith in the overall stability and continued growth of the system and thus the likely value of their virtual assets. However, the transition can be very rapid from a few market participants accepting the idea that the system could break down permanently, to large-scale acceptance. A fear-driven, positive feedback conversion of a mountain of paper virtual assets into a mole-hill of resilient real assets could develop. This would help precipitate an irretrievable collapse of the financial and economic system.

---

* Total paper assets are approximately $300Tr based upon on a GWP of $50Tr. The latter must collapse for the reasons discussed. In addition there are the monetary system risks discussed.

The Rebooting Problem

The opportunity to reboot the globalized economy from a trough in the oscillating decline model, or from a collapsed state, so as to return it to the operation and functionality of its current state, is likely to be deeply problematic. We can consider this from four standpoints.

Entropic Decay

As Germany was hit by the global economic crisis, there was a big drop in the need for commercial transport. As a result trains and locomotives were taken out of use. A year later as the economy picked up, the trains were again required. But in the interim, cylinders and engines had rusted. The trains were of no use until repairs could be carried out, which required finance, time and open supply-chains. There was a costly shortage for a while but a fully functioning operational fabric and wider economy ensured there was no disaster.[30]

If we have a major economic collapse, the longer it continues the greater the entropic decay of our productive and critical infrastructure, and the more difficult it will be to reboot.

Loss of Coordination

The global economy we have now is the result of a self-organizing process that emerged over generations. If it collapsed, we would lose the infrastructure that allowed that complex self-organization to emerge. Post-collapse, we would have to begin with top-down conscious rebuilding; this would suffice for simple projects but not the hyper-complex products with globalized sourcing we rely upon today.

Loss of Resilience and Adaptive Capacity

In this paper, I have focused on some well-defined collapse mechanisms that are to varying degrees necessary, though they are by no means exclusive. Social stresses, health crises, and the effects of climate change may all add to our difficulties.

By way of illustration we can consider climate change. We are likely to see a major (forced) drop in emissions of anthropogenic greenhouse gases. However, temperature may continue to rise for many decades. Furthermore, we are left with uncertainty as to whether we have crossed tipping points in the climate system that could accelerate terrestrial emissions.

Few studies of the economic impact assume we will be very much poorer in future. The physical effects of climate change, in the form of flooding or reduced food productivity, will amplify the effects of the collapse processes. Being much poorer, and without our current operational fabric, will mean that the relative cost of adaption and recovery from climate induced shocks will escalate beyond our ability to pay much sooner than if our economies continued on their present courses. Furthermore, we will lose the buttressing provided by insurance, and the open supply-chains and strong globalized economies that could re-distribute surplus food from elsewhere.

Focus of the Moment

In the increasing stress of the moment, available resources are more likely to be invested in dealing with immediate needs over long-term investment. The stability of the globalizing economy has provided the context in which planning and investment could occur. The inherent uncertainty in the collapse process will also tend to favor shorter-term actions. This will reduce the resources for rebooting the system to its former state.

Conclusion

An amalgam of the oscillating decline and the collapse model has been offered as a guide rather than a prediction. The irony is that people may rarely notice they are living under energy constraints. Energy retraction from the global economy can be achieved by production declines or collapses in demand, though as we have seen, they are deeply inter-related. We may experience energy use collapse not as an energy constraint, but as a systemic banking collapse and vanished purchasing power. While energy is generally regarded as non-discretionary, energy use can drop considerably and welfare can, to some degree, be maintained. Food will represent a far more persistent challenge with the strongest real price support. For collapses in food supply and/or demand may well be associated with famine.

Tainter, drawing on historical precedent, defined some of the features of the collapsed state:

- a lower degree of stratification and social differentiation;
- less economic and occupational specialization;
- less behavioral control;
- less flow of information between individuals, between political and economic groups, between the center and its periphery;

- less sharing, trading, and redistribution of resources;
- less overall coordination and organization of individuals and groups;
- smaller territories integrated within a single political unit.

The integration and speed of processes (financial information, capital movement, supply-chains, component lifetimes, etc.) within the globalized economy suggest that a collapse will be much faster than those that have gone before. Furthermore, the level of delocalization and complexity upon which we depend, and our lack of localized fallback systems and knowledge, suggests that the impacts may be very severe for the most advanced economies. No country or aspect of human welfare will escape significant impact.

Our understanding and expectations of the world have been shaped by our experience of economic growth. The dynamic stability of that growth has habituated us to what is "normal". That normal must soon shatter. Our species' *belle époque* is passing and its future seems more uncertain than ever before.

Endnotes

1. Here we are referring to the 95% drop in the Baltic Dry Shipping Index. See global economicanalysis.blogspot.com/2008/10/baltic-dry-shipping-collapses.html.
2. D. Korowicz, *Tipping Point: Near-Term Systemic Implications of a Peak in Global Oil Production* (2010), feasta.org/Riskresilience/tipping_point.
3. A. Maddison, *Contours of the World Economy 1–2030 AD* (Oxford Univ. Press, 2007), 81.
4. E. Beinhocker, *The Origin of Wealth: Evolution, Complexity, and the Radical Remaking of Economics* (Rh Business Books, 2005).
5. B. Jones, "The Burden of Knowledge and the Death of the Renaissance Man: Is Innovation Getting Harder?" *Review of Economic Studies* 76(1) (2009).
6. J. Tainter, *The Collapse of Complex Societies* (Cambridge University Press, 1988).
7. *State of the Nation: Defending Critical Infrastructure*. Institute of Civil Engineers (2009).
8. F. Braudel, *The Structure of Everyday Life (Vol. 1): The Limits of the Possible*, (Collins, 1981), 74.
9. E. Chaisson, *Cosmic Evolution: The Rise of Complexity in Nature* (Harvard Univ. Press, 2001).
10. T. Kinsella, "Politics Must Liberate Itself for Revolution to Succeed," (The Irish Times, 16th March 2009).
11. C. Cleveland et al., "Energy and the US Economy: A Biophysical Perspective, *Science* 255 (1984).
12. R. Ayres, L. Ayres, B. Warr, "Energy, Power, and Work in the US Economy, 1990–1998," *Energy* 28 (2003).

13. R. Ayres, B. Warr, *The Economic Growth Engine: How Energy and Work Drive Material Prosperity* (Edward Elgar Publishing, 2009).
14. C. Cleveland, R. Kaufmann, D. Stern, eds, "Aggregation and the Role of Energy in the Economy," *Ecological Economics* 32 (2000).
15. S. Al-Huseini, in conversation at davidstrahan.com/audio/lastoilshock.com-sadad-al-huseini-29.10.07.mp3
16. World Energy Outlook (2008). The International Energy Agency estimates a "natural" decline rate of 6.7%, which would be expected to rise as production became more dependent upon smaller fields.
17. S. Sorrell, J. Speirs, *Global Oil Depletion: An Assessment of the Evidence for the Near-Term Physical Constraints on Global Oil Supply,* UKERC Report (2009).
18. R. Heinberg, *Searching For a Miracle: Net Energy Limits and the Fate of Industrial Society,* Forum on Globalisation and The Post Carbon Institute (2009).
19. T. Trainer, *Renewable Energy Cannot Sustain a Consumer Society* (Springer 2007).
20. The evolving credit crisis has led to a drop of 19% in energy investments in 2008 according to the International Energy Agency and the cancellation of many projects that depended upon high oil prices such as the tar sands.
21. J. Hamilton, "Causes and Consequences of the Oil Shock 2007–2008," *Brookings Papers on Economic Activity* (March 2009).
22. M. Scheffer, *Critical Transitions in Nature and Society* (Princeton Univ. Press, 2009).
23. M. Scheffer et al., "Early-Warning Signals for Critical Transitions," *Nature* Vol. 461 3 (Sept. 2009).
24. stockholmresilience.org/download/18.1fe8f33123572b59ab800016603/planetary-boundaries-mentary-info-210909.pdf
25. N. Ferguson, "Complexity and Collapse: Empires on the Edge of Chaos," *Foreign Affairs* (March/April 2010).
26. P. Seabright, *The Company of Strangers: A Natural History of Economic Life* (Princeton Univ. Press., 2005).
27. H. Godfray et al., "Food Security: The Challenge of Feeding 9 Billion People, *Science* vol. 327 (2010).
28. V. Smil, *Long-Range Perspectives on Inorganic Fertilisers in Global Agriculture.* International Fertiliser Development Centre (1999).
29. F. Soddy, *Wealth, Virtual Wealth and Debt: the Solution of the Economic Paradox.* (George Allen and Unwin, 1926).
30. "Germany Faces Freight Train Shortage as Growth Picks Up, *Der Spiegel Online* (4 May 2010), spiegel.de/international/business/0,1518,687291,00.html.

Future Energy Availability:
The Importance of "Net Energy"

Chris Vernon

There is a lot of oil still left in the ground but unless, when it is put to work, it yields perhaps four times the energy it took to extract and refine it, it might as well not be there. As a result, the supply could contract very rapidly indeed and the world may have run out of useful oil by 2050.

All life needs energy. Organisms depend for their survival on their ability to gain energy from their environment with which to weather the elements, survive pathogens, fight or flee from predators and, of course, procreate. The unique genius of *Homo sapiens* lies in our ability to manipulate our environment's energy system. Tools are a means of focusing the energy in our muscles, a knife focuses energy onto a fine edge and a lever multiplies mechanical force. The development of tools elevated us beyond other species and enabled *Homo sapiens* to colonize the planet successfully.

Focusing internally metabolized energy with tools was just the first step, however. Humanity's dominance of the Earth today, which has led to the Anthropocene being regarded as new geological era, has come about because we no longer rely solely on the food we eat to energize our way of life but employ secondary and greater sources of energy. A recent book, *Catching Fire*, by Richard Wrangham, a biological anthropologist at Harvard, claims that a breakthrough in human evolution happened 1.8 million years ago when our forebears tamed fire and began cooking. This use of fire by *Homo erectus* led to anatomical and physiological changes that adapted us to eating cooked food.

Offshore Wind and Tidal Barrages Give Good Energy Returns

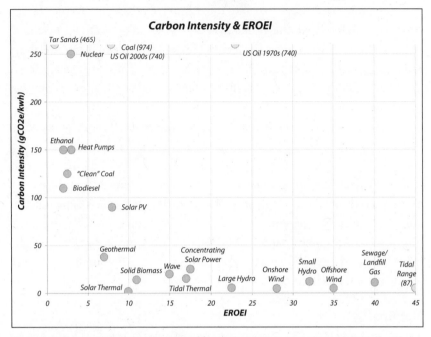

FIGURE 1: The world does not need just energy—it needs energy that is delivered with very low levels of carbon dioxide emissions (that is, a low-carbon intensity) while still giving a lot more energy back than it took to produce it. This chart, by Evan Robinson, shows the most promising technologies and those to ignore. The half dots indicate where a technology is beyond the limits of the chart. Source: http://evanrobinson.typepad.com /ramblings/science_nature/.

Wrangham argues that hominids' jaws, teeth and guts were able to shrink, and more calories were available to fuel their expanding brains, because cooking made it easier for our bodies to extract energy from food.

Then, in the Neolithic period, approximately 9,500 BC, the domestication of animals provided a new source of energy, and for the next 10,000 years, *Homo sapiens* steadily increased its access to energy by burning biomass, using draft animals and, eventually, harnessing water and the wind. The amount of energy that humanity harnessed from transient energy flows provided by the sun increased steadily for many years. The rate of growth in the energy supply accelerated somewhat when the Romans started to employ limited amounts of coal and soared dramatically after the development of James Watts' condensing steam engine in the 1770s and, more generally, the start of the industrial revolution.

Coal represented something new. For the first time, energy from a different time period was accessible and, more importantly, available on a larger time scale. Before coal, the available energy was limited to the proportion of the transient energy flows the technology of the day could capture. Coal (and the other fossil fuels) enables us to access a stock of energy sequestered over millions of years in the distant past and, to release that energy over a few short centuries.

Just as tools enabled early man to exceed the physical limits of his body by focusing the energy of his muscles, fossil fuel enables us to use more energy than we could obtain from current natural flows by tapping into vast stocks of ancient energy. The rate at which we are drawing down this ancient stock can only lead to its depletion. The characteristics of this depletion are already becoming apparent, years before its total exhaustion. As the stock diminishes, it becomes harder to extract energy from it. In other words, more energy is required by the extraction process, which reduces the *net energy* available to society.

Net Energy

A tree must gather more energy from the sun through its leaves that it expends constructing the foliage. Similarly, a fox must gain more energy consuming the hare than it took to chase it down. Our exploitation of fossil fuels is no different. In order to extract fossil fuels and utilize their embodied chemical energy, the amount of energy expended must be less than the amount we get to use. In the early days of its exploitation, a resource is abundant, easily discovered and takes little energy to extract. The principle of "best first" is adopted automatically, so the large coal seams near the surface and the large onshore oil fields are both the first to be discovered and easiest to exploit. This ease of exploitation results in large amounts of net energy as relatively little energy needs to be expended to extract the fuels.

As the resources become depleted, however, the task becomes harder. In the case of oil, new extraction is increasingly coming from deep-water deposits. The recently announced Keathley Canyon discovery in the Gulf of Mexico is under 1,259 m of water and the well depth is 10,685 m below the sea bed;[1] that's a greater distance below the surface of the earth than Everest rises above it. Unconventional resources such as shale oil and Canada's tar sands require the use of a lot of energy to produce a useful product while coal-to-liquids, biofuels and gas-to-liquids require a great deal of post-extraction processing before the fuels can be used.[2] The net energy—the energy return on invested (EROI)—delivered by all these processes is much less than the return from, say, the first oil fields in Texas.

Illustration 2 summarizes the concepts of surplus energy and the EROI ratio. E_{out} represents the magnitude of energy available after the energy extraction costs, E_{in}, have been accounted for. This is the energy available to society.

Energy Has an Energy Cost

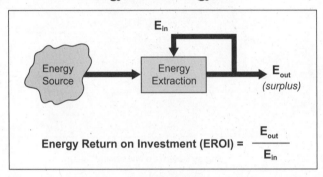

FIGURE 2. An energy source can rarely be used directly. An energy extraction process is required to discover, extract and process the resource before its energy is available to society. This process consumes energy itself, a deduction from the energy otherwise available. The energy return on invested is the ratio of surplus energy to energy required to drive the process.

EROI is a dimensionless ratio. If the extraction of 50 barrels of oil takes the energy equivalent of 1 barrel of oil, the ratio is 50:1 and 98% of the embodied energy in the source is net energy available to society. This ratio has dramatically declined over time. Professor Charles Hall at the State University of New York has calculated that for oil extracted in the US:

> The EROI for oil...during the heydays of oil development in Texas, Oklahoma and Louisiana in the 1930s was about 100 returned for one invested. During the 1970s it was about 30:1, and from about 2000 it was from 11 to 18 returned per one invested. For the world the estimate was about 35:1 in the late 1990s declining to about 20:1 in the first half decade of the 2000s.[3]

This decline has occurred almost invisibly as total extraction has increased. This has been possible as the decline from 100:1 to 30:1 to ~11–18:1 only represents a move from 99% energy availability to 97% to 93%, a trivial change in the face of the magnitude of total production which increased almost four-fold. There has been a large increase in net surplus energy compared with a small decrease in the EROI. However, projecting forward, this is not a linear system. Illustration 3 illustrates how the net energy available declines rapidly as the EROI continues to fall.

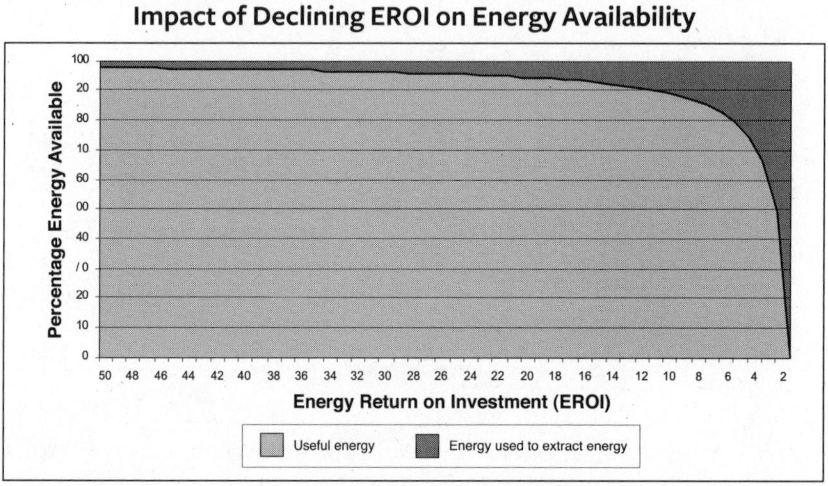

Impact of Declining EROI on Energy Availability

FIGURE 3. When an energy resource's EROI is high (>10) then most of the gross energy is available as net energy to society. Over time the EROI declines; however, the net energy does not fall significantly until the "knee" of the curve is reached at approximately 5:1. Once the knee is reached, a rapidly increasing amount of gross energy is consumed by the extraction process itself until it is no longer energetically profitable to continue to extract the resource.

Very low-EROI sources (Canadian tar sands, for example, at <5:1[4]) are already being used; their exploitation is sustained through energy cross subsidy from high EROI sources like natural gas. Large volumes of water (2–4.5 barrels of water for every barrel of synthetic crude) are also required in this case so it is likely that extraction rates will not depend on the tar sand resource at all but rather on other inputs.[5] This works in the short term, for a small volume, and whilst the gas and water is available, but does not guarantee the continued exploitation that some assume going forward.

Calculating EROI

Calculating EROI is not simple, largely because our current system is denominated in monetary terms, not energy terms. Two significant challenges are energy quality and system boundaries.

To a physicist, energy is a simple concept. Measured in joules (after 19th-century physicist James Prescott Joule), it quantifies the amount of work performed on the environment; work against gravity to raise an object, work performed to increase the temperature or velocity of an object, for example. Quality does not come into it. However, for practical applications energy can be considered to vary in quality, complicating direct comparison. The ten megajoules of chemical energy released as heat when 3 kg of coal is burnt cannot power a television for a day because the heat cannot be used directly. An indication of relative energy quality can be obtained from market price. The price for a megajoule of electricity is typically around three times higher than that of a megajoule of natural gas, and represents a willingness to waste as much as two-thirds of the primary energy in the gas when converting it to a higher quality energy, electricity.

System boundaries are particularly troublesome. A simple analysis may look at an oil well and consider the electrical energy used to pump the oil from beneath the ground compared with the energy content of the resulting oil. This is reasonable, and returns the EROI on the day the measurements were taken. However, energy will also have been expended in discovering the oil field, drilling the well (including the three preceding dry holes) and in the manufacturing and transporting of the pumping equipment itself. This will produce a fairer result because to extract oil, one must first discover it. This line of thought can be extended to include the energy costs of the petroleum engineer's education, food and health care.

Finally, simply producing surplus net energy with an EROI ratio greater than one still is not enough. A barrel of oil at the wellhead cannot be used as it stands. First, it must be refined into products such as petrol or diesel and transported to where it is required. Secondly, the infrastructure with which to use this fuel must be manufactured; the cars, trucks and the very road surface upon which they travel.

The energy used to extract the energy is only one part of the picture. Further energy must be expended in order to use the energy. Too often EROI discussion is centered upon whether a proposal is greater than unity, whether it breaks even and provides a net energy surplus. This breakeven point is not nearly enough though. If our energy system were merely to break even, human civilization would do no other activity apart from energy gathering. There would literally be no energy available for anything else.

EROI must be greater than one, but how much greater? What is the minimum EROI required for civilization? Three types of energy use can be defined: energy used to harvest energy (this is E_{in} from Ilustration 1), energy used to build and maintain the infrastructure to use the energy, and energy used for everything else that makes us civilized.

Charles Hall's research group address the first two in their paper titled "What is the Minimum EROI That a Sustainable Society Must Have?"[3] They conclude that for oil and corn-based ethanol, the minimum EROI is 3:1 at the wellhead or farm gate. Below that 3:1 figure, oil and corn-based ethanol cease to be a viable energy source because the energy output would not cover the first two types of energy use listed above: the energy used for extraction or growing and harvesting and for the construction of the roads and vehicles in which the fuel is to be used. There would be no energy left over for all the other activities of society. Civilization therefore requires energy sources to have an average EROI significantly higher than 3:1. Hall estimates that the overall EROI of the US energy system in 2005 was between 40 and 60 to one. Coal is extracted at high EROI and oil (domestic and imported) lower than this average.[6] Europe achieves similar complexity of society on approximately half the energy per capita, suggesting that significantly lower EROI can support complex society.

Peak Oil

Fossil-fuel resources are finite and, on human timescales, nonrenewable. It follows that their extraction rate starts at zero and returns to zero once the resource is exhausted. The simplistic representation of this is a bell-shaped curve with extraction rate plotted against time, and the area under the curve being equal to the extractable resource. Graphs showing the output from many oil-bearing provinces have had this bell-shaped form and their extraction rates have steadily declined after a well-defined peak. However, whilst the extraction rate may be approximately symmetrical about the peak, the first half of a province's life can be characterized by a small number of large, fast flowing fields. The EROI is high. In contrast, the second half of the province's extraction is made up of many more smaller and more complex fields, requiring secondary or tertiary recovery techniques. The EROI is low. This is only natural since the best first principle leads to the lowest-cost resources being exploited first.

Illustration 4 projects a possible global oil-extraction scenario. It is made up of a peak extraction rate in 2010 followed by a 2% per year decline rate. In the year 2000, the EROI for global oil is taken to be 30:1, which leaves 97% of the energy available to society as surplus. The blue and red curves illustrate how the surplus energy available from oil declines as EROI declines at 2% and 5% per year respectively.

By 2000, 30 years past its peak, US oil extraction had an EROI of 11 to 18:1, down from approximately 100:1 in the 1930s. This represents a rate of decline of a little over 2% per year. Under a 2% decline scenario, the global oil EROI falls to 11:1 by 2050 with 92% of the energy still available to society. However, if EROI declines at the steeper rate of 5% it passes the minimum threshold of 3:1 in 2045.

Energy From Global Oil

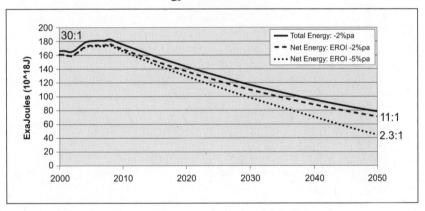

FIGURE 4. The continuous black curve projects the annual energy contained in the global · ` oil supply assuming a decline rate in extraction of 2% per year from 2010. The dashed and dotted curves illustrate the net energy available to society. In 2000, the EROI is taken to be 30:1 (97% surplus). The dashed curve assumes EROI declines at 2% per year, dropping to 11:1 by 2050, the dotted curve declines at 5% reaching 2.3:1 by 2050, below the minimum to be considered an energy source.

In other words, although there might be enough oil for global oil-extraction rates to be approximately half today's level by 2050, how much usable energy humanity will get from it depends on the rate at which EROI declines. If the EROI declines faster than it did in the US during the 20th century, it is possible that the average EROI will be so low that, by then, oil will cease to be the significant net energy source.

Conclusion

Our unique relationship with the energy system has defined our species. Our current reliance is on previously sequestered stocks of energy, which must suffer depletion and, with it, declining energy return on the energy invested in its extraction, processing and distribution. The pre-fossil fuel existence of our ancestors was reliant on the Earth's energy flows and suffered no such systemic decline. It is imperative that we find a way to move society away from its current reliance on declining, finite energy stocks and back to an energy system based on flows.

Endnotes

1. BP Press Release, BP Announces Giant Oil Discovery in the Gulf of Mexico, September 2, 2009, bp.com/genericarticle.do?categoryId=2012968&contentId=7055818, accessed 14/09/09.
2. A. R. Brandt, A. E. Farell, "Scraping the Bottom of the Barrel: Greenhouse Emission Consequences of a Transition to Low-Quality and Synthetic Petroleum Resources," *Climatic Change*, no. 84 (Springer Science, 2007).
3. C. A. S. Hall, S. Balogh, D. J. R. Murphy, "What is the Minimum EROI That a Sustainable Society Must Have?" *Energies* 2 (2009), 25–47.
4. C. A. S. Hall, Unconventional Oil: Tar Sands and Shale Oil — EROI on the Web, Part 3 of 6, theoildrum.com/node/3839, accessed 14/09/09.
5. Canada's Oil Sands — Opportunities and Challenges to 2015: An Update, National Energy Board, June 2006, pp. 38, neb.gc.ca/clf-nsi/rnrgynfmtn/nrgyrprt/lsnd/lsnd-eng.html, accessed 14/09/09.
6. C. A. S. Hall, J. G. L. Lambert, "The Balloon Diagram and Your Future, esf.edu/EFB/hall/images/Slide1.jpg, accessed 14/09/09.

Calculating the Energy Internal Rate of Return

Tom Konrad

With a constant technology mix, EROI is the most important number because you will always be making new energy investments as old investments outlive their useful lives and are decommissioned. However, in a period of transition such as the one we are entering, we need a quick return on our energy investments in order to maintain our society. We have to have energy to invest; we can't simply charge it to our energy credit card and repay it later. That means that if we're going to keep the non-energy economy going while we make the transition, we can't put too much energy today into the long-lived energy investments we'll use tomorrow.

To give a clearer picture of how timing of energy flows interacts with EROI, I will borrow the Internal Rate of Return (IRR) concept from finance. IRRs compare different investments with radically different cash-flow timings by assigning each a rate of return that could produce those cash flows if the money invested were compounded continuously. Except in special circumstances involving complex or radically different sized cash flows, an investor will prefer an investment with a higher IRR.

To convert an EROI into an Energy Internal Rate of Return, EIRR, we need to know the lifetime of the installation and what percentage of the energy cost is fuel, compared to the percentage of the energy embodied in the plant. The chart below shows my preliminary calculations for EIRR, along with the plant lifetimes I used, and the EROI shows as the size of each bubble.

The most valuable energy resources are those with large bubbles (High EROI) at the top of the chart (High EIRR). Because of the low EIRR of

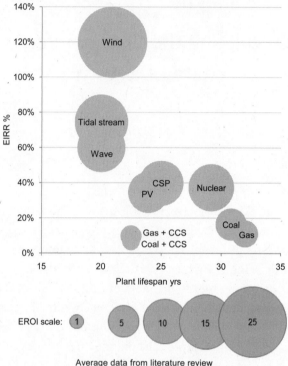

Average data from literature review
PV = Photovoltaic, CSP = Concentrated Solar Power
CCS = Carbon Capture and Sequestration

THE AREA of each bubble represents the energy return on energy invested — EROI. The most valuable energy resources are those with large bubbles — a high EROI — at the top of the chart because this shows that they also have a high Energy Internal Rate of Return — EIRR. In other words, they pay back the energy invested in developing them rather quickly. Photovoltaic, nuclear and hydropower have low rates of energy return. Graph compiled and redrawn specially for Feasta by Jamie Bull, oco-carbon.com

photovoltaic, nuclear and hydropower, emphasizing these technologies in the early stage of the transition away from fossil fuels is likely to lead to a scenario in which we don't have enough surplus energy, to make the transition without massive disruption to the rest of the economy. Jeff Vail, the author of *The Theory of Power* (see jeffvail.net) refers to this front-loading of energy investment for renewable energy and nuclear as the Renewables Hump. Note that the three fossil fuels (oil, gas, and coal) all have high EIRRs. As we transition to lower-carbon fuels, we will want to keep as many high EIRR fuels in our portfolio as possible.

Energy Efficiency and "Smart" Strategies

I have been unable to find studies of the EROI of various efficiency technologies. For instance, how much energy is embodied in insulation, and how does that compare to the energy saved? We can save transportation fuel with "smart" strategies such as living in more densely populated areas that are closer to where we work, and investing in mass transit infrastructure. The embodied energy of mass transit can be quite high in the case of light rail, or it can be very low in the case of better scheduling and incentives for ride sharing.

Many efficiency and smart technologies and methods are likely to have *much* higher EIRRs than fossil fuels. We can see this because, while their embodied energy has not been well studied, their financial returns have. Typical investments in energy efficiency in utility run demand-side management programmes cost between $0.01 and $0.03 cents per kWh saved, much less than the cost of new fossil-fired generation. This implies a higher EIRR for energy efficiency, because part of the cost of any energy-efficiency measure will be the cost of the embodied energy, while all of the savings are in the form or energy. This relationship implies that higher IRR technologies will generally have higher EIRRs as well. Smart strategies also often show extremely high financial returns because they reduce the need for expensive cars, roads, parking, and even accidents. See vtpi.org/winwin.pdf.

Brain Rather than Brawn

The Renewables Hump does not have to be the massive problem it seems when we only look at supply-side energy technologies. Demand-side solutions, such as energy efficiency, conservation and better public transport, enable us to avoid running into a situation where the energy we have to invest in transitioning from finite and dirty fossil fuels to clean renewable energy overwhelms our current supplies.

Efficiency and smart strategies are "Brain" technologies, as opposed to the "Brawn" of traditional and new energy sources. As such, their application requires long-term planning and thought. Cheap energy has created a culture where we prefer to solve problems by simply applying more brawn. As our fossil-fuel brawn fades away, we will have to rely on our brains once again if we hope to maintain anything like our current level of economic activity.

Energy and Water:
The Real Blue-Chips

Nate Hagens and Kenneth Mulder

Today's prices and costs provide a very bad basis for making investment decisions because they reflect temporary relative market scarcities rather than long-run underlying physical ones. The world needs to abandon money as its measure if it is to invest its scarcest, most limiting resources in the best possible way.

Because standard economic analysis relies on money that no longer has any link to the physical world as its measuring stick, it does not adequately account for the physical depletion of its resources. Money, credit and debt can be created with no underlying physical foundation whereas energy and scarce natural resources, not dollars, are what we really have to budget and spend.

Certainly, marginal cost pricing does not reflect true scarcity in a world of non-perfect substitutes. Oil this year (2010) is at roughly the same inflation-adjusted price as it was 35 years ago, yet the world has consumed almost 900 billion barrels in the interim as oil-powered transport became the foundation of global trade. Basing energy and economic policy on dollar-based signals alone may therefore lead to serious long-term dislocations. Instead, calculating our costs in terms of critical natural resources may be a more fundamentally sound investment paradigm.

The two most important natural resources are water and energy. In most cases, each is required to procure the other. First, we use water directly through hydroelectric power generation at major dams, indirectly as a coolant for thermoelectric power plants, and as an input for the production of biofuels. By sector, the two largest consumers of water in the United States are agriculture and electrical power plants. If we count only fresh water, fully 81% of US use is for crop irrigation. For American corn production, an average of 2,100 gallons of irrigation water is required per bushel which yields 2.7 gallons of corn-based ethanol.[1] This means that 206 gallons of water is needed per gallon of gasoline substitute, ethanol, before refining.

Several studies suggest that up to two-thirds of the global population could experience water scarcity by 2050. The shortages will be driven by the agricultural sector, which is currently responsible for up to 90% of global fresh-water consumption. Water shortages could become much more acute if there is widespread adoption of energy-production technologies that require water as a significant input, such as biofuels. If large quantities of water are diverted to energy production because the market dictates this as society's priority, there would be a significant loss of food production and a decline in human welfare.

> *The economy is a wholly owned subsidiary of the environment, not the reverse.*
>
> HERMAN DALY, *STEADY-STATE ECONOMICS* (1977)

The interdependency between water and energy goes both ways. In California, for example, where water is moved hundreds of miles across two mountain ranges, water delivery is responsible for approximately 15% of the state's total electricity consumption. Cities without nearby reservoirs require energy to pump water from below ground to their citizens. Irrigated crops also require energy, including those crops used for alternative energy production, like corn. Dryland farming produces significantly lower and more volatile crop yields. For example, from 1947–2006, irrigated corn acreage in Nebraska had a 43% higher yield than dryland corn.

Combining figures for the energy return on energy invested (EROI) with the *water invested per unit of energy* for various technologies suggests that fossil fuels also have a strong advantage in terms of their energy return on water invested (EROWI). The most water-efficient fossil electricity source we and colleagues examined yielded almost 600 times the energy per unit of water invested as did the most water-efficient biomass source of electricity reviewed.[2] So, not only is the development of bioenergy on a scale sufficient to be a significant source of energy likely to have a strong, negative

Water Requirements for Energy Production (liters per megawatt hour)	
Petroleum Extraction	10–40
Oil Refining	80–150
Oil shale surface retort	170–681
NGCC* power plant, closed loop cooling	230–30,300
Coal integrated gasification combined cycle	~900
Nuclear power plant, closed loop cooling	~950
Geothermal power plant, closed loop tower	1900–4200
Enhanced oil recovery	~7600
NGCC,* open loop cooling	28,400–75,700
Nuclear power plant, open loop cooling	94,600–227,100
Corn ethanol irrigation	2,270,000–8,670,000
Soybean biodiesel irrigation	13,900,000–27,900,000

*Natural Gas Combined Cycle

The water required for various energy technologies.[5] Unlike energy, water can sometimes be recycled. For example, cooling water withdrawn for use by a nuclear power plant may be returned and withdrawn again farther downstream to irrigate biofuel crops.

impact upon the availability of fresh water, but it would require energy inputs far in excess of what we have traditionally allocated to the fossil-energy sector.

Energy derived from finite and renewable resources is a function of multiple inputs including land, labor and raw materials — any of which may become a limiting factor for energy production. A technology might have a high EROI and yet require sufficient levels of scarce, non-energy inputs as to be extremely restricted in potential scale. For example, the amount of land required for biofuels is between 100 and 1,000 times more than the land area required for conventional fossil fuels. In addition to non-energy inputs, energy technologies vary in their waste outputs and impact on environment. Within the biofuels class itself, there is a large disparity of pesticide and fertilizer requirements. For example, per unit of energy gained, soybean biodiesel requires just 2% of the nitrogen, 8% of the phosphorous, and 10% of the pesticides that are needed for corn ethanol, inputs that impact groundwater quality and stream runoff.[1] As such, future refinements to an energy and water policy framework will probably have to look beyond energy and water supplies.

How Much Water Does It Take to Provide Energy?

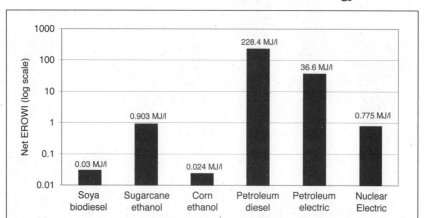

The net Energy Return on Water Invested (EROWI) for selected fuels Source: (^{2}) This graph has a logarithmic scale so the bars represent orders of magnitude. The actual amounts are shown at the top of each bar. As it takes 250 times more water to produce ethanol from sugar cane to run a car than it does to run one on ordinary diesel, the availability of water is likely to place a tight limit on biofuel production.

In a world constrained by energy and increasing environmental limitations, but with a growing human population, adherence to accounting frameworks based on natural capital will be essential for policymakers to assess energy, water and other limiting factors. Such a framework will help us discard energy dead-ends that would waste our remaining high-quality fossil sources and, perhaps equally importantly, our time and effort. The world as a whole needs to build a renewable-supply investment portfolio that achieves the highest returns on our scarcest inputs rather than on money that is based on nothing scarce at all.

Endnotes

1. Hill et al., "Environmental, Economic, and Energetic Costs and Benefits of Biodiesel and Ethanol Biofuels," *Proc. Acad. Nat. Sci.* 103:11206–11210 (2006).
2. K. Mulder, N. Hagens, B. Fisher, "Burning Water: Energy Return on Water Invested," *AMBIO — Journal of Human Environment* 39, no. 1 (February, 2010).
3. M. Webber, C. King, "The Water Intensity of the Plugged-In Automotive Economy," *Environmental Science & Technology* 42, no. 12 (2008): 4305–4311.
4. C. Cleveland, "Net Energy from the Extraction of Oil and Gas in the United States," *Energy* 30 (2005): 769–782.
5. Robert F. Service, "Another Biofuels Drawback: The Demand for Irrigation," *Science* 23, vol. 326, no. 5952 (October 2009): 516–517.

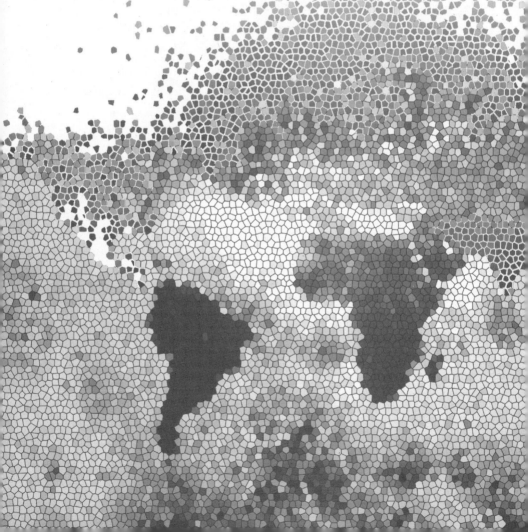

PART II

INNOVATION IN BUSINESS,
MONEY AND FINANCE

The Supply of Money
in an Energy-Scarce World

Richard Douthwaite

Money has no value unless it can be exchanged for goods and services but these cannot be supplied without the use of some form of energy. Consequently, if less energy is available in future, the existing stock of money can either lose its value gradually through inflation or, if inflation is resisted, be drastically reduced by the collapse of the banking system that created it. Many over-indebted countries face this choice at present—they cannot preserve both their banking systems and their currency's value. To prevent this conflict in future, money needs to be issued in new, non-debt ways.

The crux of our present economic problems is that the relationship between energy and money has broken down. In the past, supplies of money and energy were closely linked. For example, I believe that a gold currency was essentially an energy currency because the amount of gold produced in a year was determined by the cost of the energy it took to extract it. If energy (perhaps in the form of slaves or horses rather than fossil fuel) was cheap and abundant, gold mining would prove profitable and, coined or not, more gold would go into circulation enabling more trading to be done. If the increased level of activity then drove the price of slaves or steam coal up, the flow of gold would decline, slowing the rate at which the economy grew. It was a neat, natural balancing mechanism between the money supply and the amount of trading which worked rather well.

In fact, the only time it broke down seriously was when the Spanish conquistadors got gold for very little energy—by stealing it from the Aztecs and the Incas. That damaged the Spanish economy for many years because it meant that wealthy Spaniards could afford to buy from abroad rather than using the skills of their own people, which consequently did not develop. It was an early example of "the curse of oil" or the "paradox of plenty," the paradox being that countries with an abundance of nonrenewable resources tend to develop less than countries with fewer natural resources. Britain suffered from this curse when North Sea oil began to come ashore, distorting the exchange rate and putting many previously sound firms out of business.

Nineteenth-century gold rushes were all about the conversion of human energy into money as the thousands of ordinary 21st-century people now mining alluvial deposits in the Amazon basin show. Obviously, if supplies of food, clothing and shelter were precarious, a society would never devote its energies to finding something that its members could neither eat, nor live in, and which would not keep them warm. In other words, gold supplies swelled in the past whenever a culture had the energy to produce a surplus. Once there was more gold available, its use as money made more trading possible, enabling a society's resources to be converted more easily into buildings, clothes and other needs.

Other ways of converting human energy into money have been used besides mining gold and silver. For example, the inhabitants of Yap, a cluster of ten small islands in the Pacific Ocean, converted theirs into carved stones to use as money. They quarried the stones on Palau, some 260 miles away and ferried them back on rafts pulled by canoes, but once on Yap, the heavy stones were rarely moved, just as no gold has apparently left Fort Knox for many years. According to Glyn Davies' mammoth study, *The History of Money*, the Yap used their stone money until the 1960s.

Wampum, the belts made from black and white shells by several Native American tribes on the New England coast, is a 17th-century example of human-energy money. Originally, the supply of belts was limited by the enormous amount of time required to collect the shells and assemble them, particularly as holes had to be made in the shells with Stone Age technology — drills tipped with quartz. The currency was devalued when steel drill bits enabled less time to be used and the last workshop drilling the shells and putting them on strings for use as money closed in 1860.

The last fixed, formal link between money and gold was broken on August 15, 1971, when President Nixon ordered the US Treasury to abandon the gold exchange standard and stop delivering one ounce of gold for every $35 that other countries paid in return. This link between the dollar and energy was replaced by an agreement that the US then made with OPEC through the US-Saudi Arabian Joint Commission on Economic Cooperation that "backed" the dollar with oil.[1] OPEC agreed to quote the global oil price in dollars and, in return, the US promised to protect the oil-rich kingdoms in the Persian Gulf against threat of invasion or domestic coups. This arrangement is currently breaking down.

The most important link between energy and money today is the consumer price index. The central banks of every country in the world keep a close eye on how much their currency is worth in terms of the prices of the things the users of that currency purchase. Energy bills, interest payments and labor costs are key components of those prices. If a currency shows signs of losing its purchasing power, the central bank responsible for managing it will reduce the amount in circulation by restricting the lending the commercial banks are able to do. This means that, if energy prices are going up because energy is getting scarcer, the amount of money in circulation needs to become scarcer too if it is to maintain its energy-purchasing power.

A scarcer money supply is a serious matter because the money we use was created by someone somewhere going into debt, and if there is less money about, interest payments make those debts harder to repay. Money and debt are co-created in the following way. If a bank approves a loan to buy a car, the moment the purchaser's check is deposited in the car dealer's account, more money — the price of the car — comes into existence, an amount balanced by the extra debt in the purchaser's bank account. Consequently, in the current monetary system, the amount of money and the amount of debt are almost equal and opposite. I say "almost" as borrowers have more debt imposed on them every year because of the interest they have to pay. If any of that interest is not spent back into the economy by the banks but is retained by them to boost their capital reserves, there will be more debt than money.

Until recently, if the banks approved more loans and the amount of money in circulation increased, more energy could be produced from fossil-fuel sources to give value to that money. Between 1949 and 1969 — the heyday of the gold exchange standard under which the dollar was linked to gold and other currencies had exchange rates with the dollar — the price of oil was remarkably stable in dollar terms. But when the energy supply was suddenly restricted by OPEC in 1973, two years after the US broke the gold-dollar link, and again in 1979, the price of energy went up. There was just too much money in circulation for it to retain its value in relation to the reduced supply of oil.

The current "credit crunch" came about because of a huge increase in the price of energy. World oil output was almost flat between September 2004 and July 2008 for the simple reason that the output from major oil fields was declining as fast as the production from new, smaller fields was growing. Consequently, as more money was lent into circulation, oil's price went up and up, taking the prices of gas, coal, food and other commodities with it. The rich world's central bankers were blasé about these price increases because the overall cost of living was stable. In part, this was because lots of cheap manufactured imports were pouring into rich-country economies from China and elsewhere, but the main reason was that a lot of the money being created by the commercial banks' lending was being spent on assets such as property and shares that did not feature in the consumer price indices they were watching. As a result, they allowed the bank lending to go on and the money supply — and debt — to increase and increase. The only inflation to result was in the price of assets and most people felt good about that as it seemed they were getting richer, on paper at least. The commercial banks liked it too because their lending was being backed by increasingly valuable collateral. What the central banks did not realize, however, was that their failure to rein in their lending meant that they had broken the crucial link between the supply of energy and that of money.

This break damaged the economic system severely. The rapid increase in energy and commodity prices that resulted from the unrestricted money supply meant that more and more money had to leave the consumer-countries to pay for them. The problem with this was that a lot of the money being spent was not returned to the countries that spent it in the form in which it left. It went out as income and came back as capital. I'll explain. If I buy petrol for my car and part of the price goes to Saudi Arabia, I can only buy petrol again year after year if that money is returned year after year to the economy from which my income comes. This can happen in two ways, one of which is sustainable, the other not. The sustainable way is that the Saudis spend it back by buying goods and services from Ireland, or from countries from which Ireland does not import more than it exports. If they do, the money returns to Ireland as income. The unsustainable way is that the Saudis lend it back, returning it as capital. This enables Ireland to continue buying oil but only by getting deeper and deeper into debt.

As commodity prices rose, the flow of money to the energy and mineral producers increased so rapidly that there was no way that the countries concerned could spend it all back. Nor did they wish to do so. They knew that their exports were being taken from declining resources and that they should invest as much of their income as possible in order to provide an income for future generations when the resources were gone. So they set up sovereign wealth funds to invest their money, very often in their customers' countries. Or they simply put their funds on deposit in rich-country banks.

The net result was that a lot of the massive increase in the flow of income from the customers' economies became capital and was lent or invested in the commodity consumers' economies rather than being spent back in them. This was exactly what had happened after the oil price increases in 1973 and 1979. The loans meant that, before the money became available again for people to spend on petrol or other commodities, at least one person had to borrow it and spend it in a way that converted it back to income.

This applied even if a sovereign wealth fund invested its money in buying assets in a consumer economy. Suppose, for example, the fund bought a company's outstanding shares rather than a new issue. The sellers of the shares would certainly not spend the entire amount they received as income. They would place most of their money on deposit in a bank, at least for a little while before they bought other assets, and people other than the vendors would have to borrow that money if it was going to be spent as income. As a result, it often took quite a lot of borrowing transactions before the total sum arrived back in people's pockets.

For example, loans to buy existing houses are not particularly good at creating incomes whereas loans to build new houses are. This is because most of the loan for an existing house will go to the person selling it, although a little will go as income to the estate agent and to the lawyers. The vendor may put the money on deposit in a bank and it will have to be lent out again for more of it to become income. Or it may be invested in another existing property, so someone else gets the capital sum and gives it to a bank to lend. A loan for a new house, by contrast, finances all the wages paid during its construction so a lot of it turns into income. The building boom in Ireland was therefore a very effective way of getting the money the country was over-spending overseas and then borrowing back converted into incomes in people's pockets. Direct foreign borrowing by governments to spend on public sector salaries is an even more effective way of converting a capital inflow into income.

We can conclude from this that a country that runs a deficit on its trade in goods and services for several years, as Ireland did, will find that its firms and people get heavily in debt because a dense web of debt has to be created within that country to get the purchasing power, lost as a result of the deficit, back into everyone's hands. This is exactly why the UK and United States are experiencing debt crises too. The US has only had a trade surplus for one year — and that was a tiny one — since 1982 and the UK has not had one at all since 1983.

Table 1. The Worst External Debtors per $1,000 of GDP in 2006

1	Ireland	$6,251.97
2	United Kingdom	$3,530.89
3	Netherlands	$2,887.82
4	Switzerland	$2,836.01
5	Belgium	$2,686.21
6	Austria	$1,843.11
7	Sweden	$1,554.06
8	France	$1,551.52
9	Denmark	$1,471.46
10	Portugal	$1,413.50

DEFINITION: Total public and private debt owed to non-residents repayable in foreign currency, goods, or services. Per $ GDP figures expressed per 1,000 $ gross domestic product. Source: CIA World Factbooks 18 December 2003 to 18 December 2008

Table 2. Ireland's Gross External Debt Triples Over Five Years

CSO data for the final quarter of each year (€m)

2002	521,792
2003	636,925
2004	814,446
2005	1,132,650
2006	1,338,747
2007	1,540,240
2008	1,692,634
2009	1,611,396

Table 3. The World's Biggest Balance of Payments Deficits at the Height of the Boom in 2007

	Deficit, millions	Ranking of absolute size of deficit	Population, millions	Deficit per head
Greece	-$44,400	6	11.0	$4,036
Spain	-$145,300	2	41.1	$3,535
Ireland	-$14,120	13	4.0	$3,530
Australia	-$56,780	4	19.7	$2,882
United States	-$731,200	1	294	$2,486
Portugal	-$21,750	10	10.1	$2,153
United Kingdom	-$119,200	3	59.3	$2,010
Romania	-$23,020	9	22.3	$1,032
Italy	-$51,030	5	57.4	€889
Turkey	-$37,580	7	71.3	$527
France	-$31,250	8	60.1	$520
South Africa	-$20,630	11	45.0	$458
Poland	-$15,910	2	38.6	$412

It is notable that all the eurozone countries experiencing a debt crisis—the "PIIGS" Portugal, Ireland, Italy, Greece and Spain—appear in this table and that the three worst deficits on a per capita basis are those of Greece, Spain and Ireland. The countries with a shaded background have their own currencies and are thus better able to correct their situations. Source: CIA World Factbook, 18 December 2008, with calculations by the author.

The debts incurred by the current account-deficit countries were of two types: the original ones owed abroad and the much greater value of successor ones owed at home as loans based on the foreign debt were converted to income. Internal debt—that is, debt owed by the state or the private sector to residents of the same country—is much less of a burden than foreign debt but it still harms a country by damaging its competitiveness. It does this despite the fact that paying interest on the debt involves a much smaller real cost to the country since most of the payment is merely a transfer from one resident to another. (The remainder of the payment is taken in fees by the financial services sector and the increase in indebtedness has underwritten a lot of its recent growth.)

Internal debt is damaging because a country with a higher level of internal debt in relation to its GDP than a competing country will have higher costs. This is because, if the rate of interest is the same in both countries, businesses in the more heavily indebted one will have to allow for higher interest charges per unit of output than the other when calculating their operating costs and prices. These additional costs affect its national competitiveness in exactly the same way as higher wages. Indeed, they are the wages of what a Marxist would call the rentier class, a class to which belongs anyone who, directly or indirectly, has interest-bearing savings. A country's central bank should therefore issue annual figures for the internal-debt to national income ratio.

While internal debt slows a country up, external debt can cause it to default. In their book *This Time Is Different*, Carmen Reinhart and Ken Rogoff consider external debt in two ways — in relation to a country's GNP and in relation to the value of its annual exports.

Table 4. How Oil Imports Commandeered an Increased Share of Ireland's Foreign Earnings.

	Mineral fuel imports	GNP	Fuel cost as % of GNP	Exports	Fuel cost as % of export earnings
2001	2,219	98,014	2.26	92,690	2.39
2002	1,932	106,494	1.81	93,675	2.06
2003	1,969	117,717	1.67	82,076	2.40
2004	2,814	126,096	2.23	84,409	3.33
2005	4,020	137,265	2.93	86,732	4.63
2006	4,719	152,456	3.10	88,772	5.32
2007	5,728	161,210	3.55	88,571	6.47
2008	6,595	158,343	4.17	86,618	7.61

Source: CSO data with calculations by the author.

The second ratio is the more revealing because exports are ultimately the only means by which the country can earn the money it needs to pay the interest on its overseas borrowings. (A country's external debt need never be repaid. As its loans become due to be repaid they can be replaced with new ones if its creditors are confident that it can continue to afford to pay the interest.) The book examines 36 sovereign defaults by 30 middle-income countries and finds that, on average, a country was forced to default when its total public and private external debt reached 69.3% of GNP and 230% of its exports.

Poorer Countries Lend to the World's Richest Ones

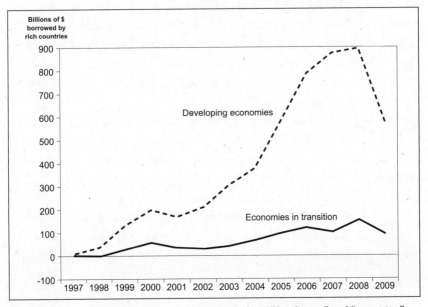

GRAPH 2. Rich countries have borrowed massively from "developing" and "transition" countries over the past ten years. This graph shows the net flow of capital. The funds borrowed came predominantly from energy and commodity export earnings. Source: World Situation and Prospects, 2010, published by the UN.

As Table 5 shows, almost a dozen rich countries are in danger of default by the Reinhart-Rogoff criteria. The total amount of debt in the world in 2010 is roughly 2.5 times what it was ten years ago in large part as a result of the spend-and-borrow-back process. This means that there is 2.5 times as much money about, but not, of course, 2.5 times as much energy. If much of that new money was ever used to buy energy, the price of energy would soar. In other words, money would be devalued massively as the money-energy balance was restored. The central banks are determined to prevent this happening, as we will discuss in a little while.

Most of the world's increased debt is concentrated in richer countries. Their debt-to-GDP ratio has more than doubled whereas in the so-called "emerging economies" the debt-to-GDP ratio has declined. This difference can be explained by adapting an example given by Peter Warburton in his

Table 5. The Most Over-Indebted Countries at the Height of the Boom in 2007

		Total state & private external debt, billions	Export earnings billions	Ratio total external debt to exports	GDP billions	Ratio total external debt to GDP
1	United Kingdom	$10,450	$442.2	2360%	2,674	391%
2	Ireland	$1,841	$115.5	1590%	268	687%
3	United States	$12,250	$1,148	1070%	14,093	87%
4	France	$4,396	$546	810%	2,857	154%
5	Switzerland	$1,340	$200.1	670%	492	272%
6	Australia	$824.9	$142.1	580%	1,015	81%
7	Netherlands	$2,277	$456.8	500%	871	261%
8	Italy	$2,345	$502.4	470%	2.303	102%
9	Spain	$1,084	$256.7	420%	1,604	68%
10	Belgium	$1,313	$322.2	410%	504	261%
11	Germany	$4,489	$1,354	330%	3,649	123%
12	Japan	$1,492	$678.1	220%	4,911	30%

Countries that exceed the average level at which countries in the Reinhart and Rogoff study defaulted are marked in a darker shade.

World Debt More Than Doubles in Ten Years

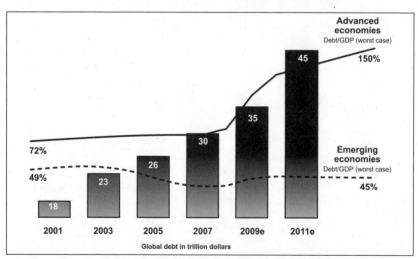

GRAPH 3. Rich-country debt has grown remarkably in the past ten years because of the amount of lending generated by capital flows from fossil energy — and commodity-producing nations was used to inflate asset bubbles. The emerging economies, by contrast, invested borrowed money in increasing production. As a result, their debt/GDP ratio declined. Source: *The Economist*.

1999 book, *Debt and Delusion*. Suppose I draw €1,000 on my overdraft facility at my bank to buy a dining table and chairs. The furniture store uses most of its margin on the sale to pay its staff, rent, light and heat. Say €250 goes this way. It uses most of the rest of my payment to buy new stock, say, €700. The factory from which it orders it then purchases wood and pays its costs and wages. Perhaps €650 goes this way, but since the wood is from overseas, €100 of the €650 leaks out of my country's economy. And so I could go on, following each payment back and looking at how it was spent and re-spent until all the euros I paid finally go overseas. The payments which were made to Irish resident firms and people as a result of my €1,000 loan contribute to Irish national income. If we add up only those I've mentioned here — €1,000 + €250 + €700 + €550 — we can see that Irish GDP has increased by €2,500 as a result of the €1,000 debt that I took on. In other words, the debt-to-GDP ratio was 40%.

As Debt Increases, US Economy Grows by Less and Less

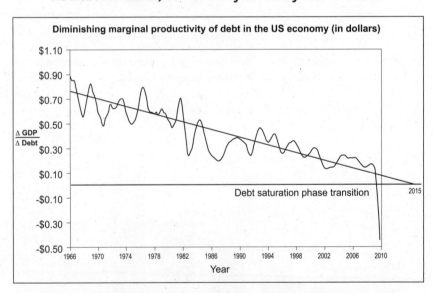

GRAPH 4. Because borrowings have been invested predominantly in purchasing assets rather than in production capacity, each increase in borrowing in the US has raised national income by less and less. The most recent bout of borrowing — to rescue the banking system — actually achieved negative returns because it failed to stop the economy contracting. Graph prepared by Christopher Rupe and Nathan Martin with US Treasury figures dated 11 March 2010. Source: economicedge.blogspot.com/2010/04/guest-post -and-more-on-most-important.html

Now suppose that rather than buying furniture, I invest my borrowed money in buying shares from someone who holds them already, rather than a new issue. Of the €1,000 I pay, only the broker's commission and the taxes end up as anyone's income. Let's say those amount to €100. If so, the debt-to-GDP ratio is 1000%.

So one reason why the debt burden has grown in "rich" countries and fallen in "emerging" ones is the way the debt was used. A very much higher proportion of the money borrowed in some richer countries went to buying up assets, and thus bidding up their prices, than it did in the poorer ones. After a certain point in the asset-buying countries, it was the rising price of assets that made their purchase attractive, rather than the income that could be earned from them. Rents became inadequate to pay the interest on a property's notional market value, while in the stock market, the price-earnings ratio rose higher and higher.

Only a small proportion of the money created when the banks lent money to buy assets was spent in what we might call the real economy, the one in which everyday needs are produced and sold. The rest stayed as what the money reform activist David J. Weston called "stratospheric money" in his contribution to the New Economics Foundation's 1986 book *The Living Economy*; in other words, money that moves from bank account to bank account in payment for assets, with very little of it coming down to earth. The fraction that does flow down to the real economy each year is normally balanced—and sometimes exceeded—by flows in the other direction such as pension contributions and other forms of asset-based saving. The flows in the two directions are highly unstable, however, not least because those who own stratospheric assets know that they can only convert them to real-world spending power at anything like their current paper value if other people want to buy them. If they see trouble coming, they need to sell their assets before everyone else sees the trouble too and refuses to buy. This creates nervousness and an incentive to dump and run.

If all asset holders lost all faith in the future and wanted to sell, prices would fall to zero and the loans that the banks had secured on their value would never be repaid. The banks would become insolvent, unable to pay their depositors, so the huge amounts of money that were created when the asset-backed loans were approved would disappear, along with the deposits created by loans given out to finance activities in the real economy. In such a situation, the deposit guarantees given by governments would be of no avail. The sums they would need to borrow to honor their obligations would be beyond their capacity to secure, particularly as all banks everywhere would be in the same situation.

No one wants such a situation so, since a decline in asset values could easily spiral downwards out of control, the only safe course is to keep the flow of money going into the stratosphere greater than that coming out. This keeps asset prices going up and removes any reason for investors to panic and sell. The problem is, however, that maintaining a positive flow of money into the stratosphere depends on having a growing economy. If the economy shrinks, or a greater proportion of income has to be spent on buying fuel and food because their prices go up, then less money can go up into the stratosphere in investments, rents and mortgage repayments. This causes asset values to fall and could possibly precipitate an investors' stampede to get into cash.

In effect, the money circulating in the stratosphere is another currency — one that has only an indirect relationship with energy availability and which people use for saving rather than to buy and sell. Because there is a fixed one-to-one exchange rate between the atmospheric currency and the real-world one, the price of assets has to change for inflows and outflows to be kept in balance. As we've just discussed, the banking system will collapse if asset values fall too far, so governments are making heroic efforts to ensure that they do not. As 20% of the assets involved are owned by 1% of the population in Britain and Ireland (the figure is 38% in the US), this means that governments are cutting the services they deliver to all their citizens in order to keep the debt-money system going in an effort to preserve the wealth of the better-off.

In 2007, the burden imposed on the real economy by the need to support the stratospheric economy became too great. The richer countries that had been running balance of payments deficits on their current accounts found that paying the high energy and commodity prices, plus the interest on their increased amount of external debt, plus the transfer payments required on their internal ones, was just too much. The weakest borrowers — those with sub-prime mortgages in the US — found themselves unable to pay the higher energy charges *and* service their loans. And, since many of these loans had been securitized and sold off to banks around the world, their value as assets was called into question. Banks feared that payments that they were due from other banks might not come through as the other banks might suddenly be declared insolvent because of their losses on these doubtful assets. This made inter-bank payments difficult and the international money-transfer system almost broke down.

All asset values plunged in the panic that followed. Figures from the world's stock markets show that the FTSE-100 lost 43% between October 2007 and February 2009 and that the Nikkei and the S&P 500 lost 56% and 52% respectively between May-June 2007 and their bottom, which was also in February 2009. All three indices have since recovered some of their previous value but this is only because investors feel that incomes are about to recover and increase the flow of funds into the stratosphere to support higher levels. They would be much less optimistic about future prices if they recognized that, in the medium term at least, a growing shortage of energy means that incomes are going to fall rather than rise.

This analysis of the origins of the current crisis leads to four thoughts that are relevant to planning the flight from Vesuvius:

1. It is dangerous and destabilizing for any country, firm or individual to borrow from abroad, even if they are borrowing their own national currency. Net capital movements between countries should be prohibited.
2. An inflation is the best way of relieving the current debt crisis. An attempt to return the debt-GNP ratio to a supportable level by restricting lending would be a serious mistake. Instead, money incomes should be increased.
3. A debt-based method of creating money cannot work if less and less energy is going to be available. New ways of issuing money will therefore need to be found.
4. New ways of borrowing and financing are going to be required too, since, as incomes shrink because less energy can be used, fixed interest rates will impose an increasing burden.

We will discuss these in turn.

1. Borrowing from Abroad

We have already discussed the problems that servicing foreign debt can create and, in view of these, it is hard to see why any country should ever borrow abroad at all. Foreign capital creates problems when it enters a country and further problems when it leaves. When it comes in, it boosts the country's exchange rate, thus hurting firms producing for the home market by making imports cheaper than they would otherwise be. It also hurts exporters, reducing their overseas earnings when they convert them into their national currency. As a result, when the loan has to be repaid, the country is in a weaker position to do so than it was when it took the loan on — its imports are higher and its exports reduced. Foreign borrowing is so damaging that it has even been claimed that the Chinese policy of pegging its currency to the dollar at a rate which makes its exports very attractive and keeping that rate by lending a lot of the dollars it earns back was designed by military strategists to destroy America's manufacturing base.[2] The strategists are said to have argued that no superpower can maintain its position without a strong industrial sector, so lending back the dollars China earned was a handy way to destroy the US ability to fight a major war.

For a country with its own currency, the alternative to borrowing abroad is to allow the value of its currency to float so that its exports and imports are always in balance and it never need worry about its competitiveness again. As eurozone countries no longer have this option, they have very few tools to keep exports and imports in balance. Indeed, it's hard to know what they should do to deter foreign borrowing because, while the state may not borrow abroad itself, its private sector may be doing so. In Ireland, for example, the net indebtedness of Irish banks to the rest of the world jumped from 10% of GDP in 2003 to over 60% four years later, despite the fact that some of the state's own borrowings were repaid during these years. All the state could have done to stop this borrowing would have been to restrict lending that was based on the overseas money. For example, it could have placed a limit on the proportion of its loans that a bank could make to the property sector, or stipulated that mortgages should not exceed, say, 90% of the purchase price and three times the borrower's income. This would have dampened down the construction boom and limited the growth of incomes and thus import demand. But such indirect methods of control are not nearly as potent as allowing the market to achieve balance automatically. Their weakness is a very powerful argument for breaking up the eurozone.

Although one might accept that borrowing abroad for income purposes comes at the cost of undermining its domestic economy, it could be argued that capital inflows for use as capital will allow a country develop faster than would otherwise be the case. Let's see if this argument stands up.

The danger with bringing capital into a country with its own currency is that part of it will become income in the ways we discussed and thus boost the exchange rate and undermine the domestic economy. So, if we restrict the capital inflow to the actual cost of the goods that the project will need to import, is that all right? Well, yes, it might be. It depends on the terms on which the capital is obtained, and whether the project will be able to earn (or save) the foreign exchange required to pay the investors. If the world economy shrinks as we expect, it is going to be harder to sell the product and its price may fall. This might mean that interest payments would take a greater share of the project's revenue than was expected, causing hardship for everyone else. So, as we will discuss later, the only safe approach is for the foreign investor to agree to take a fixed portion of the project's foreign revenue, whatever that is, rather than a fixed sum of money based on the interest rate. This would ensure that the project never imposed a foreign exchange burden on the country as a whole. The foreign capital would be closer to share capital than a loan. This should be the only basis that any country should allow foreign capital in.

At present, however, so much foreign capital is moving around that its flow might need to be limited to prevent destabilizing speculation. As Reinhart and Rogoff point out, "Periods of high international capital mobility have repeatedly produced international banking crises, not only famously as they did in the 1990s, but historically." One solution to this, again for countries with their own currencies, is to have two exchange rates; one for capital flows, the other for current (i.e. trading) flows. This would mean that people could only move their capital out of a country if others wanted to move theirs in. Rapid, speculative flows would therefore be impossible. Ireland had this system when it was part of the Sterling Area after World War II until Britain abandoned it around 1979. It was known as the dollar premium. South Africa had a capital currency, "the financial rand," which gave it financial stability throughout the apartheid period. It dropped it in 1995.

Keeping capital and current flows apart would greatly reduce the power of the financial sector. After they were divided, no one would ever say as James Carville, President Clinton's adviser, did about the bond markets in the early 1990s when he realized the power they had over the government, that they "can intimidate everybody."

Of course, the threat to its power will mean that the financial sector opposes capital-flow currencies tooth and nail. Yet its power, and income, must be reduced, especially if incomes in other sectors of the economy are going to fall. According to the OECD, the share of GDP taken by the financial sector (defined as "financial intermediation, real-estate, renting and business activities") in the United States increased from 23% to 31% between 1990 to 2006. The increase in the UK was over 10% to about 32% and around 6% in both France and Germany.

The rise in the sector's share of corporate profits was even more striking. In the United States, for example, it was around 10% in the early 1980s but peaked at 40% in 2007. Mentioning these figures, Már Gudmundsson, the deputy head of the Monetary and Economic Department of the Bank for International Settlements, told a conference in the US in 2008 that the financial sector needed to become smaller and less leveraged: "That is the only way the sector can be returned to soundness and profitability in the environment that is likely to prevail in the post-crisis period." I would put it much more strongly. The British sector's income is bigger than those of agriculture, mining, manufacturing, electricity generation, construction and transport put together, and the sector's dominance in other economies is similar. It is a monstrous global parasite that needs to be cut down to size.

The Financial Tail Wags the Societal Dog

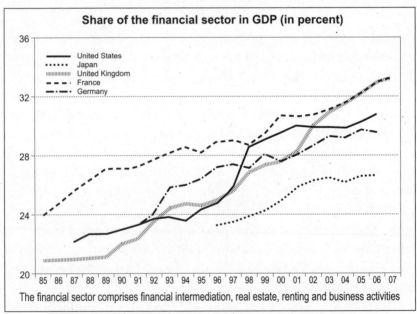

GRAPH 5. The financial sector in five rich-country economies, the US, Japan, the UK, France and Germany, has been taking an increasing share of national income over the past twenty years, in part because of the increasing debt burden. The sector is now bigger in each country than all the productive sectors put together. Source OECD.

2. Allowing Inflation to Correct the Debt-Income Imbalance

As the amount of energy in a liter of petrol is equivalent to three weeks' hard manual work, having power at one's disposal can make one much more productive. A country's income is consequently largely determined by its direct and indirect energy use. So, whenever less energy is available, incomes fall and debt becomes harder to service unless an inflation is allowed to increase money incomes and reduce the real burden imposed by the debt.

This has been demonstrated by two real-world experiments. After OPEC's first oil-supply restriction in 1973, the world's central banks allowed the inflation created by the higher oil prices to go ahead. By reducing the burden of existing debt, this made room for the commercial banks to lend out the money that the oil producers were unable to spend. The US came out of the recession quickly and Britain did not have one at all. Developing countries did well too even though they were paying more for their oil, because the prices of their commodity-exports increased more rapidly than the rate of interest they were being charged on their external debts and, although they borrowed from abroad, their debt-export ratio stayed constant.

After the 1979 restriction, however, the story was different. This time, the central banks resolved to maintain the purchasing power of their monies in relation to energy and they did all they could to fight the inflation. In Britain, an ultra-tight fiscal and monetary policy was adopted. Interest rates were set at 17% and government spending cuts of £3.5bn were announced for the following year. The result was the "Winter of Discontent" with 29m working days lost through strikes, the largest annual total since the General Strike in 1926. In the US, the prime rate reached 20% in January 1981. Unemployment, which had dropped steadily from 1975 to 1979, began to rise sharply as the deflationary measures were put into effect.

The OPEC countries themselves moved from a small balance of payments deficit of $700 million in 1978 to a surplus of $100 billion in 1980. They put most of this money on deposit in US and British banks. But what were the banks to do with it, since none of their rich-country customers wished to borrow at the prevailing interest rates, especially as their domestic economies had been thrown into recession by the central banks' policies? The answer was to lend it to the developing countries, since the loans made to these countries after 1973 had worked out well.

The result was the Third World Debt Crisis. In 1970, before it began, the 15 countries which it would affect most severely — Algeria, Argentina,

Bolivia, Brazil, Bulgaria, Congo, Cote d'Ivoire, Ecuador, Mexico, Morocco, Nicaragua, Peru, Poland, Syria and Venezuela — had a manageable collective external public debt. It amounted to 9.8% of their collective GNP and took 12.4% of their export income to service.[3] By 1987, these same nations' external public debt was 47.5% of their GNP and servicing it took 24.9% of their export earnings. This doubling had come about because they had borrowed abroad to avoid inflicting drastic spending cuts on their people like those made in the US and the UK. They could, of course, have avoided borrowing and tried to manage on their reduced overseas earnings but this would have forced them to devalue, which would have itself increased their foreign debt-to-GDP ratio. They really had very few options.

Just how deep the commodity-producing countries devaluations would have had to have been is indicated by the decline in net farm incomes in the US. In 1973, these reached a record high of $92.1 billion but by 1980 they had dropped back to $22.8 billion, largely because of a decline in overseas demand, and by 1983 they were only $8.2 billion. Not surprisingly in view of the high interest rates, many US farmers went bankrupt. In 1985, 62 agricultural banks failed, accounting for over half of the nation's bank failures that year. The high interest rates were also a factor a few years later when 747 US mortgage lenders, the savings and loans or "thrifts" had to be bailed out. The cost was around $160 billion, of which about $125 billion was paid by the US government.

Money's exchange rate with energy fell in both 1973 and 1979 because there was too much of it in circulation in relation to the amount of oil available. In 1973, the inflation removed the surplus money by requiring more of it to be used for every purchase. The results were generally satisfactory. In 1979, by contrast, an attempt was made to pull back the price of oil by jacking up interest rates to reduce the amount of money going into circulation and thus, over a period of years, bring down the "excessive" money stock. The higher rates caused immense hardship because they ignored the other side of the money=debt equation, the debt that was already there. So, by setting their faces against allowing money to be devalued in relation to energy, the central banks' policies meant that a lot of the debt had to be written off. Their policy hurt them as well as everyone else. Yet the same policy is being used again today.

So which policy should be adopted instead to remove the current surplus stratospheric money? Incomes in the real economy need to be increased so that they can support current asset values in the stratosphere and, since there is insufficient energy to allow growth to increase them, inflation has to be used instead. Attempts to use 1979-type methods such as those being promoted by the Germans for use in the eurozone will only depress incomes, thus making the debt load heavier. A lot of the debt would then have to be written off, causing the banking system to implode. Even if this could be avoided, such a policy can never work because the money is being taken from the real economy rather than the stratospheric one.

The choice is therefore between allowing inflation to reduce the debt burden gradually, or trying to stop it and having the banking system collapse, overwhelmed by bad debts and slashed asset values. In such a situation, account holders' money would not lose its value gradually. It could all disappear overnight.

The inflation we need cannot be generated with debt-based money as it was in 1973 because in today's circumstances that would increase debts more rapidly than it raised incomes. As Graph 4 shows, each $100 borrowed in 2006–7 in the US only increased incomes by around $30 whereas in 1973, the return was higher and the level of debt the country was carrying in relation to its income was about half what it is today. The same applies to most other OECD countries; their public and private sectors are already struggling with too much debt and do not wish to take on more.

The solution is to have central banks create money out of nothing and to give it to their governments either to spend into use, or to pay off their debts, or give to their people to spend. In the eurozone, this would mean that the European Central Bank would give governments debt-free euros according to the size of their populations. The governments would decide what to do with these funds. If they were borrowing to make up a budget deficit — and all 16 of them were in mid-2010, the smallest deficit being Luxembourg's at 4.2% — they would use part of the ECB money to stop having to borrow.

They would give the balance to their people on an equal-per-capita basis so that they could reduce their debts, or not incur new ones, because private indebtedness needs to be reduced too. If someone was not in debt, they would get their money anyway as compensation for the loss they were likely to suffer in the real value of their money-denominated savings. Without this, the scheme would be very unpopular. The ECB could issue new money in this way each quarter until the overall, public and private, debt in the eurozone had been brought sufficiently down for employment to be restored to a satisfactory level.

The former Irish Green Party senator, Deirdre de Burca, has improved on this idea. She points out that (1) we don't want to restore the economy that has just crashed and (2) that politicians don't like giving away money for nothing. Her suggestion is that the money being given to ordinary citizens should not just be lodged in their bank accounts but should be sent to them as special credits which could only be used either to pay off debt or, if all their debts were cleared, to be invested in projects linked to the achievement of an ultra-low-carbon Europe. These could range from improving the energy-efficiency of one's house to investing in an offshore wind farm or a community district heating system.

Creating money to induce an inflation may seem rather odd to those who advocate buying gold because they fear that all the debt-based money that has been created recently by quantitative easing will prove inflationary by itself. What they have failed to recognize is that most of the money they are worried about is in the stratosphere and has very few ways of leaking down. It is in the accounts of financial institutions and provides the liquidity for their trading. The only way it can reach people who will actually spend it rather than investing it again is if it is given out as loans but, as we saw, that is not happening. Even paying it out to an institution's staff as wages and bonuses won't work too well as most are already spending as much as they can and would use any extra to buy more assets, thus keeping it stratospheric.

A common argument against using inflation to reduce debts is bound to be trotted out in response to this idea. It is that, if an inflation is expected, lenders simply increase their interest rates by the amount they expect their money to fall in value during the period of the loan, thus preventing the inflation reducing the debt burden. However, the argument assumes that new loans would still be needed to the same extent once the debt-free money creation process had started. I think that is incorrect. Less lending would be needed, the investors' bargaining position would be very weak and interest rates should stay down. Incomes, on the other hand, would rise. As a result, if the debtors continued to devote the same proportion of their incomes to paying off any new or remaining loans, they would be free of debt much more quickly.

3. The End of Debt-Based Money

Output in today's economy gets a massive boost from the high level of energy use. If less and less energy is going to be available in future, the average amount each person will be able to produce will decline and real incomes will fall. These shrinking incomes will make debts progressively harder to repay, creating a reluctance both to lend and to borrow. For a few years into the energy decline, the money supply will contract as previous years' debts are paid off more rapidly than new ones are taken on, destroying the money the old debts created when they were issued. This will make it increasingly difficult for businesses to trade and to pay employees. Firms will also have more problems paying taxes and servicing their debts. Bad debts and bankruptcies will abound and the money economy will break down.

Governments will try to head the breakdown off with the tool they used during the current credit crunch — producing money out of nothing by quantitative easing. So far, the QE money they have released, which could have been distributed debt-free, has been lent to the banks at very low interest rates in the hope that they will resume lending to the real economy. This is not happening on any scale because of the high degree of uncertainty — is there any part of that economy in which people can invest borrowed money and be sure of being able to pay it back?

Some better way of getting non-debt money into the real economy is going to have to be found. In designing such a system, the first question that needs to be asked is "Are governments the right people to create it?" The value of any currency, even those backed by gold or some other commodity, is created by its users. This is because I will only agree to accept money from you if I know that someone else will accept it from me. The more people who will accept that money and the wider range of goods and services they will provide in return, the more useful and acceptable it is. If a government and its agencies accept it, that increases its value a lot.

As the users give a money its value, it follows that it should be issued to them and the money system run on their behalf. The government would be an important user but the currency should not be run entirely in its interest, even though it will naturally claim to be acting on behalf of society, and thus the users, as a whole. Past experience with government-issued currencies is not encouraging because money-creation-and-spend has always seemed politically preferable to tax-and-spend and some spectacular inflations that have undermined a currency's usefulness have been the result. At the very least, an independent currency authority would need to be set up to determine how much money a government should be allowed to create and spend into circulation from month to month and, in that case, the commission's terms of reference could easily include a clause to the effect that it had to consider the interests of all the users in taking its decisions.

This raises two more design questions. The first is "Should the government benefit from all the seignorage, the gain that comes from putting additional money into circulation, or should it be shared on some basis amongst all the users?" and the second is "Should the new money circulate throughout the whole national territory or would it be better to have a number of regional systems?" I am agnostic about the seignorage gains. My answer depends on the circumstances. If the new money is being issued to run in parallel with an existing currency, giving some of the gains to reward users who have helped to develop the system by increasing their turnover could be an important tool during the setup process. On the other hand, if the new money was being issued to replace a collapsed debt-based system, giving units to users on the basis of their previous debt-money turnover would just bolster the position of the better off. It would be better to allow the state to have all the new units to spend into use in a more socially targeted way.

A more definite answer can be given to the second question. Different parts of every country are going to fare quite differently as energy use declines. Some will be able to use their local energy resources to maintain a level of prosperity while others will find they have few energy sources of their own and that the cost of buying their energy in from outside leaves them impoverished. If both types of region are harnessed to the same money, the poorer ones will find themselves unable to devalue to improve their exports and lower their imports. Their poverty will persist, just as it has done in Eastern Germany where the problems created by the political decision to scrap the ostmark and deny the East Germans the flexibility they needed to align their economy with the western one has left scars to this day.

If regional currencies had been in operation in Britain in the 1980s when London boomed while the North of England's economy suffered after the closure of its coal mines and most of its heavy industries, then the North-South gap which developed might have been prevented. The North of England pound could have been allowed to fall in value compared with the London one, saving many of the businesses that were forced to close. Similarly, had Ireland introduced regional currencies during the brief period it had monetary sovereignty, a Connacht punt would have created more business opportunities west of the Shannon if it had had a lower value than its Leinster counterpart.

Non-debt currencies should not therefore be planned on a national basis or, worse, a multinational one like the euro. The EU recognizes 271 regions, each with a population of between 800,000 and 3 million, in its 27 member states. If all these had their own currency, the island of Ireland would have three and Britain 36, each of which could have a floating exchange rate with a common European reference currency and thus with each other. If it was thought desirable for the euro to continue so that it could act as a reference currency for all the regional ones, its independent currency authority could be the ECB. In this case, the euro would cease to be the single currency. It would simply be a shared one instead.

The advantages from the regional currencies would be huge:

1. As each currency would be created by its users rather than having to be earned or borrowed in from outside, there should always be sufficient liquidity for a high level of trading to go on within that region. This would dilute the effects of monetary problems elsewhere.

2. Regional trade would be favored because the money required for it would be easier to obtain. A strong, integrated regional economy would develop, thus building the region's resilience to shocks from outside.

3. As the amount of regional trade grew, seignorage would provide the regional authority with additional spending power. Ideally, this would be used for capital projects.

4. The debt levels in the region would be lower, giving it a lower cost structure, as much of the money it used would be created debt free.

In addition to the regional currencies, we can also expect user-created currencies to be set up more locally to provide a way for people to exchange their time, human energy, skills and other resources without having to earn their regional currency first. One of the best-known and most successful models is Ithaca Hours, a pioneering money system set up by Paul Glover in Ithaca, New York, in 1991 in response to the recession at that time. Ithaca Hours is mainly a non-debt currency since most of its paper money is given or earned into circulation but some small zero-interest business loans are also made. A committee controls the amount of money going into use. At present, new entrants pay $10 to join and have an advertisement appear in the system's directory. They are also given two one-Hour notes – each Hour is normally accepted as being equivalent to $10 – and are paid more when they renew their membership each year as a reward for their continued support. The system has about 900 members and about 100,000 Hours in circulation, a far cry from the days when thousands of individuals and over 500 businesses participated. Its decline dates from Glover's departure for Philadelphia in 2005, a move which cost the system its full-time development worker.

Hours has no mechanism for taking money out of use should the volume of trading fall, nor can it reward its most active members for helping to build the system up. It would have to track all transactions for that to be possible and that would require it to abandon its paper notes and go electronic. The result would be something very similar to the Liquidity Network system that Graham Barnes describes in the next article.

New variants of another type of user-created currency, the Local Exchange and Trading System (LETS) started by Michael Linton in the Comox Valley in British Columbia in the early 1990s, are likely to be launched. Hundreds of LETS were set up around the world because of the recession at that time but unfortunately, most of the start-ups collapsed after about two years. This was because of a defect in their design: they were based on debt but, unlike the present money system, had no mechanism for controlling the amount of debt members took on or for ensuring that debts were repaid within an agreed time. Any new LETS-type systems that emerge are likely to be web-based and thus better able to control the debts their members take on. As these debts will be for very short periods, they should not be incompatible with a shrinking national economy.

Complementary currencies have been used to good effect in times of economic turmoil in the past. Some worked so well in the US in the 1930s that Professor Russell Sprague of Harvard University advised President Roosevelt to close them down because the American monetary system was being "democratized out of [the government's] hands." The same thing happened to currencies spent into circulation by provincial governments in Argentina in 2001 when the peso got very scarce because a lot of money was being taken out of the country. These monies made up around 20% of the money supply at their peak and prevented a great deal of hardship but they were withdrawn in mid-2003 for two main reasons. One was pressure from the IMF, which felt that Argentina would be unable to control its money supply and hence its exchange rate and rate of inflation if the provinces continued to issue their own monies. The other, more powerful, reason was that the federal government felt that the currencies gave the provinces too much autonomy and might even lead to the breakup of the country.

4. New Ways to Borrow and Finance

The regional monies mentioned above will not be backed by anything since a promise to pay something specific in exchange for them implies a debt. Moreover, if promises are given, someone has to stand over them and that means that whoever does so not only has to control the currency's issue but also has to have the resources to make good the promise should that be required. In other words, the promiser would have to play the role that the banks currently perform with debt-based money. Such backed monies would not therefore spread financial power. Instead, they could lead to its concentration.

Even so, some future types of currency will be backed by promises. Some may promise to deliver real things, like kilowatt hours of electricity, just as the pound sterling and the US dollar were once backed by promises to deliver gold. Others may be bonds backed by entitlements to a share an income stream, rather than a share of profits, as Chris Cook describes in his article in this book. Both these types of money will be used for saving rather than buying and selling. People will buy them with their regional currency and either hold them until maturity if they are bonds, or sell them for regional money at whatever the exchange rate happens to be when they need to spend.

These savings currencies could work like this. Suppose a community wanted to set up an energy supply company (ESCo) to install and run a combined heat and power plant supplying hot water for central heating and electricity to its local area. The regional currency required to purchase the equipment could be raised by selling energy "bonds" which promise to pay the bearer the price of a specific number of kWh on the day they mature. For example, someone could buy a bond worth whatever the price of 10,000 kWh was when that bond matured in five years. The money to redeem that bond would come from the payments made by people buying energy from the plant in its fifth year. The ESCo would also offer other bonds with different maturity dates and, as they were gradually redeemed, those buying power from the ESCo would, in fact, be taking ownership of the ESCo themselves.

These energy bonds will probably be issued in large denominations for sale to purchasers both inside and outside the community and will not circulate as money. However, once the ESCo is supplying power, the managing committee could turn it into a bank. It could issue notes for, say, 50 and 100 kWh which locals could use for buying and selling, secure in the knowledge that the note had real value as it could always be used to pay their energy bills. Then, once its notes had gained acceptance, the ESCo could open accounts for people so that the full range of money-moving services was available to those using the energy-backed units. An ESCo would be unlikely to do this, though, if people were happy with the way their regional currency was being run. Only if the regional unit was rapidly losing its value in energy terms would its users migrate to one which was not.

Conclusion

Up to now, those who allocated a society's money supply by determining who could borrow, for what and how much, determined what got done. In the future, that role will pass to those who supply its energy. Only this group will have, quite literally, the power to do anything. Money once bought energy. Now energy, or at least an entitlement to it, will actually be money and energy firms may become the new banks in the way I outlined. This makes it particularly important that communities develop their own energy supplies, and that if banks issuing energy-backed money do develop, they are community owned.

As energy gets scarcer, its cost in terms of the length of time we have to work to buy a kilowatt-hour, or its equivalent, is going to increase. Looked at the other way round, energy is cheaper today than it is ever likely to be again in terms of what we have to give up to get it. We must therefore ensure that, in our communities and elsewhere, the energy-intensive projects required to provide the essentials of life in an energy-scarce world are carried out now. If they are not, their real cost will go up and they may never be done.

Working examples of both backed and unbacked forms of modern regional and community monies are needed urgently. Until there is at least one example of a non-debt currency other than gold working well somewhere in the world, governments will cling to the hope that increasingly unstable national and multinational debt-based currencies will retain their value and their efforts to ensure that they do will blight millions of lives.

Moreover, without equitable, locally and regionally controllable monetary alternatives to provide flexibility, the inevitable transition to a lower-energy economy will be extraordinarily painful for thousands of ordinary communities, and millions of ordinary people. Indeed, their transitions will almost certainly come about as a result of a chaotic collapse rather than a managed descent and the levels of energy use that they are able to sustain afterwards will be greatly reduced. Their output will therefore be low and may be insufficient to allow everyone to survive. A total reconstruction of our money-issuing and financing systems is therefore a *sine qua non* if we are to escape Vesuvius' flames.

Endnotes

1. William R. Clark, *Petrodollar Warfare: Oil, Iraq and the Future of the Dollar*, (New Society Publishers, 2005), p. 31. See books.google.com/books?id=q6efPw hWIHUC&pg=PA31&lpg=PA31&dq="us+saudi"+arabian+joint+commission +on+economic+cooperation+in+june+1974&source=web&ots=1hDQ7lQDEL&s ig=ukyrXqNPUAhGdZaO1550C95sD-M#v=onepage&q=%22us%20saudi%22%20 arabian%20joint%20commission%20on%20economic%20cooperation%20in%20 june%201974&f=false.
2. Qiao Liang and Wang Xiangsui, both colonels in the Chinese army, wrote a book, *Unrestricted Warfare*, which appeared on the internet in English 1999 about strategies China could use to defeat a technologically superior opponent such as the United States through a variety of means including currency manipulation. Extracts from the book can be found at cryptome.org/cuw.htm.
3. Yanhui Zhang, *Debt Crisis in the Third World* (2003). See grin.com/e-book/39036/ debt-crisis-in-the-third-world.

Liquidity Networks:
Local Trading Systems Using
a Debt-Free Electronic Currency

GRAHAM BARNES

No currency will work unless people accept it from each other so this novel money will be put into circulation as a way of rewarding those who are accepting and spending it most.

Around the world, conventional currencies such as the euro, the dollar and the pound are in short supply because of the current economic crisis. A liquidity network (LQN) is designed to ease this shortage by creating and distributing a supplementary debt-free currency so that businesses and individuals can trade locally without needing the conventional sort.

Money essentially performs three functions: it acts as a means of exchange, as a store of value and as a unit of account. A liquidity network aims to fulfil only the first of these. It would enable people to buy and sell goods and services in a specific geographic area. The generic name for an LQN's electronic currency is the quid but each local system will probably give a special name to its own version. For example, the emerging Kilkenny LQN group has named their unit the Katz after a very successful local hurling team, the Cats.

As quid can be spent only inside the local area, a healthy quid supply will boost local trade. If euros become scarcer and scarcer, the relative importance of an LQN will increase. Quid will free up euros for "out-of-area" transactions and places with an LQN will become more competitive than those without.

Imagine if a million euros went into circulation in your town overnight but they were super-euros — euros that could be spent only in your area and which spawned extra super-euros in your account if you spent them quickly. A much higher level of trading would take place as the new currency passed rapidly from person to person and from business to business. This super-euro is the quid.

Liquidity Network Structures and Design

Each LQN will be run by a local organization within a framework and guidelines set down by a national support organization to which they all belong. An important function of both the local and the national organizations is that they recognize and reward Positive Behavior — behavior considered to be beneficial to the specific LQN or to the acceptance and success of the LQN movement in general.

The key aspects of the LQN design are:

- Accounts are not allowed to go into the red. Transactions are processed instantly and because there is no debt, there is no need for credit checks nor a legal process for debt recovery.
- Quid are given rather than lent into circulation, the only condition being an expectation of (defined) Positive Behavior by the recipient.
- Some Positive Behaviors — for example, spending one's quid quickly after one gets them or dealing with an increasing number of people — are rewarded after the event.
- If someone fails to maintain a trading level for which they have been rewarded, the quid they were given can be gradually withdrawn. This is to ensure that the supply of quid can be reduced to maintain its value if the overall level of trading falls.
- All trading is carried out electronically by mobile phone or over the internet. This enables the LQN to calculate rewards or account reductions. There is no paper currency.

The LQN design team also have strong preferences:

1. for Open Source software development and Open Hardware
2. for organizational structures recognizing the advantages of the Viable Systems Model and sociocratic approaches

3. for the development of publicly visible Trading Reputations based on Positive Behaviors, as a means of building mutual trust among LQN users

The detailed design of each LQN will be developed with local LQN partners and local circumstances may dictate specific tactical decisions. The team's preferences above should be seen in that context.

Wherever the LQN concept is discussed, people are excited by it. The challenge now is to design and implement strategies that will create the critical mass of earning and spending required for a successful LQN. The Feasta group is concentrating on two particular approaches:

i) **A local authority–backed LQN:** The LQN would give the local authority a specific amount of currency, for example 1 million quid, to spend into circulation by paying a portion of its staff salaries with them. In return, the council would agree to carry on accepting quid, at par with the euro, in payment of local rates, rents and service charges until it had either earned-out its advance in performance rewards or had returned any unearned advance to the LQN. We are currently discussing this arrangement with councils in Dundalk, Kilkenny and Ennis.

ii) **The "TradeTrust" route:** A trade exchange network using euros is set up with the support of the local Chamber of Commerce. This network has all the features of an LQN, i.e. instant electronic transactions and no credit, except that the transactions are in euros, so users have to provide (or be provided with) a euro float. Once the exchange is running, the trading levels provide a good guide to the amount of quid that each account needs to provide the liquidity for the amount of trading it is doing. The appropriate quid amounts can then be issued and the euros withdrawn. A group in Cork intends to follow this route.

The Drawbacks of Free Money

The fact that in both of the above cases quid are given into circulation is one of the obstacles facing an LQN, as the idea that money can be "given away" encourages the thought that quid are of no value. In addition, there is an initial worry that there is no way to sanction participants who retire from the scheme immediately after spending the quid they have been given. But then the penny drops and the worriers realize that all the quid already spent are in other accounts and will be spent again and again and again around the local network.

Once an LQN is operating on a reasonable scale, fear of losing trade to rivals will be a key factor in encouraging traders to stay in the network and others to join. Getting people to join in the start-up phase may be more difficult. It is becoming more obvious that we need to appeal to both intrinsic and extrinsic motivations. We have been somewhat surprised recently to notice that while our own motivations for developing LQN are largely intrinsic, we have assumed that we needed exclusively extrinsic (economic) motivations to encourage participation. But does an LQN project grounded squarely in a distrust and dissatisfaction with mainstream economics really need to couch its propositions solely in terms of economic benefit?

For traders the advantages of joining — their extrinsic motivations — are administrative efficiencies:

- instant transactions with no credit. If insufficient funds are in place the transaction doesn't happen.
- simplified electronic transactions with well-designed user interfaces.
- low transaction costs (compared to banks) and maintenance fees.
- and being on the inside track of a new growing local marketplace, such as that offered by the members' directory section of the LQN website.

However, we are beginning to suspect that intrinsic motivations — support for one's local community, local activism vs. national "sitting on hands," building trust via transparent transaction behavior — may be as or more important than extrinsic ones and that LQNs should harness these feelings in their marketing messages.

Rewarding Positive Behavior

A progressive and proactive local council will want to be seen as a driving force at the heart of an LQN initiative that embodies the social cohesion needed for competitive modern localities. To earn their advances, councils will be required to pay a portion of their employees' wages in quid. The advantage of this is that it enables the council to avoid redundancies and reduce short-time working. Other positive LQN messages should also be adopted and communicated by the council, such as the extra quid given when users spend quickly.

Individuals and traders are rewarded when they accept quid for the first time, quickly spend the quid they have earned, increase their monthly quid turnover and have more quid dealings with more people. They will also be aware that although some of the quid they are given as a reward may be taken away if they fail to maintain the performance for which it was given, quid that they have actually earned through their wages or trading will never be taken except to pay the normal monthly account maintenance fee.

Limitations of the Quid

I noted at the start of this article that the quid is not a store of value. It is designed to incentivize local spending. Of course, individuals and businesses need to save — for retirement, to even out good and bad years and for capital purchases — but they will need to use currencies (or goods) other than the quid for these functions.

Nor is the quid suitable as a unit of account except within an individual LQN. Quid are not "backed" by the euro or by any other source of value. LQNs will not offer formal quid-exchange services between LQNs, although we expect to see such services being offered by LQN participants and would see their emergence as evidence of success.

Over time, quid will almost certainly lose their value against the euro. If the euro gets scarcer, its value in terms of quid will rise and the one-for-one parity maintained by a council will need to be broken. The quids used by different LQNs will acquire different exchange rates with the euro and thus with each other.

The Urgent Need to Get the First LQN Running

The Feasta group has already completed much of the groundwork to enable communities to get started on developing their own LQNs. We have written the basic software, demonstrated the transfer of quid from mobile phone to mobile phone, defined and modeled the reward algorithms and drafted the legal documents under which a local LQN and the national support organization would be set up. We also have an opinion from a senior counsel that an LQN would comply with Irish and EU law. All we need now is a sound, broadly based invitation from a community.

So far, though, community leaders seem not to regard their situations as desperate enough yet to overcome their reluctance to try novel solutions and risk failure. In fact, that was exactly what we were told at a meeting with officials from a Regional Development Authority. In any case, the officials said, the unions would reject the idea of their members being part-paid in quid even if they knew that all the major local shops would accept them.

Nevertheless, the group believes that the liquidity crisis will worsen and that communities will increasingly want to respond locally rather than wait passively for national interventions that may or may not arrive.

Sometime soon, then, we expect the first visionary community leader from among the councils and communities where LQN dialogues are taking place to ask for help. He or she will realize that the risk to their personal credibility is unimportant compared to the potential beneficial impact of an LQN to their friends and neighbors. They will see that "business as usual" is not an option. When they do, the LQN team will use all the energy, commitment and creativity at its disposal to make sure that these pioneer adopters gain the maximum benefit for the places from which they come.

Equity Partnerships:
A Better, Fairer Approach
to Developing Land

CHRIS COOK

The conventional way of financing property development entangles those involved in a web of debt and conflicting business interests. A new way of organizing developments promises better buildings, more affordable rents and a stake in the outcome for everyone.

We are accustomed to thinking that property is an object—typically, a productive asset—that may be bought and sold, but as Bentham points out above, this is incorrect. Property is the relationship between an individual—the subject—and the asset, which is the object of the individual's property. So the productive asset of land is not property but rather the object of a man's property or something that is "proper" to the man. It follows that property is the bundle of rights and obligations that connect the subject individual to the object asset.

The Land Equity Partnerships that I describe in this chapter (I'll just call them equity partnerships from now on) are an example of the new types of arrangement that can be made when people think of property in terms of rights and obligations rather than ownership.

Land, or perhaps more accurately location, has a value when it is put to use. Its value may perhaps derive from crops that grow on it, or from animals or fish that feed there. It may also derive from its use by individuals to live there, or to conduct business there, or for use as public infrastructure such as transport. This use value then has a value in exchange; individuals are prepared to exchange something of value in return for the use of land at a specific location.

The bundle of rights and obligations relating to land/location is typically recorded in the form of legally binding protocols, although in less-developed nations the rights and obligations relating to land may be a matter of oral tradition. Some cultures are unable to understand that anyone can have absolute rights over land. Others insist that absolute ownership is God's alone; but the convention in many societies is that the state has absolute ownership of land and that exclusive property rights may then be granted to individuals or to enterprises with legal personality (corporate bodies).

Conventional private-sector property development is transaction based. Land-owners sell land to developers who obtain any necessary permissions, improve or build on the land and sell it to a buyer. Developers typically obtain as much of the development finance as possible by borrowing at interest from a credit institution or investor. Buyers typically finance their purchase with loans secured by a legal charge or mortgage. After a time, they will sell the property to another debt-financed buyer, or find a tenant, and so on through the years.

> *It is to be observed, that in common speech, in the phrase "the object of a man's property," the words "the object of" are commonly left out; and by an ellipsis, which, violent as it is, is now become more familiar than the phrase at length, they have made that part of it which consists of the words "a man's property" perform the office of the whole.*
>
> JEREMY BENTHAM, "AN INTRODUCTION TO THE PRINCIPLES OF MORALS AND LEGISLATIONS" (1789)

In most cases a developer has no interest in high-quality standards or energy efficiency because he will not be associated with the site once the development has been sold. He simply wishes to maximize the transaction profit. He will therefore attempt to ensure that any investment in amenities, infrastructure or transport is made by the public sector rather than by him.

A New Legal Entity

On 6 April 2001, a new legal entity, the Limited Liability Partnership (LLP), came into effect in the UK and, despite the fact that its objective was to protect professional partnerships from the consequences of their own negligence, it made possible a new way of handling and financing property development. Confusingly, an LLP is not legally a partnership. It is, however — like a company — a corporate body with a continuing legal existence independent of its members. Also, as with a limited liability company, members cannot lose more than they invest in an LLP.

An LLP need not have a Memorandum of Incorporation or Articles of Association and is not subject to the laws governing the relationship between investors and the directors who act as their agents in managing the company. The "LLP agreement" between members is totally flexible. It need not even be in writing, since simple provisions based upon partnership law apply by way of default. As a result, an equity partnership set up as an LLP is a consensually negotiated contractual framework for investment in and ownership, occupation and use of land.

An equity partnership (EP) does not own anything, do anything, contract with anyone or employ anyone. In other words, it is not an organization: it is a framework agreement within a corporate "wrapper." The EP agreement sets out the relationship between the different stakeholder groups, and each stakeholder group may also have its own specific sub-agreement at whatever level of formality (e.g. an organizational constitution) its members agree. The EP encapsulates the entire property relationship within a corporate entity and related framework agreement.

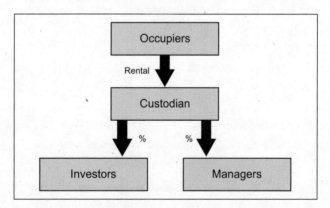

An EP has a minimum of four types of partner:
1. **The custodian:** who holds the freehold of the land in perpetuity
2. **The occupier(s):** individuals and/or enterprises occupying the property
3. **The investor(s):** individuals and enterprises who invest money and/or money's worth (such as the value of the land)

Potential Partners in an Equity Partnership

The landowner	The landowner may be a private individual or investor, a local authority or a developer. The landowner transfers the land to the custodian, and becomes an investor in the partnership.
The custodian	Holds the freehold of the land in perpetuity on behalf of the partners. The custodian is probably a board of independent experts with legal, financial, property and construction expertise. The custodian sets up a Charter of Cooperation between equity partners.
The developer	The developer may be the owner of the land, or he may have set up an agreement with the landowner, or he may be brought in as an investor to contribute his expertise to the development. He may also be the contractor.
The manager	The manager is appointed by the custodian to manage the development, its maintenance and transfers of investors. The manager is likely to be a property management company with valuation and property transaction expertise.
The local authority	The local authority zones and grants planning permission, which adds value to the land. It also imposes obligations such as Part V and charges for infrastructure services. It may be the owner of the land. If not, it may be an investor to maintain a say in the development on behalf of its tenants under the Part V requirements or other community interests.
The investors	The investors would include the site owners. They could also include the bank or the housing finance agency funding the local authority, or the bank funding the developer. Once the development is completed and fully let, it would be an ideal, low-risk investment for a pension fund or other investment fund, which could buy out the equity shares held by the landowner, and/or the local authority, the developer and the contractor if they wished to sell.
The contractor	The contractor may be brought in as an investor by the custodian, the local authority or the developer. He would be expected to invest at least part of his profits from the contract to align his interests with those of the other partners.
The insurer	The development will require insurance once it is occupied. This is normally obtained by the manager. The insurance company providing the insurance could be an investor in return for preferential rates.
The occupier	The community of individuals who occupy the properties on the land. While the majority of occupiers will be residents, equity stakes can also be built by enterprises operating on the land, e.g. a local shop or hairdresser. The occupier rents the property at an affordable basic rent. This should be sufficient to cover interest charges due to the investors. The occupier has a right to pay an additional amount to purchase equity shares in the development. Once the income from these equity shares is equal to the rent being paid, the occupier effectively owns the dwelling but not, of course, its site. This feature enables them to buy their dwellings over the years without taking out a loan. Occupiers vacating their dwellings receive the full value of any equity shares they hold.

(Source: James Pike)

4. **The developer/operator:** who provides development expertise and manages the EP

How An Equity Partnership Works

Landowners invest the agreed value of their land/location in the partnership in exchange for "equity shares" which are millionths of the flow of rentals to be paid by the occupiers when the development is complete. This gives the landowner a share in any development gain. While not every development goes to plan, the partnership model ensures that everyone involved has an interest in ensuring that it does. If the land invested does not have planning consent, the local authority can invest the value of that consent, hoping to receive a greater return on its equity shares than it would conventionally.

The custodian becomes steward over the land in perpetuity, with rights of veto over land use, and also safeguards the EP's purpose and values as expressed in the EP agreement. The custodian may be an individual, a board of independent experts with legal, financial, property and construction expertise, or a public body such as a local authority.

Investors then invest "money's worth" or money to allow the development to be carried out, and in return they receive a proportionate number of equity shares. Once the development is complete, the occupiers pay an agreed rental in money or "money's worth" of services for the use of the capital that has been invested in the location. This capital rental is set at an affordable level initially and may rise according to an agreed index of inflation. The occupiers also make a payment or provision for the maintenance/depreciation (and possibly heating) of the building. The developer/manager manages the development or use of the building in return for equity share in the rentals. If an occupier pays more than the affordable rental, he invests automatically in equity shares, and thereby acquires a stake in the property in which he lives. Once he has acquired enough shares, the income which he derives from them cancels out the capital rental he has to pay.

The pool of rentals created by development is shared out amongst the holders of the equity shares in proportion to their holdings. This form of EP is essentially a Real Estate Investment Trust (REIT). REITs have become extremely popular recently because rents flow through them without tax having to be paid by it. Instead, any tax due is collected from the shareholders.

Investors, who have seen their income dwindling as interest rates spiral toward zero, should be extremely interested in an investment such as this.

Equity shares offer a reasonable, index-linked return based on property. There is a very low risk that the return will not be paid since affordable rentals are by definition more likely to be paid. Equity shares are a perfect investment for risk-averse investors such as pension funds and sovereign wealth funds. In particular, this investment is perfect for Islamic investors since no debt or interest is involved.

Worked Examples

Capital Rental to Develop Five Eco-Houses

A landowner invests land in exchange for a 20% equity share in the rentals from the developed property. A provider of eco-friendly and energy-efficient wooden buildings is prepared to sell five units at a cost of €200,000 plus a 10% equity share since he is investing part of his profit margin. The occupiers-to-be dig the foundations and provide other non-skilled labor. In return they receive a 10% equity share. In addition to the €200,000 spent on the houses, a further €100,000 is used to purchase heat pumps, a wood-chip boiler and pay for other investments in energy efficiency.

As 40% of the rental income has been allocated, 60% is left to pay for ongoing maintenance and management and to give a return on the €300,000 money investment. Let us suppose that a 10% share goes to maintenance and 50% goes to pay the investors. A 4% initial return on investment requires a capital rental of €24,000 in the first year. It would be divided as follows.

- Management and maintenance charge is 10% or €2,400.
- The former landowner receives 20% i.e. €4,800.
- The building manufacturer receives €2,400.
- Investors receive €12,000.

The occupiers pay €4,800 per house per annum gross initially. This is reduced by €480 (their equity share), to give an affordable rent of €360/month each.

Capital Rental and Land Rental to
Reconstruct Seven Local Authority Dwellings

Seven existing properties are in municipal ownership. Two of them are to be converted into three units of 1-bed each, while the other five will each be converted to give a 1-bed unit on the ground floor and a 2-bed unit on each of the two floors above. Accommodation for, say, 20 people in 11 1-bed flats and five 2-bed flats will result. A common space and shared facilities will also be provided at ground level and ground-source heating and other energy-efficient features will be installed.

Capital Rental

Each of the seven sites on which the dwellings stand is valued at €100,000. The current value of the two buildings to become 1-bed units is put at €125,000 each and the five other buildings at €100,000. The redevelopment cost is €70,000 per building or €490,000 so the total cost of the scheme, allowing €10,000 contingencies, is €1,950,000.

The municipality puts in half the value of the land (€350,000) and 20% of the value of the buildings (€150,000) in return for equity shares. The remaining €1,450,000 is contributed by an investor prepared to accept an initial 3% return or €43,500 per year. This capital rental would be inflation-linked and would therefore provide a real asset-based return of 3% to the investor regardless of movement in interest rates. The 20 occupier members would pay €2,175 each per year in rent, or just under €42 per week.

Land Rental

In addition to the capital rental, the equity partnership members agree to include a land rental payment in their EP agreement. This rental is a pre-distributive mechanism internal to the EP and utilizes two separate parameters: an income pool and a land-use pool.

i) **Income pool:** Assume a contribution to a "pool" at the rate of 5% of income.

5 members on €50 per week state benefits pay in total	€12.50
5 members on €100 per week pay in total	25.00
5 members on €150 per week pay in total	37.50
5 members on €200 per week pay in total	50.00

The outcome is a total income pool of €125 per week, which is then divided between the 20 members giving a dividend of €6.25 each. This gives a net rebate to those earning less than €125 per week and a net contribution by those earning more. This is intended to subsidize the capital rental payments for those least able to afford them. The contribution rate could be higher or lower than 5%.

ii) **Land-use pool:** The land occupied by the EP members would be assessed using Land Rental Units (LRUs). In the example, five properties each occupy three units of land, while the other two are bigger and occupy five units — a total of 25 LRUs. The members agree a value payable per LRU by the occupants of each property into a pool. Again, net-value transfers (payments or receipts) result from those enjoying above-average land use per person to those with below-average land use.

A Comparison with Conventional Refinancing

EPs may be used to refinance existing secured debt through "unitization." Take a €1bn nominal value portfolio consisting of 5,000 25-year mortgage loans averaging €200,000 and paying interest at 6% per annum. On average, each borrower must currently repay €1303.77 per month or €15,645.24 p.a. for the life of the loan.

Under an EP arrangement, a capital rental could be set at an "affordable" level, say, an average €500 per month or €6,000 p.a. This would be index-linked. The total rental income would be €30m in the first year and would rise with inflation. The 5,000 properties would be "unitized" into (say) a million "units" or "millionths", each consisting of one millionth of the economic interest/"ownership" of the relevant properties. A unit would bring an income of €30.00 in the first year, rising with inflation thereafter. What would the market price of these units be?

 i) At €1,000 per unit the initial return is 3%, and the proceeds €1bn which refinances the debt at 100% of nominal value;

 ii) At €750 per unit the initial return is 4%, and the proceeds €750m or 75% of the nominal value. And so on.

It will be seen that the absence of debt repayment dramatically reduces financing costs.

Improved Affordability and Sustainability

Affordability

The problem in most urban areas is not the affordability of housing but rather the affordability of land, since construction costs are relatively uniform. In essence the issue relates to land rental values, since a land purchase price is simply the capitalized net present value of future land rentals. The issue of supply relates primarily to planning, land use and an absence of incentives to bring land into use. The use of a land rental will tend to incentivize occupiers to bring land into productive use.

The use of the EP allows land-owners to invest the value of their land and to receive an agreed share of the rental value of the developed land. Similarly, local authorities' participation in EPs allows them to invest the value of planning consents, and to use their resulting share of the rental value of developed land to cross-subsidize affordable property rentals. If local authorities were to specify that development could only take place within an EP framework, then the result could be a major increase in development of affordable housing. This might require legislation. In fact, the structure is similar to the use of statutory Development Corporations in the UK, except that land-value capture is addressed consensually within the EP framework, rather than adversarially within a statutory framework.

In the UK, the statutory "right to buy" in the public sector has seen a transfer of housing from the public to the private sector. The EP gives occupiers both an indefinite "right to rent" and a "right to invest" in the co-owned property in which they live.

They may not only buy equity shares conventionally, but also acquire them as "sweat equity" through:

- self-build or partial self-build;
- carrying out maintenance to agreed standards, to be monitored by the EP operator member.

As occupiers acquire equity, then their net capital rental obligation gradually falls so when their investment reaches a level at which the notional capital rental income equals their capital rental obligation they are, in economic terms, the owner, although the land remains in custody. Moreover an investor/occupier may flexibly release equity at any time simply by selling equity shares.

Governments that give rental subsidies, grants or subsidized loans for property merely increase rents or the price of land. The EP model takes landownership out of the equation by putting the land into the ownership of a custodian, and the land price therefore cannot become inflated because it is never sold again.

Where landowners are reluctant to give up ownership, it is possible for them to retain ownership as the custodian member. In that case, the EP agreement essentially operates as an evergreen lease of indefinite duration—

that is, the occupier is entitled to use of the land for as long as he pays the rental. The measure of control, such as restrictions on use, retained by the owner would affect the amount and nature of the return they could expect through the EP, in their other stakeholder role as an investor of the value of the land.

An EP improves affordability by drastically cutting long-term financing costs because:

- there is no return of capital, as there would be with debt, since the capital value is unitized into tradable equity shares in the EP, just like the units in a unit trust;
- the return on capital bears no relationship to interest rates. It gives an index-linked return reflecting the risk of property-based investment.

Stakeholders' participation means that the need for development finance is minimized. For example, the land is not bought with loan finance but invested in return for equity shares.

Sustainability

In the EP model the developer/operator is a service provider, rather than an intermediary, and need neither risk equity capital nor put his business at risk by obtaining secured loan finance. His interests lie in minimizing the total cost of occupation over time, because this will maximize the rental revenues and therefore the value of the units that he gets in return for his services, expertise and time committed.

Similarly, any contractors responsible for design and construction can be given the option of being paid in equity shares instead of money. Even if they chose money, they would be expected to take their profit in units so that their stake in the outcome was aligned with the interests of the other stakeholders. As a result, it is in the interests of all stakeholders that the buildings are constructed to high standards of quality and energy efficiency, since to do so minimizes the total cost of ownership over time. The result is a genuinely sustainable development.

Implementation

There are three key areas to which attention must be given in order to set up an equity partnership: the availability of the necessary legal form; the taxation regime; and the regulatory regime.

The Legal Form

The enabling legislation is the recognition of an "open corporate" enterprise. This is a new type of legal entity, which is a corporate body with no stipulations about what its governing agreement should be, and only simple default provisions based upon partnership principles about its governance. In the UK this was achieved in two pages of legislation and one page of default provisions. The other (relatively few) provisions in the UK legislation dealt with technical matters relating to taxation and limitation of liability. Anyone wishing to set up an EP in the Republic of Ireland could do so in Northern Ireland under the British legislation until equivalent legislation is passed by the Dail.

If open corporates are permitted, then limitation of liability could be available subject to payment of a bond (as in Jersey); an insurance premium; or a provision into a default fund. However, since an EP is a framework agreement linking all stakeholders and the EP doesn't actually do anything, there is no need for limitation of liability because no one outside the EP can be adversely affected by it.

Taxation

An EP is "tax transparent." It does not pay tax on any capital gains or income that flow through it. Its members pay instead according to their personal or corporate liability.

Regulation

Statutory provisions that protect investors in relation to the actions of financial services intermediaries are unnecessary in relation to an EP, because any financial services take place within the EP framework and are subject to the EP agreement.

Using Equity Partnerships
to Rescue Building Projects
Hit by the Downturn

JAMES PIKE

Community land partnerships provide an alternative way of becoming a property owner and gaining a voice in the management of the development in which one lives. They should also be very stable and secure investments for pension funds.

As an architect working on both public regeneration projects and private residential and mixed-use developments which have run into serious problems over the past two years, I have an obvious interest in finding alternative ways to finance such developments. I have also been aware for some years of the problems of managing residential developments, where the current model is selling individual apartments or houses to investors who then rent them on short-term leases. The tenants have no say in the management of the development and the investors no interest. The result is that the owner-occupiers, often a very small proportion of the occupiers as a whole, are the only active participants in the management company. I know from managers of such developments and as an owner-occupier myself that this creates many problems.

One other major problem with public or private developments is rebuilding or redeveloping them when they become obsolete. Currently, each house or apartment is owned freehold and many local authority estates have been sold to the tenants. I have found over the years that bringing a large number of owners together is an almost impossible task.

When I came across the Community Land Partnership ideas put forward by Chris Cook of the Nordic Enterprise Trust, I recognized that this model could be an answer to both our financial and management and redevelopment problems. It offers an alternative path to property ownership and a stake in the management of developments for all tenants. It also presents a very stable and secure development model which should be attractive to pension and other investment funds. It shares some features with current tenant-purchase schemes and rent-to-buy schemes but provides a much more flexible framework.

I got together with an accountant, Kieran Ryan, who has considerable experience in property development, and a solicitor, Kevin Ryan, to investigate the feasibility of the model in the context of current finance, tax, management and property legislation in Ireland. We have consulted a number of interested parties, including banks, property developers, local government officers and property managers.

We consider that the proposed model can work satisfactorily in Ireland without any change in legislation though some adjustments might be made if it became common practice. There could also be considerably wider benefit in revising current 100-year-old legislation on Limited Liability Partnerships in line with recent legislation introduced in the UK and many other countries.

Applying Equity Partnership to Urban Regeneration Projects

Set out below is a worked example of a major urban regeneration project in central Dublin within the canal ring. The calculations are based on a scheme selected following consultation with the existing tenants.

The land is owned by the local authority and its value is taken as nil when calculating "Capital Rent." If land is valued at €1m or say €23,000 per dwelling, this would be added in calculating sum required to purchase Equity Shares. If own-door duplex/apartments are located at ground level in all apartment blocks, except those with commercial uses, more than one-third of all dwellings would have own-door access. This represents the general proportion of households with children across the city.

Therefore, the "capital rental" is very affordable and there should be no problem letting the whole development. Tenants of the existing development or other prospective occupiers on the local authorities list would receive the appropriate level of subsidy.

Calculations for residential units and common areas only:

Construction Cost	Houses (31 × 100m² × € 900/m²)	€2,790,000
	Duplex (90 × 100m² × €1000/m²)	€9,000,000
	Apartment (636 × 100m² × €1200/m²)	€76,320,000
	Underground Parking (800 spaces at €20,000)	€16,000,000
		Say €104,000,000
Infrastructure Levy	€10,000 per dwelling (757 × €10,000)	€7,570,000
	Community Buildings etc.	Say €1,630,000
		€9,200,000
Fees & other costs	€12,000 × 757	€9,084,000
		Say €9,000,000
Total cost for dwellings and parking		**€122,200,000**
Add 10% for Management costs, demolition, contingencies		€12,220,000
TOTAL COSTS		**Say €134,400,000**

Projected rental income at current market rents:

31 — 3 bed house — €1,250 p.m. = €15,000 p.a.	€465,000
90 — 3 bed duplex — €1,200 p.m. = €14,400 p.a.	€1,296,000
124 — 1 bed apartment — € 700 p.m. = € 8,400 p.a.	€1,041,600
86 — 2 bed duplex — €1,000 p.m. = € 1,200 p.a.	€1,032,000
385 — 2 bed apartment — € 950 p.m. = € 1,040 p.a.	€4,389,000
38 — 3 bed duplex — €1,200 p.m. = €14,400 p.a.	€547,200
3 — 4 bed duplex — €1,250 p.m. = €15,000 p.a.	€45,000
	€8,815,800
	Say €8,800,000
Operating/maintenance/sinking fund 12.5%	€1,100,000
Available for payment of capital rent (i.e. initial return is 5.73%)	€7,700,000

Payments required for Capital Rent:

If return for investors is 3.0% average payment per dwelling:
    €5,390 p.a. €1,466 p.a. = €7,856 p.a.
If return for investors is 4.0% average payment per dwelling:
    €7,765 p.a. €1,466 p.a. = €9,231 p.a.

Once the development is fully let, therefore it presents a very secure form of investment, so that if tenants or occupiers leave they can be easily replaced. They are not under pressure to pay more than the "capital rent" but even at low current market rents they can build up a substantial equity share within a reasonable period. If they have financial difficulties such as losing their job, they can just pay the current capital rent or even reduce their equity share until they are in a position to pay the required level of rent. If, on the other hand, their financial position improves, they can purchase additional equity shares.

The Potential Role of a Pension Fund

Such a secure form of investment must be attractive to pension funds. The basic capital rent at, say, 2,5% currently represents a good return for a pension fund but the figures also show that a 3% return does not make the scheme unaffordable. This return is independent of service charges. In addition to their basic capital rent, which is index linked, the occupiers are buying equity shares with their surplus rent which goes to pay off the original capital invested which the pension fund can now invest in further projects, but they are likely to hold a substantial share in perpetuity because, when occupiers leave, they are paid the full value of their share but the dwelling reverts to the partnership. It is proposed that a pension fund could purchase a portion of the equity partnership to either buy out the original investors or a substantial portion of their investment. The payment would include the sum invested plus a reasonable return in the current market for that sum. A reasonable figure in the current situation would be say 10%. This would increase the capital rental required by 10%.

The Occupier

As shown in the above figures, equity partnerships offer many attractions to a potential occupier. It gives him/her much more certainty than current rent-to-buy schemes. It requires no borrowing and offers great flexibility depending on his/her financial circumstances at different times. It also involves occupiers in ownership and an input into the management of the scheme which tenants to not normally have. If occupiers want to leave the scheme, they are paid the full value of their equity share. If they have bought out their full share, they will receive the full market value of their dwelling.

The level of total rent required by the tenant to acquire the full equity share over a thirty-year period is calculated as the capital rent which will reduce by the proportion he pays above the capital rent each year plus an annual repayment at 1/30 of the capital cost, plus the operating/maintenance cost:

Payments required to purchase full equity share over 30 years
Capital Rent at 3.0% requires a total rent of: €11,641 p.a. = €10,574
Capital Rent at 4.0% requires a total rent of: €12,533 p.a. = €11,861
Average projected net market rental payment is: €11,784 p.a.

Therefore the owner can purchase a full equity share in thirty years at a net rental payment less than market rents if Capital Rent is at 3.0% or just above if Capital rent is at 4.0%.

I have not included the commercial elements of the project. If the density was increased to achieve say 900 units it would reduce the land cost per dwelling to €19,000. The density would still be a relatively low 51/acre for an inner city site and could be achieved in a low height format. This demonstrates the attraction for occupiers who may well be able to purchase their equity shares in a much shorter period if their financial circumstances improve. If their circumstances deteriorate then they can revert to paying the capital rent only or even sell some of their equity shares if necessary. Note: the figures shown are for 2010. Future rents will vary with the cost of living index.

The Investor

For a local authority or a government agency, particularly one wishing to undertake a regeneration scheme, the equity partnership model offers an attractive alternative to conventional finance particularly if a pension fund can be persuaded to take on the bulk of the funding once the development is fully occupied. It also offers an excellent management structure in which the tenants can be engaged and is much better alternative than selling dwellings to tenants in the current way because the local authority or agency does not lose the opportunity to redevelop schemes when they eventually deteriorate after a long period.

The Operator

Housing associations might be strong candidates for the Operator role, as some of them have a good reputation for managing not only their own social element in current housing projects but also the public realm in the private element of such schemes. They could perhaps also act as the Developer/Operator on behalf of local authorities or government agencies and take on the Custodian role as their boards and senior staff include a wide range of appropriate professionals.

Advantages and Disadvantages
Advantages:
- The model is not a straitjacket; it is inherently flexible and would be tailored to each regeneration opportunity.

- The model offers the potential to attract outside investment when fully let and demonstrably in successful operation. It should be particularly attractive to pension funds.
- For occupiers, they can own their dwelling, in time, without having to borrow. They also have an input in the management of the development as a member of the equity partnership: something they would not have as a renter of an investment property. They also become members of a community of stakeholders with a shared future. This core feature should make for more stable tenancies and a better experience for the occupier than possible in the private rental sector. An equity partnership also offers greater security of tenure compared to the private rental sector.
- For the local authority/investor — the model has many advantages, particularly its flexibility; it can give the local authority continuing control over key issues of social policy, while being able to dispose of a substantial element of its investment at early stage, to a pension fund or other investor.
- The development company has a project which it can easily let and which, when let, has a ready market for investors to buy out its share.
- It presents a much better framework for reconstruction or redevelopment, when the development becomes obsolete.

Disadvantages:
- The model is new and unproven in Ireland. While we do not see it as unduly complex or "over-engineered," it may be viewed in that light.
- For those on low incomes and / or paying social rents, the possibility of building an equity stake may remain quite abstract.
- Residents may be reluctant to commit resources toward an equity share until the regeneration scheme is a proven success.

Examples of additional projects are shown on the next two pages. These figures show that the occupants can buy their full equity share at around current market rents.

Conclusion
I consider that the equity partnership model presents a much better alternative to the current public-private partnership one as it does not require

1. New Development in an Inner Suburban Site

280 units (At estimated current land values and construction costs)

Land cost: €40,000/dwelling

Build: €120,000 (90m^2 gross x €1,333 per m^2)

Levies: €15,000/dwelling

Fees + other costs: €15,000/dwelling

Gross cost: (€190,000/dwelling) €53,200,000

Add 10% to cover other overheads and profit: €58,520,000

Rental income at current market rates

60 — one bed — € 800/month — € 9,600/year: € 576,000

170 — two bed — €1,100/month — €13,200/year: €2,244,000

50 — three bed — €1,250/month — €15,000/year: € 750,000

Rental income: € 3,570,000

Operating Cost / Maintenance / Sinking Fund 12.5% - €446,000

On the basis that interest relief restriction would not apply to

equity partnerships — no additional charges

Available for "capital rental" say: €3,124,000

i.e. Initial Return: 5.30% on €58,520,000

Payments required for capital rental

If additional 10% is added to the gross cost, payments required are as follows:

If return for investors is 3.0% then payments for an average dwelling would be: € 7,936 p.a

At 4% return it would be: € 10,028 p.a.

Payment required to purchase full equity share over 30 years

Capital Rent at 3.0% requires a total rent of: €12,471 p.a.

Capital Rent at 4.0% requires a total rent of: €13,517 p.a.

Average projected net market rental payment is: €12,750 p.a.

These figures show that the occupants can buy their full equity share over 30 years at around current market rents.

a private development company but only a contractor. It can recover the capital invested by the public body at an early date at a much lower cost to the taxpayer. It could form a major element in current proposals by the Construction Industry Council for funding major infrastructure projects using pension funds.

In the private sector, particularly in relation to projects whose funding loans will bring them into the NAMA portfolio, the equity partnership model must be a strong candidate as an appropriate development structure.

Current Irish legislation for Limited Liability Partnerships probably needs bringing up to date in line with recent legislation in the UK and

2. New Development in Suburban Backland Site

100% at affordable rent

54 houses: 1.75 acres

Land Value: €30,000/dwelling

Construction Cost: 110m^2 x €1,000/m^2 = €110,000/dwelling

Infrastructure Levy: €12,000/dwelling

Fees & other costs: €10,000/dwelling

Total cost/dwelling: €162,000

Gross cost: €162,000 × 54 = €8,748,000

Add 10% to cover other overheads and profit: €9,623,000

Projected rental income at current rental levels

54 — 3 bed — €1000/month — €12,000pa = €648,000

Operating / Maintenance / Sinking Fund at 7.5% = € 48,600

Available for repayment of "Capital Rent" = €600,000

i.e. initial return is 5.9% on = €9,623,000

Payments required for capital rental

If additional 10% is added to the Gross Cost payments required are as follows

If return for investors is 3.0% then payments for an average dwelling would be: €5,900 p.a.

At 4% return it would be: €7,867 p.a.

Payments required to purchase full equity share over 30 years

Capital Rent at 3.0% requires a total rent of: €9,934 p.a.

Capital Rent at 4.0% requires a total rent of: €10,918 p.a.

Average projected net market rental payment is: €10,500 p.a. = €875 p.m.

elsewhere. The Limited Company is not a suitable vehicle for such developments. Equity partnership presents a model for future housing and mixed-use development which is very flexible and which promises home ownership to the occupier without the burden of a mortgage while at the same time offering a stake in the management of the development. For the developer and a bank, it substantially reduces the risk which has been so catastrophically exposed in the current market collapse. For the public authority, it presents a much more economically and socially sustainable model for development. If we wish to reduce the risk of future property bubbles, we should seriously consider using equity partnerships.

Trying to Form an Equity Partnership to Buy a Welsh Farm

TIM HELWEG-LARSEN

Pioneering any new approach isn't easy. Because there isn't a market yet for shares in an equity partnership, it proved hard to convince would-be investors that someone would pay a fair price for their holding when they wanted to move on.

Mariska and I had been living on Pantperthog Farm with six other people for two years when, just before Christmas 2009, our landlord announced that he was going to sell the farm and offered those of us living here first refusal. The eight of us explored various ways in which some or all of us might purchase the property so that we could continue to live on and improve the farm.

All of us felt that a cooperative would give us little incentive to invest time and our own money in improving the property. "Shared ownership" had its drawbacks too. In particular, it might make raising the purchase price harder as would-be investors might worry that they would find it hard to sell their portion of the property when they needed to do so in future. Moreover, substantial decisions about how we should invest our time and money in developing the property would become very difficult.

So Mariska and I came up with a proposal that drew on Chris Cook's ideas about equity partnerships and what we had read about Islamic financial structures such as that designed by used by Tarek El Diwany for the Ansar housing development in Manchester. This approach separates the investment element from the ownership and the management of the property.

Pantperthog Farm - Bond Issue
Machynlleth, Wales, SY20 9AU

£400,000 Equity Bonds offered *
3% Annual Return, index linked to local rental prices
* This is not an investment prospectus but an invitation for business partners.

The Pantperthog Farm bond issue is an opportunity to participate in the purchase and sustainable development of a zero-carbon property in the Snowdonia National Park.

The property includes a **five-bedroom farmhouse, three barns, 5 acres of land and its own hydro-electricity and water supply.** Pantperthog Farm is currently owned by Nick Mills, and has been run as a rental property for the last three years. Nick now lives in Stroud and has decided to sell the property. As current tenants, Nick has offered us first refusal on the property at below market price.

We are forming a corporate partnership (LLP) for the special purpose of issuing equity bonds and the purchase of the property. Investors will become "Investor Partners' in the LLP and have the opportunity to buy bonds up to a total value of £400,000. Equity bonds will provide an annual return initially of 3% indexed to local rental prices.

The business of the LLP will be to run the farm as a rental property, collecting a rent from the Managing Partner and paying an annual return on bonds to Investor Partners.

We (Tim & Mariska) will act as the 'Managing Partners' of the LLP, with responsibility for the property and paying a rent to the LLP. Over time we may buy back the equity bonds of the corporate partnership.

If this investment is of interest to you or someone else you know, please get in touch. Yours Sincerely,

Tim Helweg-Larsen and Mariska Evelein
www.propertybonds.org

Our idea was to form a Limited Liability Partnership (LLP) as I had the experience of forming two LLPs in the past. This would buy the property using money raised by the sale of bonds to Investor Partners. We would become the Managing Partner of the property and give the other tenants longer tenancy agreements than they had from the owner. We sent out our draft proposal to people we knew, asking for £400,000. We got a good bit of interest including two firm offers totaling £50,000 and the possibility of a further £100,000.

However, by August 2010, we had run out of time to raise the money. Our housemates were able to find enough finance from their families to buy the farm collectively and while Mariska and I don't want to take on the risks of sharing the ownership with them, we will be able to rent our part of the farm from them.

The whole exercise has set us thinking about how we can apply the property bonds model elsewhere and Mariska and I are keen to find a home we can call our own. We are looking at how we can apply what we have learned to a smaller property, one that isn't trying to accommodate so many people and also one at a lower price. "Smaller" and "less expensive" will make it easier to trial something new. Right now we are looking to see how we could apply a similar model to buying a houseboat. Mariska is Dutch and we may be taking a trip to Holland to look at their famous barges.

The main feedback we got from people who were interested in our proposal, but chose not to go ahead, was that they needed a clearer way to get their money out. With only one property's worth of bonds, there would have been a very small market for them and investors would probably have had to find purchasers themselves even though, in the proposal, we had said that we would advertise the bonds to make the market work. The reality was, of course, that there was a risk that an investor wouldn't find someone to buy what would have admittedly been a rather unusual investment product.

We think the lack-of-a-market problem would go away if lots of houses were financed with bonds. The Holiday Property Bond company has financed 1,300 holiday properties this way, and if there were a similar number of houses financed with Sustainable Property Bonds then there would be a liquid market in the bonds and it would be quite straightforward for someone to sell their bonds and get back their money.

We spoke to a few housing-finance organizations to see if they would be willing to take a risk on our property and guarantee to buy back any or all of the bonds in 5 years' time at a price agreed today. We offered to pay the bank a fee for giving bondholders this option to sell up. We thought we could also invite a think tank to study what we were doing and pass on recommendations to the housing-finance companies, so that they could learn from the experience and see if they would like to apply the model on a larger scale. This is something we are still exploring.

There are a few hurdles for a debt-free financing structure to jump but the potential is there for one to take root and challenge the idea that "mortgages or rental" are the only options. We will continue to think about this and if we can pull it off, you will be able to find us at propertybonds.org

Vision

Our hope is that this model can find application on a wider scale. Sustainable property bonds will enable the following:

Greening of the Housing Stock

Once purchased, the property will never again be sold, supporting good long-term planning and decision-making. Properties are held in trust and are managed in accordance with environmental objectives, enforceable by the Custodian Partner.

Resolves the "Landlord Tenant Dilemma"

Tenants may themselves buy back the bonds from the initial Investor Partners, giving them a stake in the property and helping to overcome the "landlord tenant dilemma." Tenants can also invest time, energy and money in return for a larger stake in the properties bonds.

Removes Inflationary Pressure on the Property Market

By packaging the usage value of the property as a bond, and taking the property itself permanently off the market, upward pressure on property prices is reduced.

Robust During Recession

Returns to bond holders are linked to an index of rental prices, ensuring returns can always be paid even during deflationary times. The mortgage industry by contrast is open to a spiral of defaults and repossessions undermining its usefulness during recession.

The Mondragon Bank:
An Old Model for a New Type of Finance

A new type of institution is needed to handle non-debt finance. It should help promoters plan their projects and then find outside investor-partners in return for a share of each project's income rather than its profits. This is essentially how the Mondragon coops' bank used to work.

Imagine yourself as a bank manager in a small community 50 years ago. Your friends and neighbors have their current and savings accounts with you and when they need to borrow they come to tell you about their ideas. You know most of the locals and it is not difficult for you to tell whether a proposal is going to work. Your decision is based not only on the idea's potential commercial viability but also on the individual's personal ability, skill and support network.

But times have changed. Bank managers in small communities do not have the authority to give bigger loans anymore. Instead, the bank that owns the branch channels the community's savings into what it believes to be the most profitable segments of a near-global capital market. It will only lend to the people in the community if it can get a safe mortgage charge over their houses but, even here, the bursting of the housing bubble has made the bank wary about their ability to repay. On average today, people, companies and governments carry much more debt than in the past.

Banking worked very well as long as there was steady economic growth and customers were not too heavily in debt. However, economic degrowth will make it much harder for banks to find customers with a good chance of being able to repay the loan with interest in due time.

The coming energy crunch will lead to volatile prices and an overall long-term economic contraction. The opportunities for banks to lend in this environment will shrink for two main reasons. The first is that peak oil will change the relative prices of land, labor and capital and make our contemporary society uneconomic because it uses too much energy. All our capital assets will lose value because they are energy inefficient. That will force everybody to reduce their debts much more than we have so far during the current financial crisis. The second reason is that the price volatility will make the risk of losing money on new investments much higher than in the past, especially as the process of developing a new technological and institutional structure and a new way of organizing production is inescapably unpredictable.

So, the Golden Age of banking lies behind us, and yet we are facing the biggest need for investment in history in order to make the transition to a sustainable way of life. But if that need cannot be financed by the existing banking system, a new non-debt system for saving and finance has to be developed.

In principle, this new system should do the exact opposite of what ordinary banks are doing. They try to avoid risk by forcing entrepreneurs to bear as much of it as possible. That will not be possible in the future. The higher level of risk has to be shared by all, under arrangements that make savers and entrepreneurs partners in their investments — for profit or loss.

Two sorts of arrangements along these lines have been discussed in this book already. Under one, savers could exchange their money for a bond that promises to deliver real things like electricity when it matures (Douthwaite). Under the second, savers could become equity partners with the entrepreneurs (Cook). It is, however, not an easy task to knit partnerships like these together and somebody needs to have the knowledge, skill and time to do it. In other words, we need a new type of institution that would arrange the "meeting" between savers and entrepreneurs where they can develop their relations and discuss their ideas. We need professional, trustworthy and respected financial experts who can help us find sound financial solutions and create the partnership agreements.

It is not possible for existing banks to shift from making loans to building profit-and-loss partnerships; they are much too big and too disconnected from local communities. Moreover, they are tightly regulated by the state, particularly after recent events, and they have a bureaucratic risk-avoiding outlook that does not equip them well to become members of a risk-sharing partnership.

The institutions I envisage would work in much the same way as did the bank at the heart of the Mondragon cooperatives in the 1960s. There, if a group wanted to start their own business as a workers' cooperative, one of the group would join the bank staff, on normal pay, to work on the business plan with a "godfather" — someone who specialized in helping new businesses start up. Then, when the godfather judged that the plan and the group were ready, he (they were all men in those days) put the project to the bank board and funding would be approved. The godfather then helped the new business establish itself, perhaps by advising on equipment and making sure the accounting system was running well. The money the group received from the bank was nominally a loan, so the business knew how much it was expected to pay its partner each year; but in reality the risk was shared and the bank's agent, the godfather, and the members of the group were equally committed to the project's success. No projects failed under this arrangement.

In its modern form, the institution we need could be a mixture of a (non-debt) savings bank and a meeting place for all the savers and entrepreneurs in a community. Instead of being a "credit union" it could be called an "investment union" (IU) to emphasize its cooperative character. The job of those running the IU would be to help an entrepreneur develop his or her idea, until the IU had sufficient confidence in it, and in the people involved, to be able to recommend that savers put up the required capital in exchange for a specific share of the project's income. The IU would be paid for its efforts by taking a share of the income itself, as would the entrepreneurs. This would ensure that all the partners were fully committed to the project's success. Once the project was running, the IU would make a market in the shares and, while savers would be allowed to sell whenever they wished, the IU and the entrepreneurs would only be allowed to reduce their holdings with the consent of everyone else involved.

Some investment unions could be purely local and deal with a wide variety of projects. Others could be more specialized and work over a wider area. For example, they might confine themselves to energy projects and build up a lot of technical expertise. Some might be akin to unit trusts, so that every member had a stake in everything. Others might allow savers to decide on their investment portfolio themselves.

Whatever form they took, investment unions would need to perform their social financial process continuously — because a continuous flow of saved money is required to help entrepreneurs finance their continuous stream of projects. Equally, savers need to be able to get frequent access to their money to build their houses, to educate their children and to spend in old age. This continual process would be an incredible learning opportunity for the local community, over the years, as a stream of investment projects began as ideas were evaluated, financed and launched and then evaluated again and again while in operation. Apart from the incomes, much knowledge would be accumulated and strong personal ties, the bedrock of every community, would be developed.

Rethinking Business Structures: How to Encourage Sustainability Through Conscious Design Choices

PATRICK ANDREWS

Business could be the most powerful force in the world in achieving higher levels of sustainability and resilience. Unfortunately, its potential is blocked by laws and by hierarchical structures that mean that shareholders' interests are put before those of society and the planet. Some firms, however, are adopting new structures that free them to place proper emphasis on social and environmental concerns.

Our generation faces a massive challenge. We have to steer human society away from its present destructive path and toward a new era of peace, responsibility, social justice and low carbon emissions. If we are to succeed, we need everyone working together: individuals, communities, governments and, perhaps most of all, businesses. Business has become the greatest power on the planet but can we rely on businesses, and the talented people who work for them, to help?

Frankly, the signs are not good. Big businesses seem to have their own drivers, detached from ordinary life. They are focused above all on wealth maximization. Saving the planet may be important but it cannot get in the way of short-term profit and long-term growth. As the CEO of oil giant Shell, Peter Voser, explained recently when asked why Shell was cutting back on its investments in renewable energy: "I have a business to run, and the purpose of a business is to achieve returns, to achieve long-term sustainable growth."[1]

We cannot expect governments to step and in and correct this. Even if we could dream up legislation that would oblige businesses to make environmental considerations their highest priority, it is too much to expect our political system to adopt such a radical measure until there is far greater consensus about the need for urgent action. So, what can be done?

The premise of this chapter is that if we organize business differently we will see different behavior. My contention is that the structure of most businesses, and particularly of large public corporations, holds back the people in them from acting to address climate change and other social and environmental issues. These structures are a hangover from a bygone age of feudalism and slavery; they are ripe for change. They foster unhealthy relationships amongst participants and uphold a belief system that places financial interests above human and ecological needs.

That government is best which teaches us to govern ourselves

JOHANN WOLFGANG VON GOETHE

In this chapter I will examine the way in which business structures influence the development of these unhealthy relationships, and look at the root causes. I will also share some examples of businesses that have already adopted alternative structures, pointing the way to a healthy and more sustainable future. In doing so I hope to encourage us all to re-think the purpose of business in society and to support the development of alternative businesses consciously designed to bring out the best in their people and to serve the entire community of life.

About Business

Business at its best can be something creative and beautiful — one person or a group of people meeting the needs of other people, for mutual benefit. The hairdresser, the corner shop, the local plumber, all have a significant and meaningful place in the community, as their predecessors have done for hundreds or thousands of years.

What stood out in the 20th century was the emergence and rapid growth of large businesses in the form of corporations, wielding huge power and influence. Such businesses now dominate our airwaves, our high streets and our supermarket shelves. Through their lobbyists they exert a powerful influence over our public policy.

Their list of achievements is impressive. They have helped shape our modern world, achieving miracles in engineering (cars, aeroplanes, high-rise buildings), medicine (vaccines, low-cost drugs such as aspirin), retailing (low-cost food distribution), communications, computing and world trade.

At the same time there is much that these corporations do that is frivolous and, in the worst cases, positively harmful. They profit from the sale of weapons, drugs, tobacco, alcohol and polluting chemicals. They dig up wildernesses in pursuit of minerals and lobby governments to water down environmentally friendly regulations. They pay their staff as little as they can get away with while systematically increasing executive remuneration well above the rate of inflation.[2]

They hop from country to country in search of higher subsidies, lower taxes, lower wages and more relaxed labor and environmental standards.[3] And every now and then they crash spectacularly, leaving society and the planet to pick up the pieces. Think of Enron and WorldCom, Railtrack, the banks recently in Ireland, the US, UK, Switzerland and elsewhere, to name but a few.

To many outsiders, corporations have a disturbing amorality, caring little for what they do so long as it makes money. You might say the corporation is the ultimate cynic — knowing the price of everything and the value of nothing. I have seen all this as an insider.

> *It is in exchanging the gifts of the earth that you shall find abundance and be satisfied. Yet unless the exchange be in love and kindly justice it will but lead some to greed and others to hunger.*
>
> KAHLIL GIBRAN.

Employed by powerful corporations, I plied my trade as a lawyer for 14 years. I had my generous salary and bonuses, my company car, my business class flights around the world and sojourns in fancy hotels. I enjoyed the lavish Christmas parties, and conferences in sunny places. And, in return, I knuckled down to help these corporations grow and profit.

For a long time I saw nothing wrong with what I was doing. I earned a good living, I liked and admired my colleagues and the work was stimulating and challenging. It didn't occur to me to question the aims or morals of the businesses where I worked. But at a certain point a personal crisis caused me to wake up and start asking questions. What was the purpose of business, I wondered? The answers I received seemed banal. Business is about "making a profit" or "creating wealth", or "delivering long-term sustainable growth." Yet I knew that money can never be an end in itself but merely a means to an end. There had to be something more meaningful.

The only answer that really made sense came from the poet Kahlil Gibran. In *The Prophet* he wrote: "You work that you may keep pace with the earth and the soul of the earth.... When you work you are a flute through whose heart the whispering of the hours turns to music.... Work is love made visible."[4]

Work is love made visible. This spoke to my soul in a way that talk of profit and long-term sustainable growth never could. So what was I to make of my role at the time, which was to lead merger and acquisition projects for a multinational retailer? Did helping this behemoth grow have any meaning for me? I realized with increasing dismay that it didn't. My work had become fundamentally disconnected from my deepest values. I had to leave.

That was the start of a journey of exploration, as I sought to make sense of my experience. I read widely, spoke to lots of people and took on various roles in charities and social enterprises. Slowly a pattern began to emerge from the fog in my head.

We Are Not Free

It all starts with individual human beings. Every single action or omission by an organization ultimately translates into a decision by an individual or group of individuals at some level in that organization. In order to understand an organization we need to understand humans.

> *Aboriginal man always been free...just Aboriginal. But white man...he was slave one time...maybe he slave himself.*
>
> BILL NEIDJIE

Our starting point is to understand that we are not free. We feel that we are our own person, free to make our own decisions. Yet we are unconsciously influenced in all sorts of ways from many directions. Our upbringing, our life experiences, what our peers, our family, our parents think or expect, societal norms of behavior, the physical environment,[6] the weather, our physical and mental health, all affect our decisions in subtle ways and to varying degrees.

In organizations we are influenced by the rules, the practices and the culture of the group we belong to, particularly in large organizations or those with a long history. The influence of this institutional framework can be so powerful that the people can change with no effect on the institutional behavior. This can be seen in the grand old institution of Britain's parliamentary democracy, where it gets harder and harder to distinguish between one party in power and the next.

Over time, in response to these influences, we adopt habitual patterns of thinking and behavior, which become part of us, in the way a tall man who continually stoops ends up with a permanent hunch, unless he exercises to correct it. This is what Buddhists refer to as a *samskara*: a habit of thinking that locks us into patterns of behavior over which we have less and less control with every succeeding repetition. We don't react appropriately to a new situation, we react out of habit.

Sometimes these patterns of behavior are passed down from generation to generation. As Karl Marx put it: "Men make their own history but they do not make it just as they please; they do not make it under circumstances chosen by themselves, but under circumstances directly encountered, given and transmitted from the past."[7]

One of the common patterns we have inherited is the habit of obedience to authority. Historian Theodore Zeldin observed that we are all descended from slaves[8] and the history of work is rooted in feudalism and slavery. You can see this in language; for example the Russian word for "work" is derived from the word "slave."[9]

The institutional structure of the corporation exploits this tendency. This is not surprising since

Non voglio piu servir

[I no longer want to serve]

DA PONTE[5]

the structure has been passed down for centuries, as Canadian law professor Joel Bakan points out in his book *The Corporation*. This structure has been designed to allow capital (the shareholders) to control labor (the managers and staff). And it works. Each day across the planet millions of people come together to offer obeisance at the altar of "shareholder value."

In a corporation, so-called "shareholder value" is the highest value — higher than basic human values such as honesty, respect, compassion or responsibility. It is the bottom line, the alpha and omega. As Bakan puts it: "in all corporate decision-making, life's intangible richness and fragility are made invisible by the abstract calculations of cost-benefit analyses."[10] Did BP really give proper weight to environmental considerations when designing their deep-drilling rig in the Gulf of Mexico, the one that failed so dramatically? It seems likely that cost savings had too high a priority.

Prioritizing the interests of capital is so embedded in the corporate culture that it is rarely, if ever, questioned by those involved. I never heard a fellow employee challenge those two great pillars of shareholder value, the pursuit of growth and the primacy of profit. But don't take my word for it. Listen to the words of Roger Carr, Chair of the Board of iconic British chocolate maker Cadbury, which was taken over in early 2010 by the American corporation Kraft after a long, proud history of independence. You might think the board decision to agree to the takeover would be a complex matter, involving consideration of issues such as the effect on staff and the local community. Yet Roger Carr didn't worry himself with such matters. "I am paid to do a job and that job is to deliver the best value for shareholders," he told the London *Evening Standard*.[11]

The power that shareholders wield is somewhat mysterious. Why do people serve shareholders at all? After all, it seems quite unnatural for human beings to willingly serve a group of people they have never met, have no connection with and no ability to influence.

Of course shareholders do provide the money, and money has long been associated with power in our society. Those who pay our wages expect to be able to control us. There is also the law. For example, in Britain, section 172 of The Companies Act 2006 requires directors to consider first the interests of shareholders and then of other participants such as staff when making decisions. This was intended to oblige directors to take their responsibilities to stakeholders more seriously. However, the way the law is drafted, shareholders' interests still prevail, as law professor Andrew Keay has pointed out.[12]

There is another factor, operating on a more subtle level, which is the power of capital at the top of the hierarchical order. Shareholders are too remote to interfere with the day-to-day business but they hold a very powerful weapon, the ability to sack the executive, and they don't have to use this weapon very often to ensure they get what they want. All they need is for executives and employees to be aware that the weapon is there and may be used at some point.

Professor Stephen Lukes of New York University[13] points out that there are different ways in which power is manifested. At the most obvious level there is coercion — using force or threat of force to get what you want. At the opposite end of the spectrum is latent power, power so subtle that people don't know it is being exercised. As he puts it: "...is it not the supreme exercise of power to get another or others to have the desires you want them to have?" This is the nature of shareholder ownership. Like Big Brother in

George Orwell's book *1984*, shareholders do not show themselves in public yet their influence is felt everywhere.

Critics see corporations madly pursuing growth and blame the executives. Yet it is the subtle influence of capital, in the shape of the shareholders, which encourages such a strategy. In this sense, shareholders as a group are just as much responsible for the near-collapse of the Royal Bank of Scotland as the CEO, Sir Fred Goodwin.

In effect we have a "tragedy of the commons" situation.[14] Everyone in the system is behaving rationally in their own self-interest, but the system as a whole is not serving anyone. In this situation it is largely unproductive (although satisfying!) to blame individuals. It is far more useful first to look at how the system affects each individual and then look to change the system.

How the Corporate Structure Affects Individuals

The Shareholders

Shareholders are the owners of the corporation but it is a strange sort of ownership; they have no involvement in or legal responsibility for the actions of the business. Like absentee landlords, they only need to turn up and collect their rent. They are not expected to care about anything other than returns.

You might think that the shareholders, as human beings, would care about the behavior of the corporation they own, and its social and environmental impact, but they are too distant from the business to know or care.

> Men should not be ruled by an authority they cannot control.
>
> R.H. TAWNEY

As humans we care for things we feel a connection to. Something close to us matters more than something far away. We are interested in a flooding 15 miles from our home, not so much in a flood that happens 2,000 miles away.

Small shareholders feel distant from the business and very insignificant in the scheme of a large corporation. Their holding is a tiny fraction of the whole, they are one among tens of thousands, and lack the detailed information to question effectively the full-time executives who run the business. How could they hold these people to account? The only formal chance to express their views is the annual general meeting, which is controlled very tightly by the board.

As for the large institutional investors, they are run by professional fund managers who are very focused on the financial bottom line (they have to be, since their remuneration depends on it). They have no incentive to take a long-term perspective — many of them "churn" their shares regularly, buying and selling in rapid succession to take advantage of temporary rises or falls in prices. Why should they care about the long-term social or environmental record of individual corporations?

Thus investors are discouraged by the system from taking an interest in anything other than returns. A German investor in a British utility provider has no incentive to care how much the company charges or overcharges its customers, so long as he gets dividends and capital growth. It is a question of distance. By contrast, distance does not stop investors caring about money. £1 is the same whichever bank account it is in.

In summary, the role of the shareholder is a remote one, marked by lack of emotional involvement and undue attention on financial returns.

The Executives

The senior executives sit at the heart of the corporation. Wielding huge power and carrying huge responsibility, these are our modern-day generals, leading armies of foot soldiers in the brave fight for greater efficiency, lower prices and wealth creation.

Heroes or villains, it is hard to say. In many people's eyes the executives are the real cause of corporate wrong doing. Yet before we blame them we need to understand the pressures they are under. For they, too, are not free.

When a CEO sits down to write his list of things to do for the day, it is a long one. Every day he (or she) has to consider the needs and expectations of many people including staff, customers, suppliers and shareholders. At the same time he has to keep an eye out for what the competition are doing whilst ensuring the business complies with the law. He also has his own personal needs and dreams to consider.

At the bottom of his list are some nice-to-haves. These are things that he hopes to get around to but will never be fired for failing to achieve. These include social and environmental matters.

Not surprisingly, few CEOs reach the end of their daily list. They simply don't have the time or the energy or the thinking space to deal with all these often-conflicting matters. Fortunately for them, they usually don't have to. Provided they keep shareholders happy, and don't break the law, they will keep their jobs. No one can hold them to account for failing to serve social or environmental needs, provided they hit their financial targets.

In fact, CEOs have considerable autonomy. Uniquely in the corporate structure, they have no direct supervisor. What's more, they amass great power through the hierarchy, which concentrates power just as a magnifying glass concentrates light. This is what concerns many people, because the combination of autonomy with power can lead to moral corruption and excess.

Power is intoxicating — it goes to people's heads. Not to everybody's, perhaps, but to most ordinary mortals' heads. They begin to believe that they are wiser, more charismatic and more beautiful than ordinary men or women. They start to listen less and become detached from reality. They surround themselves with people who tell them what they want to hear.

> *I was having a drink with the CEO of one of the largest oil companies in the world and he admitted, "Yes I'm concerned. You are absolutely right. This world is going to pieces." And then he said, "But, hey, what can I do?"*
>
> ICHAK ADIZES[15]

They also, given half a chance, pay themselves and their close colleagues extremely generously. Executives as a group have proved adept over the years at systematically increasing their salaries, bonuses and share options, irrespective of the company's performance.[16]

Looked at from a human perspective, these patterns of behavior are understandable. As we have seen, the executives are obliged by law and by the corporate structure to put money for shareholders first. Yet the pursuit of money on its own is meaningless; it can never satisfy our highest yearnings as human beings. The need for meaning in our lives is hardwired into our system, as the social observer Dana Zohar has commented.[17] Without meaning or purpose, we lose our bearings and sink to a frivolous pursuit of wealth, power or other distractions.

The Staff

Below the senior executives are layers and layers of managers, supervisors and low-level staff, arranged in a rigid hierarchy. A hierarchy is a power structure that lowers some and elevates others in an often arbitrary manner, with the aim of achieving control from above. It is inefficient at distributing information and, as we have seen, leads to excessive power at the top, but the main trouble with hierarchy is its effect on the human spirit.

A hierarchy does not teach employees to accept responsibility for their actions — it encourages them to hand over responsibility to their "superiors." There is little need to think for themselves; they can simply follow orders and blame the manager when things go wrong. Equally, it can be demoralizing for managers since they have the unrewarding task of motivating staff whilst trying to keep their own bosses happy.

Hierarchy could theoretically work well in an ideal world where all the managers were talented leaders with no ego, who lead by example and inspire their staff to give their best, while the staff were self-motivating, enthusiastic and humble. In the real world, however, this is rarely the case. Managers and staff are humans, with human failings, and a hierarchy doesn't bring the best out of them.

We all like to feel in control of our work; in fact psychologists point out that this is a vital ingredient in mental and emotional health.[19] Being given orders can undermine our self-respect. The result is that in these institutions, staff seek survival routes. Some rebel and eventually leave. Some choose blind conformance, relinquishing responsibility in return for a steady income and a quiet life. Others become cynical, pretending to work while quietly doing as little as possible and passing the hours until it is time to go home.[20]

The Net Result

If we understand each individual's position, we can start to explain why corporations systematically subordinate social and environmental interests. It is a natural tendency in humans to care for others and for the environment but these instincts are suppressed by the corporate structure.

> *Organizations of all kinds are cluttered with control mechanisms that paralyze employees and leaders alike... We never effectively control people with these systems, but we certainly stop a lot of good work from getting done.*
>
> MARGARET WHEATLEY[18]

Many, including Joel Bakan, think that if we want to improve standards of corporate behavior, we should increase regulation,[21] but regulation is rarely the best long-term solution. Regulators are always playing catch-up since they lack the detailed knowledge of what is really going on.

Far better, to my mind, would be to change the institutional framework to encourage the sort of behavior we want to see. If organization is the "mobilization of bias," as one social observer suggested,[22] let's change the bias of the corporation. R. H. Tawney put it best 90 years ago:

> It is obvious indeed that no change of system or machinery can avert those causes of social malaise which consist in the egotism, greed or quarrelsomeness of human nature. What it can do is create an environment in which those are not the qualities which are encouraged. It cannot secure that men live up to their principles. What it can do is establish their social order upon principles to which, if they please, they can live up and not down. It cannot control their actions. It can offer them an end on which to fix their minds. And as their minds are so, in the long run and with exceptions, their practical activity will be.[23]

There are two things we need to change. We must make the ownership of corporations more democratic and their governance systems more open and less hierarchical. The good news is there are existing models we can learn from, as I discovered once I left the corporate world.

Alternative Approaches

In the last 15 years or so we have seen the emergence of a new term, the social enterprise, which I think of as "business with a purpose." Social entrepreneurs tend to have a sense of mission; they are not simply trying to make money, but using business as a way to achieve something meaningful.

A leading example of a social entrepreneur is the Nobel Prize winner from Bangladesh, Professor Muhammed Yunus. He founded the Grameen Bank, a microcredit provider owned by its customers, and subsequently set up 31 other social enterprises, including a phone company that is now the largest company in Bangladesh.

If you want to build a ship, don't herd people together to collect wood and don't assign them tasks and work, but rather teach them to long for the endless immensity of the sea.

ANTOINE DE SAINT-EXUPÉRY

There is no single legal structure associated with a social enterprise, but very few are owned by external shareholders. Mainly they are owned by "stakeholders," those directly involved in the business. Many are customer-owned businesses, such as building societies, consumer cooperatives and mutual insurance businesses and some are employee-owned, such as workers' cooperatives.

One notable group of social enterprises are fair-trade businesses. The whole fair-trade movement can be seen as a reaction to the inherent unfairness of the shareholder-ownership model. Not all fair-trade businesses have adopted a stakeholder-ownership structure[24] but they all share a commitment to serving the interests of their supplier producers and placing them above or at least equal to the interests of investors.

The beauty of stakeholder ownership is that it aligns the interests of the participants, thus encouraging the formation of a genuine community of interest, with a high level of trust and cooperation, an invaluable asset to any business. It also reduces, but does not solve, the governance issues of excessive executive power and staff alienation. We have to look elsewhere for solutions to these issues.

The most compelling solution to excessive executive power is what Australian academic Shann Turnbull describes as a "compound board."[25] This is where the traditional responsibilities of the board are divided up between several bodies, rather than being concentrated in one. Well-known examples of compound boards can be found in Mondragon, the highly successful Spanish federation of workers' cooperatives, and in the John Lewis Partnership (see below).

And what can you do about motivating staff and bringing the best out in them? Perhaps the answer can be found in the quote above from Saint-Exupéry. You have to inspire people and unite them around a common goal. The most passionate and articulate advocate of this way of organizing is Dee Hock, the first CEO of VISA International and the driving force behind its creation. He emphasizes clarity of shared purpose as a key organizing principle, uniting people in pursuit of something meaningful.[26]

Another source of inspiration for me has been the work of Elinor Ostrom. The first woman to win the Nobel Prize for Economics, this US professor studied communities that have successfully managed and maintained common resources, many of them for hundreds of years. These communities serve as a reminder that people are more than capable of sharing fairly the planet's natural wealth, if we can just organize ourselves properly.[27]

We can then remove the control systems and scrap the hierarchy. This is not unheard of in creative, people-based businesses but it can also work in more traditional manufacturing industries. W. L. Gore, manufacturers of Goretex and other hi-tech products, has been in business since 1958 and has 9,000 staff. It has what it describes as a "team-based, flat lattice organization that fosters personal initiative. There are no traditional organizational charts, no chains of command, nor predetermined channels of communication."[28]

Finally I need to mention one of the most radical and exciting organizational developments of the last 20 years, which is the emergence of on-line communities collaborating to produce free software (Linux and Mozilla), free encyclopaedias (Wikipedia) and even a map of the human genome. These adaptable, anti-hierarchical structures hint at the radical possibilities opened up by new communication technology and particularly the internet.[29]

There is a question in my mind. Given that there are options available, and they appear to be successful, why have they not been more widely adopted? Why do people cling to the established corporate model? The answer I believe is in the mindset.

The Mindset

The mindset is the fundamental beliefs that lay behind a system. If you want to cause a significant change in a system, according to systems theorist Donella Meadows, the mindset is the highest place you can intervene.[30] We seem to be stuck with an out-of-date mindset. I have identified four key beliefs that lie behind the corporate structure:

An Acceptance of Domination and Subservience.

Our society views it as normal that the powerful dominate the weak. This manifests itself in many ways, in particular through male dominating female, humans exploiting the non-human world, and shareholders ruling over staff and the board.

Some would say the root of this is in the book of Genesis: "And God said, Let us make man in our image, after our likeness: and let them have dominion over the fish of the sea, and over the fowl of the air, and over the cattle, and over all the earth, and over every creeping thing that creepeth upon the Earth."[31]

Property Rights as a Superior Form of Right.

Property rights are treated as superior even to human rights. If you are starving and take an apple from a tree on someone else's land, you can go to jail (in Saudi Arabia, you might even lose your hand!).

Shares are a form of property, and the ownership rights that come with shares are not counterbalanced by matching responsibilities. Power without responsibility breeds immorality.

Growth is the Best Measure of Success.

In businesses, as in most of our society, there is the unchallenged assumption that growth is the best, indeed the only valid, measure of success. We are obsessed by it and recognize no limits to it. By contrast, once a natural organism attains maturity it stops growing and develops in other ways.

If we are willing to go deeper and look at root causes, we might consider this fixation on growth is rooted in fear of death. By making believe that we

Michel Aumont playing Harpagon, the rich moneylender, in Moliere's play *The Miser* in a scene from a 1969 production.

can grow forever, we temporarily forget our mortality.

Profit is Pursued Above All Other Values.

We have become a society of Shylocks, Scrooges and Harpagons. As E. F. Schumacher put it "Economically, our wrong living consists primarily in systematically cultivating greed and envy and thus building up a vast array of totally unwarrantable wants." [32]

Choosing an Alternative Mindset

An alternative mindset, one that serves us better, might look something like this:

Old mindset	New mindset
An acceptance of domination and subservience.	Equality (but not sameness), balance, dialogue, no one in control. Giving back to Mother Earth more than we take.
Property rights as a higher form of right.	Human and ecological rights as more important than property rights. Ownership rights balanced with responsibilities.
Growth as the best measure of success.	Growth as one of many measures, and not the most important one.
Profit is pursued above all other values	Profit and wealth as a means to an end, not as ends in themselves.

It may seem too much to hope that a new mindset will emerge in the near future. Yet I see signs that change is coming. For example, there are signs of recognition of ecological rights at the international level.[33] The power structures we have lived with for so long are being shaken. The rich Western countries are saddled with debt, while new powers such as Brazil, China and India are growing in strength and confidence. Many corporate giants of the past are collapsing (investment banks, the American auto majors) and more will follow.

We are near the end of the industrial age and moving into the information age. Information in the form of words or data is being shared at the speed of light and this is having a profoundly disruptive impact on business and society.

The country of Bhutan has shaken off the constraints of GNP and officially adopted the measure of Gross National Happiness (GNH). Even President Sarkozy of France recently suggested that happiness and well-being should be part of a country's gross national product.[34] Most significantly I feel, change is coming because we are approaching a major global crisis, a combination of the ecological, economic, social and energy crises, and this will precipitate the adoption of new thinking and new approaches. From this new mindset, new structures will emerge.

The Way Forward

What might these new structures look like? I cannot give you one set recipe; each organization will need to work out how to make these approaches work in their own particular circumstances. But I can give you four essential ingredients:

1. The business is owned by those who are involved with or affected by its activities, and the executives are obliged to balance the interests of all involved.

2. The business has a meaningful purpose, one that inspires and unites all participants.

3. The business adopts governance systems that strive for balance between two apparent opposites, freedom and accountability.

> *You never change things by fighting the existing reality. To change something, build a new model that makes the existing model obsolete.*
>
> BUCKMINSTER FULLER

4. The participants are prepared to accept the responsibility that freedom brings!

Some Inspiring Examples

John Lewis Partnership: Large-Scale Employee Ownership

The John Lewis Partnership, including the John Lewis department stores and the Waitrose supermarket chain, is very familiar in the UK. In 2009 it was voted by readers of the Consumer Association *Which* magazine as the best UK retailer.

The purpose of the partnership is the happiness of the staff. The business is structured accordingly; it is owned by a trust on behalf of the staff. The original owner, John Spedan Lewis, started sharing profits with staff in the 1920s and transferred ownership of the business in 1950. Since that time it has thrived and now boasts nearly 70,000 employees in 29 department stores and over 200 food supermarkets.

John Lewis is owned on behalf of, but not controlled by, the employees. In fact, no one is really in control; control is shared amongst employees and management. Half the board are appointed by the Partners' Council, a representative body elected by staff. The other half are appointed by the Chair, who presides over the meeting. The Chair is powerful, but ultimately he can be dismissed by the Partners' Council.

Two more key elements to the governance structure are the registrars, a type of ombudsman responsible for ensuring that the partnership remains true to its principles, and the in-house newsletter, produced by staff for staff to allow free flow of information within the organization. Thus, as Australian academic Shann Turnbull has pointed out,[35] the John Lewis structure has the four elements of a democracy: executive, legislature, judiciary and free press.

John Lewis is intriguing because it is a rare example of a large-scale employee-owned business. Employee ownership is not uncommon at a small scale (up to around 50 staff), but when such businesses try to grow beyond that size, the complexity increases significantly. With so many owners, the management can get tied down in too much explaining or politicking. Just imagine a democracy where every decision is made by referendum! It appears that John Lewis, by adopting a relatively sophisticated structure that balances control amongst the board and the staff, has found a way to avoid the problems of simple democracy where one person equals one vote. As a consequence the business has grown and prospered.

OBI and Media Markt: Local Autonomy

OBI and Media Markt are two German retailers, leaders in their fields (respectively home improvement and electrical goods). Both have thrived in what is reckoned by many to be the toughest, most competitive retail market in Europe. They are each very different but they share a belief in the power of local autonomy. Most large retailers retain tight, centralized control of how their stores are run. They have a powerful head office that decides strategy, locates new stores, determines store layout and negotiates with suppliers.

OBI and Media Markt, by contrast, entrust the stores and their local managers with considerable responsibility. At OBI, for example, it is the store manager who decides the range of goods the stores will sell. Rather than a "head office," OBI has a central service center that supports the stores by delivering a range of services on request.

The principle of local autonomy extends to store ownership. OBI has a mixed franchise model—some stores are owned 100% by OBI, some by local franchisees and others are joint ventures, part owned by OBI and partly by locals. Media Markt gives each store manager a 10% ownership stake in his or her store.

These two retailers represent another example of a healthy balance of power, in this case between the center and the stores. The center has the high-level strategic view, gathering information from across the network of stores, sharing best practice and helping to coordinate activity. The stores have sufficient freedom to ensure that they respond to the particular needs of their customers, and they hold the center to account whenever it fails to deliver a good-quality service.

The Forest Stewardship Council: Stakeholder Ownership in a Not-for-Profit

The FSC is the world's leading timber certification body. It is a not-for-profit business, reinvesting its profits rather than distributing them. The FSC ownership concept is based on the triple bottom line of

economic, social and environmental. Its members are divided into three "chambers": in the economic chamber there are retailers, wholesalers and plantation owners; in the social chamber there are trade unions and indigenous peoples groups; and in the environmental chamber there are NGOs like WWF and Friends of the Earth.

There is a similar structure at board level. The board has nine members, three appointed from each chamber, and no decision can be passed at the board unless a majority of each chamber approves it (this ensures consensus but prevents any one person blocking a decision).

The FSC has been very successful — it now certifies more than 13% of the world's managed timber, and has seen off a number of commercial competitors. The former CEO of the FSC, Heiko Liedeker, accredits this success in large part to the ownership structure. As he points out, the FSC is the only timber certification body endorsed by Greenpeace and other NGOs; it thus has legitimacy, a priceless marketing asset that commercial certification bodies can't compete with. As Liedeker commented to me once: "If a commercial organization were structured this way, it would be unbeatable."

There are certainly challenges with this structure. In particular the board, who lead the business, is composed mainly of amateurs rather than professional business people. According to Liedeker, this means they don't always appreciate the commercial necessities of running a business and need to learn a lot before they can usefully contribute. Board meetings last three days and need a lot of facilitation.

Its main strength is that by embedding the triple bottom line into the structure, it forces those who usually oppose each other, such as retailers and NGOs, to sit around a table and thrash things out. As with the other companies described here, there is a healthy balance of power, from which well-thought-out decisions emerge.

Riversimple: A Shared-Ownership Model

The last business I want to describe is still at an early stage in its development, and its structure is relatively untested. However, there are reasons to believe it represents a new paradigm, where stakeholder ownership is truly embedded in the business. Riversimple is a revolutionary transport business, which is developing a highly efficient hydrogen-fuel-cell-powered electric vehicle. Its purpose is to build and operate cars for independent use whilst systematically pursuing elimination of the environmental damage caused by personal transport.

Riversimple began life in 1999 as a gleam in the eye of Hugo Spowers, an Oxford-trained engineer and former racing driver. A committed environmentalist, he quit the motorsport world in 1997 when he became convinced that the internal combustion engine would have to be replaced with something more benign. He decided he would have nothing more to do with cars! However, he was introduced to the work of US physicist Amory Lovins, who had conceived of a lightweight electric vehicle powered by a hydrogen fuel cell. Spowers decided to take on the challenge of developing this concept, pursuing his vision of truly sustainable transport.

Riversimple's technology demonstrator June 2009

The first milestone came when he successfully led a research project, in collaboration with Morgan Cars, Oxford University, Cranfield University, BOC and others, and part funded by the UK Department of Trade and Industry, to create an energy-efficient sports car. Known as the LIFECar, the vehicle drew much attention when shown at the Geneva Motor show in 2008.

In 2007, Hugo and a team of collaborators formed Riversimple LLP, with funding from the family of Ernst Piech, part of the Porsche dynasty, who have committed nearly £2m to the project to date. The funding was used to develop the strategy and build a demonstrator vehicle which was unveiled to the public at London's Somerset House in 2009. The vehicle is a two-seat local car powered by hydrogen, with the following characteristics:

range on 1 kg tank of hydrogen	240 miles
top speed	50 mph
fuel consumption	300 mpg (energy equivalent)
carbon emissions	31 g CO_2/km

As this book goes to press, Riversimple is in the middle of a round of capital raising, aiming to raise £25m to go to the next stage, which is further development of the vehicle, and pilot projects in the UK cities in 2012, leading to vehicle production in 2013.

When looking at the corporate structure, Spowers took the same approach as he did to the car design, starting with a blank piece of paper. The aim was to harness the goodwill and support of the various stakeholders in the business. The challenge was how to do this while attracting and retain capital. The structure that Riversimple devised looks like this:

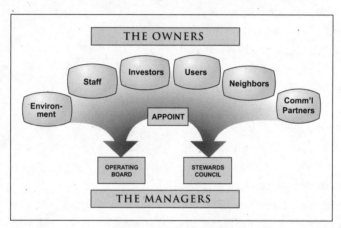

There are three particular features I want to point out. Firstly, the business is owned by six "custodians" who serve and protect the various benefit streams that the business is aiming to deliver to the environment, investors, staff, users/customers, commercial partners (e.g. suppliers) and neighbors (e.g. local government). The board is instructed to strive to deliver multiple benefits, serving the community as a whole, not any one group.

Secondly, the intention is that profits will be distributed amongst all stakeholders. Of course investors will receive the lion's share, since this is their primary interest in the business. But since the business is a creation of all stakeholders, it is right that all should share in the financial rewards.

The other notable feature is the stewards' council, which has a function rather like the Registrar in John Lewis Partnership. This function is really important for holding the board to account and encouraging high standards of decision-making. The theoretical justification for the stewards' role can be found in the famous experiments by Stanley Milgram at Yale University in the 1960s.[36] Milgram conducted tests on students and members of the public, asking them to give electric shocks to a volunteer (in fact it was an actor, and no shocks were actually given). The results showed that the average person, when ordered to by an authority figure, would inflict a surprising amount of pain on another. Milgram found that people were far less likely to obey orders automatically if there was someone else present in the room putting the case against — a rival authority figure. In Riversimple's structure, this is the role played by the stewards.

This structure is very new so there is not much else to say, except that those involved in devising it are convinced that it matches the purpose of the business and provides a solid basis for future success.

But Are They More Sustainable?

Are these businesses more ethical, more caring, more kind to the planet than their shareholder-owned competitors? I can't pretend to have done any rigorous analysis. To my eyes, compared to their peers, the John Lewis Partnership food stores put more focus on quality and customer service and less focus on pushing cheap food to cash-strapped consumers at any price. They play less with prices and use fewer gimmicks. Rightly or wrongly, I trust them more.

I am not a regular customer of OBI or Media Markt. What can be said is that these businesses have proved successful over the long term and long-term success is a fairly reliable indicator of a business that finds a balance between its various stakeholders. As for the Forest Stewardship Council, it is the only timber certification body supported by WWF and Greenpeace, which speaks for itself.

These businesses succeed because, fundamentally, they acknowledge that to thrive they need to get the best from the people involved. They empower their staff, and they stretch their organizational boundaries to encompass those who are normally considered to be outside, such as customers and suppliers. They make them all feel like owners, whatever level they work at. The result is that the people show a greater sense of commitment, stewardship, compassion and joy in their work, and the business thrives as a consequence, as does the community as a whole.

Treat your customers like friends and they will return and recommend you. Treat your suppliers like partners and they will work harder to deliver a better service. Treat your staff like collaborators, rather than "human resources," and you'll see the difference. Brad Bird, director of the blockbuster cartoon films "The Incredibles" and "Ratatouille" for Pixar, explained it this way: "In my experience, the thing that has the most significant impact on a movie's budget…is morale. If you have low morale, for every $1 you spend you get about 25 cents of value. If you have high morale, for every $1 you spend you get about $3 of value."[37]

Conclusion

Ultimately it is up to each of us. We can choose to see ourselves in our daily lives as powerless, subject to the whims of politicians and corporate leaders and awaiting our fate with trepidation. Alternatively, we can choose to see ourselves as free, powerful, self-regulating, autonomous and creative individuals with a role to play in the birth of a new age of responsible business.

> *We are the ones we have been waiting for.*
>
> THOMAS BANYACYA SR,
> ELDER OF THE HOPI NATION

Individuals who "resist more, and obey less,"[38] as Walt Whitman urged. If we do this, we free ourselves to make better, more conscious choices about the type of organizations we buy from, work with, participate in, create and own. The result will be businesses that demonstrate the best that humans are capable of. I can't wait.

Endnotes

1. See shell.com/home/content/aboutshell/swol/2010/pv_jan_2010/.
2. Thomas Clarke, in his recent paper "A Critique of the Anglo American model of Corporate Governance" (2009), pointed out that in the 1980s the average CEO in a publicly traded company in the US earned 42 times what the average worker earned. In 2002 this had risen to 400 times. As William McDonough, President of the New York Federal Reserve Board, said in 2002: "I can assure you that we CEOs of today are not 10 times better than those of 20 years ago."
3. For examples of this behavior pattern, see Naomi Klein, *No Logo* (Flamingo, 2000).
4. Kahlil Gibran, *The Prophet* (1926).
5. Words sung by Leporello, the servant to Don Giovanni, at the beginning of Mozart's *Don Giovanni* opera. First perfomed 1787.
6. Architect Christopher Alexander wrote a trilogy of illuminating books discussing the influence of physical space on human activity. These are *The Timeless Way of Building* (1980), *A Pattern Language* (1978) and *The Oregon Experiment* (1978). Published by Oxford University Press.
7. Karl Marx and Freidrich Engels, "The Eighteenth Brumaire of Louis Bonaparte," *Marx and Engels Selected Works*, vol 1:247 (1962).
8. Theodore Zeldin, *An Intimate History of Humanity* (Sinclair-Stevenson, 1994).
9. The Russian word for work is "rabota" and the word for slave "rab."
10. Joel Bakan, *The Corporation* (Constable and Robinson, 2004), 65.
11. Quote from *London Evening Standard*, 25th November 2009.
12. Andrew Keay, "Moving Towards Stakeholderism? Constituency Statutes, Enlightened Shareholder Value, and All That: Much Ado About Little?" available for download

at hq.ssrn.com/Journals/RedirectClick.cfmurl=http://papers.ssrn.com/sol3/papers
.cfm?abstract_id=1530990&partid=503514&did=61040&eid=82567606.

13. In *Power* (second edition 2005), Professor Stephen Lukes suggests that power manifests itself in three ways: (i) decision-making and behavior; (ii) non-decision making, a refusal to countenance discussion of certain matters; and (iii) our very wants are influenced and shaped by the influencing force. It is this third type of power, which is tremendously subtle and all the more powerful as a result, that is exerted by shareholders.

14. In a now famous article in 1968 published in the journal *Science*, Garrett Hardin described a situation in which multiple individuals, acting independently and rationally consulting their own self-interest, ultimately deplete a shared resource even though it serves no one's interest for this to happen. He called this dilemma "the tragedy of the commons."

15. Ichak Adizes, founder of the Adizes Institute, quoted in the magazine *What is Enlightenment?* (March 2005).

16. According to *The Guardian* newspaper survey of executive pay, salaries amongst corporate executives rose by 10% in 2009 in a time of world recession and fall in share prices. See guardian.co.uk/business/2009/sep/14/executive-pay-keeps-rising.

17. Danah Zohar, Ian Marshall, *The Quantum Society* (William Morrow and Co., 1994), chapter 11.

18. Margaret Wheatley, *Goodbye, Command and Control* (1997). Available for download at margaretwheatley.com/articles/goodbyecommand.html.

19. For example see R. Karasek, "Job Demands, Job Decision Latitude, and Mental Strain: Implications for Job Redesign," *Administrative Science Quarterly* 24 (1979), 285–308.

20. This is the approach recommended by Corinne Maier, an economist at state-owned Electricité de France, in her bestselling book *Bonjour paresse* (Hello Laziness) (2004), subtitled "The Art and the Importance of Doing the Least Possible in the Workplace."

21. See *The Corporation* (cited above), chapter 6.

22. Elmer E. Schattschneider, *The Semi-Sovereign People: A Realist's View of Democracy in America* (Holt, Rinehart and Winston, 1960), 71.

23. R. H. Tawney, *The Acquisitive Society* (G. Bell And Sons, 1921).

24. Those that have adopted such a structure include Cafedirect, Liberation and Divine Chocolate.

25. Shann Turnbull, "A New Way to Govern: Organisations and Society After Enron" (2002), available at papers.ssrn.com/sol3/papers.cfm?abstract_id=319867.

26. Dee Hock, *The Birth of the Chaordic Age* (Berret-Koehler Publishers Inc., 1999).

27. Elinor Ostrom, *Governing the Commons* (Cambridge Univ Press, 1990). For her work in this field, she received the 2009 Nobel Prize for Economics.

28. gore.com/en_xx/aboutus/culture/index.html

29. For a thorough analysis of the potential for new technologies to transform our society, see *The Wealth of Networks* (2006) by Yochai Benckler, available for download at benkler.org.

30. Donella Meadows, *Places to Intervene in a System* (The Sustainability Institute, 1999), available from: sustainer.org/?page_id=106.

31. *The Bible*, King James edition, Genesis 1:26.

32. E. F. Schumacher, *Small is Beautiful* (Abacus edition published by Sphere Books, 1974), 30.

33. See treeshaverightstoo.com for more information.
34. See guardian.co.uk/business/2009/sep/20/economics-wealth-gdp-happiness.
35. See "A New Way to Govern" cited at 25 above.
36. Described at en.wikipedia.org/wiki/Milgram_experiment.
37. Quoted in an interview in the McKinsey quarterly, April 2008, see mckinseyquarterly.com/innovation_lessons_from_pixar_an_interview_with_oscar-winning_director_brad_bird_212.
38. Walt Whitman, *Leaves of Grass* (Random House, 2001), first published in 1855.

Why Pittsburgh Real Estate Never Crashes: The Tax Reform that Stabilized a City's Economy

Dan Sullivan

Pittsburgh and Cleveland have adopted diametrically opposed strategies, with dramatically different results. In Pittsburgh, foreclosure rates are low despite the downturn, home prices are climbing slightly and construction rates are increasing. Cleveland, meanwhile, is struggling to stem a complete collapse of its housing market. The difference lies in the fact that Pittsburgh has had a site-value tax, which steadies the market, and Cleveland has not.

One hundred and thirty miles apart, Pittsburgh and Cleveland are similar cities in many ways. Pittsburgh lies at the junction of three major rivers and Cleveland on a natural harbor on Lake Erie. These navigable waters connected them to coal and iron ore mines and made them industrial hubs but the decline of steelmaking and related industries has left them as two of the largest "rust belt" cities. At the beginning of the last century, Cleveland was the nation's fifth largest city and Pittsburgh was eighth, and Cleveland was the third largest corporate headquarters (behind New York and Chicago) until it fell in rank to Pittsburgh. Both have seen their populations decline with migrations to the suburbs and to the south and west of the United States. Both now have fewer than half the residents they had during their peak years.

Cleveland has never fully recovered from the collapse of "big steel," while Pittsburgh rebounded easily. This was because Ohio never gave Cleveland the option of having a land tax similar to that in Pittsburgh, and as a result, it relied less on real estate taxes for raising revenue. Its lack of a land tax means that its property prices tend to be higher than in Pittsburgh and purchasers consequently have to borrow more. In 2005, Cleveland had an affordability index [median house price divided by median household income] of 3.61 compared to 2.44 in Pittsburgh. Although 3.61 was not high by national standards, it was the highest of any northeastern industrial city.

In 2008, just after the housing bubble broke, Cleveland led the nation in mortgage foreclosures per capita while Pittsburgh's foreclosure rate remained exceptionally low. Since then, the foreclosure rates in Las Vegas and many Californian cities, none of which collect significant real estate taxes, have passed Cleveland's foreclosure rate. However, on September 15, 2010, the *Pittsburgh Post-Gazette* reported that while at the end of the second quarter of 2010, 21.5% of America's single-family homes had underwater mortgages (the American term for negative equity), only 5.6% did in Pittsburgh. As a result Pittsburgh was top of a list of the ten markets with the lowest underwater mortgage figures.[1]

How Land Value Tax Prevents Speculation

Land value taxes discourage the bidding up of land prices and it is cheap land coupled with lower taxes on productivity that attracts productive investors to Pittsburgh. During the boom decades, land-taxing cities like Pittsburgh could not offer the speculative gains that California did but now they not only offer lower land prices and lower productivity taxes, but, importantly in these volatile times, they also offer land prices that are unlikely to fall in the future simply because they never became inflated in the first place.

This came about because investors are not just interested in the return to their investment but in the *after-tax* return. If land is increasing in value by 9%, and there is a 1% tax on land values, the net return is 8%. However, a 5% tax on land values cuts the net return to only 4%. Similarly, if the return to a productive investment such as a building is 9% and the taxes on productivity are only 1%, the net return is 8%. If the productivity taxes take 5%, they reduce the return to only 4%. If an investor has the choice of putting all his money into building a small number of houses or into buying up a much larger number of vacant lots, he will choose whichever course of action yields the highest after-tax return. That is, he will choose to build in a land-tax economy and choose to buy up land in a productivity-tax economy.

Pittsburgh has not always done so well during recessions as it is doing today. It suffered badly in the real-estate crashes up to and including the 1906 depression but its property market has been remarkably stable ever since and is continuing to attract investors despite the present recession. This transformation is linked to a series of economic reforms adopted between 1906 and 1913. Before 1906, Pittsburgh gave special tax breaks to large landholders under "agricultural" and "rural" classifications. During Pittsburgh's reform era, the city not only eliminated those breaks but also changed its property tax to fall more heavily on land and more lightly on improvements. Productive land use became less costly while idle speculation became unprofitable. As a result, city real-estate prices did not crash during hard times because they hadn't inflated during boom times.

America's early depressions were sometimes as severe as the Great Depression, which was "great" partly in the sense that it was global, just as World War I was originally called the Great War because it was global. (In fact, far more Americans lost their lives in the Civil War than in both "great wars" combined.) America's most severe panic was probably in 1837, which closed more than 40% of the banks[1] and wreaked havoc on the economy.

According to historian Stefan Lorant, "The panics of 1819, 1837 and 1857 hit the city [Pittsburgh] with particular severity. Business slackened and factories closed; and workingmen and merchants alike felt the impact of the hardships."[2] Lorant notes that the depressions of 1873, 1884 and 1893 were also severe in Pittsburgh. He quotes *The Growth of the American Republic*, by professors Morrison and Commager:

> Prices and wages hit rock-bottom and there seemed to be no market for anything. Half a million laborers struck against conditions which they thought intolerable, and most of the strikes were dismal failures. Ragged and hungry bands of unemployed swarmed the countryside, the fires from their hobo camps flickering a message of warning and despair to the affrighted townsfolk.[3]

In 1894, "Coxey's Army" of unemployed began its march on Washington, D.C., from western Ohio, with members having arrived by train from as far as Texas. Their ranks nearly doubled when they passed through Pittsburgh and Homestead.

The Russell Sage Foundation's famous Pittsburgh Survey of 1910 showed how severe the poverty was here. "One third of all who die in Pittsburgh... die under five years of age. One fourth... die under one year of age."[4]

Fighting Land Monopoly and Speculation

Until recently, Americans had always opposed the kind of land monopoly that had oppressed Europe. The Articles of Confederation called for even the federal government to be funded from a tax on the value of privately held land.[5]

The minor parties that formed the Republican Party also formed the roots of the progressive movement. They regarded land monopoly as a second form of slavery, and opposed both forms vigorously. The Free Soil Party advocated "the free grant to actual settlers," as opposed to selling large tracts of land to privileged elites.[6]

Abraham Lincoln had gained his reputation defending homesteaders against "land sharks" who would file counterclaims and demand payment to drop the challenges. In 1843, Lincoln wrote:

> "An individual, or company, or enterprise requiring land should hold no more than is required for their home and sustenance, and never more than they have in actual use in the prudent management of their legitimate business, and this much should not be permitted when it creates an exclusive monopoly. All that is not so used should be held for the free use of every family to make homesteads, and to hold them as long as they are so occupied....
>
> The idle talk of foolish men, that is so common now, will find its way against it, with whatever force it may possess, and as strongly promoted and carried on as it can be by land monopolists, grasping landlords, and the titled and untitled senseless enemies of mankind everywhere."[7]

After the Civil War, progressives witnessed the closing of the frontier and saw land speculators out-bidding those who wanted to put the land to use during the boom years, fueled by the expansion of bank credit that contracted during recessions. Besides monetary and banking reform, progressives advocated real-estate taxes, particularly on land, to make such speculation unprofitable.[8]

The Pittsburgh Battle for Reform

Although land speculation was a problem everywhere, it was particularly bad in Pittsburgh, which had been carved up for the benefit of officers in the Revolutionary War. Speculators and large estates in the city got special "farmland" and "rural" tax rates at the expense of urban properties. The price of land, and the taxes on urban real estate, became so high that workers lived in tiny houses on tiny lots.[9]

Henry W. Oliver, president of the Pittsburgh Common Council, complained in an 1872 speech of "the great landholders and speculators, and the great estates which have been like a nightmare on the progress of the city for the last thirty years."[10]

The same *Pittsburgh Survey* that exposed Pittsburgh's poverty showed that this classification system had "enabled big real estate holdings to get out from under the full share of their local responsibilities."[11] Corrupt assessment practices also shifted taxes off of speculators. However, that government was swept away after perhaps the largest municipal scandal in American history resulted in 41 indictments against city councilmen, bankers and industrialists.

In 1911, the reform government abolished special tax breaks for large estates[12] and abolished the taxation of machinery.[13]

In January 1912, the Pittsburgh Civic Commission, headed by H. D. W. English and H. J. Heinz, reported that land prices were extraordinarily high in Pittsburgh at that time, second only to those in New York City. "Industries will be slow to locate in Pittsburgh if rents or prices of land are higher than in other cities," the report stated.

It also noted that a few individuals and families had owned large tracts and that some owners, by making ground leases or by improving to a very small extent, had received sufficient income to enable them to hold their land for increases in value due to the city's rapid growth:

> A few individuals have been enabled by circumstances to place and hold land prices at a figure which prevents the profitable use of the land by others. Can this paralyzing grip on Pittsburgh's growth be broken? We recommend twice as heavy a tax on land values as on building values as the remedy. This means to place a penalty on holding vacant or inadequately improved land and to offer special inducements and premiums for improving land.[14]

Mayor Magee endorsed the measure on learning that Vancouver, British Columbia, had enjoyed considerable success after replacing their building tax with a land value tax (LVT).[15] Supporters got a state law introduced for second-class cities (Pittsburgh and Scranton) requiring those cities to adopt the Civic Commission's proposal, with a phase-in spread over ten years.

Even the Pittsburgh Real Estate Board (now known as the Association of Realtors) had joined with the Single Tax Club of Pittsburgh, the Civic Commission, the Pittsburgh Board of Trade, the Civic Club of Allegheny County and other organizations in support of the bill. The Pittsburgh Dispatch wrote: "The realty board endorsed the act and recommended its passage and is anxious to have the Governor approve it." They sent a delegation to Harrisburg to urge passage of the bill.[16]

It passed in the House by a vote of 113 to 5 and in the Senate by a vote of 40 to 0.[17] A repeal campaign was launched by the largest landowners, including agents of the Schenley estate, the biggest of all. Some opponents of the graded tax said that "unimproved landowners are the poorest of property owners" and that the graded tax was disturbing to the economic and financial situation in Pittsburgh and that it would bring depression and hard times.[18] Former Mayor Magee traveled to Harrisburg to defend the bill. He said the opposing delegation from Pittsburgh didn't represent the small property owner but the large interests of the city. "They come here weeping and wailing," said Magee, "and you would think the small property owner would be wiped out of existence. They tell you it is a terrible experiment."[19]

The *Pittsburgh Press* also defended the law, stating:

> The law is working to the complete satisfaction of everybody except a few real estate speculators who hope to hold idle land until its value is greatly increased by improvements erected on surrounding territory. Everybody endeavoring to gain a big profit in this parasitical manner is naturally opposed to the law and to the principle which it represents; it is nevertheless endorsed by and is clearly in the interest of the vast majority of the public.[20]

The repeal bill passed both houses, but was vetoed by Governor Brumbaugh, who said:

> This repealer is opposed by the largest group of protestants that have been heard on any bill.... It is advocated by those in charge of the fiscal policy of one of the two cities concerned. Inasmuch as there is such a conflict of opinion, and inasmuch as the law has scarcely yet

been tried, it is well to allow it to operate until a commanding judgment decrees its fate. To disturb it now, when a preponderance of opinion favors it, is unwise." [21]

Pittsburgh's Experience with Land Value Tax

Land prices only rose 14% in Pittsburgh during the 12 years after the graded tax was adopted in 1913, while they boomed in the rest of the nation. [22] Real-estate interests complained that LVT was robbing Pittsburgh landowners of gains enjoyed elsewhere. However, Mayor Magee saw these gains as speculative, and stood by his actions. He noted in 1924:

> I am principally interested in two things regarding taxation: the progress of the graded tax law and the problem of assessments for public works. Both concern the unearned increment, the profit of land owner who becomes rich through growth of the community without effort on his own part. I am frankly opposed to him.... [H]e is a parasite on the body politic." [23]

Magee was proved correct. National land prices peaked in 1925 and plummeted with the Great Depression, except in Pittsburgh. Despite the great flood of 1936, Pittsburgh's land prices fell only 11% between 1930 and 1940, compared to 58% in Detroit, 50% in Los Angeles, 46% in Cleveland, 28% in Boston, 27% in New Orleans, 26% in Cincinnati, 25% in Milwaukee and 21% in New York. Land prices in Pittsburgh even fell less than in Washington, D.C., where the New Deal was booming. [24]

Of course, times were still tough in Pittsburgh, especially for those who depended on steel or other industries tied to the global economy. Still, Pittsburgh was spared the added problem of a real-estate crash because its graded tax had discouraged speculators from bidding up land prices during the previous boom.

After World War II, other industrial cities got hammered once again, but even though Pittsburgh had been the world's number-one supplier of armor plate during the war, it enjoyed a renaissance that was the subject of at least 26 national and international news articles. [25]

The most amazing aspect of Pittsburgh's renaissance is that it had a construction boom without a real-estate price boom. In 1960, when real estate went into another recession, Pittsburgh continued building.

During that recession, *House & Home*, the construction industry's leading trade journal, recommended that other cities prevent land bubbles by doing what Pittsburgh was doing—taxing land values more heavily than building values. It quoted Pennsylvania governor and former Pittsburgh mayor David L. Lawrence as saying: "There is no doubt in my mind that the graded tax law has been a good thing for the city of Pittsburgh. It has discouraged the holding of vacant land for speculation and provides an incentive for building improvements." [26]

Over the years, Pittsburgh adopted other taxes that eroded the effect of LVT on speculation. In December 1978, however, Pittsburgh council president William J. Coyne rejected the mayor's call for increased wage taxes and convinced council to nearly double the LVT. The next year Pittsburgh raised the LVT to five times the building tax rate, and two years after that raised it again. These were also Pittsburgh's last overall tax increases for twelve years.

Another spectacular surge in construction followed as owners of underused land became more willing to sell. The only eminent domain controversy involved land acquisition for the PPG complex the year *before* LVT increases went into effect. [27]

1978 was also the year that California passed Proposition 13, which sharply curtailed real-estate taxes in that state. From that point on, cities in California got smaller shares of their revenue from property taxes than cities in any other state. While Pittsburgh enjoyed steady land prices in the midst of a building boom, California was consumed by a land-speculation frenzy. Foreign interests acquired more California land within the first 18 months after Proposition 13's passage than they had accumulated in the entire history of that state. [28]

Most foreign land acquisition was by Japanese concerns. How did they get enough US dollars to buy up California land? Early in 1980, US Steel chairman David Roderick accused Japan of "dumping" cars on the US market, noting that Toyotas sold for 17% less in the US than in Japan. [29] Japan had already been increasing exports to the US for some time, but lightly taxed California land made American dollars even more attractive to Japanese land speculators.

In 1979, Pittsburgh's largest employer, the Jones & Laughlin steel mill, shut down. Even this didn't prevent Pittsburgh from enjoying the biggest construction surge in its history. The real-estate editor of *Fortune* credited the LVT with playing a major role in Pittsburgh's "second renaissance." [30]

Councilman Coyne was elected to Congress in 1982. In 1983, council president Ben Woods convinced council to reduce taxes on buildings and make up the shortfall from higher taxes on land values, even though there was no need for more revenue.

However, Pittsburgh and its school district also levied an aggregate 4% wage tax, and research requested by mayor Masloff indicated that this tax was driving renters and potential home buyers out of the city at an alarming rate. In 1988, Masloff determined that the city had a surplus, and reduced the wage tax by five-eighths of one percent.

In 1989 she proposed to lower the wage tax by another 0.5 % and make up the revenue with a conventional property tax increase of 10 mils (1 percent) on both land and buildings. Council president Jack Wagner proposed to put the entire increase on land values instead. A storm of protest raged at the public tax hearing against increasing overall property taxes, but most testimony with regard to Wagner's LVT alternative was in favor of it. In a compromise with the mayor, Wagner's council increased the tax on land value by 33 mils and on buildings by 5 mils. Pittsburgh's real-estate values and construction levels remained steady during the recession of 1990.

As Pittsburgh's economy continued to grow and land values remained stable, California's land prices rapidly rose and its economy became strained. California's housing affordability index (median house price divided by median income) had been only 10% higher than the national average when Proposition 13 passed. By 2005, it was three times the national average. 23 of the nation's least affordable cities were in California. The median house price in San Francisco rose to 12.8 times the median income. Even dusty, miserable Bakersfield, the most affordable city in California, had an affordability index of 5.6. Pittsburgh's index was 2.44, among the lowest of any northeastern industrial city.[31]

Once again, the real-estate collapse missed Pittsburgh because LVT prevented the bidding up of Pittsburgh's land prices during the national boom decades of the '80s and '90s. In 2008, with the nation's construction industry coming to a near standstill, the business agent of Pittsburgh's Carpenter's Union announced that they were looking for 250 additional carpenters and apprentices to fill the increased demand Pittsburgh was enjoying. Meanwhile, California, which had curtailed real-estate taxes at the behest of those who said that those taxes were "forcing people out of their homes," led the nation in housing foreclosures.

Undoing the Graded Tax

Support for taxing land values more than buildings remained so strong in the City of Pittsburgh that efforts to repeal the policy consistently failed.[32] Many years, the chief city assessor was also the head of the Henry George Foundation of America, which championed LVT throughout North America.[33]

In 1942, however, responsibility to assess land values was shifted to the county, where opposition to LVT was stronger and support weaker.[34] A provision of Pennsylvania law was added to the second-class county code requiring Allegheny County to assess the value of land and improvements separately. Although the law reflects preferred assessment practices anyhow, it was put in place to protect the city's LVT.

County assessors gradually came to ignore land values, keeping those the city assessor had put in place and putting subsequent changes onto building values whenever possible. 1980 assessments were a fairly accurate reflection of 1950 land values.

This meant that land values became relatively over-assessed in declining neighborhoods and under-assessed in advancing neighborhoods. However, the city's shifts to LVT in the 1980s were followed by substantial land-assessment reductions in Shadyside, the trendiest neighborhood in the city, and smaller reductions in Oakland and Squirrel Hill, the city's two most prosperous and politically prominent neighborhoods after Shadyside. This marks the point when county assessors crossed the line from neglect to overt malfeasance. Even so, home owners in the poorest neighborhoods still saved under LVT, and many in the richest neighborhoods paid more. Middle-income neighborhoods saved the most.

However, opponents of LVT dominated the county board of assessors. They hired a private assessment firm, Sabre Systems, which assessed land values with such a terrible lack of uniformity that the city was forced to abandon the tax in 2001. Sabre Systems assessed lots with buildings on them six to ten times as high as identical, adjacent vacant lots. They did this only in Pittsburgh, even though there were three smaller cities in the county, Clairton, Duquesne and McKeesport, that also relied on LVT.

Wildly erratic land-value assessments forced Pittsburgh City Council to abandon LVT in 2001. The increased cost to home owners was partly offset by special exemptions, but this was done at the expense of renters and business properties, who have had to pay higher taxes into a shrinking budget. Many council members blamed the assessments and said the tax change was temporary. Only one council member blamed the LVT itself.

After losing a long series of court cases and appeals, the county is today finally addressing assessment irregularities under court order. The city controller and several city council members have expressed interest in returning to LVT if realistic land assessments are made because, if Pittsburgh is to be protected from the next recession, it must end these abuses and reinstate LVT before the next boom era.

Pittsburgh Is Not Alone

Every one of the 19 land-taxing cities in Pennsylvania enjoyed a construction surge after shifting to LVT, even though their nearest neighbors continued to decline. Clairton, Altoona and Aliquippa have shifted farther than any other cities toward a pure LVT, and are enjoying unrivaled economic vitality. LVT has also been far more extensively employed in Canada, Australia, New Zealand, Denmark and other countries, with similar success. Those who dispute the effects of LVT and suggest that Pittsburgh is prospering for other reasons have not put forward an answer as to why virtually *all* land-taxing cities in the world out-perform their neighbors.

Even states that rely heavily on conventional property taxes (with equal rates on land and buildings) have done far better than states that have curtailed property taxes.

Claims that Pittsburgh is prospering because of its efforts to become a "green" city do not explain how Pittsburgh held its land values during the Great Depression, when it was the dirtiest, smokiest, most polluted city in the nation, nor why Pittsburgh land values failed to inflate as it cleaned itself up during what were boom years for other cities, nor why the much greener cities of Portland and Seattle have suffered serious economic setbacks.

Claims that Pittsburgh was saved by its economic development projects try to gloss over the many disastrous projects, where one subsidy after another went to businesses that opened, sucked out the subsidies and then failed, or to over-subsidized corporate businesses that drove out competing, fully-taxed smaller businesses in a process known as "economic cannibalism." Those who suggest that the new casino helped the economy have to admit that the city with the highest foreclosure rate in the US is Las Vegas, the casino capital of the nation.

If anything good can be attributed to our changing policies, it is that the changes were either thwarted or came too late to do the damage done in other cities. Pittsburgh fought unsuccessfully to get a "commuter" wage tax like the 2% tax in Cleveland or the roughly 4% tax in Philadelphia. However, those cities' commuter taxes drove out businesses even faster than residency taxes drive out residents. Some suburbs of Cleveland even made a science of stealing businesses by charging the tax on workers and then rebating half of it back to the employers. Meanwhile, Philadelphia's flight of businesses has been so bad that even the Philadelphia Association of Realtors has advocated shifting from wage tax to LVT.

What Will Become of Pittsburgh?

If Pittsburgh can either force the county to assess land properly or retake control of its own assessments, it will once again be able to boast the most recession-proof real estate in the nation. However, if it does not do so before the next real-estate price boom, it will not be able to prevent the next crash either. This is because LVT prevents booms and preventing the booms is the only way to prevent busts.

Lessons for Environmentalists

Extending LVT to Air, Water and Nonrenewable Resources

Some pollutants are so noxious that they must be banned outright, but most must merely be reduced. The principle that the earth is a commons applies to air, water and nonrenewable resources. A pollution tax on emissions begins with the premise that everyone has an equal right to enjoy the air and water, and that those who use the air and water to hold their pollutants owe rent to the rest of us, whose enjoyment of that air and water is diminished. Thus, while a local LVT might not prevent factory pig farms, local taxes on water pollution certainly would.

The difference between land and nonrenewable resources is that the latter are consumed, while land is merely held. Therefore, nonrenewables cannot be rented. Still, the principle that resources are part of the commons means that it is proper for the community to decide how quickly or slowly it wants those resources to be consumed, and to set royalty charges accordingly.

Cap and Trade and the Enclosure Acts

Cap and Trade, on the other hand, is based on the idea that those who have been polluting all along have somehow earned a "property right" to continue polluting, and that those who want to pollute, even if they produce more and pollute less, must purchase "pollution rights" from the entrenched polluters.

It is put forward as a liberal environmentalist idea, but it has its origins in the "pollution tax credit" schemes of Ronald Reagan and Margaret Thatcher. It is a very dangerous approach, as it not only rewards past polluters, but enables them to punish cleaner, greener competitors.

For example, a company that can produce electricity with half the emissions must first purchase pollution credits from the established polluters. If the established polluters don't want to sell, or want to charge enough to make the greener alternative unprofitable, their Cap and Trade privileges actually hinder the transition to greener technology.

The burden of Cap and Trade falls on ordinary people for the benefit of the privileged. It is analogous to the Enclosure Acts of England and other countries, where, "for the sake of game," ordinary people were prohibited from hunting or disturbing wilderness land, while nobles were allowed even more latitude to run roughshod over the environment.

There are various sound alternatives to Cap and Trade, from pollution taxes to Cap and Share, in which every citizen gets pollution tax credits to sell to the polluters. The differences between these proposals are minor, and the best alternative is probably the one that is simplest to administer. The essential feature is that polluters must pay the community to pollute, rather than greener industries paying dirtier industries to pollute less.

LVT vs. Rural Building Restrictions

Many environmentalists think of sprawl as building in rural areas, and try to fight sprawl with restrictions that hamper the economy. Supporters of LVT see the demand for rural land as caused by the failure to build compact development in urban and inner suburban areas. Rural land is prized by developers for one reason only: it is less expensive to buy than urban and suburban land. A tax on the value of land draws that development inward and reduces the demand for rural and agricultural land. Removing land speculation as an obstacle to urban development has a positive effect on the economy, compared to imposing restrictions on rural land. The notion that "good environmentalism is good economics" is true with regard to LVT. It is hard to make a case that it is good with regard to building restrictions and the bureaucracy that inevitably accompanies them.

Problems with Exemptions

Some environmentalists argue for exemptions for landowners who hold their land as farmland or in a "clean and green" state. Those who hold "clean and green" land are invariably wealthy, for who else can afford to hold large tracts of land out of use? Often, land is held back where demand is high, forcing development to "leapfrog" over that land into more rural areas. As the editors of *House & Home* noted half a century ago,

> Suburban sprawl is what makes homebuyers drive past miles of un-used or underused countryside to get home to their tiny 60' × 120' lots. (Open fields, cow pastures, private golf links, and millionaire estates are fine, but it is much better to drive out five miles *beyond* your home to enjoy seeing them when you want to than to have to drive five miles past their "No Trespassing" signs when all you want is to get home.)
>
> *House & Home* thinks "development easements" are the worst idea yet. They just aggravate and perpetuate the sprawl by using tax money to keep golf links, orchards, and cow pastures where houses should be built, and push homebuilding out beyond to where the golf links, etc., should be. Green belts should be planned for maximum, not minimum, public use and enjoyment of the land. The 1,200 acre Field estate will make a fine state park, but as a fenced-in private property it was little or no good to anybody except the owners.[35]

Many who first hear about LVT fear that it will lead to "overdevelopment" of land, with no green space or human scale. However, Pittsburgh is reputed to have more trees than any other city in the US. While this is partly due to the city's hilly terrain, it is also due to very large city parks, many of which were sold or donated to Pittsburgh by its largest landowners.

Municipal parks are an appropriate way to maintain green space; that is, space that is maintained for the benefit of all should be under the control of democratic institutions. In contrast, open land has often been held by private interests that enjoyed tax breaks while waiting for land values to "ripen," and was then sold at a profit. Meanwhile, development leap-frogged over that land.

"Special farmland assessments" whereby land is assessed at its farm value instead of its market value, are similarly flawed. In genuine farming areas, the farm value is the market value. Farmland assessments mostly protect farms within or adjacent to the suburbs, and force the suburbs to leapfrog into farming areas.

"Smart Growth" Development Zones and Density Zoning

Development zones, often based on the Portland model, are artificial attempts to offset the effects of automobile-based sprawl. They impose incentives for developing within the zone and penalties for developing outside the zone. However, where land is inadequately taxed, the price of land inside the zone will simply rise until it swallows the value of the incentives, and the price of land outside the zone will fall until it offsets the cost of the penalties.

The problem is further aggravated by density limits within the smart-growth area. Laws that prohibit high-rise buildings in low-rise zones, low-rise apartments in townhouse zones, and townhouses in zones for free-standing houses with minimum lot sizes, prevent development from occurring within the zone, both by preventing the developer from doing more with less land, and by keeping land prices high within the smart-growth zones. Abolishing density limits within urban areas is a lot smarter than imposing arbitrary smart-growth zones.

These smart-growth zones assume that development should occur within a large circle, but a look at development patterns prior to the automobile reveal that this was rarely the case. Rather, development was dominated by small, self-contained towns, connected to urban hubs by rivers, rail lines, or even roads. However, the roads were lightly traveled, as people tended to work and shop in the same small towns where they lived, and buy a substantial share of their foodstuffs from local farmers.

The bottom line is that it doesn't matter how far a new development is from the center city. What matters is how far the people in the development will travel from their homes to the places where they routinely work and shop. This is impossible to manage via zoning laws, but substantial taxes on pollution and resource consumption will give people an incentive to arrange their lives accordingly, while substantial LVTs would make it easier for them to do so. Meanwhile, taxes on their own productivity could be reduced.

Alternative Energy Subsidies

Alternative energy subsidies take money from ordinary taxpayers, including those who have arranged their lives to consume very little energy and give it to people who consume energy, merely because they consume "less." Thus the person who bundles up and lives in a cold house subsidizes high-efficiency furnaces, and the person who mostly gets around by walking and bicycling subsidizes electric and hybrid vehicles for those who cling to the automotive lifestyle. Replacing productivity taxes with LVTs and resource consumption taxes still gives the owner of the high-efficiency furnace and the electric car an advantage over the person with a dirty furnace and a gas-hog car, but it also gives the sweater-wearing walkers and cyclists an advantage over all energy wasters.

The same is true of public transit, which is extended via subsidies into sprawling suburbs where it just doesn't work. Taxing land values and eliminating zoning creates the kind of environment where transit can compete with very little subsidy. What subsidies transit needs can come from the land-value increases that transit creates.

Ecological Economics

The bottom line is that ecology and economics come from the same root and mean almost the same thing, the former from "study of the house" and the latter from "management of the house." However, it is not enough for environmentalists to insist that good ecology is good economics, for the corollary is that bad economics makes for bad ecology.

Environmentalists naturally rankle at economics, which has been a tool for maximizing wealth from the time when kings sought to out-produce rival nations to modern times when corporate monopolies seek to out-produce rival corporations. That obsession has caused economics to become increasing divorced not only from environmentalism, but also from principles of justice and even from rationality.

Still, disdain for economics on the part of environmentalists perpetuates that logical disconnect. Fortunately, environmentalists do not have to wade through neoclassical econobabble. Rather, if they start with the same key premises that classical liberal economists and philosophers started with, the solutions become clear. Those premises are:

1. that the Earth is a commons and that the rent of land belongs to the whole people,

2. that the right to the Earth is a usufruct right, not a right to leave it in worse condition than one found it in, and

3. that what a human being produces is entirely his own, so long as he has compensated the community for what he has taken from them or foisted on them.

Following these principals, one no longer has to argue whether global warming is apocalyptic or merely detrimental. The one form of energy that is wasted when it is not consumed is human energy. So long as human energy is taxed, following these principles make it obvious, even to global warming deniers, that taxes on nonrenewable energy should replace taxes on human energy. So long as human beings sit in forced idleness, it becomes obvious that keeping nonrenewables out of use is preferable to keeping human beings out of use.

The limits of resource consumption were not an issue in Thomas Jefferson's day. Yet Jefferson recognized that forced idleness was caused by monopolization of the earth. Observing wretched poverty in France, he wrote:

> Whenever there are in any country uncultivated lands and unemployed poor, it is clear that the laws of property have been so far extended as to violate natural right. The earth is given as a common stock for man to labor and live on.[36]

The global warming issue has been polarized into a battle between what may be called the alarmist camp and the denier camp, to the detriment of all. Stepping back from this battle, environmentalists can "cut the Gordian Knot" by realizing that it is not necessary for others to agree with their analysis of the problem, but only for others to agree with their solutions.

Shifting taxes off labor and legitimate (labor-produced) capital by placing as much of the tax burden as practible on land, natural resource extraction and pollution is a proposal that many in the "denier" camp can support.

Endnotes

1. post-gazette.com/pg/10258/1087527-28.stm?cmpid=business.xml#ixzz0z0mHgS8m.
2. Stefan Lorant, *Pittsburgh, The Story of an American City* (1999), 101.
3. Ibid, p. 196.
4. Ibid. p. 287, citing Homestead chapter of The Pittsburgh Survey.
5. Articles of Confederation, Article VIII, "All charges of war, and all other expenses that shall be incurred for the common defense or general welfare, and allowed by the

United States in Congress assembled, shall be defrayed out of a common treasury, which shall be supplied by the several States in proportion to the value of all land within each State, granted or surveyed for any person...usconstitution.net/articles .html#Article8

6. Article 14, Free Soil Party Platform of 1848. angelfire.com/indie/ourcampaigns/1848 .html.

7. Letter from Lincoln to Martin S. Morris, Springfield, March 26, 1843, included in Basler, *Collected Works of Abraham Lincoln.*

8. Terence Powderly, head of the Knights of Labor, wrote that, if not for banking privilege, there would be no need for labor unions. The KoL listed one of its purposes as "To prevail upon governments to establish a purely national circulating medium, based upon the faith and resources of the nation, and issued directly to the people, without the intervention of any system of banking corporations, which money shall be a legal tender in payment of all debts, public or private." –*Thirty Years of Labor,* chapter 9, "The Circulating Medium." Powderly also wrote, "The demand of the order of Knights of Labor is, 'that all lands now held for speculative purposes be taxed to their full value.' The great difficulty is to ascertain to what extent lands are now held for the purpose of speculation.... If the Knights demanded that 'all lands held by parties, other than the government, shall bear an equal proportion of the taxation required for the maintenance of the government, and unimproved lands shall be assessed at the same rate as the nearest improved land,' they would come nearer to the establishment of a just rate of taxation, and whether lands were held for speculation or not, they would not escape their just proportion of taxation. –ibid, chapter 8, "Land, Telegraphy and Railroads." savingcommunities.org/docs/powderly.terence/. See also, George, Henry, *Progress and Poverty,* Book V, Chapter 1, "The primary cause of recurring paroxysms of industrial depressions." schalkenbach.org/library/george .henry/pp051.html.

9. Some of these tiny-house neighborhoods survive today, most notably in the bottoms of Lawrenceville.

10. Henry W. Oliver, *Henry Oliver Evans, Iron Pioneer,* (Dutton, 1942), 65–6.

11. "The Disproportion of Taxation in Pittsburgh," *Civic Frontage: The Pittsburgh Survey,* pp. 156–213; 455–68.

12. *Pennsylvania Laws,* 1911, p. 273, approved by Governor John K. Tener, May 11, 1911.

13. Ibid, pp. 287–88, approved, May 12, 1911.

14. Pittsburgh Civic Commission, *Civic Bulletin,* January, 1912; also An Act to Promote Pittsburgh's Progress, published by Pittsburgh Civic Commission in 1913.

15. "But before finally committing himself to the plan, he [Mayor Magee] sent a special investigator, Thomas C. McMahon, a member of the board of assessors, to visit municipalities in western Canada where similar tax systems had been in operation and were attracting favorable attention. The City of Vancouver had entirely exempted buildings from taxation by gradual steps over a period of fifteen years. That community was enjoying a remarkable building boom, conditions were very prosperous, and the city was receiving ample revenue under its new tax plan. "Mayor L. D. Taylor of Vancouver came to Pittsburgh about this time to address the Oakland Board of Trade and gave a first-hand report which was decidedly in favor of shifting the tax burden from improvements to land values. Mayor Magee then gave his endorsement to the proposed law and ever thereafter was a consistent supporter of the graded tax plan,

bringing to its support many of those who were closely associated with him in political life." –Williams, Percy, *The Pittsburgh Graded Tax Plan, Its History and Experience*, citing Robert M. Haig, *The Exemption of Improvements from Taxation in Canada and the United States*, 1915, pp. 170–171 (a report prepared for the Committee on Taxation of the City of New York). savingcommunities.org/docs/williams.percy/gradedtax .html#g128.

16. "Real Estate Board Committee Goes to Confer with Governor," *Pittsburgh Dispatch*, May 6, 1913.

17. *Pennsylvania Legislative Journal*, 1913, vol. 2, pp. 1635–36, 2453.

18. Pittsburgh *Post*, April 28, 1915.

19. Op. cit., Williams, Percy savingcommunities.org/docs/williams.percy/gradedtax .html#g139.

20. "Graded Tax Repealer Jolted," *Pittsburgh Press*, May 18, 1915.

21. *Pittsburgh Press*, June 10, 1915, p. 1.

22. Op. cit., Williams, Percy, appendix, table 2, "Assessed Valuation — Land and Buildings — City of Pittsburgh" savingcommunities.org/docs/williams.percy/gradedtax tables.html#table2.

23. Ibid, savingcommunities.org/docs/williams.percy/gradedtax.html#f128.

24. Ibid, savingcommunities.org/docs/williams.percy/gradedtax.html#f159.

25. *Saturday Evening Post*, August 3, 1946; June 9, 1956; *Commonwealth*, September, 1947; *Pittsburgh Bulletin Index*, January, 1948; *Business Week*, March 12, 1949; June 21, 1952; April 2, 1955; *Greater Pittsburgh*, April, 1949; *National Geographic*, July, 1949; *Time*, October 3, 1949; *Architectural Forum*, November, 1949; *The American City*, July, 1950; *Town and Country*, August, 1950; *Harper's*, January, 1951; August, 1956; *The Atlantic Monthly*, May, 1951; *Fortune*, June, 1952; *The Spectator* (London), December 19, 1952; *Real Estate*, March, 1953 ; January, 1960; *Collier's*, May 30, 1953; *USA, Tomorrow*, October, 1954; *National Municipal Review*, March, 1955; *Reader's Digest*, May, 1955; *Liberty Magazine*, February, 1956; *Life*, May 14, 1956; *Look*, January 8, 1957; *The Nation*, February 8, 1958; *Holiday*, March, 1959; *Engineering News-Record*, November 19, 1959; *Esquire*, September, 1960; *Newsweek*, October 24, 1960.

26. *House & Home*, Time-Life Inc., August 1960, p. 139.

27. "Plan in Pittsburgh on Building Fought; Merchants Oppose Taking of Their Property for Downtown PPG Industries "Headquarters Protest from Diocese," New York Times, June 3, 1979, p. 51.

28. California Department of Agriculture. (Further citation needed.)

29. "Steel exec thinks Japan 'dumping' cars in America," *The Bulletin*, Bend, (Deschuttes County), Oregon, Feb. 5, 1980, p. 24.

30. "Pittsburgh raised its tax rate on land from 4.95% to 9.85% of assessed valuation in 1979, while leaving the rate on buildings at 2.475%. New construction, measured by the dollar value of building permits issued, rose 14% as compared with the 1977–78 average. In 1980 the city widened the differential still more, to a tax rate of 12.55% on land vs. the .475% building rate, a ratio of 5.07 to 1.... Construction in 1980 leaped 212% above the 1977–78 average, reflecting ground-breaking for a new crop of office skyscrapers that is giving the city its so-called second renaissance (the first came in the 1950s with the redevelopment of the Golden Triangle). The adoption in 1980 of three-year tax exemptions on all new buildings — but not the land — also boosted construction. In 1981 construction peaked at nearly six times the 1977–78 rate. "Some

of the dozen new office towers that have gone up in Pittsburgh would have been built with or without tax concessions; downtown office space had been growing scarce. But the widening differential between the taxes on buildings and land undoubtedly helped. It cut the annual bill for owners of some skyscrapers by more than $500,000 a year when compared with conventional 1-to-1-ratio taxation." — Breckenfeld, Gurney, "Higher Taxes that Promote Development," *Fortune*, August 8, 1983, pp. 68–71 local tax.com/fortune/hightax.html.

31. Buffalo is the only large northeastern industrial city with a lower affordability rank, but Buffalo is notoriously slum-ridden. "Housing Affordability Rank of 243 US cities with populations of over 100,000." savingcommunities.org/issues/taxes/property/affordabilityrank.html.

32. A study by the Pennsylvania Economy League (Weir and Peters, 1986) alleged that a consensus of experts claimed land value tax did not aid development and hurt home owners in poor neighborhoods. However, this study was so tortuously contrived and so easily refuted that city council ignored it and continued shifting the tax burden to land values. Statements from development experts who had contradicted the PEL's desired conclusions were either twisted or ignored by the researchers. For example, former director of economic development Ed DeLuca had said land value tax did encourage development, but thought that further shifts would be necessary to have a sufficient effect. They claimed there was a consensus that the tax had no effect and that further shifts would also have no effect. Donald Stone, professor of economic development at Carnegie-Mellon University's School of Urban and Public Affairs said that interviewers responded to his positive comments about land value tax by changing the subject. Also, a check of the poor neighborhoods cited in the PEL study showed that most properties paying more were absentee-owned, and that owner occupants actually saved in those neighborhoods. A subsequent study by city finance director Ben Hayllar suffered from exactly the same failure to distinguish owner-occupied from absentee-owned properties. Owner-occupied properties in Hayllar's own sample also saved in poor districts where he alleged land value tax was punitive.

33. Percy Williams was executive secretary of the Pittsburgh Real Estate Board from 1918 to 1921. A Democrat, Williams was appointed to the board of assessors by Mayor Magee, a Republican, in 1922. The first Democrat mayor appointed him Chief City Assessor in 1934, where he remained until the county took over assessing in 1942. He had been secretary and a trustee of the Henry George Foundation since it was chartered in 1926 until his passing in 1978. savingcommunities.org/docs/williams.percy/gradedtax.html.

34. Almost all of the testimony against land value tax in the city's public hearings came from non-city residents within the county, particularly from the affluent Mount Lebanon Township. These suburban residents either owned city real estate or represented organizations of real estate interests. In contrast, most civic leaders and ordinary voters in the suburbs do not live in the four cities that have taxed land values (Pittsburgh, McKeesport, Duquesne and Clairton) and are oblivious to the issue.

35. *House & Home*, August, 1960, p. 115.

36. "Property and Natural Right," Letter to James Madison, Sr. from Fontainebleau, France, Oct. 28, 1785.

Definancialization, Deglobalization and Relocalization

Dmitry Orlov

Countries' current attempts to recover from their difficulties are driving up oil prices. The world economy will be unable to cope and will collapse, just as it did in 2008. Future attempts at recovery will also fail. Anyone who recognizes this should spend whatever money they have engaging with their neighbors and the land in new ways so that they stand a chance of saving something for themselves and their children.

What I want to say can be summed up simply: we all have to prepare for life without much money, where imported goods are scarce, and where people have to provide for their own needs, and those of their immediate neighbors. My point of departure is the unfolding collapse of the global economy. This started in the financial markets in 2008, and is now affecting the political stability of various countries around the world. A few governments have already collapsed, others may be on their way, and before too long we may find our maps redrawn in dramatic ways.

What does achieving sustainability mean, exactly? Is becoming sustainable sustainable itself? Chris Clugston summarized[1] his analysis of what he calls "societal over-extension" on The Oil Drum website. Here is a summary of his summary, in round numbers. I won't trifle with his arithmetic, because it's the cultural assumptions behind it that I find interesting. His idea is that if we shrink our ecological footprint by an order of magnitude or so, that should make humanity's impact on the planet sustainable once again. He expresses the shrinkage in financial terms: the GDP of the US would drop from, say, $100,000 per capita per annum to, perhaps, $10,000. Clugston draws a distinction between making this reduction voluntarily or involuntarily: we should make it easy on ourselves and come along quietly, so that nobody gets hurt. I find the idea that Americans will voluntarily lower their GDP by a factor of 10 rather outlandish. We keep the same system, just shut down 9/10 of it? Wouldn't that make it a completely different system? This sort of sustainability seems rather unsustainable to me.

I would like to offer a more realistic alternative. Everybody should have one US dollar for purely didactic purposes. This way, all Americans will be able to show their one dollar to their grandchildren, and say: "Can you imagine, this ugly piece of paper was once called The Almighty Dollar!" And their grandchildren will no doubt think that they are a little bit crazy, but they would probably think that anyway. But it certainly would not be helpful for them to have multiple shoe-boxes full of dollars, because then their grandchildren would think that they are in fact senile, because no sane person would be hoarding such rubbish.

Clugston himself offers an alternative to the big GDP decrease: a proportionate decrease in population. In this scenario, nine out of 10 people die so that the remaining 10% can go on living comfortably on $100,000 a year. I was happy to note that Chris did not carry the voluntary/involuntary distinction over to this part of the analysis, because I feel that this would have been in rather questionable taste. I can think of just three things to say about this particular scenario.

First, humans are not a special case when it comes to experiencing population explosions and die-offs. The idea that human populations should increase monotonically *ad infinitum* is just as preposterous as the idea of infinite economic growth on a finite planet. The exponential growth of the human population has tracked the increased use of fossil fuels, and I have yet to see a compelling argument for why the population would not crash along with them.

Second, shocking though this seems, it can be observed that most societies are able to absorb sudden increases in mortality without much fuss at all. There was a huge spike in mortality in Russia following the Soviet collapse, but it was not directly observable by anyone outside of the morgues and the crematoria. After a few years, people would look at an old school photograph and realize that half the class were gone! When it comes to death, most people make it easy on themselves and come along quietly. The most painful part of it is realizing that something like that is happening all around you.

Third, this whole budgeting exercise for how many people we can afford to keep alive is a good way of demonstrating what monsters we have become, with our addiction to statistics and numerical abstractions. The disconnect between words and actions on the population issue is by now almost complete. Population is very far beyond anyone's control, and this way of thinking about it takes us in the wrong direction. If we could not control it on the way up, what makes us think that we might be able to control it on the way down? If our projections look sufficiently shocking, then we might hypnotize ourselves into thinking that maintaining our artificial human life-support systems at any cost is more important than considering their effect on the natural world. The question "How many will survive?" is simply not ours to answer.

What's Actually Happening

There seems to be a wide range of opinion on how to characterize what is happening in the world economy now, from recession to depression to collapse. The press has recently been filled with stories about "green shoots" and the economists are discussing the exact timing of economic recovery. Mainstream opinion ranges from "later this year" to "sometime next year." None of them dares to say that global economic growth might be finished for good, or that it will be over in "the not-too-distant future" — a vague term they seem to like a whole lot.

A consensus seems to be forming that the 2008 financial crash was precipitated by the spike in oil prices when oil briefly touched $147/bbl that year. Why this should have happened seems rather obvious. Since most things in a fully developed, industrialized economy run on oil, the fuel is not an optional purchase: for a given level of economic activity, a certain level of oil consumption is required, and so one simply pays the price for as long as access to credit is maintained and, after that, suddenly it's game over.

The actual limiting price, beyond which the economy breaks down, was experimentally established to be less than the $147/bbl reached in 2008. We may never run out of oil, but we have already at least once run out of money with which to buy it, and will most likely do so again and again, until we learn the lesson. We will run out of resources to pump it out of the ground as well. There might be a little bit of oil left over for us to fashion into exotic plastic jewelry for rich people but it won't be enough to sustain an industrial base, and so the industrial age will effectively be over, except for some residual solar panels and wind generators and hydroelectric installations.

I think that the lesson from all this is that we have to prepare for a nonindustrial future while we still have some resources with which to do it. If we marshal the resources, stockpile the materials that will be of most use, and harness the heirloom technologies that can be sustained without an industrial base, then we can stretch out the transition far into the future, giving us time to adapt.

US Crude Oil Consumption as a Percent of GDP 1970–2009

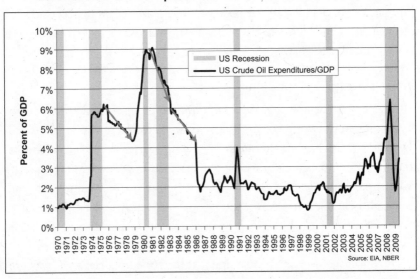

In the past forty years, three US recessions have been preceded by rapid increases in the amount of national income going to purchase oil. The bigger oil bills left less money for spending in the rest of the economy. 4% of GDP seems to be the maximum the country can afford. Source: What oil price can America afford? by Steven Kopits, at dw-1.com /files/files/438-06-09_-_Research_Note_-_Oil_-_What_Price_can_America_Afford _-_DWL_website_version.pdf

I Hold These Truths to be Self-Evident, Roughly Speaking

1. It is sometimes helpful to ignore various complexities to move the discussion forward. I believe that these points are all true, roughly speaking.

2. Global GDP is a function of oil consumption; as oil production goes down, so will global GDP. At some point, the inability to invest in

oil production will drive it down far below what might be possible if depletion were the sole limiting factor. Efficiency, conservation, renewable sources of energy all might have some effect, but will not materially alter this relationship. Less oil means a smaller global economy. No oil means a vanishingly small global economy not worthy of the name.

3. We have had a chance to observe that economies crash whenever oil expenditure approaches 4% of their GDP.[2] Attempts at economic recovery will cause oil price spikes that break through this ceiling. These spikes will be followed by further financial crashes and further drops in economic activity. After each crash, the maximum level of economic activity required to trigger the next crash will be lower.

4. Financial assets are only valuable if they can be used to secure a sufficient quantity of oil to keep the economy running. They represent the ability to get work done, and since in an industrialized society the work is done by industrial machinery that runs on oil, less oil means less work. Financial assets that that are backed with industrial capacity require that industrial capacity to be maintained in working order. Once the maintenance requirements of the industrial infrastructure can no longer be met, it quickly decays and becomes worthless. To a large extent, the end of oil means the end of money.

Now that the reality of Peak Oil has started to sink in, one commonly hears that "The age of cheap oil is over." But does that mean that the age of expensive oil is upon us? Not necessarily. We now know (or should have learnt by now) that once oil rises to over 4% of GDP, the world's industrial economy stalls out, and as soon as that happens, oil ceases to be particularly valuable, so much so that investment in maintaining oil production is curtailed. The next time industry tries to stage a comeback (if it ever does) it hits the wall much sooner and stalls again. I doubt that it would take more than just a couple of cycles of this market whiplash for all the participants to have two realizations: that they cannot get enough oil no matter how much they pay for it, and that nobody wants to take their money even for the oil they do have. Those who still have it will see it as too valuable to part with for mere money. On the other hand, if the energy resources needed to run an industrial economy are no longer available, then oil becomes just so much toxic waste. In any case, it is no longer about money, but direct access to resources.

No Need to be Gloomy

Now, I expect that a lot of people will find this view too gloomy and feel discouraged. But I feel that it is entirely compatible with a positive attitude to the future, so let me try to articulate what that attitude is.

First of all, we do have some control. Although we shouldn't hold out too much hope for industrial civilization as a whole, there are certainly some bits of it that are worth salvaging. Our financial assets may not be long for this world, but in the meantime we can redeploy them to good long-term advantage.

Secondly, we can take steps to give ourselves time to make the adjustment. By knowing what to expect, we can prepare to ride it out. We can imagine which options will be foreclosed first, and we can create alternatives, so that we do not run out of options.

Lastly, we can concentrate on what is important: preserving a vibrant ecosphere that supports a diversity of life, our own progeny included. I can imagine few short-term prerogatives that should override this — our highest priority.

It will take some time for these realizations to sink in. In the meantime, we will no doubt keep hearing that we have a financial crisis on our hands. We must do something to shore up the banks, to deal with the toxic assets, to shore up our credit ratings and so forth. There are people who will tell you that this was all caused by a mistake in financial modeling, and that if we re-regulate the financial sector, this won't happen again. So, for the sake of the argument, let's take a look at all that.

Financial management is certainly not my speciality, but as far as I understand it, it is mostly about assessing risk. And to do that, financial managers make certain assumptions about the phenomena they are trying to model. One standard assumption is that the future will resemble the past. Another is that various negative events are randomly distributed. For instance, if you are selling life insurance, you can be certain that people will die based on the fact that they have been born, and you can be reasonably certain that they will not all die at once. When someone dies is unpredictable; when people in general die is random, most of the time. And so here is the problem: the world is unpredictable, but classes of small events can be treated as random, until a bigger event comes along. It may seem like an obscure point, so let me explain the difference in a graphical way.

The square on the left is a random collection of multicolored dots. Actually, it is pseudo-random, because it was generated by a computer, and computers are deterministic beasts incapable of true randomness. A source of true randomness is hard to come by. The square on the right is not random, even to a layman. It is like oil expenditure going to 6% of GDP. That certainly wasn't random. But was it unpredictable? We had a few years of monotonically increasing oil prices, and the high prices failed to produce much of a supply response in spite of record-high drilling rates, investment in ethanol, tar sands and so on. We also had some good geology-based models that accurately predicted oil depletion profile for separate provinces, and had a high probability of succeeding in the aggregate as well. So the high oil expenditure was definitely not random, and not even unpredictable.

At a higher level, what sort of mathematics do we need to accurately model the inability of our financial and political and other leaders and commentators to see it, or to understand it, even now? And do we really need to do that, or should we just let this nice brick wall do the work for us. Because, you know, brick walls have a lot to teach people who refuse to acknowledge their existence, and they are very patient with students who need to repeat the lesson. I am sure that the lesson will sink in eventually, but I wonder how many more full-gallop runs at the wall it will take before everyone is convinced.

One person I would like to have a close encounter with the brick wall is Myron Scholes, the Nobel Prize-winning coauthor of the Black-Scholes method of pricing derivatives, the man behind the crash of Long Term Capital Management. He is the inspiration behind much of the current financial debacle. Recently, he has been quoted as saying the following: "Most of the time, your risk management works. With a systemic event such as the recent shocks following the collapse of Lehman Brothers, obviously the risk-management system of any one bank appears, after the fact, to be incomplete." Now, imagine a structural engineer saying something along those lines: "Most of the time our structural analysis works, but if there is a strong gust of wind, then, for any given structure, it is incomplete." Or a nuclear engineer: "Our calculations of the strength of nuclear reactor containment vessels work quite well much of the time. Of course, if there is an earthquake, then any given containment vessel might fail." In these other disciplines, if you just don't know the answer, then you just don't bother showing up for work, because what would be the point?

The point certainly wouldn't be to reassure people, to promote public confidence in bridges, buildings and nuclear reactors. But economics and finance are different. Economics is not directly lethal, and economists never get sent to jail for criminal negligence or gross incompetence even when their theories do fail. Finance is about the promises we make to each other, and to ourselves. And if the promises turn out to be unrealistic, then economics and finance turn out to be about the lies we tell each other. We want to continue believing these lies, because there is a certain loss of face if we don't, and the economists are there to help us. We continue to listen to economists because we love their lies. Yes, of course, the economy will recover later this year, maybe the next. Yes, as soon as the economy recovers, all these toxic assets will be valuable again. Yes, this is just a financial problem; we just need to shore up the financial system by injecting taxpayer funds. These are all lies, but they make us feel all right. They are lying, and we are buying every word of it.

The Five Fastest Ways to Lose All Your Money and Have Nothing To Show For It

These are difficult times for those of us who have a lot of money. What can we do?

1. We can entrust it to a financial institution. That tends to turn out badly. Many people in the United States have entrusted their retirement savings to financial institutions. And now they are being told that they cannot withdraw their money. All they can do is open a letter once a month, to watch their savings dwindle.
2. We can also invest it in some part of the global economy. I know some automotive factories you could buy. They are quite affordable right now. A lot of retired auto workers have put all of their retirement savings into General Motors stock. Maybe they know something that we

don't? (Actually, that's part of a fraudulent scheme perpetrated by the Obama administration, to pay off their banker friends ahead of GM's other creditors.)

3. How about a nice gold brick or two? A bag of diamonds? Some classic cars? Then you could start your own personal museum of transportation. How about a beautifully restored classic luxury yacht? Then you could use the gold bricks to weigh you down if you ever decide to end it all by jumping overboard.

4. Here's another brilliant idea: buy green products. Whatever green thing the marketers and advertisers throw at you, buy it, toss it and buy another one straight away. Repeat until they are out of product, you are out of money, and the landfills are full of green rubbish. That should stimulate the economy. Market research shows that there is a great reservoir of pent-up eco-guilt out there for marketers and advertisers to exploit. Industrial products that help the environment are a bit of an oxymoron. It's a bit like trying to bail out the *Titanic* using plastic teaspoons.

5. Another great marketing opportunity for our time is in survival goods. There are some websites that push all sorts of supplies to put in your private bunker. It's a clever bit of manipulation, actually. Users log in, see that the stock market is down, oil is up, shotgun shells are on sale, so are hunting knives, and if you add a paperback on "surviving financial armageddon" to your shopping cart you qualify for free shipping. Oh, and don't forget to add a large tin of dehydrated beans. Fear is a great motivator, and getting people to buy survival goods is almost a matter of operant conditioning: a marketer's dream.

If you want to help save the environment and prepare yourself for a life without access to consumer goods, then doing so by buying consumer goods doesn't seem like such a great plan. A much better thing to do is to BUY NOTHING. But that is not something you can do with money. But there are useful things to do with money, for the time being, if we hurry.

How to Spend All Your Money But Have Something to Show for It

Most of the wealth is in very few private hands right now. Governments and the vast majority of the people only have debt. It is important to convince people who control all this wealth that they really have two choices. They can trust their investment advisers, maintain their current portfolios, and eventually lose everything. Or they can use their wealth to re-engage with people and the land in new ways, in which case they stand a chance of saving something for themselves and their children. They can build and launch lifeboats, recruit crew and set them sailing.

Those who own a lot of industrial assets can divest before these assets lose value and instead invest in land resources, with the goal of preserving them, improving them over time, and using them in a sustainable manner. Since it will become difficult to get what you want by simply paying for it, it is a good idea to establish alternatives ahead of time, by making resources, such as farmland, available to those who can put them to good use, for their own benefit as well as for yours. It also makes sense to establish stockpiles of non-perishable materials that will preserve their usefulness far into the future. My favorite example is bronze nails. They last over a hundred years in salt water, and so they are perfect for building boats. The manufacturing of bronze nails is actually a good use of the remaining fossil fuels — better than most. They are compact and easy to store.

Lastly, it makes sense to work toward orchestrating a controlled demolition of the global economy. This calls for a new financial skill set: that of a disinvestment adviser. The first step is a sort of triage; certain parts of the economy can be marked "do not resuscitate" and resources reallocated to a better task. A good example of an industry not worth resuscitating is the auto industry; we simply will not need any more cars. The ones that we already have will do nicely for as long as we'll need them. A good example of a sector definitely worth resuscitating is public health, especially prevention and infectious disease control. In all these measures, it is important to pull money out of geographically distant locations and invest it locally. This may be inefficient from a financial standpoint, but it is quite efficient from the point of view of personal and social self-preservation.

Beyond Finance: Controlling Other Kinds of Risk

It seems rather disingenuous for us to treat economics and finance as a special case. Do we have any examples of risks we understood properly and acted on in time? Have there been any really serious systemic problems that we have been able to solve? The best we seem to be able to do is buy time. In fact, that seems to be what we are good at — postponing the inevitable through diligence and hard work. None of us wants to act precipitously based on what we understand will happen eventually, because it may not happen for a while yet. And why would we want to rock the boat in the meantime? The one risk that we do seem to know how to mitigate against is the risk of not fitting in to our economic, social and cultural milieu. And what happens to us if our entire milieu finally goes over the edge? Well, the way we plan for that is by not thinking about that.

The biggest risk of all, as I see it, is that the industrial economy will blunder on for a few more years, perhaps even a decade or more, leaving environmental and social devastation in its wake. Once it finally gives up the ghost, hardly anything will be left with which to start over. To mitigate against this risk, we have to create alternatives, on a small scale, that do not perpetuate this system and that can function without it.

The idea of perpetuating the status quo through alternative means is all-pervasive, because so many people in positions of power and authority wish to preserve their positions. And so just about every proposal we see involves avoiding collapse instead of focusing on what comes after it. A prime example is the push to develop alternative energy. Many of these alternatives turn out to be fossil-fuel amplifiers rather than self-sufficient resources: they require fossil-fuel energy as an essential input. Also, many of them require an intact industrial base, which runs on fossil fuels. There is a pervasive idea that these alternatives haven't been developed before for nefarious reasons: malfeasance on the part of the greedy oil companies and so on. The truth of the matter is that these alternatives are not as potent, physically or economically, as fossil fuels. And here is the real point worth pondering: If we can no longer afford the oil or the natural gas, what makes us think that we can afford the less potent and more expensive alternatives? And here is a follow-up question: If we can't afford to make the necessary investments to get at the remaining oil and natural gas, what makes us think that we will find the money to develop the less cost-effective alternatives?

How Long Do We Have?

It would be excellent if more people were thinking along these lines and had started making their lives a bit more sustainable, but social inertia is considerable, and the process of adaptation takes time. So the question is, is there enough time for significant numbers of people to realize the situation and to adapt, or will they have to endure quite a lot of discomfort? I believe that people who start the process now stand a fairly good chance of making the transition in time but that it would be unwise to wait and try to grab a few more years of comfortable living. Not only would that be a waste of time on a personal level, but we'd be squandering the resources we need to make the transition.

Collapse Without Preparation is a Defeat;
Collapse with Preparation is an Eccentricity

I concede that the choice is a difficult one: either we wait for circumstances to force our hand, at which point it is too late for us to do anything to prepare, or we bring it upon ourselves ahead of time. If we ask the question, "How many people are likely to do that?"—then we are asking the wrong question. A more relevant question is, "Would we be doing this all alone?" And I think the answer is, probably not, because there are quite a few other people who are thinking along these same lines.

Even so, it is very important to understand social inertia for the awesome force that it is. I have found that many people are almost genetically predisposed to not want to understand what I have been saying, and many others understand it on some level but refuse to act on it. When they are touched by collapse, they take it personally or see it as a matter of luck. They see those who prepare for collapse as eccentrics; some may even consider them to be dangerous subversives. This is especially likely to be the case for people in positions of power and authority, because they are not exactly cheered by the prospect of a future that has no place for them.

There is a certain range of personalities that are most likely to survive collapse unscathed, physically or psychologically, and adapt to the new circumstances. I have been able to spot certain common traits while researching reports of survivors of shipwrecks and other similar calamities. A certain amount of indifference or detachment is definitely helpful, including indifference to suffering. Possibly the most important characteristic of a survivor, more important than skills or preparation or even luck, is the will to survive. Next is self-reliance: the ability to persevere in spite of loneliness and lack of support from anyone else. Last on the list is unreasonableness: the sheer stubborn inability to surrender in the face of seemingly insurmountable odds, opposing opinions from one's comrades, or even force.

Those wishing to be inclusive and accommodating, who want to compromise and to seek consensus, need to understand that social inertia is a crushing weight. Translated, "We must take into account the interests of society as a whole" means "We must allow ourselves to remain thwarted by people's unwillingness or inability to make drastic but necessary changes; to change who they are." Must we, really?

There are two components to human nature, the social and the solitary. The solitary is definitely the more highly evolved, and humanity has surged forward through the efforts of brilliant loners and eccentrics. Their names live on forever precisely because society was unable to extinguish their brilliance or to thwart their initiative. Our social instincts are atavistic and result far too reliably in mediocrity and conformism. We are evolved to live in small groups of a few families, and our recent experiments that have gone beyond that seem to have relied on herd instincts that may not even be specifically human. When confronted with the unfamiliar, we have a tendency to panic and stampede, and on such occasions people regularly get trampled and crushed underfoot: a pinnacle of evolution indeed! And so, in fashioning a survivable future, where do we put our emphasis: on individuals and small groups, or on larger entities — regions, nations, humanity as a whole? I believe the answer to that is obvious.

"Collapse" or "Transition"?

It's rather difficult for most people to take any significant steps, even individually. It is even more difficult to do so as a couple. I know a lot of cases whether one person understands the picture and is prepared to make major changes in the living arrangement, but the partner or spouse is nonreceptive. If they have children, then the constraints multiply, because things that may be necessary adaptations post-collapse look like substandard living conditions to a pre-collapse mindset. For instance, in many places in the United States, bringing up a child in a place that lacks electricity, central heating or indoor plumbing may be equated with child abuse, and authorities rush in and confiscate the children. If there are grandparents involved, then misunderstandings multiply. There may be some promise to intentional communities: groups that decide to make a go of it in rural setting.

When it comes to larger groups — towns, for instance — any meaningful discussion of collapse is off the table. The topics under discussion center around finding ways to perpetuate the current system through alternative means: renewable energy, organic agriculture, starting or supporting local businesses, bicycling instead of driving and so on. These certainly aren't bad things to talk about, or to do, but what of the radical social simplification that will be required? And is there a reason to think that it is possible to achieve this radical simplification in a series of controlled steps? Isn't that a bit like asking a demolition crew to demolish a building brick by brick instead of what it normally does? Which is, mine it, blow it up and bulldoze and haul away the debris?

Better Living Through Bureaucracy: A 10-Step Program

1. Formulate a brilliant plan.
2. Generate community enthusiasm.
3. Get support from industry, government, the UN, the Vatican and the Dalai Lama.
4. Use mass media to generate public awareness.
5. Form action committees.
6. Propose new legislation. Lobby parliaments.
7. Secure corporate sponsorship.
8. Execute pilot programs.
9. Publish papers, present results at conferences.
10. COLLAPSE!

There are still many believers in the goodness of the system and the magic powers of policy. They believe that a really good plan can be made acceptable to all—the entire unsustainably complex international organizational pyramid, that is. They believe that they can take all these international bureaucrats by the hand, lead them to the edge of the abyss that marks the end of their bureaucratic careers, and politely ask them to jump. Now, don't get me wrong, I am not trying to stop them. Let them proceed with their brilliant schemes, by all means.

There are far simpler approaches that are likely to be more effective. Since most wealth is in private hands, it is actually up to individuals to make very important decisions. Unlike various bureaucratic and civic bodies, which are both short of funds and mired in social inertia, they can act decisively and unilaterally. The problem is, what to do with financial assets before they lose value. The answer is to invest in things that will retain value even after all financial assets are worthless: land, ecosystems and personal relationships. The land need not be in pristine or natural condition. After a couple of decades, any patch of land reverts to a wilderness, and unlike an urban or an industrial desert, a wilderness can sustain life, human and otherwise. It can support a population of plants and animals, wild and domesticated, and even a few humans.

The human relationships that are the most conducive to preserving ecosystems are ones that are in turn tied to a direct, permanent relationship with the land. They can be enshrined in permanent, heritable leases payable in sustainably harvested natural products. They can also be enshrined as deeded easements that provide the community with traditional hunting, gathering and fishing rights, provided human rights are not allowed to supersede those of other species. I think the lifeboat metaphor is apt here, because the moral guidance it offers is so clear. What has to happen in an overloaded lifeboat at sea when a storm blows up and it becomes necessary to lighten the load? Everyone draws lots. Such practices have been upheld by the courts, provided no one is exempt — not the captain, not the crew, not the owner of the shipping company. If anyone is exempt, the charge becomes murder. Sustainability, which is necessary for group survival, may have to have its price in human life, but humanity has survived many such incidents before without descending into barbarism.

Gift-Giving as an Organizing Principle

Many people have been so brainwashed by commercial propaganda that they have trouble imagining that anything can be made to work without recourse to money, markets, the profit motive and other capitalist props. And so it may be helpful to present some examples of very important victories that have been achieved without any of these.

In particular, Open Source software, which used to be somewhat derisively referred to as "free software" or "shareware," is a huge victory of the gift economy over the commercial economy. "Free software" is not an accurate label; nor is "free prime numbers" or "free vocabulary words." Nobody pays for these things, but some people are silly enough to pay for software. It's their loss; the "free" stuff is generally better, and if you don't like it, you can fix it. For free.

General science works on similar principles. Nobody directly profits from formulating a theory or testing a hypothesis or publishing the results. It all works in terms of mutuality and prestige — same as with software.

On the other hand, wherever the pecuniary motivation rises to the top, the result is mediocre at best. And so we have expensive software that fails constantly (I understand that the Royal Navy is planning to use a Microsoft operating system on its nuclear submarines; that is a frightening piece of news). We also have oceans full of plastic trash — developing all those "products" floating in the ocean would surely have been impossible without the profit motive. And so on.

In all, the profit motive fails to motive altruistic behavior, because it is not reciprocal. And it is altruistic behavior that increases the social capital of society. Within a gift-giving system, we can all be in everyone's debt, but going into debt makes us all richer, not poorer.

Barter as an Organizing Principle

Gifts are wonderful, of course, but sometimes we would like something rather specific, and are willing to work with others to get it, without recourse to money, of course. This is where arrangements can be made on the basis of barter. In general, you barter something over which you have less choice (one of the many things you can offer) for something over which you have more choice (something you actually want).

Economists will tell you that barter is inefficient, because it requires "coincidence of wants": if A wants to barter X for Y, then he or she must find B who wants to barter Y for X. Actually, most everyone I've ever run across doesn't want to barter either X for Y, or Y for X. Rather, they want to barter whatever they can offer for any of a number of the things they want.

In the current economic scheme, we are forced to barter our freedom, in the form of the compulsory work-week, for something we don't particularly want, which is money. We have limited options for what to do with that money: pay taxes, bills, buy shoddy consumer goods and, perhaps, a few weeks of "freedom" as tourists. But other options do exist.

One option is to organize as communities to produce certain goods that the entire community wants: food, clothing, shelter, security and entertainment. Everyone makes their contribution, in exchange for the end product, which everyone gets to share. It is also possible to organize to produce goods that can be used in trade with other communities: trade goods. Trade goods are a much better way to store wealth than money, which is, let's face it, an essentially useless substance.

Misleading Idea 1: Local/Alternative Currencies Can Help

There is a lot of discussion of ways to change the way money works, so that it can serve local needs instead of being one of the main tools for extracting wealth from local economies. But there is no discussion of why it is that money is generally necessary. That is simply assumed. There are communities that have little or no money, where there may be a pot of coin buried in the yard somewhere, for special occasions, but no money in daily use.

Lack of money makes certain things very difficult. Examples include gambling, loan sharking, extortion, bribery and fraud. It also makes it more difficult to hoard wealth, or to extract it out of a community and ship it somewhere else in a conveniently compact form. When we use money, we cede power to those who create money (by creating debt) and who destroy money (by canceling debt). We also empower the ranks of people whose area of expertise is in the manipulation of arbitrary rules and arithmetic abstractions rather than in engaging directly with the physical world. This veil of metaphor allows them to mask appalling levels of violence, representing it symbolically as a mere paper-shuffling exercise. People, animals, entire ecosystems become mere numbers on a piece of paper. On the other hand, this ability to represent dissimilar objects using identical symbols causes a great deal of confusion. For instance, I have heard rather intelligent people declare that government funds, which have been allocated to making failed financial institutions look solvent, could be so much better spent feeding widows and orphans. There is no understanding that astronomical quantities of digits willed into existence and transferred between two computers (one at a central bank, another at a private bank) cannot be used to directly nourish anyone, because food cannot be willed into existence by a central banker or anyone else.

Misleading Idea 2: Science and Technology Can Help

One accusation I often hear is that I fail to grasp the power of technological innovation and the free-market system. If I did, apparently I would have more faith in a technologically advanced future where all of our current dilemmas are swept away by a new wave of eco-friendly sustainability. My problem is that I am not an economist or a businessman: I am an engineer with a background in science. The fact that I've worked in several technology start-up companies doesn't help either.

I know roughly how long it takes to innovate: come up with the idea, convince people that it is worth trying, try it, fail a few times, eventually succeed and then phase it in to real use. It takes decades. We do not have decades. We have already failed to innovate our way out of this.

Not only that, but in many ways technological innovation has done us a tremendous disservice. A good example is innovation in agriculture. The so-called "green revolution" has boosted crop yields using fossil-fuel inputs, creating generations of agro-addicts dependent on just one or two crops. In North America, human hair samples[3] have been used to determine that fully 69% of all the carbon came from just one plant: maize. So, what piece of technological innovation do we imagine will enable this maize-dependent population to diversify their food sources and learn to feed themselves without the use of fossil-fuel inputs?

We think that technology will save us because we are addled by it. Efforts at creating intelligent machines have failed, because computers are far too difficult to program, but humans turn out to be easy for computers to program. Everywhere I go I see people poking away at their little mental-support units. Many of them can no longer function without them: they wouldn't know where to go, who to talk to, or even where to get lunch without a little electronic box telling them what to do.

These are all big successes for maize plants and for iPhones, but are they successes for humanity? Somehow I doubt it. Do we really want to eat nothing but maize and look at nothing but pixels, or should there be more to life? There are people who believe in the emergent intelligence of the networked realm — a sort of artificial intelligence utopia, where networked machines become hyperintelligent and solve all of our problems. And so our best hope is that in our hour of need machines will be nice to us and show us kindness? If that's the case, what reason would they find to respect us? Why wouldn't they just kill us instead? Or enslave us. Oh, wait, maybe they already have!

We'll Need to Re-Skill and Toughen Up

Supposing all goes well, and we have a swift and decisive collapse, what should follow is an equally swift rebirth of viable localized communities and ecosystems. One concern is that the effort will be short of qualified staff.

It is an unfortunate fact that the recent centuries of settled life, and especially the last century or so of easy living based on the industrial model, have made many people too soft to endure the hardships and privations that self-sufficient living often involves. It seems quite likely that those groups that are currently marginalized would do better, especially the ones that are found in economically underdeveloped areas and have never lost contact with nature.

And so I would not be surprised to see these marginalized groups stage a comeback. Almost every rural place has its population of people who know how to use the local resources. They are the human component of the local ecosystems and, as such, they deserve much more respect than they have received. A lot of them can't be bothered about fine manners or speaking English. Those who are used to thinking of them as primitive, ignorant and uneducated will be shocked to discover how much they must learn from them.

Rules for Your New Life

1. Conserve energy. Get plenty of rest and sleep a lot. Sleeping burns 10 times less energy than hard physical labor.
2. Save time. Avoid living to a schedule. Work with the weather and the seasons, not against them.
3. Pick and choose. Always have more to do than you ever plan to get done.
4. Have plenty of options. You don't know what the future holds so (don't) plan accordingly.
5. Think for yourself. The popularity of the stupid idea doesn't make it any less stupid.
6. Laugh at the world. Make sure to maintain a healthy sense of humor.

So what are we to do while we wait for collapse, followed by good things? It's no use wasting your energy, running yourself ragged and aging prematurely; so get plenty of rest, and try to live a slow and measured life. One of the ways industrial society dominates us is through the use of the factory whistle: few of us work in factories, but we are still expected to work a shift. If you can avoid doing that, you will be ahead. Maintain your freedom to decide what to do at each moment, so that you can do each thing at the most opportune time. Specifically try to give yourself as many options as you can, so that if any one thing doesn't seem to be working out, you can switch to another. The future is unpredictable, so try to plan so as to be able to change your plans at any time. Learn to ignore all the people who earn their money by telling you lies. Thanks to them, the world is full of very bad ideas that are accepted as conventional wisdom, so watch out for them and come to your own conclusions. Lastly, people who lack a sense of humor are going to be in for a very hard time, and can drag down those around them. Plus, they are just not that funny. So avoid people who aren't funny, and look for those who can laugh at the world no matter what happens.

Endnotes

1. theoildrum.com/node/5381, dated 3 May 2009.
2. The average price of a barrel of oil in 2007 was $65.61 and production was 73.78 million barrels per day. The Gross World Product was $65,610 billion. This means that 2.7% of world output was spent on buying oil. In 2008, the average price rose to $91.50, thus pushing the share of world output figure to around 4%.
3. R. H. Tycot et al., "The Importance of Maize in Initial Period and Early Horizon Peru," chapter 14 in *Histories of Maize: Multidisciplinary Approaches to the Prehistory, Biogeography, Domestication, and Evolution of Maize*, eds. J. E. Staller, R. H. Tykot and B. F. Benz (Elsevier, 2006), downloadable from shell.cas.usf.edu/~rtykot/14%20 Tykot%20et%20al.pdf.

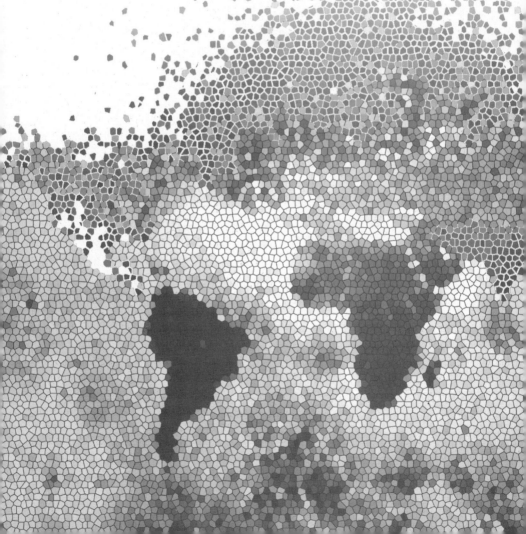

PART III

NEW WAYS OF
USING THE LAND

Proximity 2.0:
Cutting Transport Costs and Emissions Through Local Integration

Emer O'Siochru

Rather than bringing similar activities closer together to reap the benefits of scale and agglomeration, different activities should be situated beside each other to be more energy and carbon efficient.

This old saying tells us there was a time when it was an uncontested fact in Ireland that living close to each other was essential for a happy human life. That human life thrives when human actions are so confined in space as to impact on others today seems strange given our current desire for ever more expansion and separation in our living and working arrangements. Did this old saying emerge from a need to make the best of a bad situation or is it a forgotten but essential truth that still has resonance today?

is ar scáth a chéile, a mhaireann na daoine

SEANFHOCAL GAEILGE

In the shadow or shelter of each other, live the people

OLD IRISH SAYING

This paper will advance the case that closeness, or "proximity," was valued as life enhancing in the past—and for good reason, despite the propaganda of the rural revisionists. It describes what I call the Proximity Principle 2.0, the idea of a redefined and augmented "proximity" that has a great deal to offer communities in the troubling times ahead. There's more than a little bit of magic about the notion that something unexpected and wonderful can come simply by confining and combining existing elements differently, but that's exactly what the Proximity Principle 2.0 offers us.

In Ireland over the past 50 years, we've invested heavily in putting distance into our living and working arrangements. We live apart from each other, work far from where we live, shop far from where we work, grow food far from where we eat and so on. Our support systems are all far-flung and invisible; electricity is generated remotely, waste is processed remotely, knowledge is generated remotely to our everyday experience. Something profound has happened to the way we live.

FIGURE 1. The way we live now: scattered houses, Co. Galway, Ireland.

This paper does not explore what happened; others better able to do so will contribute to that topic in this book. Instead it will look to the past for clues to the immediate future.

Irish Settlement Patterns Myths

First we need to debunk some myths. Contrary to what is generally believed, the Irish people are not culturally predisposed to isolated settlement patterns. In fact, the historical records and the maps show that Irish people consciously chose to live close together where and when they had the freedom to do so. The Vikings founded many of our coastal towns but the Irish had their own proto town, set in the fertile plains and river valleys. These were the monastic settlements of the early Christian era and were centers of trade as much as of learning and piety.

What is less well known is that as the population increased, Irish society was developing the village structure along the European model in the 16th and 17th centuries, i.e. farmer and farm laborer families living alongside artisans and small-scale merchants in compact mixed settlements. In these villages, farmers traveled from the village every day to the tillage and orchard in-fields and further to the out-field pastures.

The Cromwellian reconquest put an abrupt halt to this evolution; towns and villages were broken up and new settlers and the non-rebellious installed on isolated farms. Only in the areas protected by the powerful Norman Butler family around Counties Kilkenny, South Tipperary and Waterford can we see surviving evidence for this farm/village from the 1830 OSi map records.

FIGURE 2. The way we lived then, 1: this 1816 map of Listrolin, a farm village in Co. Kilkenny, shows how farms and houses were clustered together in the past.

The displaced Irish were prevented from coming together in the better lands, but, given the relative freedom of the poorer lands on coasts and hillsides, they again formed settlements. We can see evidence of this in the many clachán settlements on Ireland's western seaboard, today mostly abandoned. This seaboard contained the highest density of rural population in Europe in the first half of the 19th century, when the entire island hosted and fed eight million people.

This evidence is countered by those who claim that the Irish had little choice but to live in these dense settlements because all of the better land was retained by the absentee landlords and let out to conforming tenants. Another argument is that famine was brought on by the unrestrained breeding of the Irish, who foolishly ignored the fact that the poor land could not maintain their families. In fact, the land maintained them pretty well for many generations; they did this by using the nutrients from the sea to feed the soil, having well-organized pasturage systems and using the efficient lazy-bed system of cultivation — until, of course, the potato failed. Contemporary accounts tell of healthy, handsome, happy people, even if a bit unwilling to take instruction from their "betters."

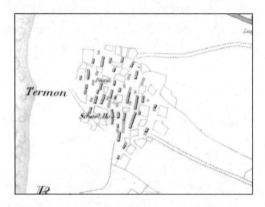

FIGURE 3. The way we lived then, 2. Terman, a clachan village in Co. Kerry, demonstrates how densely people once chose to live together.

The native Irish had to wait until the 18th century for the political and economic conditions that would foster the founding of the market villages and towns most of which survive today. These new villages and towns were centers of trade and exchange, not the homes of farmers. While they were often laid out by the freehold-owning landlord, they were built by Irish Catholics who had won a significant interest in their property in the form of long leases and lifelong leases.

This model was in complete contrast to the village-development model in England, where the landlord offered only limited tenancies in buildings that he built. This newly propertied merchant and professional class of Catholics led the struggle for the Land Acts, a struggle that was ultimately to redistribute the agricultural land and which, from that platform of security, later led to the national struggle for nationhood. So it can be said, not unreasonably, that the Irish villages and towns can be thanked for national independence.

The Loss of Proximity 1.0

Over the years the native Irish began to accept that living in isolated farmsteads was the natural order, its original imposition forgotten. This loss in folk memory led to a second great scattering, this time guided by well-intentioned motives.

After the terrible Famine of the 1840s, the improving Congested District Boards consolidated the fragmented holdings of clachán dwellers into separate freehold farms and individual farmhouses, breaking up the settlements in the processes. It never crossed the minds of these public servants that the villages had any value in the new Ireland they were building, nor that consolidated farms could be provided at the same time as retaining the existing settlements in use.

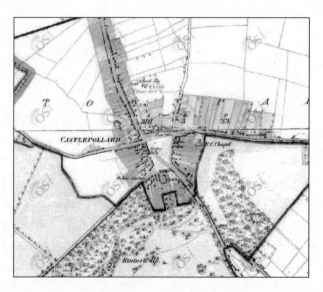

FIGURE 4. Castlepollard, a market village in Co. Westmeath, also shows a compact development pattern

Not only did this policy undermine the survival of the Irish language by making it synonymous with isolated rural life, it also destroyed much of the potential for economic development by destroying the potential for specialization.

The evidence for this conclusion is convincing. Today, the area where the Congested Districts Board operated along the western coast coincides almost exactly with the areas of disadvantage and population loss identified by the government's "Clar" designation (Figure 5b) and the areas identified in the National Spatial Strategy (NSS) as having weak village structuration (Figure 5c).

The loss of village structure and thus of the benefits of proximity led to the loss of opportunity, especially for non-farming families, which in turn led to mass emigration of the young and enterprising. Martin Charlton's

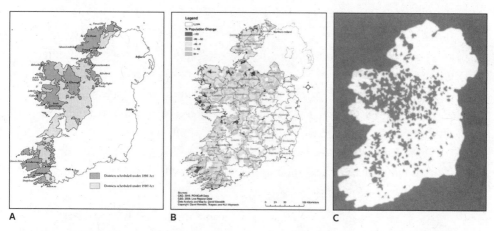

A   **B**   **C**

FIGURE 5. The Congested Districts of the 19th century shown in the map on the left were in most of the same places as today's Clar areas of Disadvantage (middle map) and where the National Spatial Strategy has identified a "weak" village structure.

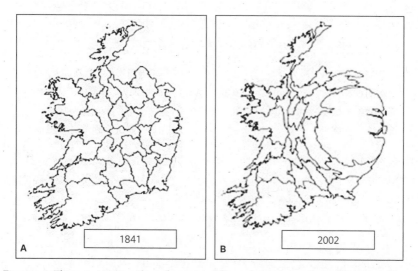

FIGURE 6. These cartograms show the areas of the counties drawn in proportion to their populations. They reveal how some populations, particularly in the West, shrank from their level before the Famine while the population of Dublin soared. Source: Martin Charlton, (2007), NUI, Maynooth. ncg.nuim.ie/content/media/downloads/Cartograms QuantumLeap.pps

cartographic project which adjusts the areas of counties according to their population makes the results of this very clear. The first map illustrates the population before the Famine; the second population loss and gain by county size in 2002 (Figure 6).

Proximity 2.0: Some Definitions

Proximity has recently been rediscovered and to a certain extent reinvented as a positive principle, having earlier been eclipsed for many years by the potential of globalization and the elimination of distance by cheap fossil fuels. A Google search brings up a surprising number of incarnations in widely differing contexts. Each context illustrates a particular attribute, and the combination of all these is what I term Proximity 2.0.

Definition 1, the most familiar interpretation or use of the term, comes from the environmental sector and refers to waste-management systems.

> "The proximity principle advocates that waste should be disposed of (or otherwise managed) close to the point at which it is generated, thus aiming to achieve responsible self-sufficiency at a regional/or sub regional level."　　　　　　　　　— Basel Convention 1989

In this case, the proximity principle enables and delivers "responsible self-sufficiency" which is something we will need in times of emergency.

Definition 2 comes from the technical field of industrial processes.

> "Proximity is the main tool used in manufacturing to enable one-piece flow, flexibility and to quickly assist another station on the U shaped production line."
> 　　　　　　　— Principles of Product Development Flow 2009

Here, proximity fosters smooth-flowing processes where glitches can be spotted and rectified quickly. This kind of flexibility is essential to resilience building, again a useful attribute in uncertain times.

Definition 3 comes from the knowledge economy discourse.

> "In spite of increasing global flows of ideas, capital, goods and labor, the rise of a knowledge-based economy and changes in the organization of the innovation process have actually increased the value of geographical proximity to innovation."
> 　　　　　　　　　　　— Sonn and Storper 2003

Geographical nearness fosters the random encounters that spark new ideas, something that no IT media has been able to replicate. This runs counter to the argument that all you need for innovation in the countryside is fast broadband.

Definition 4 comes from town and country spatial planning and is familiar to local government administrators, professionals and social and environmental advocates.

> "Proximity should be favoured over dispersal in settlements to encourage community interaction, make public transport, local services and environmental initiatives more viable."
>
> — Campaign to Protect Rural England 2008

Rural services are in decline in Ireland and will be under greater threat with the New Emergency. The more dispersed the settlement, the greater the cost of providing its population with the services and maintenance it needs. Even though councils coped reasonably well with floods and snow of Winter 2009–10, rural roads remain potholed and pitted as budgets were exhausted by the immediate emergency measures. A second harsh Winter would render some roads impassible.

Definition 5 stems from economics and the theories of US economist and writer Henry George.

> "This premise that parks have a positive impact on property values is known as the 'proximity principle'. It suggests that the value of living near a park is captured in the price of surrounding properties."
>
> — Frederick Law Olmstead 1856
> (Olmstead was the architect who laid
> out Central Park, New York City)

This aspect of proximity is the most revealing and useful when we plan for the future because it tells us that investing in useful infrastructure or desirable amenities can be paid for from the increased value of the nearby/adjacent land. Proximity, here, generates value, and if recouped by the community, also generates money to pay for further services.

In sum, then, Proximity 2.0, combining all of its benefits of its various aspects, offers the following:

1. Enables recycling of waste especially for energy.
2. Creates flexibility and resilience.
3. Fosters innovation.
4. Makes services viable.
5. Adds value to land.

What Proximity 2.0 is *not* is about is agglomeration. Agglomeration is a term used to describe the benefits of putting similar uses together. It is familiar in retail studies i.e. retailers benefit from other retailers selling similar goods nearby as consumers are attracted to the choice and convenience offered and increased footfall leads to increased turnover for everyone. The agglomeration effect often outweighs the advantage of a local monopoly in particular classes of goods. Neither is Proximity 2.0 linked to "benefits of scale," such as the efficiencies made possible by building and servicing a large number of similar houses or other buildings in a limited area.

On the contrary, Proximity 2.0 describes the advantages of placing very *different*, not similar, uses and functions in close relationship. The advantages that accrue to agglomeration and scale are dependent on cheap energy and globalization, and this produces an apparent simplification locally that masks a remote and therefore opaque and potentially vulnerable complexity.

"Localization" is an emerging concept used by environmentalists advocating the reversal of globalization. But it is a modest and uninspiring concept on which to base an emergency response. Proximity 2.0 goes beyond negative definitions to suggest potential synergies that emerge when different activities and functions are linked at the local scale. The next section describes some examples of these benefits.

Applications of the Proximity Principle

The Natural Step[1] is a framework for industry and business covering the generation and processing of waste. The framework builds on a basic understanding of what makes life possible, how our biosphere functions and how we are part of the Earth's natural systems. It points out that in a sustainable society, nature would not be subject to systematically increasing concentrations of substances extracted from the Earth's crust or created by scientists and that people would not be subject to conditions that systemically undermined their capacity to meet their needs. The Natural Step seeks to make these systems apparent to producers through a rigorous checklist process and the use of a non-political logic that eliminates pollutants through design.

Similarly, Natural Capitalism,[2] developed by the US-based Rocky Mountain Institute that researches and advises on sustainable settlement, building and transportation design, describes the objective of "industrial ecology." This strategy discourages forms of amoral purchasing arising from ignorance of what goes on *at a distance* and implies a political economy that greatly values natural capital and relies on what Amory Lovins calls "instructional capital" to design and maintain each unique industrial ecology.

These principles converge and locate in the concept of "Industrial Symbiosis." The tasks of identifying and eliminating the unsustainable increase in substances and deleterious conditions and of eliminating ignorance of far-flung effects is solved through the Proximity Principle 2.0 because it places different but related production systems physically adjacent to each other. This makes the problems and solutions clear without the need for checklists and renders those problems solvable without a huge investment in instructional capital.

The Municipality of Kalundborg in Denmark was one of the first to introduce the world to Industrial Symbiosis when it applied the Proximity Principle 2.0 in industrial-estate planning. In Kalundborg, all waste is someone else's raw material. Symbiosis here means the coexistence of diverse organisms that may benefit from one another. A symbiosis network links a 1500 MW coal-fired power plant with the community and other companies. Surplus heat from this power plant is used to heat 3,500 local homes in addition to a nearby fish farm, the sludge from which is then sold as a fertilizer. Steam from the power plant is sold to Novo Nordisk, a pharmaceutical and enzyme manufacturer and a Statoil plant. This reuse of heat reduces the thermal pollution of hot wastewater discharged to a nearby fjord. Additionally, a by-product from the power plant's sulfur dioxide scrubber contains gypsum that is sold to a wallboard manufacturer. Almost all of the manufacturer's gypsum needs are met in this way, reducing the amount of open-pit mining needed. Furthermore, fly ash and clinker from the power plant are utilized for road building and cement production.

This kind of symbiotic cooperation has developed spontaneously over several decades and today comprises some 20 projects. The exchange of residual products between the companies is laid out in Figure 7. The collaborating partners also benefit financially from the cooperation because the individual agreement within the symbiosis is based on commercial principles. All projects are environmentally and financially sustainable. It's a win-win scenario for all concerned.

Industrial Symbiosis

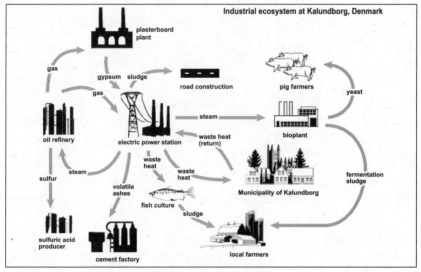

FIGURE 7. This flow chart illustrates how the waste and by-products of companies on a municipal industrial estate in Kalundborg, Denmark, become the raw materials for other companies. Source: *Ecodecision*, Spring 1996.

According to Amory B. Lovins of the Rocky Mountain Institute, 19th- and 20th-century model power plants had a higher cost and outage rate than the grid, so both supply and demand had to be aggregated through the grid to make sure that electricity production continued without interruption. In the 21st-century model, in contrast, power plants have a lower cost and higher reliability than the grid, so affordable and reliable supply should now logically originate at or near the customer for security of electricity supply. Indeed this has been happening — in Figure 8 below we can see that non-utility i.e. non-power company electrical generation, has been increasing since the mid 1980s.

In his book *Small is Profitable*, Lovins measured the benefits of "distributed" or electrical generation in proximity to consumption at two to three times that of remote generation, more if the grid is congested or reliability required. If the heat from electrical generation can be used, then the benefits double again. There are often other extra-over benefits or positive side effects or "externalities" as economists call them for certain sites.

We can see these benefits in Güssing, a small town in Austria that today has a rape-oil refinery for the production of bio-diesel, a district heating

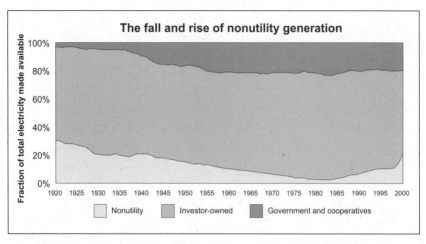

FIGURE 8. This graph, from Amory Lovins' book *Small is Profitable*, shows how, after a period in which very few US consumers produced their own electricity, more are beginning to do so at the expense of the commercial utility companies.

unit supplied with wood, and a state-of-the-art biomass-power plant with a generation of 2 MW electricity and 4.5 MW heat. The town is now 45% self-sufficient in energy and has attracted 50 new companies, more than 1,000 new jobs, and total increased sales volume of 13m Euro per year. An eco-tourist business now sees 1,600 visitors per week visit the town, eager to learn how it reinvigorated itself.

The German town of Lünen, north of Dortmund, will use organic material from local farms to provide electricity for its 90,000 residents, producing 6.8 MW to power and heat 26,000 houses. The gas is distributed through a new biogas pipeline network being built underground using a horizontal drilling robot.

Using the process of anaerobic digestion (AD), biogas can be produced from agricultural wastes, mainly slurries, of which there is an abundance in parts of Ireland. However, manure-only AD will not generate enough biogas and thus sufficient electricity to give a good return on its costs, as manure at best produces

FIGURE 9. Farm anaerobic digester Wexford.

189

20 cubic meters of biogas per tonne. Mixing biowaste from commercial and municipal brown bins transforms the economics of farm-based ADs. An AD facility would be financed easily through gate fees (the fee chargeable for accepting wastes for processing or transformation), along with the money earned from the extra energy production that comes from the higher energy content of biowaste. Hauling bulky manure from many widespread locations to a central point is expensive; taking the smaller quantity of pasteurized biowaste to a rural location near or in a livestock farm has lower costs and lower CO_2 emissions. It also returns food waste to where it was generated, thus closing the nutrient cycle.

If the 1.5 million tonnes of manure produced annually by 200,000 adult cattle, about 5% of the Irish herd, was augmented with 300,000 tonnes of biowaste to give a 60/40% mix in dry matter terms, rural ADs could produce 180GWh per year. This digestion of 1.5 million tonnes of manure would also reduce greenhouse emissions by about 150,000 tonnes per year in terms of CO_2 or its equivalent in other gases. This is 2.5 times the reduction required from manure management by the Irish government's 2000 Climate Change Strategy, and there are also energy-related savings. Another significant benefit would come from the reduction in artificial fertilizer nitrogen use by around 400 tonnes per year of nitrogen, thereby preventing about 100 tonnes per year of nitrogen getting into watercourses.

Simply combining food production and consumption close together brings benefits to consumer and producer by cutting out the middleman and eliminating transport costs. Traceability is not a problem in the Herrmanndorf farm market in Hanover, Germany. Herrmanndorf, originally a sausage manufacturer, vertically integrated all aspects of food production, processing and sales in one location. Beef, milk and pork are produced on

Figure 10. Herrmannsdorf shop and animal housing, Hanover, Germany.

the farm and neighboring farms using own-grown grass and cereals. Animals are farmed, slaughtered and processed on site using energy from their wastes. Beer is brewed and bread is baked from local cereals and sold in the farm market in the same way. Accommodation for workers and trainees is provided on site. The farm is a popular weekend destination for Hanover residents who enjoy a day out while doing their shopping.

Rural settlements in Ireland are uniquely well-positioned to respond to the developing crisis. Local agriculture can produce food, biomass for energy and structural materials and fiber for construction, providing all the materials for village production and reproduction. Hemp a neglected but particularly versatile crop that offers seeds and oil for human consumption, fiber for paper and clothing and hurd for use as an insulant and binder in construction. Combined with lime, hemp forms a composite material that has many useful qualities. Hemp-lime is insulating, fire-proof, rot-proof, vermin-proof and moisture-buffering. With passive design, it can eliminate the need for space-heating systems in new homes. Hemp-lime with timber construction saves 50 tonnes of CO_2 and stores 5 tonnes of CO_2. Hemp can be grown locally in normal crop rotations with low inputs, and is easily harvested and processed with conventional machinery. Lime and other additives are widely available in Ireland.

We now come to the most overlooked form of waste, human sewage. It's not usually included in waste-management plans but lumped under a special category called "wastewater" in government and local government regulations. Water could hardly be described as a waste so it must be something we have put into the water and the question is why? Conventional sewage systems consume scarce freshwater and dilute useful nutrients. The nutrients are carried to rivers and the sea, where they are extremely harmful causing eutrophication. In turn, more nutrients have to be produced for agriculture, causing depletion of fossil resources and high energy demand. Considerable fossil energy is used to treat sewage and graywater this way. There is, however, a better way than gravity sewerage pipework to transport human waste to treatment and processing facilities. Vacuum-based transportation, another Victorian invention, is already used successfully in virtually every train, airplane and ship.

External and/or internal vacuum wastewater systems give design flexibility; small pipes 25–100 mm can go up to 6 meters vertically and 3 km on the flat. Costs are low for installation, maintenance and future modification as the many vents and traps of the gravity system are eliminated. Importantly, water is conserved; a vacuum system uses 1 liter of water per flush. Multiple collection tanks and pumps can be used to separate different types of wastewater. Vacuum transportation is the final component of a redesigned domestic system that can recover all energy and nutrients in the food cycle. There are a few examples of such a complete system in place. A small housing development in Lubeck, Germany installed completely independent sewage and domestic food waste-treatment systems (Figure 11).

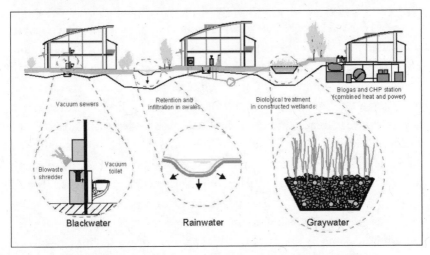

FIGURE 11. A chart illustrating the flows of energy and nutrients in a small housing development in Lubeck, Germany, which has installed completely independent waste-treatment systems for sewage and domestic food.

Cellulosic waste or woody wastes, of which there is a vast amount left over from food production, forestry and construction, are not suited to anaerobic digestion, which deals better with green or wet biowastes. Burning cellulosic waste recovers energy but leaves little of the original nutrients or carbon to return to the soil. Far better is pyrolysis, the process of heating without oxygen to release the volatile gases of the cellulosic material. Pyrolysis is a new name for the old-fashioned process of charcoal making. If applied in a certain way, it produces a "biochar" that locks up the CO_2 of the biomass and returns it to the soil where it stimulates and supports the soil organisms. (Others will describe the benefits of biochar in this volume.) (Figure 12).

Pyrolysis is not yet a commercial reality in Ireland, nor has it been convincingly established elsewhere. Its promise is enormous, as it can deliver

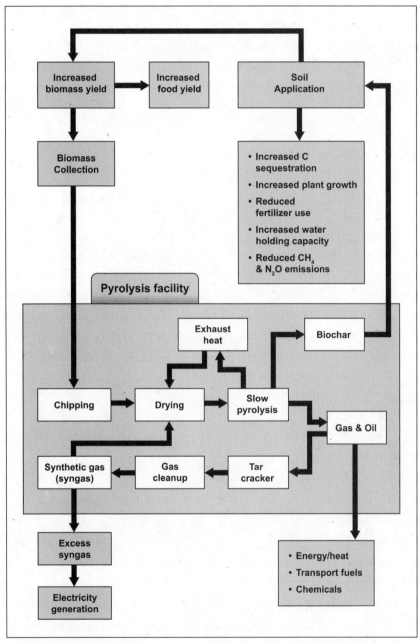

FIGURE 12. Positive feedback: turning biomass into biochar and applying the char to the land increases fertility and enables more biomass to be produced, along with fuels and a wide range of chemicals.

renewable electricity to the grid, considerable heat for a local factory, bio-oil for heating and transportation, and biochar for commercial agriculture and possible future carbon-credit sales. High rate of investment return can only be delivered if all of the co-products are realized i.e. when production of biochar is in the right location and is integrated into other production and consumption activities. In other words, proximity is a *sine qua non* for biochar to reach its potential as a climate-saving technology.

ENLIVEN Study

Energy was an already an important element of proximity 1.0 in the past. Before oil was exploited for energy, settlements were often established near energy sources. An example can be found in Co. Offaly on the foothills of the Slieve Bloom mountains, where a necklace of villages grew up around watermills on the Silver River. In the 1930s, the source of energy changed to exploitation of the bogs for turf. As the source of energy shifted, so too did the economic and political power. Ballyboy ceased to be the chief county town, and little-known Frankfort, renamed Kilcormac, rapidly developed with new worker housing because of its proximity to the turf works. As the bogs lost their importance as the importation of oil and gas rose, Kilcormac also fell into sleepy decline.

FIGURE 13. The watermills in Ballyboy and Cadamstown villages were once the heart of the community.

In 2005, EOS Future Design participated in a research project entitled ENLIVEN to prepare for a European funding submission exploring how renewable energy resources could once again be used as an engine for village development. We identified hydro, wind, forestry bioenergy and agricultural biowaste resources available to the villages of Cadamstown, Ballyboy and Kilcormac. It was a first attempt to outline a new vision for rural communities using renewable energy sources located close by. In the past, rural development policies have sought to preserve threatened ways of life or to revive those that had already passed into history. The ENLIVEN study looked to the future instead of the past and actively prepared for largely predictable events. But the report did not overlook local place and local culture; the plans were rooted in specific natural and social contexts. The study easily identified a potential 43% reduction in fossil-fuel use and CO_2 emissions in a rural community of 1,200.

We proposed a new plan-led process of village development that would shift from incremental one-off house development in the rural village hinterland, or the sudden huge developer-led anonymous housing estate at the edge of the village, to a more controlled process. The following is a slightly amended version of this process that takes into account political fiscal changes.

The first stage of the ENLIVEN development process covers planning and design.

- The community of a village in decline or under potentially damaging development pressure would request a framework plan for the village.
- A revolving fund would be available to manage the upfront costs of the plan and the infrastructure development that follows.
- The local authority would contract a team of consultants directly or approve a set chosen by the community and would partner the team in the preparation of the plan.
- A "Charrette" in which all stakeholders participate to plan their village is facilitated by the planning and design team on location over a number of days.
- Agreement would be sought as much as possible with landowners about what land should be developed within a five-year time horizon guided by sustainability objectives and community needs.
- These identified lands would be prioritized for new infrastructure and investment.
- New access roads, parks, water, drainage and waste-treatment and energy-generation facilities and amenities and services required would be located, sized and costed.
- A three-dimensional plan would show the new roads, squares, parks and also the heights, shapes and uses of the buildings that enclosed them.

- A design guide would be developed which reflected the local building vernacular and the distinctive qualities of the local settlements, and set energy and other ecological standards for the construction.

Implementation would be carried out in two stages: a) Infrastructure, services and public spaces and amenities; and b) building construction on sites.

- The local authority would use its powers to clear title and/or acquire key land where the community and authority as a whole thought it was necessary for the benefit of the wider community.
- The local authority or, in partnership with a private or not-for-profit infrastructure developer(s) — under building licences from the landowners, would carry out the infrastructure works and agreed amenities and service buildings. Equity partnerships are the optimal vehicle to align everybody's interests.
- Landowners would build on the fully developed sites or sell them to self-builders or in small groups to local builders in accordance with the design guide.
- The community, or at least the landowners in the community, would have control of the sale price and to whom it sold the houses and sites.
- In addition a portion of the land (equivalent to Part V of 2000 Act) should be given over to a Community Land Trust in the form of an Equity Partnership, which would provide housing for rent or purchase at a lower-than-market cost as it would not include the land element. This would ensure that locals were never priced out of their own area despite the high values created and that the key skilled people (mechanics, teachers or nurses, for instance) that the community needs for its development and maintenance would be attracted into the area.

The Proximity Principle tells us that the land values created by the development of infrastructure, services and amenities can be recouped by the upswing in land values of served and adjacent property. Section 49 of the 2000 Act provides for the recouping of investment by a local authority directly relating to a served site i.e. roads and pavements. The value added by the combined renewable-energy and waste-processing plant will attach to all land in the vicinity including developed properties. A new Site Value Tax (SVT) promised in the program for government will provide the means to collect that value created. The SVT will also ensure that the developed sites are sold quickly and the revolving fund recouped to be made available to other communities.

Over a year, ENLIVEN showed that it could deliver 100% net renewable-energy services through electricity and hot water mini-grids in the participating villages. However, at any one time, the villages could be exporting or importing non-renewable energy from the national grid. The balancing of supply by suitable demand uses will be pursued through the planning process (the Framework Plan) and by the active participation of local development agencies to identify energy-hungry, job-creating uses.

It may be advantageous to involve an ESCo (an Energy Services Company) to undertake the "top up and spill" technical and pricing interface with Eirgrid and the billing of customers. Again an Equity Partnership structure would include consumers, investors and energy producers in a sustainable relationship. Activities that are flexible enough to use off-peak electricity generated by the wind turbine, such as refrigeration or kilns, will be attracted by very cheap rates to the participating rural villages.

A local ESCo could make the extra costs of peak electricity use visible to users so that they have the option of postponing discretionary electricity use, such as the drier or dishwasher, until the energy demand and price are lower. Metering and billing systems should be intelligent so that using electricity or hot water at the high demand times will cost more than the off-peak times.

We estimated that the energy savings arising from intelligent design, construction and retrofit could eventually reach 6,282,000 kWh as a direct result of the ENLIVEN project for the three villages which amount to 3,700 tonnes of CO_2 saved every year. At €22.47 per tonne, this represents a saving for tax-payers of €83,228 per annum if emission rights have to be bought by the government.

Because of the insolvency of Irish banks and the pressure on public funds due to the crash in fiscal receipts, the more pessimistic observer might argue that the funding is simply not available for this kind of ambitious energy and waste infrastructure. But the Proximity Principle tells us otherwise.

Funding has been allocated under two different category streams for rural development. The first is the **Rural Development Programme** which was set up to tackle the quality of life in rural areas and to promote diversification within the rural economy. 50% funding for private projects up to

€150,000 is available which not-for-profit community groups will be eligible for a higher rate of aid at 75%. Administration and training is funded up to a generous 100%. €30,000 per project is offered for analysis and project development.

This funding is appropriate for the Plan and Design Stages of the ENLIVEN process and would be available for reuse by further communities when recouped under SVT and Section 49 of the 2000 Planning Act.

The second major source of funding is that allocated under the **Water Services Investment in the NDP**, a total €4.7 billion. €89 million investment was planned in the 2009 budget although final figures were reduced. To illustrate, small wastewater plants for six villages in North and South Tipperary cost €10.80m (€1.9 million each on average).

€1.9 million will easily cover the costs of a combined agricultural and human waste-processing anaerobic digester with combined heat and power energy generation and nutrient recovery to ensure the agricultural input quality for a rural village. The private sector will be willing partners in such a facility, thereby making these funds work for other communities.

Opportunities for Proximity 2.0 in Ireland

- The Environmental Pillar is now recognized as a "Social Partner" at national level. Social Partners have to be included in "partnership structures" at every level and every Leader Company (32) has to have an environmental representative, as do City and County Development Boards. So for the first time, environmental activists have a voice at local government level.
- Many of these representatives have taken their places on these boards. I am on the County Westmeath Special Policy Committee for Environment and Water Services and I have put an item on the agenda to reconsider Westmeath's existing specification and procurement of wastewater-treatment systems. Others will follow.
- Site Value Taxation is now contained in the Programme for Government thanks to policy-development work by the environmental network Smart Taxes, which is led by Feasta. As the time of going to press, the network had been invited to discuss implementation issues with the Department of Finance. Those who follow Irish governance will know that this is a big advance.

Obstacles to Proximity 2.0 in Ireland

- The myth of an historic model for single houses and the under-valuation of the rural village still persist today as remote "one-off" houses are still being granted planning permission and built despite the downturn, even by self-proclaimed environmentalists.
- There's no easy way to capture the land value created by new energy and waste facilities to help fund investment until SVT is implemented and it has many enemies. Worse, even SVT political friends underestimate its vital underpinning of the economics of sustainability as it can be a difficult concept to explain.
- Outdated drainage and wastewater building regulations and planning practices that stifle any innovation. On the positive side, these are under revision not least because of budget constraints.
- Outdated electricity grid and cost/reward structure. The new "Refit Tariff" for bioenergy is an advance, but more is needed, especially commitment to the distributed and embedded energy model by government and a Cap/Tax and Share of carbon allowances.
- The Limited Liability Partnerships legal structure needed for Equity Partnerships is not yet available under Irish Company Law.
- Specialist, siloed scientific, technical and professional education and practice is a persistent obstacle to proximity 2.0 and one that is difficult to solve in the short term but keeping our young qualified graduates from emigrating would be a good start.

Conclusion

As I have shown, there are numerous tangible benefits that come from applying the Proximity Principle 2.0, not least greater energy and food security in the long term, and in the short term — rural jobs in waste treatment and energy generation. The kind of synergy that comes from placing different services and uses in proximity to each other in rural settlements is a matchless opportunity to rapidly build circuit breakers at the mid or community scale to halt complete systemic collapse. Proximity Principle 2.0 really is a case of the whole being greater than the sum of its parts, always allowing that the different parts are close enough to interact. There's no sleight-of-hand involved; it is simply good integrated design using best-practice technical knowledge.

The payment for these manifold benefits is the abandonment of a desire for isolated living in the countryside — a settlement pattern that was never native to us anyway.

Endnotes

1. The Natural Step is a non-profit organization founded in Sweden in 1989 by a scientist, Karl-Henrik Robèrt, which promotes a systematic, principle-based definition of sustainability. See naturalstep.org/.
2. Paul Hawken, Amory Lovins and L. Hunter Lovins, *Natural Capitalism: Creating the Next Industrial Revolution* (Little Brown and Company, 1999).

The Nutritional Resilience
Approach to Food Security

BRUCE DARRELL

*Very few soils have a perfect balance of minerals. As a result, their fertility
is limited and the crops grown on them cannot provide all the nutrients
people need. As people can get food from elsewhere at present, these local
deficiencies do not matter too much. However, if the option of filling one's
plate from all over the world disappears, human health will likely decline
unless the missing minerals are applied over the next few years.*

We all talk about food but our discussions are generally confined to our own
spheres of interest. So, while food links farmers to CEOs, advertisers to aid
agencies, community activists to urban planners, gardeners to chemical engineers, geneticists to nutritionists, lorry drivers to commodity traders, and
cooks to economists in a complex web, crucial relationships and unifying
issues are missing from most conversations.

Moreover, we usually assume that the issues we don't discuss are unrelated and unchanging. Indeed, those working on one issue usually have beliefs that preclude engagement with those working on others. For example,
urban planners assume that farming yields are the same regardless of scale
and context. This leads them to discount urban agriculture as a fringe pursuit rather than a productive and essential use of urban and peri-urban
land. The disconnect between production and nutrition is perhaps more
critical. Farmers and nutritionists rarely discuss the nutritional quality of
a carrot and how it could be improved through farming practices. Farmers
are more concerned with yield and appearance while nutritionists typically
assume that all carrots are created equal.

201

At this critical point in human history it is essential that we gain a more holistic understanding of food. We need ways of thinking about food which not only encourage engagement between specialists but also allow more integrated systems-wide approaches to develop.

Food security is perhaps the most effective lens through which to see the complexity of food systems as an integrated whole. There are numerous definitions of food security but most would have a lot in common with that used by one of the world's largest food security organizations:

> The Community Food Security Coalition (CFSC) is a non-profit North American organization dedicated to building strong, sustainable, local and regional food systems that ensure access to affordable, nutritious, and culturally appropriate food for all people at all times. We seek to develop self-reliance among all communities in obtaining their food and to create a system of growing, manufacturing, processing, making available and selling food that is regionally-based and grounded in the principles of justice, democracy, and sustainability.[1]

Described this way, food security is a positive goal, in much the same way that financial security is. It can be approached incrementally — the numerous components of the food systems, and each of the many transformations that are made, can be evaluated to determine whether they increase or degrade food security. Alternatively, the entire food system can be evaluated holistically to identify key weaknesses or opportunities. Food security is a scalable concept, useful for a community or region, or at an individual family scale, or for the entire global population. It is also descriptive without being prescriptive, recognizing that there are many ways of achieving food security and the forms that it takes could vary radically for each person, community or region.

There are two general approaches within the broader food security movement, neither of which have adequately addressed the critical issues facing us. This is because both generally assume that the broader context of economic growth, cheap energy, resource abundance and environmental stability will continue. The first approach, and the most common, focuses on achieving an advanced degree of self-reliance. This approach, which is evident in the CFSC statement, is more likely to ensure the security of a community's food supplies in an economic collapse as well as during energy and resource shortages. The supply will be protected through greater reliance on local inputs, better relationships between producer and consumer, and the increased resilience of the local social and economic systems that results from having a local food system. However, the supply will likely falter in the event of extreme weather conditions in the region, sustained social disruption or war.

The second approach is to ensure a diversity of supply. This is often the goal of global organizations such as the FAO[2] which recognize the need to ensure "timely transfers of supplies to deficit areas" in order to respond to "harmful seasonal and inter-annual instability of food supplies" caused by climate fluctuations, drought, pests, diseases, war, as well as natural and man-made disasters. This approach is essential if regional disruptions in food security are to be mitigated but will be less useful during a global economic collapse and while energy supplies are contracting rapidly after the energy supply peaks. However, it is overly dependent on the global supply of energy-intensive inputs, stable economic and political systems, and complex financial relationships.

In view of the complexity of crises we face, we need both approaches — for now. In future, though, the global system that ensures the diversity of supply will be weakened by economic collapse and decreased fossil fuel availability and the self-reliance approach will inevitably turn out to be more effective at achieving and sustaining food security. Even so, we will need to increase the resilience of local production to make up for the fact that surpluses from other areas may not be available in times of crisis.

A resilient system is one that is able to withstand or recover quickly from difficult conditions. While several factors contribute to making food production more resilient, nutrient and water availability are by far the most important. Water is a renewable resource, at least on a global level, and in many places its availability can be managed through careful conservation and use. Water is also very visible; we can see it flow and it is relatively easy to determine when there is too little or too much.

This paper will not focus on water directly, despite its importance, but will instead concentrate on nutrients as these are essentially invisible and do not regularly fall from the sky. Although there are natural processes that renew nutrient levels, they tend to be slow, working on long timescales. We do not see nutrients flow through our systems, nor can we easily determine through casual observation which field or food is deficient in which nutrients, or where there is toxic excess. Yet without sustainable and balanced nutrient availability, a decline and eventual collapse of the food supply is inevitable. Moreover, it is far easier to develop resilient food systems if we start by establishing high and balanced fertility in the soil.

The global industrialized food production system is very poor at managing nutrients. It relies on energy-intensive processes to pull nitrogen from the air and to mine a few other nutrients, primarily phosphorus and potassium, from depleting geological reservoirs. These concentrated fertilizers are then dumped in excess on fields, causing ecological contamination, unbalanced growth and the depletion of other nutrients in the soil. Nutrient cycling, the process of returning nutrients to the land, is virtually impossible because of the great distances between the fields and consumer, and there is inevitable contamination of the waste streams as they pass through cities and communities.

Organic farming methods are much better at sourcing and managing nutrient resources but as most organic food is produced for distant markets, nutrient cycling is just as difficult. Local food systems are more capable of developing sustainable nutrient cycles, though very few of them have done so, especially in the developed world. Instead, the small scale of many of these systems permits a reliance on relatively abundant supplies of clean organic material, nutrient reserves in the soil or imported concentrated fertilizers. The supply of many of these resources will diminish as the number and scale of these systems increase to meet the challenges we face.

There are very few examples of holistic approaches to nutrient management that incorporate strategies for increasing and balancing nutrient levels as well as developing efficient nutrient cycling. Perhaps this is not surprising when dealing with something that is essentially invisible and which has no generally recognized name as a concept. I use the term nutritional resilience for an approach that extends from ecosystem resilience and productivity, to soil health, plant health and productivity, human health, resource management, community viability and systems resilience.

There are two strategies for developing nutritional resilience whether one is dealing with the global food system, a broader community, or a small garden plot. One is a transition strategy, the other a sustaining one. The transition strategy combines aspects of the globalized, industrial food systems with those of local, predominately organic food systems to build fertility where it is most useful. The sustaining strategy focuses on balancing and maintaining fertility through nutrient cycling and would develop as the transition was completed or after the decline or collapse of the global industrial system.

Nutrients

We rarely think of the origins of the components of the food we consume. The bulk of what we eat is energy in a variety of forms. It was created by plants using solar energy to extract carbon, oxygen and hydrogen atoms from carbon dioxide and water and then to recombine them into simple sugars. These simple sugars are then further combined into more complex carbohydrates (literally carbon and water) by plants, and the fungi, bacteria and animals that consume them, all of which contain C, H and O in a wide variety of structures. Fats, which are essentially another form of carbohydrate, contain C, H and O in different proportions and structures. So are alcohols. All of these forms of energy are relatively easy for an ecosystem to produce except where air, water or sunlight are lacking.

Proteins are created by combining amino acids, which are essentially nitrogen atoms mixed in with the carbohydrates, adding an N to the C, H and O mix. N is the most important nutrient that cannot be readily added to the mix that becomes our food. Despite its abundance in the atmosphere, it takes a significant amount of energy to "fix" it to oxygen or hydrogen atoms. This can be done by industrial processes using fossil fuels, by lightning or by special bacteria that are fed a lot of sugars by their host plants. Once fixed, nitrogen is a volatile, energetic and valuable nutrient that can easily become unfixed and escape back into the atmosphere. In many natural ecosystems, productivity is limited by the amount of available nitrogen.

All the other nutrients we need can be divided into two general groups — minerals and compounds. The minerals include calcium, iron, magnesium, phosphorus, potassium, sodium and sulfur as well as numerous trace minerals including boron, copper, iodine, manganese, nickel, silicon, tin, zinc and many more. These nutrients are needed by our bodies as basic elements, though we rarely eat them in their pure form. Over 30 different minerals or elements are needed in total[3] (and perhaps over 60[4]), some in significant quantities, some in a few parts per billion, but all of them essential for healthy life. The compounds include vitamins and other complex molecules produced by plants and animals which we need to eat in their organic compound form. These compounds contain C, H, O, N as well as the diversity of other elements.

The old saying "you are what you eat" reminds us that our bodies are composed of the reconstituted pieces of what we eat, and, more subtly, that the quality of what we eat will be reflected in our bodies. In his book *In Defense of Food*, Michael Pollan takes this concept one step further with the statement that "you are what what you eat eats, too,"[5] highlighting the fact that the quality of what an animal eats is reflected in the meat that we eat. The same can be said of plants. Although we generally don't think of plants eating in the same way, plants are made up of what they "extract" from the soil, water and air, and the quality of what they eat is reflected in the plant tissue that we consume directly or by eating the animals that eat the plants. We can trace this chain of consumption back to its origins and say that "we are what is in the soil or water that produced our food."

Nutritionists and many other people working in the fields of food and health are very aware of the complexity of carbohydrates, proteins, fats, minerals, vitamins and other organic compounds that we need to eat in order to stay healthy. All of the minerals needed by humans and other animals — either directly or in compound form — are also needed by plants to be healthy. Unfortunately, most farmers are unaware or unconcerned about most of the diversity of minerals that are needed, and are concerned only with supplying the major nutrients of nitrogen, phosphorus and potassium. Calcium and occasionally other minerals are added too but only when they show up as serious deficiencies. This is the most critical disconnect in our food systems. If these minerals are not in the soil or water, in a form that the plants can use, then they can't be in the plant and thus can't be in our food. Deficiencies progress up the food chain. In many ways deficiencies in our diet are more critical to our health than avoiding excess consumption of sugars, fats, etc. We are told to eat our vegetables to get essential nutrients and other compounds, but if the plant cannot extract the essential nutrients from the soil because they are not there, they cannot be in our food. A different way of thinking starts to form: "you are what you don't eat" or "you are what what you eat can't get."

Most farmers assume that, beyond the major fertilizers, everything that a plant needs they can get from the soil. To understand why this is rarely the case, we must understand how soils form and the processes of mineralisation. Soil is essentially ground-up rock, which is nothing more than solid aggregates of minerals. As the rock is broken down, most of the minerals remain as essentially inert chunks of smaller and smaller pieces of rock; from gravel, to sand, to silt and finally to the smallest particles of clay. Some of the minerals dissolve in water and wash away. A wide range of minerals stays in the soil either as inert elements, or chemically bound to other minerals, perhaps clinging to particles of clay; or they can be absorbed into the cycle of growth and decomposition involving microorganisms, fungi, plants and animals. This cycle of life brings additional elements, particularly carbon and nitrogen, out of the air and into the soil. The decomposition of the carbon-based life forms adds an additional component to the soil in the form of humus which plays a role similar to clay by holding onto loose minerals and compounds in the soil, as well as holding onto water.

While many microbes can extract the mineral nutrients that they need from the rock particles and complex compounds within the soil, the higher plants, the ones we eat, need a more refined diet. They generally absorb nutrients that are dissolved in water, loosely held in the soil by clay and humus, or which are fed directly by symbiotic microorganisms. This bio-availability is a critical aspect of the extent to which soil can support life.

It is important to understand that C, H, O, N and sulfur can all be found in gases in the atmosphere. This allows them to be transported easily to any ecosystem. All the other nutrients can only be transported in a solid or liquid form,[6] making them more difficult for an ecosystem to obtain.

Of course, the Earth is a very dynamic place, and the extent of soil building and mineralization is not limited to what can be extracted from the bedrock in a particular place. There are many processes that move minerals and soil particles from one place to another. The most dramatic — and the slowest — process is the advance and retreat of glaciers which grind up rock from one place and transport it long distances to where it is washed away by the melt water to form alluvial plains. Another process is the wind blowing smaller particles across continents. This has created huge deep drifts of loess soil in places such as the fertile farmlands of China and the midwestern United States.

As water falls on land as rain and flows toward the sea, it washes away dissolved minerals and silt and deposits them on floodplains as both soil and fertility. Ancient Egypt was sustained for thousands of years by the annual transportation of soil from the uplands of Ethiopia to the lower floodplains of the Nile valley. Volcanic activity brings fresh nutrient supplies from the molten core of the Earth to be deposited in the form of ash on the surrounding land, sustaining fertile ecosystems and productive farming such as those that developed in Java and Bali. Most of the early large human settlements developed in areas with significant deposits of soil and minerals.

Animals are responsible for significant movements of nutrients from one place to another. Some species of salmon make a remarkable journey from the sea to spawn and then die in the smallest tributaries inland. Their journey transports the valuable nutrients that make up their bodies from the fertile sea to points high up in the mountain. This is a substantial annual flow of nutrients on which the entire ecosystem depends. Similarly, seabirds have created huge reservoirs of fertility under their nesting grounds, bats leave huge piles of guano in caves, and numerous other animals have deposited nutrients over wide areas along their migration routes. Humans have participated in this process throughout the ages, often for their own benefit through farming and, more recently, on a much more advanced, pervasive and damaging scale.

This movement of nutrients and soil leads to concentrations in some places and deficiencies in others. However, the basic reason for most mineral deficiencies is that not all bedrock contains the full spectrum of minerals in the proportions needed by plants and animals. In addition, when rain falls on the land, many of the minerals that are there dissolve in the water and either filter deep down into the soil, beyond the reach of plant roots, or flow downstream. Floodplains and other landforms do trap and hold some of the nutrients and silt but this is only a temporary pause on the inevitable path to the sea. Unfortunately, the water cycles that evaporate from the sea and deposit rain far inland do not bring back any of the nutrients. The increasing amount of nutrients dissolved in the sea and settled on the sea floor only gets back inland through the relatively small-scale actions of animals, the rising of the sea bed and the movement of tectonic plates to create mountains of new rock to be eroded into life.

Human activities over thousands of years have accelerated the natural nutrient loss through inappropriate land-management practices such as burning vegetation cover and plowing the soil, both of which increase erosion. Humans have also removed large quantities of organic material to use as food, fodder, fuel, wood and other materials. All this organic material contained valuable nutrients that the ecosystem had worked hard to obtain, which were then concentrated in other areas or lost to the sea. Since the development of larger communities and broad-scale agriculture, this removal process has accelerated. Now, rather than removing a small portion of material from an ecosystem, agricultural processes generally remove much of the organic matter from the land, or at least the nutrient-dense fruit, vegetables, oils, protein and seeds. Even if the soil was very deep and fertile initially, nutrients are removed with every harvest, generally much faster than they are naturally replaced. It does not take long for deficiencies to develop and the only way to stop this depletion is to add nutrients to the soil either by recycling those that were extracted or importing new ones from elsewhere.

> Agronomists are confident about which minerals are required, and in what proportions. As an example, most plants use a lot of calcium, but for every six to eight measures of calcium, they'll also need one measure of magnesium, maybe a sixteenth measure of sulfur, and one ten-thousandth measure of boron. If they have heaps of calcium but are short of magnesium, then they won't grow any more than the amount allowed by the quantity of magnesium they've got. If they have adequate calcium, magnesium, and sulfur, all in the right proportions for ideal growth, but are desperately short of boron, then they will grow as poorly as though they were short of calcium and magnesium and sulfur.[7]

This passage from Steve Solomon's book *Gardening When it Counts* describes why mineral balance is critically important in soils. Plants will take up unbalanced proportions of minerals, if that is what they find in the soils, but their health and productivity suffer. Plants, like humans, will struggle on in less than optimal conditions.

A natural woodland, bush or grassland ecosystem, on reasonably good soils, will generally develop a balanced but low mineral fertility level in the soil. Minerals that are in excess won't be absorbed by the plants and as a result are more likely to wash away or otherwise become unavailable. Minerals in short supply will be sought out. Once a reasonable balance is achieved, an increase in balanced fertility develops very slowly as more of the limiting nutrients are found. David Holmgren, in his book *Permaculture: Principles and Pathways Beyond Sustainability*, describes what happens when humans move into this landscape, disrupt the ecological processes and transform the land for agriculture. In the first stage they degrade the soil and create imbalances, producing low and imbalanced soil fertility. The second stage sees the introduction of imported fertilizers. "However, imbalances typically remain or new imbalances have been created that are reflected in the poor quality of food and the increased rates of fertility loss,"[8] he writes. Most farmland and gardens remain stuck at this stage, requiring considerable effort and resource-input to maintain a high level of fertility, but persistent and serious imbalances remain. Very few farmers attain the "Holy Grail" of balanced but high fertility.

In view of this, perhaps we should assume that all soils throughout the world are deficient, that all food produced on that land is therefore deficient in minerals and has minimal nutritional value, and that it is consequently very difficult for people to have a nutritionally complete diet, even if they eat all their vegetables.

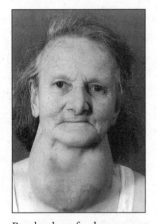

People whose food was grown mainly on the limestone soils of Derbyshire in England suffered so frequently from goitre, which is caused by an iodine deficiency, that the complaint became known as Derbyshire Neck. Since the 1930s, a diet grown over a wider area has led to its disappearance but it could return if most food had to be grown locally again before the mineral balance of the Derbyshire soils had been improved.

Fairly similar fertility-management practices using concentrated soluble fertilizers have been used on much of the world's farmland over the past half-century. This will have produced common mineral imbalances — excess amounts of nitrogen, phosphorus and potassium, but general deficiencies in minerals such as magnesium and calcium. But the bedrock and mineral reserves in the soils vary widely. As most of the food grown on these soils is distributed through the globalized system, on any given day we could be eating food that had its origins on dozens of different fields spread all over the world. While general mineral imbalances may persist, and the overall nutritional quality may be low within this system, it is unlikely that specific trace minerals will be deficient in all the food we eat. If we had an industrialized farming system without the global distribution system, then local deficiencies would become much more apparent when clusters of illness and disease developed. Soil mineral deficiencies and the effects that they have on health are currently hidden by the global trade and distribution system.

As many families and communities begin the process of developing localized food systems, and get much more of their food from a single allotment plot, a few neighboring fields, or a broader region with similar bedrock and soil conditions, deficiencies could begin to damage the people's health. This is a fundamental flaw in local food initiatives and the grow-it-yourself movement. Growing your own food is a great idea, and is perceived as an easy thing to do, but most people growing food do not know how to produce healthy plants, or even what a really healthy plant looks like. While the freshness and the unforced quality of the produce will convince people that they are eating truly healthy food, especially when compared to what they buy in the supermarket, in many cases they won't be. Unless there is a fortunate choice of growing sites and fertility management, people growing their own food or producing for a local community will need to focus on the nutritional balance and fertility level of the soils if the short-term benefits of local food systems are not to create long-term difficulties.

Health of Plants, People and Communities

What happens when a soil has achieved the Holy Grail of soil fertility—high, balanced levels of minerals? David Holmgren describes how, in following the work of William Albrecht and others in creating an ideal balanced soil, all crops grown on this soil will produce high yields of good-quality food, and that the structure and water-holding capacity of the soil will improve, as will the processes of decomposition and nutrient cycling within the soil. Holmgren suggests that:

> ...this represents the biological optimum soil in which all plants will thrive. Within the constraints of climate, this balanced soil will support the most productive biological systems in terms of total energy capture and storage. Thus balanced and fertile soil is nature's integrated and self-reinforcing design solution for maximizing power of terrestrial life.[8]

In this way, balanced fertility in the soil is the key to a productive garden, farm or natural ecosystem, allowing all of the ecological processes to work effectively in producing a greater yield of better food or material. This is the primary objective in developing nutritional resilience.

Many organic gardeners and farmers believe that the best way to minimise damage by pests and disease is to provide the conditions in order for the plant to be as healthy as possible, with the purpose of strengthening the plant's immune system and defenses. Elliot Coleman approaches the issue of pests in a more direct way:

> There is a direct relationship between the growing conditions of plants and the susceptibility of those plants to pests. Problems in the garden are our fault through unsuccessful gardening practices rather than Nature's fault through malicious intent. The way we approach pest problems in the garden is to correct the cause, not treat the symptoms. The cause of pest problems is inadequate growing conditions.[9]

Taking this idea further, Francis Chaboussou, author of *Healthy Crops: A New Agricultural Revolution*, believes that "the relations between plant and parasite are above all nutritional in nature" and that "plants are made immune to the extent that they lack the nutritional factors that parasites require for their development. In short, what is involved is a deterrent effect not a toxic action."[10] A pest will essentially starve on a truly healthy plant, or at least will not be able to obtain the energy needed to reproduce or develop. The basis of this theory is that most pests and parasites depend on an abundant supply of amino acids — they are reliant on an easy source of nitrogen — but in a healthy plant amino acids are quickly used to synthesize proteins, and are therefore unavailable to the pests. A fertile, balanced soil is one of the key elements to plant health (together with adequate water availability, appropriate weather, etc.) and this leads to the possible elimination of the need for pest and disease control, both chemical and organic. Reducing the risk of disease and pests also significantly increases food security.

Food from plants grown on soil with balanced minerals should therefore be nutritionally complete, in that there will be no deficiencies, and yields should be greater as less is lost to pests and disease. But there is more to the story. The overall nutritional value of the food can also be substantially increased, so that it gives higher quantities of sugars, minerals, proteins, etc. per kilogram. Wine producers have known this intuitively for centuries, and more recently have used simple optical refractors to measure the amount of sugars dissolved in the juice, picking or purchasing grapes only when they have a certain concentration. This concentration of sugars, vitamins, minerals, amino acids, proteins, hormones, and other solids dissolved within the juice is measured in BRIX (ratio of the mass of dissolved solids to water) and the same method can be used to determine the nutritional density of most foods, and the sap of plants. When plants are grown in soil with balanced and high fertility, the BRIX reading of the plant sap and juice of the produce is significantly higher than the same plant grown in less than ideal conditions.[11] The BRIX reading of one carrot can be more than twice as high as that of another carrot grown in poor-quality soil, and therefore it will contain at least twice the amount of sugars, vitamins, minerals etc. Given that this is what we eat a carrot for, we can eat less than half a carrot to get the same nutrition as we can get from a whole poor-quality carrot of the same weight.

This higher nutritional value can drastically increase the real yield achieved by growing on high-quality soils. Not only is it possible to achieve a higher total yield in weight, but each kilogram can provide more nutrition. The overall nutritional yield can easily be several times higher within a given area, providing good nutrition to more people from the same piece of land. There are other advantages to high nutritional density in plants and food. The additional solids in the plant sap act as a form of antifreeze, allowing plants to better withstand frosts and deeper cold spells. This extends the growing season in many regions, and helps the crop withstand abnormal and extreme weather conditions. While low-quality food tends to begin to decompose fairly quickly, requiring refrigeration, quick delivery, and processing, food with high nutritional density tends to last much longer and is more likely to dehydrate rather than rot. This allows a significant reduction in the amount of wasted food as well as the amount of resources, energy and infrastructure needed to store and preserve food that is produced locally. But, perhaps the greatest benefit is that nutritionally dense food tastes better — you can literally taste the greater density of sugars and minerals.

If we can produce nutrient-dense food, which people (especially children) will be more likely to want to eat because of the great taste, what does this mean for their health? Many diseases and health problems are caused or exacerbated by malnutrition, and the increasing prevalence of poor health over the past few decades seems to parallel the decline in mineral content in food over the same time period.[12] How can people be healthy if their food is nutritionally deficient? Or, a more important question is: what will happen to peoples' health if they consume food with high nutritional density and no mineral deficiencies? If poor-quality food decreases the health of the population, and food of moderate nutritional quality can sustain health, will the consumption of high-quality food make a person healthier and more resilient? Can it help heal a sick person? Beyond the personal and social benefits that come with good health, a community cannot be resilient without a population that is healthy and physically capable, or if a substantial portion of its resources is spent on health care.

Progress Toward Nutritional Resilience

Nutritional resilience starts with mineral qualities of the soil and extends to plant health and productivity, nutritional density of food, human health and community viability, as well as incorporating sustainable resource management and the resilience of the entire food system. Nutritional resilience also extends to natural landscapes, through which we can assist ecosystems to become more resilient and productive with the benefits of greater biodiversity, ecosystem services, and carbon sequestration. Nutritional resilience is the foundation upon which broader resilience can be more easily built, and without it, the journey will be slower and much more difficult. Given the current economic context, the climate crisis, and the possibility of a systemic collapse in the near future, it is essential to prioritize anything that increases the speed and ease of transformations.

As I said earlier, there are two different strategies or processes for developing nutritional resilience. The transition strategy focuses on building and balancing fertility in key areas. The sustaining strategy focuses on developing effective nutrient cycles, fine-tuning mineral balance and expanding the areas of resilience. While these two strategies can in many ways progress simultaneously, it is important that sufficient attention is given to the first, as it is this aspect that will require most energy, resources and inputs, all of which may be of limited availability in the near future. Many local food initiatives and alternative farming projects currently fail to give the transition strategy enough priority.

The primary objectives of the transition strategy are to capture the existing material flow, to facilitate effective decomposition, to enable nutrient storage and to correct excessive mineral imbalances. The specific methods used will vary widely with each location, depending on the nature of the existing soils, as well as on existing infrastructure and cultural bias, but there are common approaches. There is a massive amount of organic material and fiber flowing through most settlements and capturing and using the nutrients available in this flow should be a key concern everywhere. All food and green "wastes" are very valuable sources of nutrients and many trace minerals. Although the use of human "wastes" are also important, it could be more appropriate to deal with the complexities of transforming the sewage system later in the process.

Paper, cardboard, a fair amount of other packaging and most waste wood are all valuable sources of carbon and some minerals and they should be processed and used locally. These materials are much more valuable as part of biological nutrient-management processes than they are as recycled fiber if the aim is to build local resilience. Much of this material combines well with the other, more nutrient-dense organic matter for composting, or can be used directly as mulch to facilitate the conversion and maintenance of lands, or as a substrate for beneficial fungi, or it can be converted to biochar. Through these processes, a lot of the original carbon is converted to humus, or to charcoal, which serves many of the same valuable functions as humus, but can last much longer. The processing and decomposition of this material should be done carefully to prevent the loss of minerals and carbon through leaching or off-gassing, as often happens at large municipal composting plants which treat the material as waste for disposal rather than as a resource to be valued.

This captured supply of nutrients and carbon should ideally be added to the local farmlands, fields and gardens that will be used for local food production. If the land is not available yet, then the processed material should be stored for later use in such a way that its quality can be maintained or improved over time. The lack of growing space and capacity should not prevent conversion of the easiest parts of the material flow and the building up of a store of fertility and humus. This buildup of raw material for future productivity is similar to the gradual collection of materials before you start to build a house.

The existing soil should be tested for major and trace mineral levels as well as for toxicity. Significant mineral imbalances should be corrected by importing organic or synthetic concentrated supplies. Many organic and natural farming methods emphasize more gradual processes for building fertility, primarily through composting local biomass, and tend to avoid importing concentrates as well as restricting anything synthetic. This may be the movement's Achilles heel. Although concentrated nutrients can cause problems through inappropriate application, their continued deficiency in the soil is more detrimental in the long run. Trace mineral levels should be generally improved by incorporating rock dust, seaweed meal or sea solids, or through the use of concentrates to correct specific deficiencies (such as using borax to boost levels of boron). Nutrient accumulator plants can also be used to mine supplies of both trace and major minerals from the broader landscape and concentrate them in key areas, but this process would tend to exacerbate deficiencies and undermine the health and productivity of the surrounding ecosystem.

Excessive concentrations of some minerals can cause a detrimental imbalance in the soil and care must be taken to ensure that imported supplies do not contain significant amounts of these minerals, or the imbalances will continue or worsen. Some excessive concentrations can be reduced through the use of accumulator plants or dispersion of soils over a wider area. Toxic levels of nutrients, especially of lead and other metals, and contamination by industrial and chemical compounds, should be mitigated either through careful bioremediation or avoidance. The same testing should be done with the flow of decomposed organic matter so that it does not further disrupt the balance of nutrients or introduce contamination. Within this process, it is important to focus on key areas of productivity rather than on having a diluted impact on broader areas. It is also important to see the transition stage as a temporary process. There is little sense in developing substantial facilities to handle material flow which will not be available once this phase reaches its natural end, or is abruptly halted by collapsing economies.

The sustaining strategy can start fairly early, running in parallel to the transition phase, and would take over entirely when nutrient levels have reached a high and generally balanced level, or when economic conditions interrupt the easy flow of material or cheap energy is not available to process and transport nutrients from outside. The key focus of this strategy is to prevent the loss of nutrients through leaching, erosion, exporting products, and through sewage and waste water. Nutrient cycling systems need to be developed, including composting toilets and urine separation, as well as graywater management systems to minimize loss of fertility and minerals. Trade restrictions may need to be put in place so that excessive amounts of minerals, especially those that are not in abundance in the local soil, do not leave the area in the form of food and material.

Land-management practices need to be developed to reduce the amount of nutrients and soil that washes away or leaches underground. Deep-rooting trees and plants should be used to pull leached nutrients and a fresh supply of trace elements from deep in the soil, and catchment basins should be established to intercept the nutrients that flow away during extreme weather events. As the overall ecosystem develops it will be important to continue to monitor and correct the mineral balance where possible, and to develop ways to increase the overall fertility levels gradually.

Once the key production sites have been adequately developed, it may be possible to gradually expand the land under management, either the adjacent fields, or the broader landscape. Focusing first on the key areas and then using these as a base for improving other areas, or for helping neighboring communities, is a useful strategy for developing broader nutritional resilience in the uncertain future that we face.

> In the future (perhaps within a hundred years), after the fossil fuel energy subsidy to agriculture has declined, the mineral fertility and balance of our farmlands and entire catchment landscapes will become one of the most important issues in resource management and economics, and yet the powerful means that are currently available to achieve this on a large scale will be very costly or simply unavailable. In this situation we will once again be dependent on the slower, low-energy processes of building and balancing fertility.[8]

I fear that, when writing the above passage, David Holmgren may have significantly overestimated the amount of time that we have.

Endnotes

1. foodsecurity.org.
2. FAO, Rome Declaration on World Food Security, fao.org/docrep/003/w3613e /w3613e00.htm.
3. "The Role of Elements in Life Processes," Mineral Information Institute, mii.org /periodic/LifeElement.html.
4. Folke Gunther, holon.se/folke/kurs/Distans/Ekofys/Recirk/Eng/phosphorus.shtml.
5. Michael Pollan, *In Defense of Food: An Eater's Manifesto* (Penguin Press, 2008).
6. As [4].
7. Steve Solomon, *Gardening When It Counts* (New Society Publishers, 2005), 17–18,.
8. David Holmgren, *Permaculture; Principles and Pathways Beyond Sustainability* (Holmgren Design Services, 2002), 40.
9. Eliot Coleman, *Four-Season Harvest* (Chelsea Green Publishing Company, 1999), 147.
10. Francis Chaboussou, *Healthy Crops; A New Agricultural Revolution* (Jon Carpenter Publishing 2004), 7.
11. crossroads.ws/brixbook/BBook.htm.
12. Anne-Marie Mayer, "Historical Changes in the Mineral Content of Fruits and Vegetables," *British Food Journal* 99 (1997).

Turning the Land from an Emissions Source to a Carbon Sink

CORINNA BYRNE

Farming and other land-based activities could do a lot to mitigate global warming. Ireland needs new policies to get its land to absorb CO_2 rather than release it. The large amounts of carbon locked up in the country's peatlands must be safeguarded and damaged bogs restored so that they can sequester carbon again. In addition, the use of biochar could reduce methane and nitrous oxide emissions and build up the fertility and carbon content of the soil.

Climate change is the most pressing problem of our time and one to which we all contribute in varying degrees. Those working on or closely with the land can do a lot to improve the situation. At present, their activities, especially in agriculture, contribute significantly to global warming by adding not just CO_2 but also methane and nitrous oxide to the atmosphere. However, if policies were adopted which refocused the purpose of the land and the right methods were used to manage the different greenhouse gases (GHG), agriculture could be transformed from being a source of emissions to a sink.

In order to explore what these policies and methods might be, Feasta set up the Carbon Cycles and Sinks Network (CCSN) in late 2008 with funding from the Irish Department of the Environment, Heritage and Local Government, which wanted advice on policies it could adopt to reduce GHG emissions from land-based sources in Ireland. The Network enables people with specialist knowledge of these emissions and ways of reducing them to help identify and develop the policies put forward.

Irish land-based emissions are the largest in the EU in relation to its other emissions so it is in Ireland's interest to take a lead in developing EU policy in this area. Accordingly, the CCSN has not restricted itself to developing national-level policies but is also advancing approaches that Ireland could promote at EU and possibly at UN level. We have concentrated on what can be done to reduce emissions from the most important land activities: deforestation, the management of agricultural soils and the raising of livestock.

We consider that Irish climate policy should be developed on the basis that temperatures must be prevented from rising by more than 2°C and even that figure is probably too high. The Intergovernmental Panel on Climate Change (IPCC) 4th Assessment report says that achieving the 2°C target means stabilizing GHG concentrations at about 445 to 490 ppm carbon dioxide-equivalent (CO_2-eq). This corresponds to about 350 to 400 ppm of CO_2 alone. Ireland should therefore press its EU partners to negotiate for a concentration target of 350 parts per million of CO_2 by volume or less. Four eminent climate experts — Nicholas Stern, James Hansen, John Schellnhuber and Rajendra Pachauri — have all indicated that a target of 350 ppm or less is required. The 350 level was passed in 1987 and, at present, the atmospheric concentration is around 390 and is rising by about 2 ppm a year. Returning to it means that all current emissions must stop and, at the very least, all the CO_2 released since 1987 that remains in the air must be recovered.

At present, only land plants can be considered to be natural atmospheric carbon extractors as current scientific evidence indicates that the fertilization of the ocean will not significantly increase carbon transfer into the deep ocean and thus lower atmospheric CO_2.[1] In view of this, CCSN concentrates on land-based carbon sequestration and aims to develop policies that should lead to the land taking up and holding more carbon.

Reducing and Sequestering Carbon Dioxide Emissions

Terrestrial ecosystems store about 600 billion tonnes of carbon in living organisms and decaying material and 1,500 billion tonnes in soil organic matter. The total, 2,100 billion tonnes, is almost three times the 750 billion tonnes currently in the atmosphere. Consequently, if fossil and land-based carbon emissions stopped today, reducing the atmospheric concentration of CO_2 from 390 to 350 ppm would involve increasing the amount in plants and soils by 77 billion tonnes or about 3%.

Of course, fossil- and land-based carbon emissions cannot be stopped immediately. Fossil-fuel combustion will release about 29 billion tonnes of CO_2 this year. If that release rate was phased out over 40 years on a straight-line basis, a total of 580 billion tonnes would be released before emissions stopped. Deforestation is releasing perhaps 7 billion tonnes a year. If it proves possible to stop that in ten years, it will add 35 billion tonnes to the atmosphere by the time it ceases. So, if other GHG emissions are ignored, 615 billion tonnes of CO_2 will be added to the atmosphere by 2050. This converts to 166 billion tonnes of carbon. Adding that to the excess carbon already in the air means that the amount of carbon held by plants and soils needs to increase by over 11%.

Each year's flow of carbon into and out of the terrestrial stock is huge, as Figure 1 below shows. It would only be necessary to reduce the outflow and/or increase the inflow by a small amount each year to achieve the 11% increase in the terrestrial carbon stock over, say, the next 50 years.

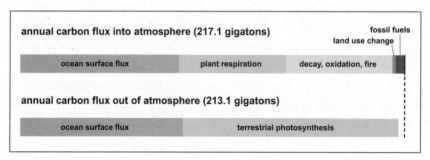

FIGURE 1. Annual carbon fluxes into and out of the atmosphere

Increasing above-ground biomass (AGB) by planting could do much more than take carbon out of the air. It could, for example, provide all the energy currently provided by fossil sources by 2035. It could also sequester 13 billion tonnes of atmospheric carbon a year, well above the 1 billion tonnes required to ensure that the 350 target is not exceeded by the end of the century.[2] It would also provide food. In addition, there is a strong possibility that the transpiration from the new growth would increase cloud cover and thus have a cooling effect. On the other hand, it would change much of the Earth's surface but in a more benign way than a runaway warming.

Several policy conclusions inevitably follow from the adoption of the 350-or-less target. The discussion focuses on those directly concerning land-based emissions.

The Carbon Maintenance Fee

Rewards should be offered for holding and sequestering carbon and penalties imposed for carbon releases. All countries, not just developing ones, should be paid an annual carbon maintenance fee for maintaining each tonne of carbon in their soils and biomass as well as a higher, once-off reward for every tonne by which the stock is increased between one assessment and the next. It will not be possible for the average reward to be as large as the price being charged for the right to release a tonne of CO_2 when fossil fuel is burned. This is because a large part of the revenue collected by governments or an international agency when emissions rights are sold will have to be recycled under an arrangement such as Cap and Share so that the poorest people in the world are not priced out of the market for energy as its price rises due to the artificial scarcity caused by a rapidly tightening cap. Governments that allowed their terrestrial carbon stock to decline should be required to pay a price based on the price of a fossil carbon emissions permit but with an allowance for the inevitable imperfections in the accuracy of the data in comparison for that from fossil-fuel use.

The carbon maintenance fee (CMF) would be paid in recognition of the fact that countries with forest or peat bog could potentially use that land in more immediately lucrative ways and that they therefore need to be rewarded for passing up those opportunities and retaining it as a carbon store. There are practical reasons for introducing a CMF too. For example, no government is going to like paying the charges involved if its terrestrial carbon stock is reduced. However, if the international agency levying the carbon-loss charge was also paying the government a carbon-maintenance fee, the deduction would be automatic.

Rewarding countries that increased their terrestrial carbon would put a very high value on maintaining forests. The Stern Review gives a figure of up to 1,000 tonnes of CO_2 being held in a hectare of standing trees. At $25 per tonne of CO_2—a figure which is likely to be far below the price that users are likely to pay for the right to burn fossil fuel—the penalty for clearing the trees would be $25,000 less the value of the harvested wood. Stern gives a figure of up to $1,035 per hectare for the income from the sale of the wood and says that the cleared land, if it were to be used for high-value crops such as soya or palm oil, would be worth $1,000 per hectare. If his figures are correct, the penalty the state suffers for allowing the land to be cleared would be ten times the amount the landowner would get from going ahead with the clearance. This should be enough to make the payment effective, particularly as tropical forest can be expected to take in carbon each year.

A 2009 report[3] on the results of monitoring around 70,000 trees in ten African countries for 40 years shows that for at least the last few decades, each hectare of intact African forest has trapped 2.2 tonnes of CO_2 per year. If the reward for each tonne of CO_2 sequestered by this natural sink was €25, ($32) the government responsible for the forest could expect to be paid about $70 a year per hectare in addition to the carbon maintenance fee. When the researchers combined their African data with earlier figures from South American and Asian forests they calculated that tropical forests remove about 4.8 billion tonnes of CO_2 from the atmosphere every year, about 18% of the annual amount added by burning fossil fuels. African forests alone account for 1.2 billion tonnes. That could give the countries that have them an annual income of perhaps $38 billion plus a carbon maintenance fee. As sub-Saharan export earnings in 2007 were $268 billion if South Africa is excluded, that is a significant sum. The forestry chapter in the IPCC's Fourth Assessment report quotes an estimate that at around the $25 figure (it actually uses $27.2 per tonne) "deforestation could potentially be virtually eliminated."

As for the CMF itself, if it were paid on all the 2,400 billion tonnes of carbon in the Earth's biomass and soil, the rate per tonne would be very low. Suppose just ten US cents per tonne of carbon was paid, which works out at 37 cents per tonne of CO_2. This would mean the annual payment for keeping the carbon in the 1,000 tonnes of CO_2 per hectare of forest mentioned by Stern would be $370 per year. The total transfer of resources involved (it would be a mistake to think of the payment as being a cost) would be $240 billion. This compares with the 2009 GWP of $70,000 billion. In other words, the transfer would involve about 0.3% of the world's incomes, which would seem to be an affordable sum.

Other ways of rewarding countries for forestry planting under offset arrangements should be ended. Offsets enable fossil-fuel users whose emissions are controlled by a cap to exceed their emissions limit by reducing emissions in a country outside the cap. As a result, offsets do not reduce emissions. Because a reduction in one place justifies extra emissions somewhere else, the best they can do is to stabilize them. But, according to FERN, the Forests and the European Union Resource Network, even this best-case scenario appears to be rare as it is not possible to verify whether any claimed reduction would otherwise have occurred. By allowing the release of extra emissions without the certainty of equivalent extra reductions elsewhere, any trading scheme involving carbon offsets may increase rather than reduce GHG emissions. On top of this, many of these projects also affect the rights of some of the world's poorest communities, resulting in increased hardship and suffering.[4]

In any case, because of the massive effort required of the land-use sector if it is to become a net sink and absorb the excess CO_2 in the air, it's unlikely to have the additional capacity to absorb the fossil-fuel CO_2 emitted under offset arrangements as well. Moreover, if, as suggested above, a global emissions cap was put in place, offsetting would be unnecessary since, if a country or a company wished to emit more than it had been allowed, it would simply buy the permits to do so from a country or company with a surplus.

EU policy maintains that tropical deforestation should be reduced by at least 50% by 2020 compared to current levels, and the global forest cover loss should be halted by 2030 at the latest. Ireland should press for each of these targets to be brought forward by five years. The EU has failed to challenge the REDD approach of paying countries for the emissions they avoid by clearing forest at a slower rate than in the past. It wants to fund REDD by using voluntary contributions from rich-country governments to cover "readiness work and capacity building," with the bulk of the remainder coming from offsetting via the sale on developed-country carbon markets of carbon credits covering the avoided emissions.

However, the EU is worried that these sales could undermine the carbon markets by overloading them with credits to such an extent that the carbon price falls and no longer acts as an incentive to developed countries to curtail their emissions. As a result, it has suggested a separate market for REDD credits. It's not clear how this would work but the idea of keeping the two markets apart as a temporary measure until a global cap is in place is in essence a good one as it would prevent the land being used to offset current fossil emissions rather than having the task of removing the excess of CO_2 already in the air.

The EU is also concerned about the possibility that carbon credits will be issued because trees are not being cut down at the previous rate in one part of a country while forests are being cleared faster in another. It therefore wants a whole-country approach to be adopted to prevent this "leakage," something that might only be possible if remote-sensing measurements are used. Ireland should urge its EU partners to reject offsetting via REDD altogether or to tighten the limits on how much can be done with a view to phasing it out completely by 2020. Funding for whole-country REDD schemes should be come from the proceeds of auctioning EU emissions trading system permits (EUAs) after 2012 until a global system can be put in place.

Using Remote Sensing for Carbon-Emissions Reporting

Because adequate whole-country measurement methods were not available when the Kyoto Protocol mechanisms were devised, the rich, high-emissions countries which signed up to it — collectively known as the Annex 1 countries because that is where their names are listed — had no option but to take an activities-based approach to measuring, reporting and accounting for their Land Use, Land-Use Change and Forestry (LULUCF) emissions. Because this approach looks solely at the emissions that result from an activity such as planting or clearing trees and assumes that everything else is unchanged, it has allowed a lot of gradual changes to be ignored. Consequently, now that remote sensing techniques are being developed to enable all the emissions and emissions absorption from a country's entire land area to be estimated with reasonable accuracy, Ireland should move toward land-based LULUCF measuring and reporting using remote sensing techniques. It may be possible for the country to achieve Tier 3, the most accurate and detailed level of emissions reporting, on this basis.

The two main types of remote sensing, Synthetic Aperture Radar (SAR) and LIDAR, can be used together and in conjunction with optical and infra-red images. SAR has been used to map ABG since the 1960s. Microwave pulses are sent out and the amount of that energy reflected back to the sensor is recorded. As it uses radar, it can operate day or night through haze, smoke and clouds. The microwaves penetrate forest canopies and the amount of backscattered energy can reveal a lot about the trees' leaves, branches and stems. Rather than microwaves, LIDAR sends out pulses of light from a laser. This means that it cannot penetrate cloud. However, it has an advantage in that it can measure the three-dimensional vertical structure of vegetation in great detail. It has revolutionized the way vegetation is measured from satellites, but for forestry operations, aircraft-borne sensors are used. A 2009 assessment[5] of remote sensing techniques by a team from Woods Hole concluded

> Satellite data enable reliable mapping of carbon stocks over large areas… This situation will improve further as new satellite missions come online in the next few years, several of which are designed specifically with the intent of improving estimates of the standing stock of carbon in biomass, and changes in those stocks through time. The UNFCCC process would benefit from refinement and application of these approaches and from improved data in developing policies designed to reduce emissions from deforestation and forest degradation.

With remote sensing, a country could report and account comprehensively for everything that affects the types of land that, like pastureland, forests and bogs, can be either a sink or a source depending on management methods and the climate itself. This is particularly important because rising temperatures and altered rainfall patterns will play a large part in determining whether land releases carbon or takes it in.

At present, under the Kyoto Protocol's Article 3.4, Ireland can choose to operate on Tier 2 and account for carbon gains and losses from forest management, cropland management and the management of pasture land. So far, Ireland has not accounted for these carbon gains and losses, mainly for lack of data, and operates on Tier 1, which uses default figures rather than country-specific ones to estimate emissions. To use Tier 2, for example, cropland and grazing land management require data going back to 1990. However, this data requirement would disappear if a switch was made to remote sensing as it would no longer be necessary to establish a trend line and estimate changes in the trend. All that would be necessary would be to use an aircraft to carry out a baseline LIDAR survey that was calibrated by on-ground sampling. The sampling would measure AGB, below-ground biomass and soil carbon. Leaf litter and deadwood could also be included if desired. The aerial survey would then be repeated regularly at the same time each year and a calculation carried out to establish the carbon gained or lost.

If the EU adopted remote sensing for its emissions returns it could pilot its use by the rest of the world at a later date. The adoption is likely to save money. Not only is it cheaper to gather the required information by remote techniques but New Zealand has also found that it can recover the cost about 22 times because it ensures that country's eligibility to offset GHG emissions above the 1990 level of emissions and to participate in international carbon trading.

At least some of the revenue each member state received for holding and, in some cases, increasing the biomass and soil carbon stock should be used by the state to encourage further increases in the carbon held. A system of rewards to individual landowners would be impractical because of the difficulty of measuring soil carbon with sufficient accuracy, especially as the remote-sensing results are optimized to show changes from year to year rather than exactly what was on the ground when the over-flight took place. As a result, Teagasc, the Irish Agriculture and Food Development Authority, suggests that a new definition of best farming practice be devised and that the adoption of this be incentivized by the program that is being developed to replace the Rural Environment Protection Scheme (REPS). This could include activities that lead to lower agricultural emissions and the increase in carbon in biomass and the soil. CCSN has been asked to help devise this "Carbon REPS."

Irish Land-Based Emissions: A Three-Gas Problem

In global warming terms, carbon dioxide is not the most important GHG produced by activities on Irish land (see Figure 2 below). Methane produced by the national livestock herd is more serious, accounting for 45% of the land-based warming effect. CO_2 makes up 32% and nitrous oxide 23%. Moreover, the CO_2 figure is only as high as 32% because the emissions from peat burning have been included, although, internationally, they would not be included in emissions in the LULUCF category.

Nationally and internationally, all three gases need reduction programmes and targets of their own and methane and nitrous oxide should not be bundled with CO_2 as "carbon dioxide equivalents" with exchange rates set at their Global Warming Potential (GWP) in relation to CO_2. The bundling approach tends to limit the priority given to reducing the emissions of each gas to the latest estimate of their GWPs whereas a more holistic view of a gas's total climate and environmental impact is desirable, something that can only come from a gas-by-gas approach.

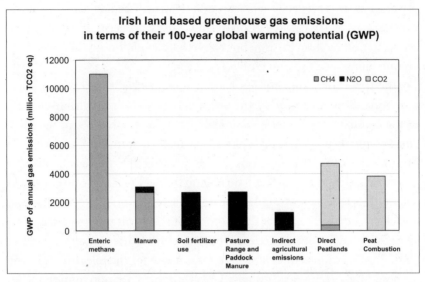

FIGURE 2. Compares the ways the emissions of the three greenhouse gases are produced by the way the land is used. Indirect nitrous oxide emissions are those produced when ammonia has escaped into the air or nitrates have been washed into rivers get broken down. Direct peat land emissions are the methane released by intact bogs and the CO_2 released by bogs that have been disturbed. (Compiled by CCSN.)

Reducing Carbon Dioxide Emissions from Peatland

Peatlands are Ireland's largest stock of terrestrial carbon, storing an estimated 1.2 billion tonnes.[6] This equates to 4.4 billion tonnes of CO_2 so, as total Irish GHG emissions were 67.44 million tonnes CO_2 in 2008, the peatlands contain 7 times the carbon in the country's annual emissions. Peat bogs and the fuel that is taken from them are also this country's largest land-use source of CO_2. They add perhaps 9.1 Mt or over 13% (there is no agreed figure) to the country's total GHGs and there is therefore no alternative but to act to bring down the emissions they generate. There are two components to these emissions; the use of peat as a fuel and the release of CO_2 from disturbed bogs, primarily as a result of the extraction of fuel. There is also the opportunity cost of disturbing bogs because the damage means they do not take up carbon from the atmosphere. In their intact or undamaged form bogs are the most efficient terrestrial sink for atmospheric carbon dioxide as their persistently high water table ensures that the carbon entering the system through photosynthesis is greater than the amount leaving as organic matter is broken down.[7] A crude estimate based on data[8] produced by a team led by Dr. David Wilson of University College Dublin that annual sequestration by near-pristine bogs in Ireland could be anything between 60,000 tonnes and 140,000 tonnes of carbon.

The Irish Environmental Protection Agency's National Inventory Report 2009 shows that in 2007, the burning of peat was responsible for 7.6% of the country's fossil-fuel emissions but provided only 3.6% of the fossil energy actually used. It is therefore a very inefficient fuel in CO_2 terms. To this must be added the emissions caused by extracting the peat. Draining a bog so that extraction can begin turns land from a CO_2 sink to an emissions source. This is because the fall in the water table allows air to get to the peat and start oxidizing it, so that the carbon in it slowly disappears. There is no specific Irish data for these releases but if Finnish figures are applied to Ireland, Bord na Móna's bogs alone are responsible for the release of 454,400 tonnes of CO_2 each year. This compares with the 2,700,000 tonnes of CO_2 released when the fuel that it supplies to the power stations was burned. It can therefore be said that extraction adds at least 17% to the combustion emissions from milled peat. Estimates of the releases from bogs used for the production of sod peat amount to over 4 million tonnes of CO_2 a year. If this figure is correct, as sod production amounts to an estimated 650,000 tonnes per year,[9] sod peat production is especially emissions inefficient as, in addition to the emissions from the peat extraction, its combustion leads to 779,000 tonnes of CO_2 being released. So for every tonne of sods burnt, over 8 tonnes of CO_2 is emitted.

But peat is not only expensive in emissions terms, it is also costly in money terms when compared with other fossil sources, which is why its use for electricity generation has had to be subsidized in periods when the price of other fossil fuels has been low. A 2009 study, *Burning Peat in Ireland* by the Electricity Research Centre at University College Dublin, showed that electricity users subsidized peat-fired power stations by around €60 million in 2008 through the public service obligation (PSO) levy. To this must be added the value of the EU Emissions Trading System permits that the three stations had to be allocated so that they could burn the peat and which they could have sold if the fuel had not been used. If a price of €25 a tonne of CO_2 is assumed, the 1.81 million tonnes of CO_2 allocated[10] would have a market value of €46 million.

There are three peat-burning power stations in Ireland. The main reason for building them was energy security, the desire to have electricity from an Irish source that could be relied upon if there was ever any difficulty importing the coal, oil or gas required by the bulk of the country's generating stations. The three stations are readily dispensable. When they are working, they supply only 6.6% of the electricity system's demand. In the climate emergency situation we face, the energy security that peat provides must be achieved in some other way and peatland use must be refocused from energy to carbon storage and sequestration.

The extraction of sod peat for domestic use has damaged an estimated 46% of Irish peatlands.[11] The protection of peatlands is required by the EU Habitats Directive and by the Ramsar and Biodiversity Conventions. Ireland is legally required to maintain the area and range of these habitats as they were when the Directive came into force in 1992. Some effort was made in 1999 when over 160,000 ha of bog were designated as Special Areas of Conservation (SACs). At present, the SAC area is estimated to have risen to over 220,000 ha.[12] However, ownership of these sites remains largely in private hands and conservation depends on a management agreement between the state and the private owners.[13] This is not a secure basis for conservation as the integrity of the reserves remains partially dependent on the goodwill of the owners. Moreover, the state is not protecting SAC bogland as required by the directive. Thirty-two raised bog sites were designated in the 1990s as SACs under the directive. However, a ten-season derogation was granted in 1999 which allowed turf cutting to continue in the "protected" sites. In 2002, a similar ten-year derogation was given for raised bog SACs designated since 1999 and in 2004, an additional ten-year extension was given to allow continued digging on raised bogs designated as Natural Heritage Areas. Blanket bog conservation areas (SACs and NHAs) are effectively subject to an indefinite derogation. There is no provision in the Habitats Directive which allows member states to derogate in this way, and in this respect Ireland is in danger of being found to be in breach of EU law.

In order for Ireland to fulfil its climate obligations and those under the Habitats Directive, peatlands and the carbon they contain must be protected. In 2003, domestic turf cutting was going on in over 80% of the designated raised bogs. It is estimated that over 20,000 turbary rights exist on these bogs, of which over 2,500 were exercised in 2003.[14] In 1999, the National Parks and Wildlife Service (NPWS) introduced a voluntary scheme to purchase turbary rights. This has met with very limited success and only about 5% of turbary rights have been purchased. This may be because the price available under the voluntary scheme, €3,500 per ha in SACs and NHAs, does not reflect the bog's earnings potential for the landowner. It is said that a worked peatland can produce a profit of up to €1,000 per hectare per year.[15]

So what is the solution? A greatly increased price would be needed to purchase turbary rights with this potential. Accordingly, an annual tax should be payable by the owner of every bog where turf cutting is being carried out or which has been drained so that it can be carried out. The tax would apply to all turf cutting, not just in protected areas. The amount payable for each site would be based on an estimate of the emissions released by the oxidation of the bog as a result of the drainage plus the emissions from the combustion of any peat dug.

It is reasonable to impose such a tax as emissions from peatlands are likely to be included in the returns that Ireland has to make to the EU in future under the Effort-Sharing Decision, and the country is almost certain to have to pay a cost per tonne to buy permits to cover its failure to meet the reduction target set for it. After the tax was in operation, the turbary rights to the protected sites, and probably the sites themselves, would be bought by compulsory purchase in cases where it had proved impossible to buy them voluntarily and the owners were not prepared or unable to restore the bogs to which they applied. The tax would obviously reduce each bog's profit potential and thus the price paid for it, compulsorily or not. Moreover, the tax on drained but unworked bogs would encourage their restoration. If the government wished, the purchase offer, but not the compulsory purchase powers, could be extended to other peatlands.

The owners of any intact peatlands that remained in private hands after the tax had been imposed, and after harvesting in the protected areas had ceased should be paid an annual maintenance fee to reward them for the carbon they were keeping safe. The income for this, and for the purchase of turbary rights, could be paid out of the income that the state can expect to receive from the auctioning of EU ETS emissions permits after 2012. Alternatively, the Land Bond system, once used by the Land Commission to buy out the landlords, could be used to buy the turbary rights or the entire bog. The bonds would pay their registered owner a fixed rate of interest.

In addition to the threats to peatlands from peat extraction for energy, there are other threats, including extraction for horticulture, drainage for agriculture, afforestation and wind-turbine installation. All afforestation and planting on peatland and high-carbon soils should cease, wind-turbine installation should not occur on areas of peat and any peatland already taken into other uses should be restored if the carbon balance is favorable.

Reducing Methane Emissions from Irish Farms

On a global level, the development of policies for the control and reduction of methane emissions is not helped by the fact that surprisingly little is known about the natural sources of methane, how long it persists in the atmosphere, the size of its warming effect in relation to carbon dioxide and what eventually causes it to break down. Figure 3 below is typical. It shows that emissions are estimated to have increased from 233 million tonnes of methane a year in pre-industrial times to about 600 million tonnes today.

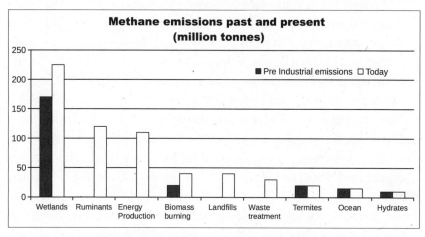

FIGURE 3. The conventional view of methane sources, based on data from the *Scientific American*, February 2007. Wetlands are thought to be giving off more methane now than in pre-industrial times because of increased rice cultivation. The chart omits tropical forests, a large, recently discovered source.

Where Does Methane Come From?

One of the biological sources of methane, are methanogens, single-celled microorganisms that belong to a major division of life, archaea. These live in anaerobic conditions like those found in a stagnant pond or a cow's rumen. After other microorganisms have split any plant material in those environments into hydrogen and carbon dioxide, the methanogens use the hydrogen to turn the CO_2 into methane.

Complexity of the Methane Problem

Uncertainty about how long methane stays in the atmosphere means that estimates of its warming effect as compared with CO_2 have recently been revised twice. Half-life figures quoted in the literature range from seven to ten years. The atmospheric lifetime relates emissions of a component to its atmospheric burden and is 8.4 years for methane. In some cases, for instance for methane, a change in emissions perturbs the chemistry and thus the corresponding lifetime. The CH_4 feedback effect amplifies the climate forcing of an addition of CH_4 to the current atmosphere by lengthening the global atmospheric lifetime of CH_4 by a factor of 1.4, making the estimate of its lifetime in the atmosphere 12 years.[16]

An important reason for this uncertainty seems to be that most methane[17] is broken down by combining with hydroxyl ions and possibly chlorine ions in the upper atmosphere to make CO_2 and water. The hydroxyl ions are produced when the sun's rays split an ozone molecule (O_3) and each of the three free oxygen radicals that result joins with a water molecule to make two hydroxyl (OH) ions. If there are a lot of hydroxyl ions about, the methane is quickly destroyed but if a lot of methane is suddenly released, the supply of hydroxyls gets exhausted and the methane lingers on, continuing its warming effect. If this is correct, methane's half-life is not a fixed number and, as a result, there is no fixed value for its warming effect in relation to CO_2. The Intergovernmental Panel on Climate Change said it was 23 times worse until 2001[18] but now prefers 25.[19] What is beyond dispute, however, is that methane has a massive short-term heating effect that dies away as it gets broken down. Accordingly, reducing the amount released is a powerful way to have a big near-term impact on the rate the world is warming.

Emissions from the global herd of ruminants (cattle, sheep, goats and camels) contribute about one quarter of the methane production that is under human control and, consequently, consideration has to be given to reducing ruminant numbers. The UN Food and Agriculture Organization is very concerned about this and produced a report in 2009 jointly with the International Energy Agency. The report, *Belching Ruminants, a minor player in atmospheric methane*, concluded:

> Since 1999 atmospheric methane concentrations have leveled off while the world population of ruminants has increased at an accelerated rate. Prior to 1999, world ruminant populations were increasing at the rate of 9.15 million head/year but since 1999 this rate has

increased to 16.96 million head/year. Prior to 1999 there was a strong relationship between change in atmospheric methane concentrations and the world ruminant populations. However, since 1999 this strong relation has disappeared. This change in relationship between the atmosphere and ruminant numbers suggests that the role of ruminants in greenhouse gases may be less significant than originally thought, with other sources and sinks playing a larger role in global methane accounting.

A Bespoke Approach to GHG Emissions

In view of these uncertainties about methane, and in particular about its comparability with CO_2, the Feasta Climate Group considers it unwise to have a single emissions-reduction program, with a common target, for the two gases. It is therefore suggesting that Ireland should advocate the adoption of a non CO_2-linked methane emissions cap-and-control program at an international level.

Having a common carbon-equivalent price for all land-use emissions would present problems because each emitting activity releases two or three different GHGs and involves a number of sub-activities. Moreover, as I have just explained, the relative importance of reducing each gas cannot be adequately expressed through Global Warming Potential calculations. To achieve the desired result, it may therefore be better to have a number of policies and prices. Emissions from the raising of livestock should not be lumped in with those from, say, deforestation or fossil-fuel use and the same carbon, or carbon-equivalent price applied. A more suitable approach to controlling the release of enteric methane might be a separate national market for livestock emissions permits, linked by a common international cap. Any flow of permits from one national market to another should be controlled by the two governments and regulated by an international authority to ensure that sales did not mean that global emissions increased because land had to be cleared to accommodate the animals or they were to be fed in a different way.

Methane: The Case for Ruminants and Other Livestock

Amongst the livestock, it is the ruminants that produce most of the methane, both as a result of their digestive process and the way their dung is

handled. It has therefore been suggested that, because the potential to reduce their methane emissions in any other way is limited, their numbers
should be reduced in response to the climate crisis. However, for any such
reduction policy to make sense, it would have to be done under a global cap
that applied to all livestock, not just ruminants, to avoid a switch to pork
and poultry production. Such a switch would mean a diversion of soya and
grain that people could eat directly for animal food. Moreover, if the land
area under crops being grown for animal food increased, it could mean increased emissions from deforestation, from the loss of carbon in the soil and
from the nitrogenous fertilizers used. The global cap would also avoid production lost in countries which accepted the cap being made up countries
which did not.

Ireland, working through the EU, should therefore seek to have global
livestock numbers capped at their current level and to have the animal units
allowed under the cap allocated to governments according to the number
of animals kept in each country at present. Once a world livestock cap was
in place, the international community would have the ability to control animal numbers. It could decide, for example, that the global herd was to be
reduced by 10% over the next ten years. In this case, each government would
be required to surrender 1% of its original allocation each year and a government that had grandfathered the initial allocation by giving them to farmers
in perpetuity would have to go into the market and buy back enough of the
permits it had given away.

However, it might be that the international community decided that no
reduction in the global herd was required. This could be for three reasons:

1. People want to eat meat and milk.
2. There are no alternative farming enterprises in many parts of the
   world. Cattle represent the best way that some types of land can be
   used for food production. Livestock-based cultures need to be preserved and poor people need sources of income.
3. The methane the herd produces does not build up in the atmosphere
   beyond the point at which the rate of its breakdown into CO_2 and
   water equals the rate at which it is being produced. Moreover, the CO_2
   from the methane is not a net addition to the atmospheric stock as it
   was originally extracted from that stock by the plants the animal ate.
   Consequently, a constant global herd has a constant global warming

effect rather than the cumulative one produced by the emissions from the burning of fossil fuels. The additional warming produced by the animals has to be set against the fact that pasture land takes CO_2 from the air and sequesters it in the soil, where it will stay unless the land is plowed. Moreover, while animals can damage land and reduce the carbon it contains, they can also be used to improve it and to increase its carbon content. Allan Savory's award-winning work[20] in Africa, the US and Australia has shown that if run-down land is very intensively grazed and trampled and then the animals are taken away completely until the grass and other plants have completely regrown, the land becomes more drought resistant and the amount of carbon in the below-ground biomass and the soil itself increases rapidly too.

The livestock sector is so complex and so important to so many poor people that it should not be expected to compete for emissions rights with fossil-fuel use. It is therefore suggested here that in terms of Irish policy, livestock emissions should become a new negotiating category alongside fossil-fuel and LULUCF emissions within the UNFCCC. Parties to the Convention should be asked to agree to the imposition of a global cap on livestock emissions and discussions should be held about the distribution of the emissions under the cap and the way they would be managed by national governments.

Agriculture is estimated to be the single largest contributor to Ireland's GHG emissions (26.8% in 2007). This is unusual for a developed country but it's much lower than in 1990 when it accounted for 35.9%.[21] The EPA believes that this reduction reflects the fall in nitrous oxide emissions due to less fertilizer being used, and a fall in methane emissions due to a decrease in cattle and sheep populations. In 2007 alone, there was a 3.8% decrease in agricultural GHG emissions. The continuing decrease in agricultural emissions is shown in Figure 4. According to O'Mara et al (2007),[22] about 49% of agricultural GHG emissions are methane from enteric fermentation in sheep and cattle. This would mean that ~13% of Ireland's entire GHG emissions arise from this source alone. Of this, 91% is from the cattle herd. Since these emissions are currently included in the non-Emissions Trading System emissions, which the country has to reduce by 20% relative to their 2005 level by 2020,[23] ways of reducing these enteric emissions need to be explored.

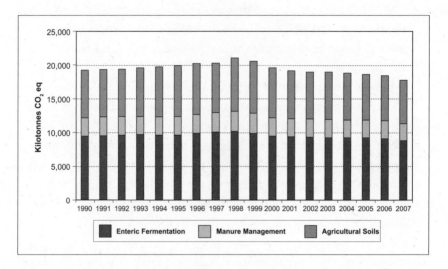

FIGURE 4. Nitrous oxide and methane emissions from Irish agriculture have fallen continuously since 1998 as a result of the decrease in livestock numbers and lower levels of fertilizer use. Enteric methane makes up just over half of these emissions in warming-effect terms. Source: National Inventory Report, 2009.[24]

Table 1 gives the best current estimates of what might be achieved in reducing enteric methane emissions from livestock. If all the techniques could be applied in conjunction with each other, enteric emissions might be cut by about 5%. These estimates could still be highly inaccurate, and some depend on market conditions. The uncertainties due to a lack of whole life-cycle analyses could also be significant, notably the amount of nitrous oxide released when concentrates and additives such as dietary oils are grown. If the principle of internalizing externalities is adopted, reducing methane emissions by any of the strategies listed in the table becomes theoretically profitable.

An effective methane-abatement policy should seek to raise emissions efficiency in relation to output rather than just cutting absolute emissions. At the current stage of research, the only feasible methane-reduction techniques are simple management strategies such as sending a beef animal for slaughter as soon as the average rate at which it is putting on weight begins to decline. These strategies could be part of the proposed Carbon REPS program. However, a further reduction in the size of the nation's herd or in milk and meat production must be opposed in the absence of a global livestock cap as otherwise "leakage" will occur.

Table 1. Summary of Potential Methane Emissions Reductions. Adapted from O'Mara et al. 2007.[25]

Practice	State of development	Financially viable without payment for emissions saved?	Abatement possible (% reduction in enteric methane)	Annual value of mitigated CH_4 when CO_2 is €25/tonne
Replacing roughage with concentrate for dairy cows	Being applied on farms	On a minority of farms	0.08	€180,000
Replacing roughage with concentrate for beef cattle	Being applied on farms	Yes (with further research required)	0.79	€1,790,000
Genetic improvement of the dairy herd	Being applied on farms	Yes	0.43	€976,000
Improvement in milk yield additional to genetic progress	Being applied on farms	Yes	1.30	€2,950,000
Genetic improvement of beef cattle	Being applied on farms	Yes		
Lifetime management of beef cattle: halve number of cattle slaughtered over 30 months	Being applied on farms	Depends on market conditions	0.88	€2,000,000
Lifetime management of beef cattle: increase number of young bulls slaughtered to 100,000/year	Being applied on farms	Depends on market conditions	1.00	€2,270,000
Feeding dietary oils to beef cattle	Ready to apply on farms	Marginal	0.69	€1,570,000
Feeding dietary oils to dairy cows	Establishing scope of measure (no program currently in place to do this)			
Propionate precursors for beef and dairy cattle	Ready to apply on farms	Not currently		
Feeding maize silage to dairy cows	Establishing scope of measure (no program currently in place to do this)			
Feeding maize silage to beef cattle	Establishing scope of measure			
Feeding other cereal silages instead of grass silage	Establishing scope of measure			
Improved grazing management	Establishing scope of measure			
Forage species and legume inclusion	Basic research stage/ Establishing scope of measure			
Probiotics	Basic research stage			
Halogenated compounds	Basic research stage			

Reducing Nitrous Oxide Emissions from Irish Farms

The reduction of nitrous oxide emissions needs to be given much higher priority than even its high global warming potential, 298, and long life in the atmosphere, 114 years, would seem to warrant. It currently contributes 7.9% of the total anthropogenic warming effect. Its atmospheric concentration, 319 parts per billion in 2005, was estimated to be 16% above pre-industrial levels.

The reason for giving nitrous oxide much higher priority is that, now that emissions of chlorine- and bromine-containing chlorofluorocarbons (CFCs) and halons are declining sharply as a result of the Montreal Protocol, nitrous oxide is now responsible for destroying twice as much ozone as the next worst ozone-depleting anthropogenic substance, CFC-11, a refrigerant.[26]

The destruction is damaging in two ways. Firstly, ozone filters out ultraviolet radiation coming from the sun, leading to an increase in skin cancers and cataract-induced blindness. Secondly, ozone destroys atmospheric methane. Consequently, an increased nitrous oxide concentration is likely to lead to an increased methane concentration and thus a greater total warming effect than from the nitrous oxide alone. It is not the nitrous oxide itself that destroys the ozone but two other nitrogen oxides, nitric oxide (NO) and nitrogen dioxide (NO_2), which some of it becomes when the gas reaches the stratosphere, the second major layer of Earth's atmosphere, between 10 and 50 km high. There, sunlight splits a fraction of it (~20%) into the nitrogen oxides via various reactions, while the major portion is converted to inert nitrogen gas (N_2).[27] Nitric oxide's destruction of the ozone is catalytic — the gas is not itself broken up by the process — so one molecule can go on doing damage until it is either broken up itself or floats out of the ozone layer, probably to fall to earth as acid rain.

The destruction of atmospheric N_2O in the stratosphere by photolysis and photo-oxidation is the only sink considered in global climate models. Very little seems to be known about other ways the gas is broken down, although two German scientists[28] working in a Norway spruce plantation in Bavaria recently found that long drought periods can turn the forest soil into a N_2O sink, while wetting it turns it back into a source. The overall global balance between the sink function of soils and the source function is unknown.

Irish agricultural N_2O emissions accounted for 9.9% of the country's total GHG emissions and 37% of agricultural emissions in 2007. Fortunately, the prospects for reducing those emissions are much better than those of cutting methane. Significant reductions of around 20% nationally can be made immediately via:

- Full adherence to the Teagasc Nutrient Advice. In general, Irish farmers still over-fertilize.[29] The Teagasc Nutrient Advice 2008,[30] coupled with a soil nutrient test, is the primary source of information on optimum fertilizer amounts, taking account of current legislation (e.g. Nitrates Directive), plant-nutrient (including nitrogen) requirements as they vary over time and with soil and crop type, and the fertilizer-replacement value of land-spread manure.
- Replacing slatted sheds with out-wintering pads. These have a purpose-built outside drained surface to replace slatted sheds for winter housing of livestock, and are becoming increasingly popular due to their lower cost (around 65%), completing the farm forestry cycle by using wood chips in its construction,[31] and increased animal health.[32]
- Partial replacement of calcium ammonium nitrate with urea; on average urea causes 80% less N_2O emissions than calcium ammonium nitrate,[33] depending on soil and environmental conditions.
- Adopting white clover-grass swards. White clover, a nitrogen-fixing legume, can be grown together with grass to add nitrogen to soil, replacing synthetic fertilizer and thus reducing fertilizer-induced N_2O emissions.
- Using only low-emission slurry spreaders. Most Irish cattle slurry is spread with a splash plate that results in high NH_3 volatilization and NO_3 leaching and hence indirect N_2O emissions. The use of low-emission surface spreaders such as band and trailing foot/shoe could reduce NH_3 volatilization by around 60%[34] and reduce the resulting indirect N_2O emissions.
- Separating slurry into liquid and solid fractions, and storing the latter as "solid storage". Emissions from slurry fertilizer can be reduced by separating into liquid and solid fractions.[35]

Cuts of a further 40–50% could be made if some or all of the following techniques were adopted:

- The urea spread on pasture and arable land had nitrification and urease inhibitors added to it by the manufacturers. This adds very little to the cost and, because less nitrogen can be applied since less is lost, promises to save the farmer money. Inhibitors could also be added to slurry before it is spread.

- More slurry was digested anaerobically. This would cut methane emissions as well. Inhibitors could then be added to the liquid digestate before it was injected into the land or the nitrates and the phosphates it contains could be secured by being taken up by biochar which would then be spread on the land.

- Changes were made to animal diets, more cover crops were grown to take up the nutrients that might otherwise be lost if the land was bare between crops, and passing run-off water through a "bioreactor", wood chips or sawdust — which absorbs almost all the nitrates it contains.

Policy should be focused on reducing nitrous oxide releases, taking in reductions in methane emissions whenever these are compatible, such as in the use of anaerobic digesters.

Biochar: A Way to Improve the Soil as a Sink?

The use of biochar is one of the few strategies that gives any basis for optimism that the excess CO_2 in the atmosphere can actually be removed. Biochar is the charcoal produced when biomass such as wood, manure or leaves is heated in a closed container with no oxygen. This treatment is known as pyrolysis. A typical biochar sample is fine-grained and consists of between 50% and 80% organic carbon. Pyrolysis also produces a gas that may be burned to provide the heat the process needs and bio-oil, a liquid that may be upgraded to a liquid fuel.

The current worldwide interest in biochar stems from the possibility of using it to sequester carbon extracted from the atmosphere in a way that boosts a soil's fertility. It does this by improving the soil's ability to retain nutrients and water while simultaneously reducing the amount of methane and nitrous oxide it gives off. It is also claimed that including biochar in the soil boosts a symbiotic relationship by which the plants themselves increase the carbon content of the soil. They are said to do this by sending sugars through their roots to feed the fungi and microorganisms living in the soil in exchange for the nutrients that the microorganisms release from the stock held by the biochar.

From a climate policy perspective, there is no point in supporting the application of biochar to the soil unless it can be shown to reduce GHG emissions and/or increase the carbon in the soil in addition to its own weight. It would be better to burn the biochar instead of coal if all that was achieved by applying a tonne of it to the soil was to sequester 600 kg of carbon.

The benefits claimed for biochar are:

- Carbon will be sequestered in the soil
- The crop yields from land to which biochar is applied will be significantly greater than those grown on untreated soil, increasing the amount of carbon sequestered by the biochar alone.
- Because biochar locks up nutrients, less fertilizer is required and this in itself cuts emissions.
- Biochar reduces methane and nitrous oxide emissions from the soil to which it is applied.
- Biochar improves the soil's water-retention capacity
- The production of biochar could lead to the development of a network of rural biorefineries that turn biomass into energy, foodstuffs and chemicals as well as producing char.

Some of these benefits would go to the farmer, while the climate-related ones would accrue to the whole world. In deciding how much support the state or the international community should give to biochar use, a value needs to be put on both categories of benefit so that farmers pay for their benefits and, if a top-up is required to get biochar into use on the scale required to reduce the atmospheric concentration of CO_2 as rapidly as required, the international community should pay the difference.

The International Biochar Initiative (IBI) has been campaigning for biochar use to generate carbon credits to offset emissions in Annex 1 countries. If this was allowed without careful and detailed planning and strict sustainability criteria in place and the value of the credits rose because of determined climate policies, the price put on biochar might rise so high that its production booms and becomes damaging. The level of demand might, for example, cause the clearance of natural forests and price the charcoal used for cooking out of the reach of the world's poor. There might also be competition between food production and biomass-for-biochar growing for land. We therefore believe that at this stage, support for biochar should be limited to financing research and village-scale demonstration projects that utilize waste feedstocks, such as municipal solid waste, forest residues and agricultural residues, that do not compete with food and other land uses. In response to these fears, the IBI recommends that waste materials from agriculture and forestry should be "the primary near-term source of biomass feedstock for biochar production." It writes:[36]

> Large amounts of agricultural residues, municipal green waste and forestry biomass are currently burned or left to decompose and release CO_2 and methane back into the atmosphere.... Using only 27% of the world's crop and forestry wastes (the portion of wastes not currently used for anything else) for biochar, could by 2030 sequester 0.25 gigatonnes of carbon a year from biochar alone. If the energy co-product of biochar production is used to offset fossil fuel use, then the annual carbon mitigation potential of biochar more than doubles to 0.6 gigatonnes of carbon annually by 2030. A scenario utilizing 80% of crop and forestry residues shows that by the year 2050, approximately 2.2 gigatonnes of carbon could be stored or offset annually, reaching the gigatonne scale of carbon sequestration that is the benchmark for significant climate mitigation technologies.

Using waste material for biochar would avoid competition with food production and land conversion from forests to plantations. It would also create none of the pressure that forces indigenous people from their land. Furthermore, food security would be greatly enhanced by integrating biochar into food-cropping systems and turning crop residues into biochar for use on the farm.

Ireland's efforts in the biochar arena should concentrate on research to demonstrate its effects in Irish soils and on developing a network of rural bio-refineries that would produce it as a by-product. This is how a local refinery might work. It could take in a crop such as miscanthus, crush it and extract the juice. These crops contain sugars and plant protein. The protein can be extracted and made into animal food and the remaining sugars can be anaerobically digested to create methane. That leaves the crushed stems, which are mostly cellulose. These could be pressure-cooked at 200°C in dilute sulfuric acid to break up the molecules into furans, levulinic acid and lignin, the glue that holds the plant fibers together. The lignin can then be charred and some of it heated with steam to produce hydrogen and carbon monoxide. These gases can then be mixed with the methane from the digester to give a synthetic natural gas that can either be piped to people's homes, used to power an engine to generate electricity or compressed for use in cars. The furans would be transported to a regional refinery to become a diesel fuel. The levulinic acid would be sent away too as it is the starting point for a whole range of chemicals including nylon. Meanwhile, the remaining char would be used by the local refinery to purify the liquor coming from the digester. The char would tie up the plant nutrients it found there and would be put back on the land both to sequester carbon and increase fertility. Taking all these steps together, a whole new set of rural activities would be born.

For this vision to be realized, a detailed research program for biochar is needed. This program should do the following:

- Identify and characterize potential feedstocks for biochar production from wastes, agricultural and forestry residues and energy crops.
- Develop a classification system for biochars produced from different feedstocks.
- Optimize pyrolysis technologies and operating conditions for different feedstocks and for biorefinery residuals.
- Examine the stability of biochar in soils (lab-based trials, leading to field trials) to determine the changes that occur when biochars are applied to different soils. The most important parameters that affect stability for carbon sequestration, plant growth and the health of the soil need to be determined.
- Investigate soil and plant growth improvement by biochar addition and the potential for fertilizer displacement.
- Investigate the potential reductions in nitrous oxide emissions from fertilizer application through the use of biochar.
- Investigate the potential human health implications from biochar production and application.
- Develop a standard system for production of biochar from different feedstocks.

Conclusions

A number of measures are urgently needed to mitigate or avoid the worst effects of climate change. A separate reduction program is needed for each major gas from each major source so that its special characteristics and the circumstances of its release can be taken into consideration rather than just its global warming potential. The four land-based programs are:

1. Enteric methane from ruminants.

2. CO_2 emissions from the clearing of forests, the extraction of peat and the conversion of land from one use to another.
3. Methane from all non-enteric land-based sources.
4. Nitrous oxide from all land-based sources.

It might be that the reduction programs for nitrous oxide and methane could take in releases from all sources rather than just land-based ones but the implications of doing so need further consideration. However, in general, emissions trading between the different programs, and thus different gases and different types of source, should not be allowed as that would effectively make them one program and would dilute the priorities and the incentives being given for those with the highest urgency.

Table 2 below shows a summary of current land-based GHG emissions in Ireland and the possible emission savings to be made by implementing the reduction measures outlined in this report. Biochar does not feature

Table 2. Summary of current land-based GHG emissions in Ireland and of possible emissions savings to be made by implementing the reduction measures outlined in this report.

	Current Emissions	Possible Emissions Savings		Note
Peatland CO_2	9.1 million tonnes CO_2eq (4 million from peat combustion; 5.1 million from peat oxidation)	3.2 million tonnes CO_2eq (>80% reduction)	4.6% of national emissions	Peat oxidation currently ignored. Peat cutting must stop.
Agricultural N_2O	37% of agricultural or 9.9% of national emissions	1.4–3.4 million tonnes CO_2eq (20–50% reduction)	2–5% of national emissions	
Manure Management CH_4	2 Mt CO_2e (14% of agricultural emissions)	Estimated 75% reduction	2% of national emissions	More research needed.
Enteric CH4	9 million CO_2e (~13% national emissions)	Reduce by 450,000t CO_2eq (5% reduction)	0.7% of national emissions	National herd not reduced.
Total			9.3–12.3% (8.6–11.6% excluding CH_4) reduction in national emissions	

in the table but it could play a significant role in carbon sequestration and emissions reduction besides bringing other benefits. A key aspect of its production is that it takes biomass that would otherwise have rotted away, dissipating the energy it contains, and the pyrolysis, besides making the char, turns the plant material into synthetic natural gas and diesel fuel and also into chemicals that are currently produced from oil.

If we are to survive the current emergency we need to look closely at how our land-based activities could mitigate global warming if we refocused their purpose. This will involve a serious rethink not only of policy and management methods, but also of our attitude and connection to the land. Land has always had a special significance for the Irish. In the future, it will continue to be important to us but in ways that are different from those at present. For the sake of our own health and that of the planet, we must use it well today if it is to be the resource we need it to be in the future.

Endnotes

1. Surface Ocean Lower Atmosphere Study, an international research group based at the University of East Anglia, issued this statement in June 2007: solas-int.org/aboutsolas/organisationaandstructure/sciencesteercomm/sscmins/positionstatement.pdf.
2. P. Read and A. Parshotam, "Holistic Greenhouse Gas Management Strategy (with Reviewers' Comments and Authors' Rejoinders)." Institute of Policy Studies Working Paper 07/1 (Victoria University of Wellington, Wellington, New Zealand, 2007), ips.ac.nz/publications/files/6e811fc9e32.pdf.
3. Simon L. Lewis, "Making the Paper," *Nature* 457, 933 (19 February 2009).
4. "Reducing Emissions or Playing with Numbers?" *Forestwatch*, no. 136 (March 2009).
5. Scott J. Goetz et al., "Mapping and Monitoring Carbon Stocks with Satellite Observations: A Comparison of Methods," Carbon Balance and Management 4:2 (2009), cbmjournal.com/content/4/1/2
6. Based on total island of Ireland. R. W. Tomlinson, "Soil Carbon Stocks and Changes in the Republic of Ireland." *Journal of Environmental Management* 76 (2005): 77–93; M. M. Cruickshank et al., "Carbon in the Vegetation and Soils of Northern Ireland," Proceed RIA, vol. 98B, no. 1 (1998), 9–21.
7. D. Wilson et al., "Rewetting of Cutaway Peatlands: Are We Re Creating Hot Spots of Methane Emissions?" *Restoration Ecology* (2007).
8. D. Wilson et al., "Carbon dioxide dynamics of a restored maritime peatland," *Ecoscience* 14 (2007), 71–80.
9. P. J. Foss, C. A. O'Connell and P. H. Crushell, *Bogs and Fens of Ireland — Conservation Plan 2005*, Irish Peatland Conservation Council, Dublin (2001).
10. 68.5% of emissions. EPA, 2008. Emissions Trading — Final Allocation Decision; Tuohy et al., 2009.
11. Ibid 10.

12. C. Douglas, F. Fernandez and J. Ryan, *Peatland Habitat Conservation in Ireland*, International Peat Congress (2008).

13. M. G. C. Schouten, "Peatland Research and Peatland Conservation in Ireland: Review and Prospects," in J. Feehan, ed., 13th International Peat Congress, International Peat Society (Ireland 2008).

14. Ibid 10.

15. According to Galway East Fine Gael TD Paul Connaughton "Turf Ban Will Hurt Galway Families," *Galway Independent* (March 2008).

16. Wuebbles and Hayhoe (2002) surmise that reaction with hydroxyl radicals account for about 90% of the removal of methane, while transport to the stratosphere (~5%) and dry soil oxidation (~5%) account for almost all the rest.

17. Ibid 16.

18. IPCC, 2007. Fourth Assessment Report: Climate Change. Intergovernmental Panel on Climate Change,

19. Ibid 18.

20. A video of a lecture by Allan Savory in which he explains his work can be found at feasta.org/events/general/2009_lecture.htm.

21. Ibid 14.

22. F. P. O'Mara et al., *Climate Change — Estimation of Emissions of Greenhouse Gases from Agriculture and Strategies for their Reduction: Environmental RTDI Programme 2000-2006*, Wexford: EPA (2007).

23. EPA, *Ireland's Greenhouse Gas Emission Projections 2008-2020* [online], available: epa.ie/downloads/pubs/air/ airemissions/ghg_Emission_Proj_08_12_30032009.pdf, accessed 30 June 2009 (2009).

24. EPA, *National Inventory Report, 2009* [online], available: coe.epa.ie/ghg/nirs/NIR_2009_IEv1.2.pdf, accessed 30 June 2009 (2009).

25. Ibid 22.

26. A. R. Ravishankara, J. S. Daniel and R. W. Portmann, "Nitrous Oxide (N_2O): The Dominant Ozone-Depleting Substance Emitted in the 21st Century," *Science* 326 (5949) (2009): 123-125.

27. P. Warneck, *Chemistry of the Natural Atmosphere* (Academic Press, 1988).

28. S. D. Goldberg and G. Gebauer, "Drought Turns a Central European Norway Spruce Forest Soil from an N_2O Source to a Transient N_2O Sink," *Global Change Biology* 15 (2009): 850-860.

29. B. S. Coulter et al., *A Survey of Fertilizer Use from 2001-2003 For Grassland and Arable Crops* (2005).

30. B. S. Coulter and S. Lalor, *Major and Micro Nutrient Advice for Productive Agricultural Crops* (2008).

31. E. Kennedy, P. French, B., O'Brien, *Low Fixed Cost Expansion Options with Increased Labour Efficiency*. TResearch 4, no. 2 (2009): 44-45.

32. K. O'Driscoll et al., "The Effect of Out-Wintering Pad Design on Hoof Health and Locomotion Score of Dairy Cows," *J. Dairy Sci.* 91, no. 2 (2008): p. 544-553.

33. C. A. M. De Klein et al., "Nitrous Oxide Emissions from Agricultural Soils in New Zealand — A Review of Current Knowledge and Directions for Future Research. *Jour. of the Royal Soc. of New Zealand* 31, no. 3 (2001): 543-574.

34. Ryan, D., *A Slurry Spreader to Meet Farming Needs and Environmental Concerns* 2005, Teagasc.
35. C. Bertram et al., "Pig Slurry Treatment Modifies Slurry Composition, N_2O, and CO_2 Emissions After Soil Incorporation. *Soil Biology and Biochemistry* 40, no. 8 (2008): 1999–2006.
36. Letter to the UK Parliament, 23 October, 2009. zerocarbonfarm.com/document%20 library/research/Oct%2023%202009,%20International%20Biochar%20Initative,%20 Letter%20to%20UK%20Parliament%20in%20defence%20of%20biochar.pdf.

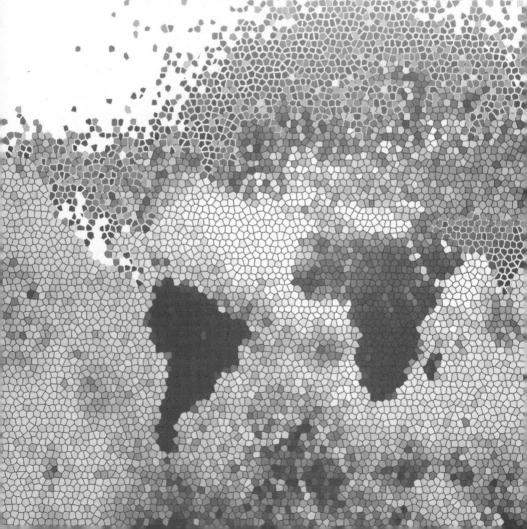

PART IV

DEALING
WITH CLIMATE CHANGE

Future Global Climate Institutions

ALEX EVANS

Any framework for dealing with the climate crisis should be based on a scientifically derived stabilization target. Such a framework should also distribute the global carbon budget among the world's nations according to a transparent, equitable formula. To achieve this, global climate institutions will have to change.

In 2009, when David Steven and I embarked on a study for the UK government of future global institutions for tackling climate change, we felt that the world had spent almost nothing investigating the sort of global institutions we'd need in future in order to solve the issue. By comparison, millions of pounds had been invested in understanding the science of climate change — above all through the Intergovernmental Panel on Climate Change (IPCC) — and the economics of the issue, especially the Stern Review.

This, we thought, was surprising. In the past, whenever nations or peoples have faced an existential, systemic challenge, the new settlement that follows is almost always marked by new institutions. Think of how national sovereignty evolved out of Europe tearing itself apart in the Thirty Years War during the 17th century, or how the UN emerged, phoenix-like, from the ashes of the Second World War.

It's already clear that climate change is the defining challenge of our age. Why then is so little thinking underway about the kind of institutions needed to solve it? It's this nagging question that motivated us to produce our May 2009 paper "An Institutional Architecture for Climate Change."

We were guided from the outset by two principles. The first was that we didn't want to fall into the trap of thinking that institutions were the same as organizations. Instead, we liked Douglass North's definition that institutions are "the rules of the game in a society or, more formally, the humanly-devised constraints that shape human interaction." He continues: "institutional change shapes the way societies evolve through time and hence is the key to understanding historical change." That sounded a good starting point to us.

The other principle we wanted to stick to was a really rigorous focus on function over form. As we know only too well, energy spent on reforming the international system all too often gets dissipated in setting up new organizations, closing them down, or otherwise trying to create some sort of perfect international organogram — without necessarily asking what it is we actually need international institutions to achieve.

So, those were the two principles underpinning our study. Which leads on to the question: what do we need international institutions to achieve on climate? David and I argue that the short answer to that question is that they need to send back *signals from the future*.

Let me explain that phrase. When you look at what determines how policy actors behave on climate change, you realize that *how they act today is fundamentally determined by their expectations of what will happen in the future*. So if countries — or companies, or citizens — expect a slow transition to a low-carbon world, then it makes sense for them to "free-ride" internationally and to protect incumbents and vested interests. Moreover, given the long investment horizons involved, everyone shares an interest in predictability. If, on balance, people expect a slow transition, then it's rational for them to reinforce that dynamic by seeking to slow the process down themselves. But if, on the other hand, perceptions tip to the other side — toward expecting a rapid transition to a low-carbon world — then a virtuous circle is much more likely to develop, because actors will have incentives to lead the change, nurture innovators and cooperate internationally.

Where institutions can make a difference, then, is by sending "signals from the future" that shape people's expectations. Institutions can give people confidence that we are going to solve this problem and, in doing so, create a self-fulfilling prophecy that brings about that very outcome.

This subtle feedback loop shows in microcosm a much wider point about where we are today in terms of international cooperation, with globalization challenged not only by climate change, but also by the credit crunch, growing resource scarcity, the risk of protectionism and so on. As these and other stresses on globalization increase, it's likely that we'll see either a significant loss of trust in the system, as globalization retreats and countries focus on narrow, short-term national interests, or a significant increase in trust, as countries move decisively to increase their interdependence and invest in the institutions needed to make globalization more resilient, sustainable and equitable.

Muddling through in some ways looks the least likely outcome. That's why we argue that the issue of "signals for the future" is so important, and why we believe international institutions matter so much in this context. How do today's climate institutions shape up?

Well, let's start with the good news. Our institutional framework has a clear objective, set out in Article 2 of the UNFCCC: stabilize concentrations of GHGs at a safe level that avoids dangerous interference with the climate. That treaty also represents a pretty much universally agreed-upon reference point, with only Iraq, Somalia and Andorra not having ratified it.

Other items on the "credit" side of the institutional ledger include the IPCC, which has been not only a neutral arbiter of the science but also a kind of anchor for the global conversation about climate change; Kyoto's system of binding targets, plus cap-and-trade, for developed countries; some basic mechanisms for emissions abatement in developing countries, including the Clean Development Mechanism; and methodologies for countries to report on their emissions.

Unfortunately, these elements don't add up to a clear signal back from the future. Here are a few reasons why not:

First, although we've defined stabilization as the goal, our institutional framework doesn't actually cohere with that end. We've neither quantified, nor even seriously discussed, the level at which GHG concentrations should be stabilized to avoid dangerous climate change, much less agreed a binding global ceiling on GHG levels in the air.

Second, Kyoto's targets for developed countries weren't in any way scientifically derived. Instead, they were based on countries' own political and economic assessments of what they could manage.

Third, the lack of quantified targets for developing countries makes it impossible to forecast overall global emissions with any certainty. On top of that, there's the problem of "carbon leakage," so in the UK, for instance, while production of GHGs fell 12.5% between 1990 and 2003, consumption of them grew by 19% over the same period. Why? In effect, it's because the

UK, like other rich countries, has "exported" its dirty industries to the developing world, which then have to pay the cost of investing in clean technologies.

Fourth, Kyoto's enforcement system is weak. Sanctions on countries that fail to meet their targets are weak; systems for monitoring, reporting and verification are ineffective; and there are no penalties on countries that refuse to join in the first place. Indeed, the fact that the US stayed out of Kyoto is likely to help it to generate a much more generous target this time around.

Fifth, there's a similar lack of clarity on finance, adaptation and technology.

- On technology, there are now numerous funds, but they lack clear terms of reference or a sense of exactly what they're supposed to deliver. The amount of public R&D spent on energy, meanwhile, is half what it was 25 years ago.
- On adaptation, debate is focusing more on the question of "how much?" than the question of "how?" National Adaptation Plans of Action are highly focused on short-term measures and far less on the challenge of really mainstreaming resilience through development programming.
- On financing, there's a lack of clarity over how financing flows on mitigation, adaptation and low-carbon technology cut across each other, and how they relate to other flows like development aid and private-sector investment.

And last but not least, there's a lack of coherence between climate change and other key policy areas, such as trade, energy, food security, land use and economic stability.

Ultimately, for all that policymakers stress the scale of the climate challenge and the need for radical action, the fact remains that our current institutional setup is saying something different. In effect, the signal actually being sent back from the future by today's institutions is that:

1. The likely impact of climate change will be considerably less than that predicted by the IPCC.
2. The cost of reducing emissions far exceeds the benefits, while there is little need to insure against catastrophic impacts.
3. Short-term economic imperatives outweigh longer-term interests, including both economic and, especially, non-economic ones.

4. The needs of the poor should be given less weight than those of the rich.

All of which poses the question: what would it look like if we had an institutional framework that provided the opposite signal from the future — the unequivocal message that the world was clearly resolved to tackle climate change over the full term of the problem, and that individual countries, companies and citizens should position themselves to get out of carbon as swiftly as possible?

Let's start by being clear about the three most fundamental functions for the system. It must:

- Constrain emissions and manage sinks in a way consistent with stabilization.
- Provide mechanisms to take account of equity, in both the mitigation and the adaptation contexts.
- Include enforcement mechanisms tough enough to make the regime effective and credible.

So what might these mean in practice? Well, first and foremost, we think countries will need to agree a quantified, binding stabilization target as the bedrock of the whole system. Today, we work from the short term — 5-year emission targets — out toward the long term: an aspiration of eventual stabilization, at some unspecified level.

It's time to reverse this trend and ensure that what happens today is driven by what needs to happen over the full term of the issue. A defined stabilization target, like 450 parts per million CO_2, would achieve that. And once we have it, we can use it to derive the size of a safe global emissions budget over the same period.

The next question is how to share out this budget. In the scenarios we did for the report, David and I argue that the only way that 192 countries are going to agree on the distribution of emission permits is through some kind of standard allocation formula to reconcile countries' different equity claims. We call this "the Algorithm."

At one end of the spectrum, emerging economies like China and Brazil want permits allocated in proportion to historical responsibility; at the other, many developed countries assume that "grandfathering" permits in proportion to GDP is the only feasible approach.

Somewhere in the middle is a compromise, probably with allocations ending up on an equal per-capita basis at the end of a negotiated convergence period.

Even then, the problem with a per-capita allocation is that it's impossible for developed countries to deliver in the short term, and a tough sell politically. At the same time, it's also inequitable for poor countries, which receive a disproportionately small share of emissions while convergence to equal per capita equity takes place; these countries are also not rewarded for having low emissions prior to taking on targets.

Happily, there's quite a lot that policymakers can do to increase equity. One is to make emission permits a tradable property right, so that emissions trading provides compensatory finance flows during the convergence period. Another approach involves directing resource flows through non-market mechanisms, like technology transfer. A third is resource flows for funding adaptation.

But we need to take a far more integrated approach to climate finance than we do today. At present, most of the push on financing is around making adaptation finance additional to the 0.7% of GNP target for development aid. And it's far from clear to me how we put ourselves on strong ground by arguing on the one hand that adaptation is all about mainstreaming, while on the other insisting on separate financial flows.

More fundamentally, imagine what a truly global cap and trade system, coupled with an equitable allocation algorithm, could do for finance for development. Official Development Assistance is currently worth about $100 billion a year. Emissions trading markets are already worth two-thirds of that level a year — $64 billion in 2008, according to the World Bank — and they're still in their infancy. Yet because they have no targets and hence own no assets, developing countries are missing out on these markets. Instead, they get the Clean Development Mechanism, which doesn't deliver real finance for development or real emissions reductions. Such inequity is startling. You couldn't make it up.

Finally, let me say just a word about enforcement. Our current setup does not work — not on enforcing targets, not on penalizing countries that stay out of the regime and not on checking that financial commitments actually get delivered.

In the long run, David and I argue that a climate deal will have to require an "all or nothing" approach to international participation. Either countries play a full part in the system, and thus have access to international frameworks on finance, trade, development, energy and other resources, and perhaps even security; or they sit outside the international system and are effectively barred from all forms of international cooperation. Carbon default would therefore become as weighty an issue as sovereign debt default or failure to comply with a UN Security Council resolution. Right now, of course, such a scenario seems totally inconceivable, but it does indicate the extent of the shift in understanding that is still needed.

We certainly don't claim to have all the answers about future climate institutions, nor does our report purport to be a full blueprint. Our aim is simply to start a broader, deeper, more engaged conversation about a dimension of the climate challenge that's been seriously under-considered. This is also why we call for a "Stern Review"–type process to look at climate institutions much more comprehensively. Only when we embark on both of these can we begin to glimpse a real, workable model for our global institutions on the horizon.

Cap and Share: Simple is Beautiful

LAURENCE MATTHEWS

Cap and Share is a fair, effective, cheap, empowering and simple way to reduce emissions from the burning of fossil fuels. It could form the basis of a wider global climate framework but how realistic is it to call for its introduction?

Humanity faces many challenges in the current crisis: development issues; global poverty and inequality; security of energy, food and water supplies; and a range of environmental problems which stretches far beyond limiting carbon emissions. Maintaining greenhouse gas concentrations at safe levels is just one requirement for survival but it is a prominent, important and symbolic one. Any response to it needs to be effective and, if possible, efficient in economic terms. But in order to be effective it has to be adopted and this means it must be acceptable in terms of issues such as equity, development agendas and parochial political struggles. If a framework is simple, it can more easily be tested for alignment with these other concerns.

Simplicity has other virtues too. Simplicity is important when rallying emotional support for a measure — no matter what the economic incentives might be. Inspirational ideas are usually simple. Simplicity fosters a feeling of inclusion, rather than the alienation and exclusion that results from discussions by "experts". An insistence on simplicity also forces naysayers to state clearly what they object to, which clarifies the discussion immensely. We are facing a planetary emergency here and we need to be clear-sighted if we are to solve our problems in time.

Simplicity should not be confused with naivety; indeed naivety is often displayed by concentrating on some aspects of a problem in sophisticated detail while completely ignoring others. Concocting elaborations and complications may be useful for addressing technicalities and can be useful for finessing stumbling blocks in negotiations, but this process risks getting out of hand and is prone to being blind to errors which would be elementary to others less immersed in the details. Proponents of a simple system might do well to consent to discussions on elaborations only if the basis for the simple framework is agreed first.

The next section describes Cap and Share, recently selected by the UK's Sustainable Development Commission as one of its "Breakthrough Ideas for the 21st Century" (SDC 2009). Cap and Share is an example of an effective, fair, efficient and, above all, *simple* method for capping carbon emissions.

Cap and Share

Cap and Share (C&S) is a system for limiting the carbon emissions from burning fossil fuels (Feasta 2008); it is an alternative to carbon rations or carbon taxes. It could work on a global scale, or nationally for a single country's economy. We'll return to this later, but for the moment imagine a national scheme. As the name implies, there are two parts to C&S:

Cap: The total carbon emissions are limited (capped) in a simple, no-nonsense way.

Share: The huge amounts of money involved are shared equally by the population.

There is a trick to each of these. First the Cap. This is set in line with scientific advice, at a level each year that will bring concentrations (of carbon dioxide in the atmosphere) down to a safe level. But how do we ensure this cap is met? The trick here is to go "upstream." This is often explained (Barnes 2008) by the analogy of watering a lawn with a hosepipe connected to a lawn sprinkler, with lots of small holes spraying water everywhere. If you wanted to save water, you could try to block up all the holes one by one — but wouldn't it be simpler to turn off the tap a bit? It's the same with fossil fuels, where the sprinkler holes correspond to the millions of houses, factories and vehicles, each emitting carbon dioxide by burning these fuels. By controlling the supply of fossil fuels coming into the economy (corresponding to the tap) we automatically control the emissions that occur when those fossil fuels are burnt somewhere down the line. So instead of focusing on the emissions, we focus on the fossil fuels themselves. The primary fossil-fuel suppliers (e.g. oil companies) are required to acquire permits in order to introduce fossil fuels into the economy (by importing them or extracting them from the ground). A permit for, say, 1 tonne of carbon dioxide entitles the fossil-fuel supplier to introduce that amount of fossil fuel that will emit 1 tonne when burnt. The number of permits issued equates to the desired cap.

Next, the Share. Since the fossil fuel suppliers have to buy the permits, they will pass on this cost by increasing the fuel price. This flows through the economy (like a carbon tax), making carbon-intensive goods cost more. This sounds like bad news for the consumer. But the trick this time is to share out the money paid by the fossil-fuel suppliers, back to the people, which compensates for the price rises. There are two possible mechanisms for getting the money to the population. In one, the version called Cap and Dividend (Barnes 2008) in the US and based on the Alaska Permanent Fund, permits are auctioned and the auction revenue distributed to the citizens on an equal per capita basis. Under "classic" C&S (Feasta 2008) each adult receives free of charge — say, monthly or annually — a certificate for his or her share. These certificates are then sold to the primary fossil-fuel suppliers (through market intermediaries such as banks) and become the permits. Under "classic" C&S people thus receive certificates instead of money, so that if they should wish to, they can retain (and destroy) a portion of their certificates — and thus are able to reduce the country's carbon footprint by that amount.

That's Cap and Share in a nutshell.

To many people, however, the "obvious" mechanism is not Cap and Share but either a carbon tax (discussed below) or a version of cap and trade applied "downstream" where the emissions take place. Such a cap and trade system has two parts, as follows. The first applies to the fossil fuels we buy directly (petrol, gas, coal) and burn ourselves, causing emissions; these direct emissions account for half of our "carbon footprint." For these direct emissions, some form of personal carbon trading is envisaged, typically based on ideas of "rationing" familiar from petrol and food rationing during the Second World War. Personal Carbon Allowances (PCAs) typically involve giving an equal allowance to each adult citizen, and each purchase of petrol, oil or gas is deducted from the allowance (typically using swipe card technology). The other half of our carbon footprint consists of indirect emissions, the "embedded" emissions in goods and services, which arise when companies produce these goods and services on our behalf. These indirect emissions are controlled with an Emissions Trading System (ETS) for companies, such as the European Union ETS. (The EU ETS is already up and running, and has had its teething problems; but its faults — lax caps through too many permits being issued, free allocation windfalls to large utility companies, partial coverage only of the economy, leaks through dubious CDM projects — are now widely accepted and these shortcomings are being addressed in the next phase).

Taken together, PCAs and an ETS-like arrangement for companies can constitute an economy-wide scheme; variants have names such as Domestic Tradable Quotas or Tradable Energy Quotas (Fleming 2005). Under the scheme individuals or companies who use more than their allowance can buy extra from those who can make do on less, but the total amount in circulation is finite, set by the cap. This downstream approach is compared with Cap and Share's upstream approach in research commissioned by Comhar, the Irish sustainable development commission, and carried out by AEA Technology and Cambridge Econometrics (Comhar 2008). C&S came out well from the comparison.

Benefits of Cap and Share

It is worth listing the benefits of C&S because they are so multifaceted. Firstly, there are some obvious consequences of the way C&S works:

- **Effective:** C&S delivers; it is not just an aspiration. Individual countries like the UK and blocs like the EU may have targets (and various institutional arrangements), but so far they have no mechanism to ensure that the targets are achieved. C&S guarantees a cap.
- **Fair:** The framework clearly has at its root a simple, robust form of equity. This serves as a focal point for agreement, in the same way that one-person-one-vote serves as the basis for democracy. C&S is exactly as fair as rationing would be, or more so, given the inequity typically built in to the ETS half of such systems.
- **Simple:** A typical country will have at most 100 or so fossil-fuel suppliers, so C&S is simple to operate and police. Meanwhile all other companies, and all individuals, are free to go about their lives without the need for swipe cards or carbon accounting, making their decisions based on price alone. Contrast this with the EU ETS, which has been described as "more complicated than the German tax system."
- **Fast:** A result of this simplicity is that the system is easy to introduce very quickly — and we don't have the time to wait another decade before getting started.

- **Cheap:** This is also a direct result of the simple, upstream nature of the cap.
- **Transparent:** With scrutiny focused on the small number of fossil-fuel suppliers, there is much less scope for cheating than with a complex system like an ETS.

Next, there is an important political point:

- **Robust:** This arises from looking at the winners and losers under C&S. Although the payments to people compensate them for price rises, this is only true on average. If you have a lower carbon footprint than the national average, you will come out ahead: your payments from C&S will more than compensate for any price rises. People with higher than average carbon footprints will be worse off, but the skewed nature of income distributions means that there are many more winners than losers (for the same reason that there are more people on below-average incomes than above-average incomes). There is thus a natural constituency (McKibbin & Wilcoxon 2007) in favor of maintaining a tight cap, to counterbalance the vested interests that would push for a cap to be relaxed or abandoned. Indeed, C&S could be sold politically under the slogan "save the world — and get paid for it." This gives a certain robustness in the face of shocks and political events, necessary for a scheme that will need to survive for decades. (Consider, by contrast, carbon taxes. These are also simple, and a carbon tax is equivalent to an upstream cap if the tax level is set high enough. But the robustness incentives disappear if the money disappears into general taxation, and so taxes are unpopular. So it is much less likely that the tax level *would* be set high enough.)

Next come some technical benefits of C&S:

- **Efficient:** Because permits are subject to supply and demand, and price signals then flow through the economy, C&S uses markets to guarantee that the cap is met with optimal economic efficiency.
- **Scalable:** C&S can operate at the level of a country, a bloc like the EU, or globally. This is discussed further in the "Global/International" section below.
- **Flexible:** An upstream system can easily form part of hybrid schemes (see the next section).

And last but not least, C&S has some intangible, psychological benefits:
- **Positive:** People can relax slightly, knowing that this problem, at least, is being addressed. They no longer need to feel guilty; on the contrary, the people are part of the solution rather than part of the problem. (Even the "losers" mentioned above have non-monetary compensations; for example, since everyone knows that the problem is being addressed, the rich can counter criticism from environmentalists by responding, "my emissions are all within the cap too, so stop criticizing!")
- **Empowering:** C&S has a lack of intrusiveness and micromanagement. People are free to get on with their lives, without any need to keep to an "allowance." There is no hassle and no intrusive tracking of individual purchasing transactions. Better still, people are in control: they are controlling the system rather than the system controlling them. You have control over "your share of the country's carbon footprint."
- **Resonant:** C&S has an "all in this together" feel to it, and resonates with many other movements concerned with equality (Wilson & Pickett 2009), justice and development issues; it also resonates with initiatives at a local community level, which need to have national and global frameworks in place if their work is not to be undermined.

To summarize, we have a combination of emotional appeal, psychology and hard cash.

Of course, C&S is not the answer to everything. A framework such as C&S is a complement to, not a substitute for, measures closer to home. On the ground, people will be making behavioral changes (improving home insulation, shopping more locally, etc.) for a variety of reasons. Some of these reasons will be financial, driven by the economic incentives provided by the framework. But technology standards can help here, as can tax regimes (e.g. support for renewables), education, and efforts to envisage and communicate a low-carbon future as a desirable one. It will not be sufficient to put the framework in place and "let people get on with it." But it is the framework that ensures that the numerical target set by the cap is met.

Elaborations

The basic idea of C&S is capable of embracing a number of elaborations quite easily. All these have merits, although each eats into the basic simplicity so should be undertaken with care.

- **Equity:** C&S is based on simple equity between all adults. Now one can argue about whether or not this equity represents justice (Starkey 2008), and arguments can be made for adjustments to simple equity — allocating extra to rural households, partial shares to children, etc. Everyone can claim to be a special case, but equity is the undoubted starting point, just as it would be for food rations in a lifeboat. Recognizing that special-case pleading could go on indefinitely, in practice there will be a compromise between adjustments that target particular groups and the simple guideline of equity. One could argue that the details of the distribution are less important than the fact that the cap is in place: the Cap is more important than the Share. But equity is an important factor in rendering the scheme publicly and hence politically acceptable, thus allowing the introduction of the cap in the first place. It may be better to keep it simple and tackle special needs with explicit, separate arrangements.
- **Scale:** As mentioned above, C&S is scalable, applicable to a nation alone, or on a global scale. But instead we could introduce C&S just for personal direct emissions, or even just in a single sector (for example, an initial introduction for the transport sector only).
- **Hybrids:** As an upstream system, C&S also could adopt a "hybrid" approach (Sorrell 2008) to dovetail with an existing ETS as a transitional measure (Matthews 2008). It is thus flexible enough to accommodate other ideas — within an underlying simple framework.
- **Transitions:** Hybrids are one way of introducing C&S "gently" to allay fears and incorporate learning from other schemes. Other pathways are possible too. For example, a government initially reluctant to impose a cap might introduce a carbon tax levied upstream; but this can easily morph into an upstream permit system with ceiling prices (see below), and then (by raising the ceiling prices) into an upstream cap.
- **Offsets:** Although leakage through spurious offset "projects" should be avoided, offsets might be allowed against sequestration, either capture at the point of combustion or direct sequestration of atmospheric carbon dioxide (by hi-tech scrubbers, or low-tech methods like biochar).
- **Extensions:** C&S is presented here for carbon dioxide, but the same principle applies to other greenhouse gases (which would be hardly feasible for a downstream system). In fact any other common resource such as a fishery could be incorporated: it is easy to maintain a cap

using permits, and distribute the share to the population. This has a deep resonance with emerging "commons thinking."

- **Funds:** Some of the revenue could be kept back to fund collective projects to smoothe the transition to a low-carbon economy. There could also be a fund to help specific countries (or individuals) with adaptation. Some proposals in fact, such as Kyoto-2 (Tickell 2008), commandeer *all* the funds for such purposes. However, hiving off a significant fraction of the revenue undermines the "robustness" incentives, and there is again a strong argument for separate arrangements to tackle these issues. C&S would complement, not replace, parallel efforts to encourage R&D, set technology standards, aid with adaptation and so on.

International/Global

In an ideal world, C&S would operate as a *global* scheme, a single policy for the planet considered as a whole, A global scheme needs a global institution such as a Global Commons Trust, presumably run by the UN, to operate a worldwide system of permits (which in this case would apply to extraction of fossil fuels only, since there are no "imports" from other planets), with the resulting revenue returned to the (world) population. Global schemes thus bypass nations, except perhaps as a vehicle for transmitting the funds to their populations.

An alternative approach is the *international* one, which seeks to add up and link together actions taken by sovereign nations. In this approach a global cap is apportioned using a formula agreed by all; each nation then operates its own scheme (such as national C&S). The apportionment formula is of course a thorny question: the formula might be based on Contraction & Convergence (C&C), promoted by the Global Commons Institute (Meyer 2000) and accepted at various times by various national governments, and under which national shares of a global emissions budget start at the current shares of global emissions and converge over (perhaps a short) time to equal per capita shares. If countries sign up to the general principle of a global cap, it is quite possible that the actual pathway ends up resembling the framework proposed by Frankel (2007), which is an ingenious set of elaborations on C&C performing a tricky balancing act of incentives. Or, as soon as the world recognizes the extent of the emergency, we may be into Greenhouse Development Rights territory (Baer et al 2007) — an approach that also explicitly addresses inequality within nations. The negotiations might get messy, but the rallying cry must be simple.

Global C&S is equivalent to C&S in each nation with national caps calculated on an equal per capita basis, so the eventual destination of many global and international frameworks would be the same. Global C&S is just C&C with immediate convergence, and with "the permits going to the people."

Now, global frameworks would require global institutions (and probably other things like monetary reform). Many authors regard this overruling of national sovereignty as hopelessly unrealistic — although others see climate change as a catalyst for wider reform, perhaps ushering in some form of global democracy (Holden 2002). Global institutions would seem to be an obvious long-term goal, but many would see the problem as simply too urgent and complex: we should not attempt to tackle too many things at once. Advocates of this view would stick with an international system. Of course, even international systems need global elements too: greenhouse gas concentrations are global entities and the cap must be set accordingly. Whatever one feels about this, it seems certain that the current emergency caused by humanity bumping up against the finite limits of the planet will force a reassessment of many of the tacit — but clearly unrealistic — assumptions underlying "conventional" economics, politics and much else.

Which leads us finally to asking, "what is realistic?"

A Choice of Realisms

There is no sign of Cap and Share being introduced by any nation, never mind as a global scheme, any time soon (although Ireland has been considering C&S for the transport sector). Instead, government communication to the public concentrates on individual "small actions": on doing one's bit, with exhortations to switch off standby electrical equipment, use low energy lightbulbs, and calculate personal carbon footprints. There is a nagging tone and a strong implication that "people are the problem." This message fosters guilt, perpetuates ignorance and misconceptions (e.g. that climate change can be halted by recycling), and encourages the perception that climate change is not important (or else the government would be doing something serious about it).

It is easy to read into this a picture of governments scared of facing up to the truth and of telling that truth to the people. But there is some truth in government assertions that the public is as yet unwilling to curb its carbon emissions. Despite a blossoming Transition Towns movement in the UK and elsewhere which seeks to build local resilience ahead of climate change and peak oil, at the moment it appears that the majority of the population want to tackle climate change only if it isn't too much "hassle," and only if it doesn't cost too much money.

So, what can we "realistically" hope for?

In the international arena, proposed international climate architectures (Aldy & Stavins 2007) lie on a rough spectrum from top-down formula-based plans aiming at universal participation by all nations, through to bottom-up arrangements of piecemeal actions taken by nations unilaterally. Let's call proponents of these schemes "Builders" and "Growers" respectively (with no disrespect intended to either group). A Builder wants to plan, and suggests building a tower, while a Grower wants to let things happen, and suggests planting trees. Growers, pointing to game theory, say that building a tower is "unrealistic." Builders, pointing to the urgent need to avert runaway climate change, say that waiting for a tree to grow is "unrealistic." These are clearly different uses of the word "unrealistic."

This Builder-Grower spectrum is correlated with another spectrum concerning transfers of wealth from rich countries to poor. Suggestions for allocation of the global "pie" range from grandfathering (pegged to current emissions, that is, rich countries get more) through equal per capita allocations (everybody gets the same) to proposals "beyond" equal per capita allocations that compensate for the legacy of historic emissions (rich countries get less). Planners' frameworks typically involve transfers of funds, whereas unlinked and unilateral actions (by default based on grandfathering) typically don't. Large transfers are dismissed by some in the developed world as utopian, unrealistic or unacceptable. But there is also hostility from developing countries to proposals that seem to limit their development, especially if these ignore "ecological debt" (Simms 2005, Roberts & Parks 2007).

There is also a correlation with another spectrum concerning strength of caps. Should they be tight, quantity-based targets related to "safe levels" of greenhouse gases; softer price-based targets balancing benefits and costs; or should targets be abandoned altogether in favor of encouraging unilateral "efforts"? A Grower might say that a quantity-based target, or cap, is unrealistic as costs must be taken into account. A Builder might say that any cost-benefit analysis that tries to put a price on a stable climate is unrealistic. Which sort of "unrealistic" do we choose?

Price-based policies often involve "ceiling" prices. To guard against the price of permits rising unacceptably high, governments undertake to issue more permits and sell them at the ceiling price. (The government may also agree to buy permits at a "floor" price, should the demand for permits fall "too much" and undermine green investment). A ceiling price offers to convert a quantity-based policy, based on "safe levels" of greenhouse gases, into a price-based one, balancing benefits and costs, when the going gets tough. Ceiling prices are often described as a "safety valve."

The safety valve metaphor conjures up the image of a steam engine or pressure cooker, where if the pressure builds up excessively it can be released before there is an explosion. By analogy the pent-up demand for permits might put excessive pressure on the permit price. (Even the phrase "ceiling price" has a comforting ring of "limiting the anguish" to it). Governments naturally seek the reassurance of a mechanism existing to release this (political) pressure, and this seems eminently sensible; after all, letting off steam is a benign image. Yet this image contains no hint of any external limits or constraints.

Consider instead the following story. Passengers are queuing at check-in at the airport; they are attending a coin-collecting convention and each wants to bring his coin collection along. Unfortunately there is a weight limit, and the passengers are unhappy about being refused their requests. The check-in supervisor nervously watches anger mounting, and worries that this might explode unless the weight limit is relaxed. Yet now we can clearly see the problem with giving in to this pressure: the plane crashes on takeoff. In hindsight it would have been better to face up to the metaphorical explosion — of anger, of tantrums at not getting one's way — in order to avoid the literal explosion (at the end of the runway).

The analogy with the global climate is clear. Seemingly sophisticated arguments about "stock-pollutants" notwithstanding, it is surely better to come to terms sooner rather than later with what a finite planet means. The view that it is naive to expect governments to agree to any scheme that does not have a ceiling price is offered as "realism." But there is a choice of realisms here.

As debate continues, the problem is increasingly urgent as scientists point to feedbacks and tipping points. To avert catastrophic climate change we will need a mobilization of resources akin to that in wartime, and if this mobilization is to be forthcoming, we need to realize and accept that we are all in the same boat — and a sinking one at that, despite claims from some that "it's not sinking at our end yet." It is in the self-interest of all that the boat does not sink. Yes, it is political realism to recognize that the temptation is to "free-ride" — to leave the effort of doing something about it to someone else — but pointing to this situation and shrugging is a wholly inadequate response. This type of realism is only a starting point. A tougher — and necessary — biophysical realism insists that this situation is addressed robustly.

A global cap may be agreed by policymakers, but should be based on science (for example as recommended by the IPCC); that is, it should be based on what is required to stop runaway climate change, not merely "what is politically feasible" or "the extent of popular or political support." In one sense it is tautological to say that the extent of popular support will set the cap, but the onus must be to change this support to align with scientific necessity. An emergency demands a scale of response commensurate with the gravity of the situation.

It is too easy to regard an acceptance of current political realities as pragmatic, and regard as utopian any insistence that they change. Human nature might be pretty fixed, but "political realities" are more malleable. We need to think through which realism we are choosing. Some types of realism are not an option — at least not an option consistent with survival. As the residents of Easter Island could tell us, scientific realism will trump political realism in the end.

Conclusion

One of our overriding needs is for statesmanship, deploying rhetoric of the caliber of Gandhi, Lincoln, Mandela, Confucius or Churchill, to prepare the world for, and lead it into, swift and far-reaching changes. The messages are not easy, and the rhetoric will need to draw on simplicity and to extend the discussion beyond economics. Governments might engage in cool calculation, but people are inspired by rhetorical appeals to deeply held values and visceral feelings. At the moment, the populations of most countries are largely in psychological denial, "yearning to be free" of the knowledge, deep down, that we are collectively on the wrong road. The abolition of slavery overrode economic arguments by appealing to basic human values. Surely averting climate chaos, and hence ensuring our survival and that of much of the natural world, is an equally inspiring goal?

Any framework such as C&S would be adopted alongside other measures, such as a push on R&D, infrastructure projects and funding for adaptation; research into geo-engineering and sequestration technologies; agreements concerning land use; and so on. We will need them all. But we will also need a dramatic change in global popular opinion — a change of worldview. Adoption of a simple, fair and realistic framework for cutting global carbon emissions — such as Cap and Share — would be inspirational, resonating with this change and with efforts to solve the other problems that face us collectively on our finite planet.

References

1. Joseph E. Aldy and Robert N. Stavins, eds., *Architectures for Agreement* (Cambridge University Press, 2007).
2. P. Baer, T. Athanasiou and S. Kartha, *The Right to Development in a Climate Constrained World: The Greenhouse Development Rights Framework* (Heinrich Boll Foundation, 2007), ecoequity.org.
3. Peter Barnes, *Climate Solutions* (Chelsea Green, 2008), capanddividend.org.
4. Comhar, *A Study in Personal Carbon Allocation: Cap and Share* (Comhar, 2008), comhar.ie.
5. *Cap and Share* (Feasta, 2008), feasta.org; see also capandshare.org.
6. David Fleming, *Energy and the Common Purpose* (The Lean Economy Connection, 2005), teqs.net.
7. Jeffrey Frankel, *Formulas for Quantitative Emission Targets* (Aldy & Stavins, 2007), 31–56.
8. Barry Holden, *Democracy and Global Warming* (Continuum, 2002).
9. Laurence Matthews, *Memorandum Submitted to the Environmental Audit Committee*, in Environmental Audit Committee (2008). *Personal Carbon Trading*. London: The Stationery Office, pp. Ev 99–112 (parliament.uk).
10. Warwick J. McKibbin and Peter J. Wilcoxon, *A Credible Foundation for Long-Term International Cooperation on Climate Change* (Aldy & Stavins, 2007), 1–56.
11. Aubrey Meyer, *Contraction and Convergence* (Green Books, 2000), gci.org.uk.
12. J. Timmons Roberts and Bradley C. Parks, *A Climate of Injustice* (MIT Press, 2007).
13. Andrew Simms, *Ecological Debt* (Pluto Press, 2005).
14. Steve Sorrell, *Memorandum Submitted to the Environmental Audit Committee*, in Environmental Audit Committee (2008). *Personal Carbon Trading*, The Stationery Office, pp. Ev 84–98 (parliament.uk).
15. SDC (2009). *Breakthrough Ideas for the 21st Century*. London: Sustainable Development Commission (sd-commission.org.uk).
16. Richard Starkey, *Allocating Emissions Rights: Are Equal Shares, Fair Shares?* Working Paper 118 (The Tyndall Centre, 2008), tyndall.ac.uk.
17. Oliver Tickell, *Kyoto2* (Zed Books, 2008).
18. Richard Wilkinson and Kate Pickett, *The Spirit Level* (Allen Lane, 2009).

Influencing High-Level Strategic Decision Making Toward a Sustainable Low-Carbon Economy

Julian Darley

Decision-making at a global level is governed by both economic and non-economic factors. If the new systems required to deal with climate change effectively are to be introduced, and a sustainable, low-carbon economy established, more knowledge of the non-economic factors will be required.

The world has changed a lot since 2008. America now has a president who is deeply concerned about climate change, the environment and renewable energy. China is showing much greater awareness of these issues and so are many smaller economies. The world economy is going through an extraordinary phase of contraction which, while both alarming and destructive, is also generating new and unexpected opportunities for change.

Across the world many thinkers are working on economic, social and policy frameworks designed to address carbon emissions, fuel insecurity and a host of environmental problems. These problems of sustainability are being confronted by scholars in an ever greater range of disciplines and analytical streams, from many of the physical sciences through to the social sciences of risk, organisational theory, decision science, behavioral economics, ecological economics, econophysics, game theory, choice theory, management science, leadership research, sociology, anthropology, social psychology, evolutionary psychology, cognitive neuroscience, cultural research and political science. Research approaches include both quantitative and qualitative techniques, scenario building, modeling, systems analysis and, increasingly frequently, combinations of different techniques and disciplines.

On this reading, the world should therefore be well on the way to a sustainable low-carbon economy. In reality, many of the government policies and industrial strategies being discussed and developed, no matter how well backed up by economic, physical and social evidence, remain calls and exhortations rather than action. They are all too rarely turned into government mandates and business plans. There are exceptions to be sure, but these still tend to be isolated, and we won't know for some time whether the economic crisis will stall these efforts.

Increasingly there is a palpable sense of frustration in some corridors of power. We know at least some of the measures we should take, but at every level, from the individual to the institutional, we see that the right action is not taking place, either at the scale or speed that is needed. Often we are still going in the wrong direction, and even when we are not, as the International Energy Agency points out, we must consider non-economic barriers concurrently with more conventional economic factors.[1]

Getting "There" From "Here"

The question that comes through powerfully from these considerations is how do we get "there" from "here"? In other words, what are the obstacles to developing a sustainable, low-carbon economy and what are the conditions that could enable such an economy?

Unless we actively and deliberately discover how to remove the obstacles and create the enabling conditions, we risk a continuation of decades of difficulties that policy researchers and sustainable business strategists have had in seeing good ideas turned into action. Civil society finds similar frustrations. Over a number of years, many people have witnessed the burnout that so often happens when good intentions at the citizen level are carried out largely in isolation from government and business.

Closing the "Sustainability Gap"

It is hard to avoid the conclusion that without high-level action, vital civil society efforts will continue to be stranded. It is arguable that the efficacious, long-term involvement of citizen and consumer may in reality depend, however ironically, on "sustainable" high-level decision-making. There is of course a reciprocity in the sense that high-level decision-making is not sustainable in any sense without the active agreement and participation of civil society.

Even as civil society has tended to have an uneasy relationship with power (be it corporate or political), so business is often not sure of what government is going to do, on the one hand, and on the other, government has tended to reduce its policy levers to market mechanisms, correlating with, though not necessarily caused by, the rise of public choice.

There are now many reasons why the relationship between those primarily engaged in supply-chain decision-making (business) and those primarily engaged in setting the direction of society (government) need to develop a different and more reflexive relationship — one that can begin to close the "sustainability gap."[1] That already complex relationship will also need to engage and keep civil society involved. The rising new tools of social media (particularly instant broadcast platforms such as Twitter) seem set to play a new and fascinating role in future relationships and engagement between the different sectors of society.

Democracy

Even if government, business and civil society do engage with each other in ways that we have not often witnessed yet, there are important questions about the potential to create a sustainable economy within a democracy. Although there are clearly special difficulties for democracies in addressing energy security and climate change, the problematic can be framed in the positive light of the dynamic possibilities of "path creation."

More specifically, on the one hand, in democratic systems, there is bound to be competition at every level, meaning that "pure strategies," such as green blueprints, tend not to fare well. On the other hand, dynamic strategies, which feature continual adjustment and frequent decision-making, are likely to be essential in a sustainable economy and will likely be much easier to foster in a democracy than in other political systems, which tend to discourage citizen innovation and be more centralized.

Innovation will be vital — and challenging — in terms of sustainable decision-making, most likely at every level. There is far more literature on business innovation than either political or civil society innovation — it is possible that the latter could learn from the former. How different kinds of innovation are perceived by high-level decision-makers and wider society will become an important factor in how different groups engage, accept or reject sustainable policies.

Against the hope of dynamic strategies there will be opposition from actors who prefer the status quo and there will be manifestations of path dependency and "lock-in." Since surely we all have an interest in discovering what can influence decision-making toward sustainability (not just what is blocking it), it will be important to investigate attitudes to and possibilities of path creation, which is an emerging positive response to policy-technology "lock-in."[9]

This leads to another key question: what influences or can influence high-level decision-makers towards a sustainable, low-carbon economy? This question focuses attention on key decision-makers in the economy, such as those running fossil-fuel and renewable-energy companies, and politicians in departments dealing with energy and climate.

The Feed-In Tariff Lens

To say anything usefully specific about the question of influence, however, one must the narrow the scope. For this essay, consideration will be given to national experiences with the Feed-in Tariff (FIT). FIT is a "policy mechanism designed to encourage the adoption of renewable energy sources and to help accelerate the move toward grid parity."[13] Generally, looking at FIT adoption allows some exploration of certain vital parameters (in particular risk) and the drawing of some larger conclusions about society, sustainability and decision-making. Here, and in brief, using the FIT lens, I shall focus on some interesting factors in decision-making and make some tentative observations based on or drawn from existing literature.

Proponents of FIT claim that it has been dramatically successful, and many nations that have adopted it have higher penetrations of solar renewable energy generation than those that haven't.[10] However, this is not the issue of most help in understanding and developing decision-making for sustainability; the real question is: why is a new and important policy, such as FIT, so much easier to introduce in some nations than in others?

Furthermore, using FIT as a case study can offer the possibility of including, in greater or lesser detail, some of the most intractable decisions now before us, including how we can shift from an economy dominated by an oil-based transport system to a renewable electricity-based system.

FIT also encourages the study of the cultural dimensions that may be some of the most significant non-economic factors influencing high-level decision-making. For instance, Hofstede[5] alludes to the possibility that nations with a high MAS (Masculinity) Index combined with high levels of individuality find collective decisions for the common good very challenging. This may be in part because liberal economics is built on privileging means over ends. Certainly, in most of the anglophone world, despite early beginnings in California, FIT has not (yet) been adopted and implemented. This may be changing; for instance, the Department of Energy and Climate Change in the UK announced in October 2008 that it will bring in FIT. However, it will remain the case that nations like Germany are far in advance of Britain and the USA in developing a renewable-energy industry, and understanding why this is so could shed light on better decision-making in future.

Path Dependency

I mentioned path dependency. This can be split into physical and policy path dependencies. An example of a physical path dependency is that of the conventional power industry, which has built an enormous physical infrastructure, including the transmission grid with its associated control systems and power generation units, which until the advent of wind power have usually been very large centralized objects. FIT is an example of a policy path dependency, though one imagines it could *in extremis* be revoked (if there were a war or some other cataclysm). Nevertheless, for practical purposes a 20-year legally binding FIT is an example of a path that cannot easily be changed and is going to enable or disable many other major decisions. There are many other vital but occluded factors in current decision-making, including historical, business and geographical factors, which may also create path dependence.

Path dependence can shed light on complex interlocking mechanisms. Two quite different examples are Prohibition in the US and the advent of collateralized mortgage obligations. Both developments have had extraordinary unintended consequences, from the growth of the Mafia to the recent financial crisis. Though not as dramatic, the development of a certain type and layout of power grid can of course have short- to medium-term benefits, but in the long run, if the grid is not flexible, as conditions change, a nation may be left with problems not dissimilar in scale to the two rather unfortunate examples just mentioned.

FIT is also an example of the kind of long-range policy making that is surely to be considered vital in combating climate change.[3] Thinking long term is also clearly indispensable for national and international energy policy, and FIT may be an example of how energy policy, as opposed to climate change policy, could be an easier pathway to the twin goals of energy security and carbon reduction.

FIT is not only a significant long-term policy with energy and climate implications, but it may also shed light on other long-term strategic policy-business problematics with international dimensions, such as cultural dimensions. Germany, for instance, has some measurable cultural similarities with the US and UK, but also some major differences, along with major differences in terms of their economic systems.

Cultural dimensions are important for any long-term policy designed to combat climate change and enhance energy security. FIT is therefore a good example to examine, since it requires government to create the long-term conditions that then allow business to create the supply chain in reality. But government can create these conditions only if the public participates and accepts higher power charges, and by implication is willing to balance long-term benefit against short-term cost. Any future study on this issue would also have to consider FIT in different economies and cultures, as this offers the possibility of examining different long-term reflexive government-business relationships, with the public's attitude measurable both at the ballot box and by survey. We already know that some nations are much more willing to think long term than others; the question that needs to be answered in detail for different nations is why and what, if anything, can be done about it. This is one of the key questions for future research.

Risk

FIT does not present an issue of dramatic, sudden or catastrophic risk, the kind that, in some ways, humans find easier to comprehend. It is not the sort of policy that is likely to elicit great fear even though it may be disliked by some with certain economic or other beliefs. FIT may be compared with nuclear power, which certainly evokes strong emotions and offers a much larger risk profile. Nuclear power is slated to undergo a major renaissance. It would be interesting indeed to explore a scenario in which nearby residents were offered a nuclear power station versus a wind farm. With nuclear power now very much part of the debate on climate change and energy security, such a comparison is no longer of merely academic interest.

Conclusions

Although specific research on how to create the conditions for and actually influence high-level, strategic decision-making for a low-carbon economy remains to be undertaken, some provocative conclusions can be drawn now in addition to the suggestions already made.

The key contention here is that there may be some non-economic factors which are more important than economic factors in strategic decision-making. If so, far more attention should be paid to non-economic factors than appears to be the case at the moment. A summary of these factors follows.

Path dependency and lock-in often severely constrain what a government or business can do to make major or sudden change in policy or product. It is true that Roosevelt famously switched the US auto industry from cars to planes and tanks practically overnight, but that was in the face of the type of threat that *Homo sapiens* knows how to deal with — an external attack. Whether President Obama will be able to do something similar — for instance turning Detroit into a hub of wind turbine manufacture and electric car production — remains to be seen and, given the difficulties he faces, looks unlikely. If major change is to become feasible or acceptable to decision-makers and/or the public, either climate change or energy security will have to seem far greater threats than they do now.

There are a number of often interlocking cultural factors that make long-term decision-making for a distant benefit difficult, such as, societies that

  i) favor the individual over the collective;
 ii) attenuate the idea of the common good;
iii) stress means over ends, in effect being unwilling to discuss the good whether it be common or personal;
 iv) stress competition as a very high virtue;
  v) promote aggression as an acceptable way to solve problems and an aggressive attitude as a preferred modus operandi.

Attitudes to risk, innovation, entrepreneurialism, fairness, justice and economic polarization also have a vital effect in enabling or disabling strategic and long-term decision-making. The level of democratic participation and engagement may play a significant role in many ways, including in the ability of policymakers to deploy policies known to be effective but only if the public is engaged at a very granular level, such as by direct personal contact with someone representing a government agency operating a particular policy.

Increasingly, it appears that much will depend on human psychology, at the individual, group and societal levels. Nowhere is this more true, perhaps, than in the matter of leadership, which is closely related to decision making. New work on leadership, informed by recent advances in the understanding of how evolution has shaped human and primate psychology, may offer powerful tools in comprehending why good decision-making is so hard to do and so hard to enact.[12] It is emerging that there are core contradictions between the kinds of leadership that we have evolved to accept (and are able to offer) and the conditions of work and decision-making we have created in late industrial society.

We evolved in quite flat, small societies where leadership was often distributed according to performance: the best hunter led hunting, an elder would administer justice and peacemaking, and so on. There should be no illusion that this was utopia; conflicts, often leading to homicide, abounded. It is only to say that we found evolutionary advantage with a very different kind of leadership from the kinds we are now usually faced with. There are several further factors compounding our difficulties with modern leadership — and by implication decision-making — including, ironically, that leadership by prestige (akin to leadership by performance), which can be a more acceptable leadership mode, may find itself in competition with and overwhelmed by leadership by dominance, or aggression, to put it more crudely.

These leadership contradictions appear to be so legion that it is not clear that it will be possible to implement many strategic decisions for sustainability without understanding these factors and putting in place some measures to ameliorate the more difficult conditions. The same can be said for the kinds of cultural factors mentioned here. They too could doom efforts to create a sustainable economy, though it is possible that cultural factors may be more malleable, at least in theory, than evolutionary factors, such as our propensity for certain kinds of leadership and our concomitant willingness to follow or not.

It may seem daunting that not only do we face the prospect that much of the low-carbon, physical infrastructure of the 21st century will need to be different from that of the high-carbon 20th century, but also that we will need to make major societal and cultural adjustments. Approached in the right way, however, these challenges could become opportunities to develop conditions to which human beings are better adapted and in which they might actually flourish and be happier. Right now, this may not seem the most likely path, and clearly some pathways are locked in, at least for the moment. But there are new pathways opening up, and sometimes the demise or contraction of a system (such as the conventional car industry) can allow something much better to be developed to replace it. Armed with careful research and appropriately prepared, we could influence decision-making in meaningful ways that effect meaningful change. That is something devoutly to be desired and clearly possible — if not yet obviously probable.

Endnotes

1. Paolo Frankl, *Deploying Renewables: Lessons Learnt from IEA RE Policy Analysis,* IEA REMAP Conference (16 December 2008).
2. Paul Ekins, *Economic Growth and Environmental Sustainability: The Prospects for Green Growth,* (Routledge, 2000).
3. Paul Ekins et al., "A Framework for the Practical Application of the Concepts of Critical Natural Capital and Strong Sustainability," *Ecological Economics* 44, no. 2-3 (March 2003).
4. Anthony Giddens, *The Politics of Climate Change* (Polity, 2009).
5. Shaun Hargreaves Heap et al., *The Theory of Choice: A Critical Guide* (Blackwell, 1992).
6. Geert Hofstede, *Culture's Consequences: Comparing Values, Behaviors, Institutions and Organizations Across Nations* (Sage, 2001).
7. Tim Jackson, *Motivating Sustainable Consumption: A Review of the Evidence on Consumer Behaviour and Behavioural Change,* Policy Studies Institute (2005).
8. Tim Jackson, *Prosperity Without Growth,* Sustainable Development Commission 2009).
9. Martin Stack and Myles P. Gartland, "Path Creation, Path Dependency, and Alternative Theories of the Firm," *Journal of Economic Issues* vol. XXXVII, no. 2 (June 2003).
10. Miguel Mendonca, *Feed-in Tariffs: Accelerating the Deployment of Renewable Energy* (Earthscan, 2007).
11. Nicholas Stern, *The Economics of Climate Change,* American Economic Review: Papers & Proceedings (2008).
12. Mark Van Vugt, Robert Hogan and Robert Kaiser, "Leadership, Followership, and Evolution: Some Lessons From the Past," *American Psychologist* (April 2008).
13. Grid parity, is "the point at which alternative means of generating electricity is equal in cost, or cheaper than grid power." — Wikipedia: en.wikipedia.org/wiki/Feed_in _tariff (accessed 2 September, 2010).

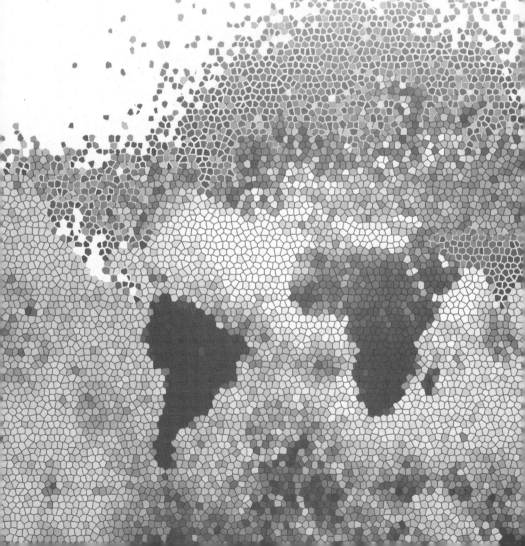

PART V

CHANGING THE WAY
WE LIVE

Danger Ahead:
Prioritizing Risk Avoidance in Political and Economic Decision-Making

BRIAN DAVEY

Now that the financial and political components of the present system have discredited themselves, a fluid situation exists that might allow more viable options to emerge. Local green initiatives, in particular the Transition Towns movement, are gaining in strength and number(s), but do they have the potential to develop the capacity needed at a national level to transform societies' energy and transport infrastructures?

In a commentary on the Great Depression of the 1930s, the German economic historian Werner Abelshauser noted that the scale of the crisis in its early stages was often underestimated. While still in office, President Hoover saw the worst as being over, and when he came to power in 1933, Roosevelt thought the same. According to Abelshauser, the main actors in the drama lacked what he called "Catastrophe Consciousness." They simply could not comprehend the scale of what was happening.

In this paper, I argue that the same now holds true for elite thinking and preparedness across a range of issues that were predicted in the 1970s by the group that wrote the Club of Rome Report, the "Limits to Growth." At the time, this report received a lot of attention but it was widely rubbished by mainstream economists, who helped create a conventional wisdom that the "Limits to Growth" theorists "had been proved wrong."

Unsustainable Growth, "Overshoot" and Collapse

The subsequent period was marked by the rise of Thatcher, Reagan and market fundamentalism and by the collapse of the communist bloc. A long period of expansion occurred from which most people in the world either did not gain or emerged worse off. The cheap energy powering modern transport and communications enabled globalized capital to move easily to where it wanted — to take advantage of the cheapest pay, most favorable tax opportunities and lowest environmental standards. It is therefore not surprising that while the index of market-based transactions (GDP) soared, the other, less-publicized well-being measures — like the Genuine Progress Indicator or the Index of Sustainable Economic Welfare — stagnated or declined. While the media was full of adverts for the latest energy-guzzling toys and stories showing the luxurious lifestyles of the celebrities, most people could only have a taste of this lifestyle if they ran down their savings or got deeper into debt on a gamble that the equity on their home would continue to rise. The consumer toys they then purchased were bought "on the cheap" because the environmental filth generated in production is offloaded onto people living in or near the new industrial zones in India, China and elsewhere.

In short, this kind of development was highly unbalanced, characterised by the running down of financial savings and natural capital, followed by the piling up of financial debts — and ecological debts too. As the system became grotesquely unequal it became correspondingly unbalanced. The money, and hence the purchasing power, accumulated to the benefit of a few. They then lent it back into circulation, which maintained aggregate demand. After a point however, those who borrowed the money were too poor to service their debts. And when energy prices rose, this finished them off. The financial debt crisis has been very painful for millions of people but they will mostly survive it; what is not clear is whether humanity will survive the crisis of ecological debt.

The "Limits to Growth" theorists had a phrase to describe all of this: "overshoot." They didn't deny that growth could occur for a time at high rates, but they argued that it couldn't last because humanity cannot permanently run down natural capital and degrade sinks — the air, seas and lands that absorb the wastes of economic activity.

Oil and gas depletion is a rundown in natural capital because natural gas and oil are non-renewable. Using them can only be described as sustainable if a proportion is set aside to build up a renewables-based infrastructure that will deliver not only an equal or greater amount of replacement energy over its lifetime, but also the energy needed to replace the renewables infrastructure itself. To date, nothing of the kind has happened.

Wherever one looks in the world, fossil water supplies have not been used sustainably. Soils are being eroded and not restored at anything near the rate required. Perhaps most seriously of all, the use of the atmosphere as a greenhouse gas dump far exceeds safe levels. In a now well-known article, scientist James Hansen and colleagues calculate that a safe level of CO_2 in the atmosphere is probably far below 350, possibly as low as 300–325 ppm. Yet the atmospheric concentration is already 387 ppm and rising.

Humanity is thus taking from future generations to feed its consumption now or, rather, a very tiny minority is doing so. And this tiny minority — the political and economic elite — is steering planet Earth toward a catastrophe far greater than the credit crunch. They are steering us directly toward an ecosystem crunch.

Seeing the Trends Together: Nature Does Not Do *ceteris paribus*

The true magnitude of this crisis can only be ascertained by viewing all the different problems together. Typically, the various threats and problems are examined by specialist media correspondents and editors, specialists in academia and specialist departments in government and local government. These experts are all working within certain conceptual and administrative conventions that parse reality into bite-size chunks that journalists, researchers, officials and policy makers can cope with. The specialization seems to help them get a better grasp of the issues.

In a generalized system crisis, the opposite is the case: the compartmentalization that specialization brings with it precludes a clear overview, one that would tell us that things are far more dangerous and the dangers likely more imminent than we thought. Thus specialists can tell us that a 1 degree Celsius rise in global temperatures will probably lead to a fall in global crop yields of 10%. But to calculate figures like these, specialists have to make assumptions about the context in which 1 degree C rise will happen. The normal assumption is *ceteris paribus*: all other things being equal or staying the same. However, in a general system crisis, most relevant "other things" are NOT staying the same. They are changing, and very often in an unfavorable way, because one problem exacerbates the others in a chain reaction that becomes a cascade of knock-on effects. Thus, for example, plants grown in warmer temperatures than they are acclimatized to will need adequate water to suit those altered conditions, and if there is a depleted level of fossil water to draw upon, then crop yields may fall a lot more.

The Food Crisis

If runaway climate change or the Energy Winters predicted by peak-oil theorists are not gloomy enough for you — if you really want to be frightened — then just consider together some of the well-established trends in global food production:

1. Climate change, leading to a rise in surface temperatures and a decline in crop yields.
2. Declining regional water availabilities. Falling water tables in countries populated by half the world's peoples. According to figures quoted by Lester R. Brown, 175 million Indians consume grain produced with water from irrigation wells that will soon be exhausted.
3. Soil degradation and erosion, bringing increasing desertification. Top soil is eroding faster than new soil formation on perhaps one-third of the world's cropland.
4. Increased urbanization and non-farming activities out-compete food production for land and water use.
5. Fossil-fuel depletion impacting on fertilizer/pesticide availability and costs, reducing access to the inputs that have increased yields over the last few decades.
6. Decline of biodiversity of food crops, bringing vulnerability to disease just as pesticide costs rise.
7. Crops used to feed animals rather than humans as affluent meat-based diets become more common.
8. Biofuels; grains and crops used to feed cars rather than humans.
9. Depletion of global phosphorous inputs. There's no research on peak phosphorous but according to the European Fertilizer Association, phosphorous may begin to run out in the second half of the century. And without phosphorous, crop yields will fall by 20–50%.
10. Global diseases of bee pollinators. British bee populations slumped 30% in the winter of 2007/8, the result either of pesticides, disease, mites and/or milder winters that encourage them to forage too soon (*The Independent*).

11. Rising world population, increasing at 1.14% per annum or an extra 75 million per year (Wikipedia). The cultivated area per person fell from 0.6 hectares per person in 1950 to 0.25 hectares in 2000 (*Limits to Growth 30 Year Update*, p. 62).

12. Overfishing, marine pollution and decline of world fish stocks. A 2003 study by a Canadian-German research team published in *Nature* concluded that 90 percent of the large fish in the oceans had disappeared over the last 50 years.

13. The bulk of global grain market in the hands of just three companies. Development of "terminator" seeds to concentrate all seed sales in the hands of a corporate elite.

Failed States

In a May 2009 article "Could food shortages bring down civilization?" in *Scientific American*, Lester R. Brown argues that some of these trends are creating the context for conflict, the breakdown of political administrations and the emergence of "failed states." Of course, the disintegration caused by resource wars is one other reason for failed states. As oil, natural gas, water, agricultural land and mineral resources become scarcer, so land grabs or destabilizing maneuvers are made to secure privileged access to them; this often underpins conflicts that, at least on the surface, are about ideology or religion.

The growing number of conflicts then has its own self-feeding dynamic. Increasingly "the market" reacts by growing a security, prisons and armaments sector with a vested interest in further sales, while mass psychology becomes more paranoid and sociopathic. Frightened, hostile groups find it more difficult to cooperate to find positive responses to the situations they find themselves in. Meanwhile, quite apart from the misery of living in them, failed states become sources of refugees, disease, piracy and drugs and, arguably as a consequence, breeding grounds for psychopaths.

Disease, Ill Health and a Global Public Health Crisis

The risks of disease and ill health are crucial. Once again, if we put the trends together the picture is far more alarming than if we look at each issue in isolation:

1. Climate change, bringing extreme temperature and natural catastrophes, and shifting boundaries for insects and pests like mosquitoes.

2. Weakened immune systems due to malnutrition, stress and water, air and soil pollution.
3. Water shortages, creating problems of basic hygiene and health.
4. A combination of resource wars, corruption and collapse of political administrations, leading to weak or non-existent public-health infra-structures and large populations forced into migration.
5. Extreme concentration of animal factory farming, creating ideal conditions for mutations of pathogens.
6. Urbanization and globalization. Rapid travel between densely popu-lated centers creates optimal conditions for rapid transmission of diseases.

Naturally, there are trends working in the other direction. Most systems have feedback effects, including negative feedbacks that act as stabilizers. Thus, when animal diseases like swine flu sweep around the world, some people stop eating meat either temporarily or for good. That the world is in an economic recession has led to a dramatic decline in air travel, which has probably slowed the spread of swine flu.

Scaremongering Versus the Reasons to be Cheerful

The threats, then, seem both real and in some cases imminent. But to pres-ent the picture wholly from the negative side is to be accused of "scare mon-gering" by those techno-optimists and politicians who are confident that while problems exist, they are still manageable. Such people argue that it is alarmist to emphasize negative trends and worst-case scenarios without also highlighting options for responding to those threats. With regard to food, water and soils there are indeed many options for organic production and ecological agriculture. Possibilities exist to improve soils, manage wa-ter resources better, enhance and extend biodiversity, integrate alternative forms of aquaculture and fish production, and disperse the concentrations of animals that have become "disease factories" and, because much of their food is made from it, act as a pressure on the price of grain. There are also ways to improve energy efficiency and to promote renewables and policies like Cap and Share that could lock in the carbon gains made.

The real problem is not a lack of potential responses to the truly colossal threats we face. What is genuinely alarming is that the political-economic establishment has a built-in inertia that stops it responding quickly, effectively and adequately to these threats as they present themselves. And while it is true that it has responded relatively quickly, and certainly on a huge scale, to the banking crisis, this is only because making money is the primary purpose of the economic system. Crucially, even though the threats it poses are far graver, as outlined above, the response to the ecological crisis has been totally different. The vast vested interests and financial clout of the corporate elite are based on a fossil fuel — and carbon-powered status quo that wants to see "business as usual" continue in perpetuity. All of which means that the money men drag their feet when it comes to addressing the ecological crisis.

Take this May 2009 quote[1] from *The Guardian*, for example

> America's oil, gas and coal industry has increased its lobbying budget by 50%, with key players spending $44.5m in the first three months of this year in an intense effort to cut off support for Barack Obama's plan to build a clean energy economy.
>
> The spoiler campaign runs to hundreds of millions of dollars and involves industry front groups, lobbying firms, television, print and radio advertising, and donations to pivotal members of Congress. Its intention is to water down or kill off plans by the Democratic leadership to pass "cap and trade" legislation this year, which would place limits on greenhouse gas emissions.

The essence of the problem can be expressed in economic terms: those with access to fossil fuel-based technologies are currently far more productive and therefore have a competitive advantage that allows them to undercut their competitors and make the most money. The wealth thus gained also allows them to undermine their political rivals where it really counts — well-connectedness. It enables direct access to those in positions of political authority so they can influence political agendas. Resources are also made available for campaigns to set agendas within the mass media, and in this way to mould public perceptions and public opinion.

Power Arrogance and Hubris

There is nothing new in the phenomena of power arrogance and hubris. Since the earliest civilizations, rulers have made decisions and overreached their power in the confident belief that they had God on their side. In more modern times our rulers have believed that nature rewards the fittest, in other words, them.

Irrespective of what point in history they emerge, the starting point of most elites is the comfortable assumption that, as things have typically gone right for them in the past, they will continue to go right in the future. This belief is compounded by the fact that for a long time it has been the "little people" who bear the costs while those higher up the food chain reap the benefits. Power means that they are effectively cocooned from the negative kickback from their actions. Long before the rulers themselves are successfully challenged and fall — and this typically happens only in the final stages — millions of others have already lost out badly and immense damage has been done.

What we term hubris is the cruel arrogance that arises from a failure of bottom-up feedback in systems where vast social and geographical distances exist between the powerful and the powerless. The punishment of Nemesis, the Greek goddess who was supposed to re-impose limits on those who overstepped their power, typically befalls entire societies before it befalls the rulers. Today the vast distance that separates the global elite from ordinary people is magnified further by the high-power technologies of communications, transport, production and weaponry. Nemesis, when she comes, will be global.

Power Relationships in the Transition

What to do? Marxist acquaintances of mine would probably suggest armed revolution but that would be futile. It would only enhance and exacerbate the current trends toward greater surveillance, paranoia, police powers and militarization, a war that the powers-that-be would win before we're all dragged into the vortex of the ecological crisis.

The situation demands that we rethink what political and economic power involves. Because there are a host of things that can and must be done to re-organize society at the level of the household and local community, there's no need for people of goodwill to wait for politicians to set an example. The Transition Towns movement has shown that immense potential exists for people to organize to do what they can now to get their homes, gardens, local transport arrangements and communities in order for the coming crisis. Increasingly, local politicians are taking their point of departure from the Transition Initiatives. This shows that power comes not solely, or even mainly, from positions of formal political authority; it comes with having the kind of initiative to which others respond and which acts through the power of personal influence and example.

The exercise of power in human society occurs by means of various initiatives. And these initiatives don't always need to be big. Many of the biggest and most powerful institutions originally started very small.

As individuals and groups we have both needs and problems. To meet the needs and solve the problems, we structure our activities in purposeful ways. And a purpose pursued over time, through an arranged sequence of activities, is an initiative. When we pursue this purpose with other people, we set up organizations and institutions to help us. We agree to (or in an authoritarian system impose!) to shared purposes, develop the skills for attaining them, and then assemble and apply the energy, material and financial resources required.

It is a challenging job to get new organizations off the ground around new purposes, bringing together people who may not know each other, developing and applying new skills, and accumulating the other resources for the job — and all from scratch, too. This process is commonly called "capacity building" and it requires all-round leadership.

Capacity building is a process of empowerment in the sense that the group has a growing capacity to achieve its aims. As groups grow they develop a capacity for planning and designing their activities over time, implementing their decisions and then monitoring and reviewing their results. The more a group can achieve, the more resources it will tend to attract and the more it will get noticed in the political process, irrespective of whether any group member occupies a formal position of political power.

Now that we have exceeded the limits to growth, the new conditions of resource scarcity require many initiatives to meet individual and community needs in different ways, closer to home, with less energy and materials. Transition Initiatives highlight a major area for change, one in which most ordinary people can and must participate: the acquisition of new skills, networking, organizing initiatives and developing projects. As this process evolves, it's inevitable that participants will recognize that the state and politics must also change to complement, rather than undermine, what they're trying to achieve.

It's obvious to many that to deal effectively with climate change or environmental chaos, energy is best spent seeking to influence or replace those in power, i.e. people in senior positions in politics and business. Politicians typically pass the buck, however, claiming that citizens should change, that they can't do much until we are ready. This, however, is nothing but an excuse for not getting down to the issues at hand. The truth is that some things we can do on our own, some with state support and some mainly (or only) at state level. If the state is unwilling to act, we can still get on with things locally and join with others nationally and internationally. And when we do, we build the organizational power and the moral authority to eventually transform the state.

Proximal and Distal Power

Personal circumstances determine the purposes that people pursue. Most ordinary people have, at best, *proximal power* — the ability to influence that which is immediate in their lives, e.g. what they buy, who they spend time with and so on. But this kind of proximal influence can be considerably extended by networking together in Transition Initiatives and skilling up on a different model. In the end, more ambitious goals for transformation means influencing and changing the structures of *distal power*.

Distal power transcends proximal power.[2] It is the world in which high politics, high finance and business operates, often behind the scenes, informally in clubs, in social networks of the well connected, in official offices of state. Distal power is the ability to determine the contexts in which others operate. In terms of political power, this means the ability to influence things like interest rates, public expenditure priorities, program priorities for grant-aid funding, legal frameworks, minimum standards regulations for health and safety, buildings etc.

The Danger of Co-Option: Sticking to Transitional Purposes

I do not wish to deny the usefulness of intervening in the political arena, nor of trying to influence policy. On the contrary, movements like the Transition Initiatives will hopefully become more able to work the system, i.e. find their way around and use the structures of distal power to develop more resilient communities. At the same time, it is to be hoped that engagement with the system does not lead to compromise. Where movements or individuals engage prematurely with more powerful networks, they tend to get co-opted, lose their own agenda and adopt the agenda of the more powerful players. The danger in our case is that that "involvement" would be manipulated to legitimize "greenwashing" and resource-wasting growth. It is important that we stick to our own purposes.

With the vital caveat about the dangers of co-option in mind, we can nevertheless envisage a process where groups like the Transition Initiatives secure changes in the structures of distal power so that they are more amenable to their different purposes. Specifically, it would involve state structures prioritizing resilience as the number one item on the public agenda. Resilience would be seen by all as being not only different from a growth agenda, but incompatible with it. Priorities like public health, social cohesion (a priority for vulnerable people who will otherwise become a source of public-health risk), the conservation and maintenance of sustainable energy supplies, would shift to a position where they have the power to trump the provision of more inessential consumer goods.

We will know we have made it in the UK when we rewrite the mission statement of the UK Treasury, which currently says that its "aim is to raise the rate of sustainable growth, and achieve rising prosperity and a better quality of life with economic and employment opportunities for all." Its aim ought to be "to secure economic resilience to protect and ensure that the basic needs of all can be met fairly through assisting transformation of the economy in the face of natural capital depletion and environmental limits."

With this kind of state it would be possible to develop a collaborative working relationship between communities, officials and a community economy sector. This last sector would establish ethical living as its goal. It would help communities provide for their basic needs while adjusting to, and coping with, difficult times. The community economic agenda would prioritize fairness and equity to help maintain social cohesion. And as resources become scarcer, social and community enterprise would stand a better chance of surviving conflicts arising from distribution.

Unless and until we can change the state to support these kinds of processes, it will be necessary to grow our abilities to develop purposes in ways that are largely independent of the structures of distal power. This means the development of confidence, skills and resources that do not rely on anything bestowed by the structures of social authority; we will need to development the ability to use our own unutilized energies for the organization and management of "powerdown" processes.

Contradictions Between Different Parts of the State and Public Sector

Firstly, confronted by the limits to growth, current political-economic establishments are having great difficulty acknowledging that citizens will have to change their lifestyles. On the one hand, there is no desire to sponsor a movement in which people might—horror of horrors—lose interest in shopping. After all, what is growth without consumption?

On the other hand, some politicians recognize that many people are having great difficulty holding onto their "lifestyle packages" and these politicians don't want to give the impression that they're going to make life even more difficult for these people. Each of us holds in balance a habitat and consumption throughput that must match an income and credit capacity related to our work and sources of income, and which sustains our dependencies and emotional relationships in ways appropriate to our age, health and aspirations. In a time of generalized crisis, people are subjected to agonizing decisions because the choices are no longer about which brands to pick on supermarket shelves, but about how to hold the entire lifestyle together without losing one's home, seeing one's relationships break up or being unable to cope in a job whose security is in any case precarious. It is therefore no surprise that establishment-based "green" thinktanks and consultants base policy frameworks on the assumption that the public would not be obliged to substantially change their lifestyles. It is simply too unpalatable a message.

As a result, mainstream politics largely cedes the very space where much of the real work of change is needed: the creation of a movement focused on post-consumerist, low-energy lifestyles. I write "largely" because health-promotion agencies and sustainability officials will typically lend their support to projects that promote allotments, community gardens, local food, warmer homes and the like. But such schemes are far from the mainstream and have tiny budgets. And in terms of political traction, they can be a bit toothless.

The politics of the future is therefore one in which these fringe groups, aided and abetted by officials and practitioners working to an increasingly important public-health agenda, are likely to move increasingly into the mainstream, while "economic development"—the industrial and financial activities of the state and the networks in which they operate—come to be seen as largely irrelevant, are discredited or are (rightly) perceived as operating in a way that is eco-socially toxic.

Government Decisions that Affect the Ways the Public Changes

While the state will increasingly recognize that it must urge the public to take action to reduce carbon emissions and unnecessary waste, the reverse of this also holds true: that the public will be more sensitive to whether, and in what ways, major government decisions either enhance or undermine what they are being urged to do. People are increasingly aware that unless society as a whole, and unless nations as a whole, take action on climate change, what they do as individuals and communities is futile.

This is a crucial part of the argument for policies like Cap and Share because it cuts through the backsliding and evasion that currently passes for climate policy. If fossil fuels create climate change they should be banned from sale unless with a permit. Period. The limited permission to sell fossil fuels now is temporary. It arises only because we cannot wean ourselves off our addiction to fossil fuels overnight. The number of permits, denominated in greenhouse gas quantities, has to be reduced as quickly as possible down to zero. A policy like this must also be administered in an equitable manner. In contrast to the European Emissions Trading System, which gives away permits, the fossil-fuel suppliers should have to buy in a Cap and Share system. The bulk of the revenue from these sales should go back to the people, shared out on a per-capita basis. The people need these revenues to invest in establishing their houses and communities as the top priority.

If people are to be encouraged to take action at the proximal level and this action is not to be undermined by actions at the distal level, the frameworks themselves must be changed in a complementary way. Cap and Share is one part of ensuring this happens. But it's not enough on its own. Consistent industrial, transport and agricultural policies are also needed.

Shaping Strategic Infrastructure Decisions

Over and above the reorganization of local space (homes, gardens and neighborhoods), some very large-scale bits of engineering are needed to create the broad-scale renewable-energy and transport systems of the future. The techno systems are so large that national-level strategic political decisions have to be made, with major implications for resource allocation. At this point in time the carbon lobby is far too dominant and well entrenched for government to get behind even the most modest non-carbon energy and transport. It will take time to grow a citizens' movement with the economic clout, momentum and networked resources needed to change this situation, though the pressure for this change will certainly build.

People who take the climate crisis seriously and start to act in their private lives and community are obviously going to be outraged when government takes the sorts of decisions that they have recently in the UK by agreeing to a third runway at Heathrow. In the age of the internet, people can see now only too clearly what is going on when big government and carbon interests cut deals to develop coal power based on the slender hope that Carbon Capture and Storage will work sufficiently and on time. We are therefore likely to see a growing polarization against big government and big carbon business alliances that currently have a stranglehold on national energy and transport policy.

The scope for change for millions of people is not simply a matter of individual wishes and willpower. The term "lock in" is often used to describe how our economies and societies operate with a technical infrastructure that is replaced only very slowly and at considerable investment cost. While individuals and communities can start to change their lifestyles at the local level to a considerable extent, further change will hinge on decisions taken about engineered infrastructures by the organizations that decide on them. At some point a full follow-through in ecological transformation will be dependent on huge collective planning and investment decisions about the technical infrastructure of society — the fabric of buildings, the transport systems and the power station architecture.

I use the word "systems" here deliberately because there is a danger of thinking in terms of individual technologies and not seeing that we are actually talking about larger techno-social systems with cross-economy complementarities. Central to the energy system, for example, is the problem of how to deal with intermittency if renewables are to be used to their maximum capacity. There are clearly ways to deal with this — through matching electricity demand to the supply when it's available (when the wind blows, batteries for electric cars are charged up) as well as through the development of electrical storage capacity. However, the decisions that need to be taken here are big strategic decisions involving industrial, energy and transport policy.

Furthermore, large-scale engineering and building programs can develop only at a certain pace, and, while it can perhaps be speeded up if we all accept that an emergency exists or is imminent, limits are still set by the time needed to plan, clarify technological, legal and administrative issues, raise finance, train people and get them together in functioning and effective teams. These time issues cannot be wished away.

Capacity Building for "Powering Up"

The Transition movement has a good chance, over several years, of making an impact on the "Power Down" agenda, but for a "Power Up" agenda to be realized, well-thought-out, strategic decisions must be made in the fields of energy, industry, agriculture and transport. Ideally, taken together these decisions would comprise a consistent plan. But getting such a plan worked up and implemented is not merely a matter of political will; we also need organization, resources, logistics and skills. The politics cannot move faster than the buildup of the eco-economic capacity.

Free-market fundamentalists might well say that the state is likely to do a thoroughly bad job if it has too much influence over big infrastructure decisions. They might thoroughly dislike my implied *dirigiste* argumentation. They might be right. However, rather than states backing the wrong systems, I fear we're more likely to see a failure of states to back any coherent large-scale system plans *at all*.

Given the short-term nature of the parliamentary system and the huge scale on which we now have to re-cast the entire energy, transport, agricultural and industrial systems, given the competing vested interests with their rival approaches, given the credit crunch, given peak oil and its capacity to bring the economy to its knees, given the enormous complexity of all these things, I believe that politicians and the state are simply incapable of making strategic decisions on the scale necessary. What we will get instead is a lot of floundering and procrastination disguised with rhetoric. Indeed, although there has been a lot of rhetoric about Green New Deals, there has been almost no spending on climate or environmental agendas.

This situation echoes the ideas of Joseph Tainter: that societies collapse not because of stress surges per se, but because, when stress surges occur, circumstances have become so complex that the authorities are overwhelmed by all the complications to the point of being unable to provide a response and see it through. This dynamic defines the larger and longer term challenge. We are threatened with a future of breakdowns, extreme weather events and epidemics, all observed by an increasingly paralyzed state and an elite that masks the collective self-deception using the machines of the PR industry and the mass media. The race will be on to develop a coherent ecological package to forestall the growth of extremist parties. These parties will focus on people's mass anger and despair and on simplistic messages of hatred — blaming and persecuting scapegoats like ethnic minorities, immigrants, the rich or the growing numbers of environmental refugees.

Can a new movement of ecological activists unfold to the extent that one is needed? Can it move from proximal to distal agendas without co-option? As it evolves, can it find within itself the necessary financial acumen, skills and organizational resources to create realistic and *realizable* plans? Will it be able to create the minimal necessary renewable-generating capacity and the minimal necessary alternative transport network and cultivational system? Given the collapse in the credibility and legitimacy of the carbon mainstream, can this nascent movement find sufficient popular political support to take over and transform the state in a peaceful process to oversee the development of an alternative ecological resilience package? I believe that yes, of course it can.

Endnotes

1. guardian.co.uk/environment/2009/may/12/us-climate-bill-oil-gas.
2. This terminology of "proximal power" and "distal power" is taken from David Smail's *The Origins of Unhappiness* (HarperCollins, 1993).

Transition Thinking:
The Good Life 2.0

Davie Philip

We need to make an evolutionary leap in the way we do things if we are to make a controlled, planned transition to a post-industrial, low-carbon society. The initiatives developed by the nascent Transition Towns movement suggest that we are up to the challenge, and provide a model for how the more resilient communities needed for the future might be built.

The Emergency

As we slide deeper into an economic recession, one question we often hear is, "how long is this downturn going to last?" There is a commonly held belief that it is only a matter of time before we get back to "business as usual." But what many fail to grasp is the severity of the problems we face and the "once-in-a-species" opportunity that these challenges offer us.

The shape of the recovery is being hotly debated within economic circles, with three possibilities being mooted. One, the possibility of a "V"-shaped recovery in which the economy quickly bounces back, is falling out of favor, displaced by the idea that there will be a "double-dip" — a rapid partial recovery followed by another sharp decline. Others still think that the recovery will be "U"-shaped — that growth will be restrained and that the economy will take a bit longer to recover. In a 2009 Post Carbon Institute posting, Richard Heinberg argued that the recovery will actually be "L"-shaped; that instead of returning to high levels of growth, society will have to get used a much lower level of economic activity. As economic growth is dependent on abundant and growing energy supplies, the expected constraints in global oil availability mean that a "V-" or "U"-shaped recovery is highly unlikely.

Of course, as well as attempting to "fix the economy," we will need to radically decrease our vulnerability to an overdependence on oil, coal and gas. This means looking beyond the obvious, i.e. electricity supply or fuel, and rethinking our food, health and almost all other systems. Currently everything we do is dependent upon a non-renewable, climate-changing source of energy: oil. I was born in the year that global oil discovery peaked and in the 45 years since we've failed to discover more oil than we had back then. Today we consume four barrels of oil for every barrel discovered and have reached, or will soon reach, the peak in global oil production.

Not that it needs to be explained here, but "peak oil" is the geological term used to describe the time when the amount of oil that can be extracted reaches its limit and begins to decline. Extracting oil after the peak becomes more difficult and expensive, and the amount of oil produced begins to decrease. The term "peak oil" usually relates to worldwide production, but the majority of oil-producing countries have now reached the point where their oil production has peaked and is now declining. Before the recent economic crash, when oil was touching on close to $150 a barrel, awareness of the oil issue was high. With the price now around $80 a barrel, and with the economy collapsing, society seems to be forgetting all about the energy problem.

Climate change has also been slipping from our awareness recently, just as the urgency of taking appropriate responses has become more apparent. According to the Climate Safety Report published by the Public Interest Research Centre in 2008, climate change is accelerating more rapidly and dangerously than even the IPCC had expected. The earlier-than-predicted onset of ice-free Arctic summers will cause additional heating, greenhouse gas emissions and sea-level rise, over and above what has been predicted to date. The melting glaciers, the famine in Darfur, the changing monsoon patterns, the enduring drought in Australia and the widespread loss of species — these all illustrate the global nature of the crisis. Climate change is already impacting the majority of people on this planet, but despite apparent scientific consensus on the issue, the debate in the media, here in Ireland at least, still focuses on whether or not it is happening at all.

Some scientists have warned that the rapid disappearance of all kinds of life, from bacteria and insects to plants and animals, is as dangerous as climate change, and closely related to it. In a Eurobarometer survey taken in 2008, most Irish people said they did not know anything about the loss of biodiversity, despite up to half of all Europe's birds, butterflies, fish and animals being threatened with extinction.

So it is clear that we are facing not a financial, energy, climate or even a biodiversity crisis per se, but a systemic crisis for which we are completely unprepared. We have now reached the long-predicted "limits to growth" and find ourselves facing a convergence of challenges that are inextricably connected. Through overpopulation and overconsumption we have overshot Earth's carrying capacity. We now urgently need to take an evolutionary leap in the way we do things and to design systems from the bottom up in a way that fits the planet's carrying capacity. And we need to do this together.

The availability of cheap and easily available energy has led to an unprecedented time of individualism; now most of us know the characters of our favorite soap opera better than the people we live amongst. We might be the first generation who has no need for real neighbors, and that loss of community means a loss of resilience. Our global economy is designed to work without any need for community. Our food and energy come from halfway around the world and we have no relationship with the people who produce it. Very little is local and as Robert Putnam notes in *Bowling Alone*, social capital has been falling in the US and over the past 25 years, attendance at club meetings has fallen 58 percent, family dinners are down 33 percent and having friends visit has fallen 45 percent. It looks like just when we are going to have to depend a lot more on our neighbors, we are actually doing less and less together.

We've been aware of these unfolding crises for a long time. The "Limits to Growth" report was written over 35 years ago, climate change has been known about for over a century and resource depletion is an issue that many have understood and been trying to alert more people to for decades. The biggest difficulty we face is that the majority of the planet's citizens still haven't grasped that a problem exists at all. Or if they do, they can't comprehend the scale of it.

What I want to explore is how we rise to the challenge of engaging as many people as possible in making the transition to a post-industrial society. How do we build sustainable communities that can survive and thrive in a future that will be characterized by change, uncertainty and surprise? Can we do this in a way that liberates the ingenuity of the human spirit and galvanizes our most powerful impulses to create and evolve? Can the new social movement called Transition Towns be a catalyst toward the development of low-carbon, resilient and healthy communities we need? Are the emerging Transition initiatives up to the challenge, and what more could this nascent movement be doing?

The Good Life 2.0

Web 2.0 is the term used to signify the new upgraded internet, which is community-based, interactive and user-driven. As the emerging crisis is too overwhelming for individuals to face alone, I want to propose a "Good Life 2.0" — a response to the challenges of the current era based on an "upgrade" of the ideas of the 1970s self-sufficiency movement and the values of community, together with everything we have learned in the 30 years since.

Do you remember *The Good Life*, the TV show that ran from 1975 to '78? One of Britain's favorite sitcoms, it popularized the notion of getting out of the rat race and being self-sufficient. Tom and Barbara, Richard Briers' and Felicity Kendal's characters, converted their suburban garden into a farm, kept pigs and chickens and grew their own food.

The first series was launched just after the first oil shock, amid one of the UK's worst economic downturns. It was actually based on the writings of John Seymour, the father of self-sufficiency. His books give a comprehensive introduction to the "Good Life," covering everything from growing your own crops, animal husbandry, wine making and beekeeping, to building, renewable energy and much, much more. John gained considerable experience living a self-sufficient life, first in Suffolk, then Pembrokeshire and then in Ireland, where he established the School of Self-Sufficiency in Co. Wexford. He also traveled around the world and wrote and made films exposing the unsustainability of the global industrial food system. Sadly, on September 14, 2004, John Seymour passed away at the ripe old age of 90.

Over the last five years of his life I had an opportunity to spend some time with John. We campaigned together to stop the planting of genetically engineered sugar beet, which culminated with seven of us in a New Ross courthouse. But that's another story.

Surprisingly, John once told me that he was actually wrong about self-sufficiency. On a visit to his smallholding in Wexford, he shared with me his conclusion that it would be too difficult to sustain the noble effort of living off-grid and providing for all your own needs on your own land. Self-sufficiency wasn't enough. His new thinking was something he called co-sufficiency—self-reliant local communities that could provide the social relationships essential for facing an uncertain future, together. Seymour predicted that we would need strong, connected communities that could work together to meet their needs and make the transition to a post-industrial economy that is not dependent on fossil fuel.

If Tom and Barbara of *The Good Life* were striving to be self-sufficient today, they would probably have joined their local Transition Town group and be engaged in the building of food and energy security with their neighbors. That's "The Good Life 2.0," a community approach to building local resilience, because, as Richard Heinberg writes in his book *Powerdown*, "personal survival depends on community survival."

Making the Transition

At the heart of the Transition Towns movement is the building of relationships with our neighbors and working with them on projects of common interest. In the coming years we will need to live more locally and work cooperatively in our neighborhoods and towns. The process is taking root throughout the world, with thousands of communities now adopting the model. Even the fictional town of Ambridge in the Radio 4 program *The Archers* has become a Transition Town.

Construction work at Cloughjordan ecovillage in early summer 2010. Photo: Albert Bates.

I often say that the Transition process was born in Ireland, a statement with some truth to it. Rob Hopkins, who is recognized as the founder of the Transition movement, lived in Ireland for 12 years and it was here that the seeds were sown. I first met Rob in 1997 at one of the Sustainable Earth Fairs at Maynooth University where I was studying. This was an early gathering of advocates of sustainability from around Ireland, and Rob's passion for Permaculture and sustainability was infectious even then. It was around this time that Marcus McCabe, one of Ireland's early adopters of Permaculture, held a meeting on the subject of eco-villages in Monaghan. He expected about 20 people to turn up but so many people arrived that it had to be relocated to a bigger venue. At this meeting Rob met Greg Allen and Gavin Harte and, with them, set up Baile Dulra, an idea for a sustainable community based on permaculture principles; they spent the next couple of years developing the idea and looking for land. This project was the precursor to the Hollies in West Cork and the Ecovillage in Cloughjordan, Co. Tipperary (where I now live).

Following an amicable parting of ways, Rob went on, with his partner Emma and Thomas & Ulrike Riedmuller, to found The Hollies, the center for practical sustainability in West Cork, Ireland. From here Rob developed and taught on the two-year Permaculture course in Kinsale community college. In the years leading up to the development of the energy-descent action plan prototype by Rob and his students in Kinsale, FEASTA had held a number of events that introduced and popularized the ideas of peak oil and explored the ramifications for our economy and society. I remember seeing Colin Campbell speaking at a FEASTA event in Dublin in the year 2000 and just not getting the importance of the geological turning point of peak oil. It wasn't until FEASTA's landmark three-day conference in Thurles in 2002 that I got it. There, Richard Douthwaite, David Fleming, Colin Campbell and many other "early toppers" really illuminated the issues at stake. Interestingly, the event was called *Before the Wells Run Dry, Ireland's Transition to Renewable Energy*. Indeed, it was this conference, and of course Greg Green and Barry Silverstone's now classic film *The End Of Suburbia*, that were responsible for many of Ireland's sustainability advocates' "peak oil moment." Sustainability, seen through the lens of resource depletion, makes even more urgent the work of developing resilient communities, permaculture and systems thinking.

In Kinsale in 2004, on the first day of a new term, Rob Hopkins and his Permaculture 2nd-year students watched *The End of Suburbia* and heard a talk that followed by Colin Campbell. This "peak oil double bill" culminated in what Rob describes as a week of PPSD, *post-petroleum stress disorder* in the college, and led to the development of the Kinsale Energy Descent Action Plan as their end-of-year project. This document, and the landmark event that launched it in 2005, changed the landscape of peak-oil response forever. David Holmgren, Richard Heinberg and a host of others including our now Minister for Energy, Eamon Ryan, spent three days in West Cork planning how we would best manage our transition to a low-energy future. This event led in turn to the formation of a new group in the town driven by some of the students, local activists and residents of Kinsale. Known as Kinsale Transition Town, the group enjoyed some initial successes, but it wasn't until Rob and Emma relocated from West Cork to Totnes in Devon, England, that the Transition process emerged. In Totnes, Rob began working with locals on what would become Transition Town Totnes, the Transition process and the Transition Network.

In a few short years, Transition culture has gone viral and an international network of Transition initiatives has rapidly grown as cities, islands, towns and rural villages sign up to the process. Thousands now exist, with communities setting out to radically reduce their carbon emissions while at the same time developing further their ability to cope with a future that is very uncertain. Transition is a process that offers pathways, new ways of thinking and a set of tools that could help us respond to the shocks that we will inevitably face.

The Transition model helps communities come together to develop the capability to provide most of its essential needs — food, energy, water and raw materials — from a number of local sources. The model ensures that in the event of a system failure, communities can look after themselves. The process comes with a "cheerful disclaimer" that states that it is a social experiment on a massive scale; it is not known if it will work.

One of the most striking characteristics of "Transition" communities is their positivity and creativity; the process is purposely designed to be non-threatening and engaging, so people feel at ease to explore different ideas and approaches. Its strength lies in its ability to bring all sorts of people together and to be greater than the sum of its parts. There is room for everyone.

Planning our Energy Descent

Through a loose process Transition initiatives set out to build the capacity of the community to plan its energy descent. The goal is to envision a desirable post-fossil fuel future and then "backcast" the incremental steps needed to realize that future. This is called an Energy Descent Action Plan, and is the process at the core of Transition thinking: planning how to wean ourselves off fossil-fuel energy and do a lot more for ourselves.

> "The concept of energy descent, and of the Transition approach, is a simple one: that the future with less oil could be preferable to the present, but only if sufficient creativity and imagination are applied early enough in the design of this transition."
>
> — Rob Hopkins, *The Transition Handbook*

Underpinning the Transition process is a belief that life with less energy is inevitable and that it's better to plan for it than be taken by surprise. This may sound like prudent advice, but it is surprisingly difficult for us to imagine the future and plan the transition needed to get there.

Instead of waiting for someone else, or some other agency, to do something about the emergency we face, the communities embarking on the Transition process are endeavoring to act for themselves, knowing that if they don't do something, no one will. Examples of Transition initiatives include starting community gardens and allotments, creating community-supported agriculture systems (CSAs), localizing energy production, starting car clubs and "future proofing" their houses and public buildings. Some have even introduced local currencies to keep money circulating in their local area. All of these build community and offer the potential of an extraordinary transformation in our economic and social systems.

From Vulnerability to Resilience

Transition initiatives maintain that building local resilience will help us weather the fast-approaching storms. The flip side of vulnerability, resilience is the ability of a system to hold together and function in the face of disruption and shock. This means having the capacity to deal with adversity and to find new ways of doing things when current approaches become redundant or fail. An authoritative definition is offered from a report commissioned by the International Council for Science (ICSU) in preparation for the 2002 World Summit on Sustainable Development (WSSD):

> Resilience, for social-economic-ecological systems, is related to
>
> (a) the magnitude of novelty or shock that the system can absorb and remain within a given state
> (b) the degree to which the system is capable of self-organization

(c) the degree to which the system can build capacity for learning
and adaptation

When massive transformation is inevitable, resilient systems
contain all of the necessary components for renewal and reorganization. Intentional management that builds resilience can sustain
social-economic-ecological systems in the face of surprise, unpre-
dictability and complexity.

Because the possibility is rising fast of abrupt breakdown in our vital social,
economic and environmental systems, we need to find ways to accelerate
the building of resilient local communities.

We in Ireland are more reliant on imported oil for our energy requirements than almost every other European country. This leaves us very vulnerable to interruptions in supply. In response to this, Transition initiatives
facilitate the design of a "powerdown" strategy that helps us cope with such
shocks and at the same time greatly increases our "well-being" and resilience. Although debate about energy futures and the top-down strategies
needed for a low-carbon economy has focused mainly on technology and
supply-side replacements for fossil fuels, much work is underway by Transition initiatives on reducing our energy demand and exploring the prospects
for community responses to this "new emergency".

Going Further

So, are Transition initiatives up to the challenge of building community resilience and preparing us for the new emergency? One problem that needs
to be overcome is that, generally, the people attracted to Transition are the
usual suspects, making it a case of preaching to the converted. This emerging social movement must therefore explore ways to move beyond the familiar demographic, get their message out to the "unconverted" and bring
much greater diversity into their initiatives.

Ecology is all about relationships; the more diverse a system, the better. In Transition initiatives in Ireland and the UK, I've noticed a predomi-
nance of greenies, slow foodies and the middle-class, middle-aged, white,
urban types. Where are the working classes, middle Ireland, the new ethnic
communities, faith communities, the youth and the traditional left? If the
movement fails to build diversity and get these sectors of society on board,
prospects are poor for a gentle descent.

One barrier to getting more people involved in Transition may be a perception that it is full of "New Age" principles or "hippy dippy" notions. Nothing turns some people off more than the thought of being asked to sit in a circle and share how they feel about the state of the world or, worse, themselves. No one wants to feel uncomfortable, that they don't know enough to participate or that it all might be some kind of cult. This constitutes a massive barrier to the building of resilient communities and the Transition movement needs to consider how to develop relationships with people that hold different values.

We need to live with those people in our communities with whom we don't necessarily share the same worldview or values. We're all in this together and we need to get through it together. Transition initiatives need to liaise with other local groups and networks as well as finding innovative ways of creating forums for bringing people together and maximizing the opportunities to share ideas and freely express opinions. That in many respects it does so already is one of its strengths; the movement offers many examples of the bringing together of young and old, rich and poor, male and female, the business man and the activist — even the right and the left.

Building a mass movement demands an understanding of where people are at. It means not turning people off before they hear what we have to say. For me, it highlights the need, above all, for flexibility and the ability to adapt the language and techniques we use. Discussing the potential for safe communities, warm homes and local jobs might be more palatable to traditional middle Ireland than attempting to, initially at least, discuss climate change and peak oil with them.

In 2008, Paul Chatterton and Alice Cutler of the Trapese Collective, a Popular Education non-profit organization, wrote a critique of the Transition process called "The Rocky Road to a Real Transition." They argued that unless we identify and confront the vested interests in the media, government and business, and reject all systems of control, we will be unable to make a real transition. This was an interesting critique as in my experience many people involved in Transition initiatives see themselves as activists and aren't opposed to challenging power. As Rob Hopkins points out in his response to the paper, "I make no apologies for the Transition approach being designed to appeal as much to the Rotary Club and the Women's Institute as to the authors of this report." One of the strengths of the Transition movement is the blame-free dialogue it encourages in this same spirit.

People involved in Transition tend not to dismiss global movements struggling for justice around the world and many, in their own capacity, do what they can to support the oppressed. However, the Transition process is more about coming together to demonstrate what is possible and what can be done rather than taking to the streets. Transition nurtures a common purpose: to facilitate the self-organization needed to rebuild community and at the same time massively reduce our fossil-fuel dependency.

In response to the Trapese Collective's argument that Transition shies away from confronting politics, Hopkins writes in his blog that, for him, "Transition is something that sits alongside and complements the more oppositional protest culture, but is distinctly different from it. It is a different tool. It's designed in such a way as to come in under the radar."

When you scratch the surface, Transition is highly subversive, but most of all it's positive and can be fun. As Richard Heinberg says, "Transition is more like a party than a protest march." We can't smash the system entirely as we are part of it. We need to short-circuit the system by building an alternative one that works.

I do think that the future will be rocky. And I understand, too, that while planning for a gentle transition is one thing, there's a concern out there that the energy descent may not be as slow as the classic slope of Hubert's curve suggests. For most, it seems, the future may be chaotic, confusing and violent. The nexus of challenges will probably lead to increases in criminal activity and, in many places in the world, to war or unrest, both civil and transnational. In some places, the new emergency will most likely bring with it a rise in extreme right-wing and religious fundamentalism. It is said that it is easier to slide down a slope rather than climb up it, but as we move into the unchartered waters of energy descent, we may find that preparing for civil disruption is just as important as building our local economies and growing our own food.

Emergency Preparedness

I am often accused by some friends of being overly pessimistic and constantly told that things are not as bad as I think they are. Conversely, many colleagues accuse me of being overly optimistic and that things are a lot worse than I think they are. On top of the credit crunch, rising unemployment and the unfolding environmental crises, what if, as Feasta's New Emergency conference suggests, we are actually on the cusp of collapse?

Will the community building and bottom-up approaches of Transition be enough? At the 2009 Transition gathering in London, Richard Heinberg was beamed through the internet to give a presentation titled "Emergency Preparedness." In this session he introduced the idea of top-down emergency planning and the formation of disaster-management groups. He stressed that the development of these would not compete with Transition strategies; they would just be working at a different level.

While disaster-management groups don't sound as much fun as Transition initiatives, this approach will be very much required as part of our response to the problems we face; the two are not mutually exclusive. Heinberg also stressed that we will all have to get ready for rapid and deep shocks and play a part in the development of short-term emergency plans for our communities, regions and nations. Emphasizing the need for more preparedness for such rapid change, he proposed that Transition initiatives should form working groups to identify people and organizations with something to offer emergency planning. He suggested contacting mainstream organizations responsible for the systems needed in an emergency in our area, working with them to develop contingency plans and strategies for emergency preparedness in their own fields and helping them scale these up quickly.

Building Resilient Communities

For ten years I have been involved with a disparate group of people in a unique and innovative project that is striving to create a fresh blueprint for modern sustainable living in rural North Tipperary where resilience and community are very much to the fore.

I have moved into one of the first houses to be occupied in this innovative development, which is integrating with the existing town of Cloughjordan; this makes it a very different model to most established eco-villages. Work has started on over 30 eco-homes and 45 families from the project have now located to Cloughjordan. The development, which is being progressed by a community-owned educational charity, Sustainable Projects Ireland, is a lot more than an eco-housing estate and has many elements that will provide community resilience.

Homes will be surrounded by an edible landscape of fruit and nut trees, vegetables and herbs. A tree nursery has been established to nurture hundreds of trees for planting along the pathways and in the community gardens that are dispersed throughout the residential area. Larger community and personal allotments have been established to provide more space for growing food. The remaining eco-village land is dedicated to farming and woodland. The Cloughjordan Community Farm is located on 28 acres on the outskirts of the village and also utilizes two fields on the eco-village land. This example of CSA, Community Supported Agriculture, has been a fantastic way to build a bridge between the residents of the new community and the old.

This paper has focused on the need to build community resilience in a world that is rapidly crashing around us. From its Irish roots the Transition process has taken off and provides a way to mainstream the ideas of sustainability and help us to revitalize our local economies. I believe that Transition, although still a young movement, can be a catalyst toward the development of low-carbon, resilient and healthy communities. Its strength will be its ability to share what is working and what is not through a global network of motivated and enthusiastic people who are learning how to cope and adapt to the challenges of these turbulent times.

There is an old African proverb, quoted by Al Gore in his Nobel Prize acceptance speech: "If you want to go quickly, go alone. If you want to go far, go together." To make the transition, we need to go far and we need to go quickly. To maintain a good life in the 21st century we will need to rebuild our social, economic and environmental systems, localize our communities and most importantly, we will have to learn to do all this together.

Here are ten steps or action points that I think could help us to develop our personal and community resilience.

- **Understand the context:** We need to understand where we are at and be observant of limits, both ecological and our own. Awareness of what the converging challenges facing us are and what the responses might be is an essential first step in developing our resilience to cope.
- **Take a helicopter view:** We live in a complex living system so we have to be able to see systems at work. Being able to take a whole systems perspective is of the highest importance and it is fundamental to understand our human systems through the lens of living systems. Taking a permaculture course will give us the tools to begin to apply this thinking to the development of local resilience.
- **Build community:** Make social networks real, get to know your neighbors and develop a stronger sense of place. Focus on building relation-

ships with others and developing trust. In these times it is vital that we break out of our specialist silos of interest, establish partnerships and strengthen the bonds with others pursuing similar objectives. Join or start a Transition Initiative.

- **Map your assets:** As a community, identify and strengthen your physical, social and human assets. Value the tangible and the intangible, especially the skills and talents of local people.
- **Develop new skills:** In a changing world new skills and knowledge will be needed. Identify what capacities you and your community need to build.
- **Powerdown:** Do everything you can to reduce your dependency on fossil fuels. Future proof your homes and buildings and minimize your need to travel.
- **Eat locally:** Learn to produce food, start a garden and build relationships with local food producers. Develop community food systems.
- **Lead:** As a key aspect of resilience is the ability to self-organize; a leader in this context needs to help people move away from a culture of dependency and become leaders themselves. We need to equate leadership not with being in charge but rather with the ability to inspire initiative and new thinking with those around us.

500 square metres of flat plate solar thermal panels, part of the community-owned district heating system at Cloughjordan ecovillage. Photo: Davie Philip

- **Catalyze:** The journey to resilience will be a challenging one. New capacities are required — ones that catalyze new thinking and action. The ability to kindle a shared vision or a common purpose is vital.
- **Keep learning:** Education happens throughout life, formally and informally and reflecting on, and learning from, our collective experiences will build resilience.

Sailing Craft for
a Post-Collapse World

DMITRY ORLOV

Land transport will be costly, difficult and dangerous after the industrial system has broken down. Moving goods and people by water will be a better option even for quite short distances but what sort of boats will be needed and what materials will be available to build them?

At present, whether you need to move around yourself, or whether everything you need is delivered straight to your door, you depend for transport on industrial products whether they be cars and lorries, planes, trains, ships, bicycles or even just a good pair of shoes. Is *any* means of transport available that you could provide, build or even service yourself that does not require access to industrial materials, products or services?

Even human bipedal locomotion has been industrialized: just to get from the bedroom to the bathroom you might want to put on slippers, and they probably say "Made in China" on them. They were made in a large factory, and were brought to you on an even larger container ship. Few of us know any cobblers who live within walking distance, whereas, were the global industrial economy to unravel, bipedal locomotion would become, pardon the pun, our sole recourse. It is an old experimentalist tradition to try experiments on oneself, and so, as an experiment, I spent a few months going about barefoot. I found it quite possible, reasonably safe, and even perfectly pleasant, in the warmer seasons and climates, following a few weeks of somewhat uncomfortable adaptation. But that's a minor matter; my other, more ambitious experiments have made me quite optimistic

A Thames barge, a traditional 80ft shoal-draft craft designed for estuaries and coastal waters, could carry large amounts of cargo and be sailed by a man and a boy. Photo: Steve Birch.

regarding one's ability to cover huge distances and generally move about the planet, even after jet aircraft, container ships and other leviathans of industrial civilization go off to join the dinosaurs. Provided, that is, that one makes some timely preparations.

Although a complete and instantaneous collapse of global industry doesn't seem particularly likely just at this very moment, its likelihood begins to approach 100 percent as we move through the 21st century. The opposing view — that industrial civilisation can survive this century — comes up rather short of facts to support it and rests on an unshakable faith in technological miracles. In an echo of medieval alchemy, the hopes for technological salvation are pinned on some element or other: yesterday it was hydrogen; today it's thorium. Fusion reactors are currently out of fashion, cold fusion doubly so, but who knows what new grand proposal tomorrow will bring?

In the meantime, we have far more mundane problems to consider. We've had ample chance to observe that when key supplies run short, industrial economies crumble. Throughout their relatively short history, industrial economies have tended to do well as they were given more and more of everything they needed (energy, raw materials, fresh water, land, cheap/

free labor and so forth). There are no examples of industrial economies surviving chronic shortfalls of key commodities — especially ones that have no
readily available substitutes. Quite the opposite: we have the stunning example of the USSR, where the peak in domestic crude oil production precipitated a financial collapse and a political dissolution just a few years later,
events which were followed by a severe and prolonged economic decline.
It was only by integrating with the global economy, which had plentiful resources at the time, that the Russian economy was able to recover. No such
rescues will be available when the shortfalls become global.

We also have the example of the current Great Recession, which occurred as soon as the global economy encountered a physical limit to oil
production. These events are like canaries in a coal mine, because over the
course of the century the global industrial economy is destined to encounter not just global peak oil, but peak just about everything else it runs on:
coal, natural gas, iron ore, strategic metals and minerals — in short, just
about everything that industry requires to maintain itself and to grow. Since
most footwear is now made of polymers, which are synthesized from oil
and natural gas, we are also likely to pass peak shoes. Such facts can now be
gleaned from a number of authoritative reports published by international
and governmental agencies.

Why, then, don't these facts inform the discussion on the future of
transport? If one were to assemble a panel of professionals and experts on
transport technology and ask them to propose transport solutions that
could continue to operate for the remainder of this century, one would no
doubt hear of various hi-tech products — electric cars, light rail, high-speed
trains, hydrogen fuel cells, plug-in hybrids and so on. These would enable
our contemporary, industrialized society to perpetuate its current lifestyle,
and everyone to keep their jobs. That's all well and good, but as a follow-up
question one might wish to inquire as to how their plans will be impacted by
a variety of factors, some of which are already present, some certain to happen at some point during this century, with only the exact timing in dispute.
The list of such factors might reasonably include:

1. The inability to supply/afford transport fuels in the amounts needed
   to run existing transportation networks, construction and industrial
   equipment. Transport fuels are made almost entirely from oil, and
   global oil production has probably already entered terminal decline.
   Since coal and natural gas are set to follow within the next 15 years,

they can scarcely provide substitutes. Renewable energy sources such as solar, wind or biomass either do not provide transportation fuels or provide them in comparatively tiny quantities.

2. A lack of the resources required to build new transportation infrastructure due to a permanent and deepening economic depression. Economies that fail to grow, or grow more slowly than the population, would not produce a surplus sufficient to maintain their existing infrastructure and vehicle fleets, never mind investing in ambitious new schemes.

3. Shortages of strategic metals and key rare earth elements needed to manufacture high-technology components such as electric vehicle batteries, photovoltaic panels and high-efficiency electric motors. These are mined predominantly in China and are only available in restricted quantities.

4. Social disruptions and political upheavals caused by population pressures in the face of a shrinking economy. These are unpredictable but would predictably result in disruptions to global supply chains, shortages of parts, and project delays and cancellations.

5. Disruption of ocean freight once rising ocean levels begin to inundate port facilities. The current authoritative worst-case estimates are for a 1.5 meter sea level rise this century, but it is based on incomplete understanding of global warming effects and dynamics of polar ice cap melt. As knowledge improves, the estimates tend to double every few years, but they have not been keeping up with observed reality. The ultimate sea level rise may be as high as 20 meters.

In response, one would no doubt hear that solving such problems is outside of the area of expertise of transport technology professionals. Transport might be able to overcome some combination of such external problems, given enough time and money. For instance, a way might be found to manufacture high-technology components without using the rare earth elements in short supply. Or, if rising sea levels inundate ocean freight terminals, then, clearly, the terminals would have to be rebuilt again and again. However, if the resources were not available for such an ambitious and ultimately futile undertaking, then that would be regarded not as a technological but as a financial or even a political problem. Working one's way up the technological food chain from the transport sector to the energy sector, one finds that energy professionals always blame production shortfalls and high prices on lack of sufficient investment. Why do they always say that the problems they face are not physical but economic? Economists, in turn, are perfectly content to ignore physical realities and treat all problems as problems of economic policy.

And so it would appear that the overall working assumption of every specialist, expert and professional in every discipline is ceteris paribus — all other things being equal. They will work just on those problems on which they are qualified to work, provided that sufficient research and development funds, materials and facilities are made available to them. They would prefer to assume that future demand patterns will be much like the present ones: to-be-developed electric cars and light rail lines would be used to convey commuters to and from their jobs and consumers to and from nearby businesses and shopping centers. It must be inconceivable to them that this equipment would be idled while the former commuters and shoppers, bankrupted by wasteful and ineffective investments in technology, would be forced to spread out across the rural landscape in search of hand-to-mouth sustenance. They would no doubt prefer to think that their profession will continue to exist and have relevance: jobs will lead to pensions, graduate students will grow up to be post-doctoral students and hope to become junior faculty members some day, grant money will continue to flow, conferences will be organized and peer-reviewed journals will be published. In every field of research, from oil field analysis to climatology, no matter how conclusively morbid the results, more research will always be needed. But won't the sort of disruption we are going to encounter deal the coup de grace to the industrial-scientific establishment? This perfectly reasonable question is answered either with quiet despondency or with entirely unjustified accusations of defeatism or extremism. Such emotional responses are woefully unprofessional; we can and must do better.

One approach to doing better seems to have already exhausted its possibilities. A branch of science known as systems theory was once seen as a way to de-compartmentalize thinking and to formulate interdisciplinary solutions to the problems of large, complex systems. An echo of that approach can still be heard in some of the current thinking on climate science, which attempts to leverage conclusions based on observations and climate models to formulate international public policies to reduce global greenhouse gas emissions. Experience with both the Kyoto Treaty and the more recent failure to agree a Copenhagen Treaty has laid bare a critical flaw in such thinking: it confuses knowledge with power.

The ability to analyze a complex system does not in any way imply an ability to influence it. Scientists appear, as a group, to be naïve about politics, and are misled into accepting as fact a fiction of control perpetuated by politicians and industry and business leaders, who find it useful to pretend that they possess the power to alter systems over which they merely preside. Be it the fossil fuel industry, or mining and manufacturing, or industrial agriculture, or the weapons industry, or the automotive industry — all of these can be modeled as machines lacking an "off" switch. Yet each one requires energy, raw materials, and financial and social stability and can only continue to operate as long as these needs continue to be met, after which point they undergo systemic breakdowns and cascaded failure. Although an analysis based on systems theory cannot do anything to prevent them, perhaps it can offer valuable insights into how long these systems should be expected to continue functioning, or provide some detail on how their demise will unfold.

If we are willing to concede that the global industrial economy will not last through the 21st century, then, while it is still possible, we can put together technologies and designs appropriate for the post-industrial age, and set in motion forward-looking projects with the goal of creating enough momentum, in the form of strong local traditions, institutions, practices and skills, to carry them through periods of economic disruption and political dissolution. Future generations will have to learn to make do with much less of everything, and with much less research and development in particular. Working in the twilight years of the industrial era, we could offer them a great service by leaving behind a few designs that they will actually be able to build and use.

In particular, post-industrial transport is a subject that until now has been quite neglected. Quite a lot has already been done to elucidate some of the available options for post-industrial construction, agriculture, medicine and other areas. Yet the ability to travel, on foot or otherwise, is the Achilles' heel of our ability to implement solutions in any other area: innovation and diffusion of new practices, technologies and ideas is bound to come to a near-standstill without the ability to move materials and people. Without long-distance transport, long-distance communication is bound to break down as well, and the current unified view of the planet and of humanity will dissolve. Unlike other components of the industrial life support system, industrial transport systems have no post-industrial back-ups worth mentioning. Post-industrial agriculture has its organic and permaculture alternatives, post-industrial architecture its passive solar, cob, straw bale, rammed earth and round timber alternatives, post-industrial medicine its traditional Chinese medicine and other alternative medical traditions and practices, but when it comes to transport there do not appear to be any presently available post-industrial alternatives beyond horses and our very own scantily shod feet.

Our contemporary transport systems are almost entirely dependent on refined petroleum products for both the maintenance of transport infrastructure and most of the actual movement of passengers and freight. It took decades to phase in large-scale transport technologies such as coal-fired steam engines or marine diesels. Moreover, these transitions could only have taken place in the context of an expanding economy and resource base, and with the older modes of transport still functioning. Thus, it seems outlandish to imagine that a gradual, non-disruptive transition to alternative transport technologies might still be possible. A resilient plan should be able to survive an almost complete shutdown and provide for bootstrapping to an entirely new mode, within a new set of physical limits. Take away petroleum, and none of the contemporary industrial transport systems remain functional. Even electric rail or electric cars, or even bicycles, which do not use petroleum directly, require an intact industrial economy that runs on fossil fuels, and on petroleum-based fuels for the delivery of spare parts and infrastructure maintenance. The current global recession and trends in the global oil market make it possible to sketch out how a Great Stranding will occur: transport fuels may still be plentiful in theory, but in practice they will become unaffordable, and therefore unavailable, to much of the population.

Two factors play a key role. The first is the maximum price that consumers can pay. Beyond this price, demand is destroyed and the recession deepens. Each time this price is reached, a great deal of wealth is destroyed as well, and when subsequently a partial recovery occurs, consumers are poorer, and the maximum price they can pay is lower. Thus the maximum price decreases over time. The second factor is the minimum price that oil producers can charge, as determined by their production costs, which rise over time as easy-to-produce resources become depleted. Beyond putting a floor under prices, this trend cannot continue past a physical limit: as the easy-to-exploit resources are depleted, a point is reached when the resources that are left, though they may yet be plentiful, cannot be produced profitably at any price, because the amount of energy required to do so would exceed the amount of energy they would yield. Thus the minimum price increases over time.

Although an argument can be made that this trend can be offset to some extent by developing alternative energy sources, such as solar, wind, nuclear or biomass, a careful study of this question reveals that the net energy yield of alternative energies is, in all, rather poor, that the overall potential quantity of energy delivered by the alternatives is rather low, and that the massive financial investment that would be necessary to exploit them is increasingly unlikely. Most significantly, while individual countries may find solutions, there are simply no alternative sources of transport fuels in the quantities required globally for current systems to continue functioning, nor are there resources available to replace existing systems with anything else on a similar scale.

Thus we have two trend lines: a falling maximum price that consumers can afford, and a rising minimum price that producers have to charge. When the two lines cross, production shuts down. Since there is finer structure to both the supply and the demand, this is likely to happen in stages. On the demand destruction side, consumers can forgo holiday airline trips; they can stop driving cars and switch to walking or bicycling; they can heat just one room of the house; they can go back to the older tradition of the weekly splash in the tub (whether they need one or not) in place of the daily hot shower. This will allow them to make do with far less energy, and to sustain much higher energy prices. In turn, energy producers can cut their costs by producing less and closing wells or mines that are expensive to operate.

As the oil industry shuts down, maintenance requirements for roadways and bridges, seaports and other infrastructure will no longer be met, while the price of transport services will come to exceed what businesses and consumers can afford to pay. There are already signs that we are in the early stages of such a slow-motion train wreck. In 2009 the northernmost State of Maine could no longer afford to continue maintaining many of its paved rural roadways, which were being allowed to revert to dirt. At the opposite end of the transport spectrum, global airline travel had begun to decline, with most airlines reporting losses, and with air traffic still expanding only in the oil-rich Persian Gulf region. Such a gradual winding down of the industrial economy will leave little room for many non-essential activities, such as safety and efficiency upgrades, infrastructure maintenance, fleet replacement, and research and development. We can expect priority to be given to keeping existing equipment in running order by cannibalizing and reusing parts as fewer and fewer vehicles remain in use. As this happens, safety and reliability will suffer, with many more cancellations and accidents, and cargoes being lost due to spoilage.

One can reasonably imagine that certain internal combustion vehicles will stay in sporadic use longer than others. For instance, limousines for weddings and hearses for funerals will perhaps remain motorized the longest, moving slowly over unpaved roads, since people would still be willing to pay extra for dignity on special occasions. We can also foresee that certain groups, such as governments, mafias, armed gangs and other social predators will be able to secure a supply of fuel the longest.

It is difficult to imagine that such a winding-down can happen uniformly, smoothly and peaceably. Inevitably, geography will be the determining factor: remote population centers, to which fuel must be brought overland, will have their supply curtailed long before those that are close to pipelines, railway lines, seaports or shipping channels. In communities that find themselves without access to transport fuels, much of the remaining economic activity will center around gathering the necessary resources to escape, and they will steadily depopulate. Only the old and the sick will be left behind.

To see where this process might eventually lead — if we are lucky — it is helpful to look at pre-industrial settlement and transport patterns. After all, industrial, fossil fuel-powered transport has existed for just a blink of an eye in the long history of global trade and migration. By the time the fossil-fuel age arrived, the vast majority of the planet's surface was already explored and settled. People moved about on foot, on horseback, by boat and by sailing ship, and these are the transport modes to which humanity will return once the fossil fuel-driven episode is over.

Transport costs can be grouped into two categories. The first is energy cost, encompassing consumables such as fuel, food and fodder, as well as the energy embodied in the equipment used — draft and pack animals, carts, boats, ships and so on. The second is cost of predation, which includes tributes, bribes, taxes, tariffs, duties and tolls, some officially sanctioned, some criminal. Efforts to avoid predation, by choosing pack animals over draft animals, or by taking detours to avoid toll roads, or by fording rivers instead of paying tolls at bridges, or by sailing random courses instead of following sea-lanes, or by sailing smaller vessels so as to pose a smaller, less desirable target, or by traveling in armed convoys to dissuade would-be robbers, and so on, form a gray area between the two. The upper limit on the amount of transport that is feasible is limited by the sum of the two costs. There is also a trade-off between the two: higher energy efficiency allows for more and fatter prey, and, in due course, for more and fatter predators. On the other hand, successful efforts at avoiding predation may increase energy costs but lower predation costs, resulting in greater overall efficiency and a larger volume of cargo that actually reaches its destination. In this case, greater resilience is achieved by "wasting" energy on predation avoidance rather than by striving to be maximally energy-efficient while inadvertently maximizing the level of predation.

For some cargoes in the past, the cost of predation as a result of official tolls and unofficial tributes collected along the way could double the goods' final price. Tolls were collected along inland waterways and at bridges and river crossings on major roadways. In more remote areas, and especially near mountain passes, brigandage was widespread. Often the only distinction between official and unofficial predation was that the former was sanctioned by the local aristocracy.

For bulk commodities, the energy cost of transport imposes hard limits on the maximum distance that is feasible. For instance, if the product is hay, and the mules pulling the cart eat half of it by the time they reach their destination, then either the trip was futile, or the mules would have nothing to eat on the way back. The energy value of the cargo also imposes an upper limit on the level of predation that is sustainable; if the limit was exceeded frequently, the predators would deplete their prey. Since moving bulk goods by barge is more energy efficient, canals could charge higher and more frequent tolls than toll roads. But the ease with which tolls could be collected along canals often led to abuses by rapacious local officials, forcing canal traffic back onto the less energy-efficient roads and depressing the overall level of trade.

Wheeled vehicles were used for local transport of bulk goods (hay, firewood, grain and other bulk commodities) but not for long-distance transport, which relied on caravans of pack animals. Energy considerations made long-distance overland transport impractical for bulk commodities, restricting it to high-priced items, such as specie (gold and silver), works of art and craftsmanship such as porcelain and cloth, and spices and medicinals. For such high-priced goods, transport costs represented a much smaller fraction of their final price, making avoidance of predation far more important than conserving energy. Wheeled vehicles make predation avoidance more difficult, because they have to use roads and bridges, whereas pack animals can use footpaths, steep mountain passes, dry riverbeds, and can ford rivers and streams. Unlike wheeled vehicles, pack animals can be pulled off the road and hidden by making them lie down behind vegetation, to avoid confrontations with both highwaymen and local officials.

Overland transport is orders of magnitude less energy-efficient than water transport. Before the advent of railways and coal-fired steam locomotives, it cost more to move freight a few kilometers overland than it did to ship it across the ocean by sail. The fortunes of coastal cities were determined by the quality of their harbors. In the New World, cities such as New York, Boston, Charleston and San Francisco became transport hubs because of the large numbers of oceangoing vessels their harbors could easily and safely accommodate. Inland transport relied on navigable rivers and canals, making use of wind and tide to move cargo as far as possible up tidal estuaries. Where wind and currents were unfavorable or unavailable, propulsion had to be provided by draft animals (including imprisoned or enslaved humans) either rowing or pulling the vessel from the towpath. For this reason, inland cities were often built in tidal estuaries at the uppermost reach of the tides and along rivers, lakes and canals.

Coal never fully supplanted sail either in coastal freight or on the high seas, and it was not until the widespread adoption of the marine diesel engine in the mid-20th century that the last sail-based merchant vessels were finally decommissioned. With the exception of very profitable routes and cargoes, such as the China tea trade, which was served by large and fast tea clippers, most sailing vessels were rather small, with large numbers of schooners of around 60 feet (18 meters) and crews of about a dozen, and with the vast majority of oceangoing vessels under 100 feet (30 meters) in length. There was a tendency to build larger merchant vessels in the richer trading nations and during politically stable and prosperous times but, even there, less prosperous and uncertain times brought a reversion to norm.

There were many reasons for this, from the inability to secure financing for an ambitious shipbuilding endeavor, to lack of profitable cargo with which to fill a large vessel.

A different logic applied to building military vessels, where ability to project force was prioritized above economy, and where large crews could be obtained cheaply from the ranks of young men who were pressed into service by the simple expedient of denying them any other option. Conditions on board could be almost arbitrarily brutal, with discipline imposed through flogging. Disgruntled seamen swelled the ranks of pirates and privateers, who were often unopposed in their confrontations, because the seamen often sympathized with the pirates rather than with their own loathed and despised officers.

Although, within the larger naval empires, the horrid naval traditions often carried over to the merchant fleets, including the megalomania, the brutality and the purpose-bred viciousness of the officer class, in general merchant vessels could not exceed a size that could be sailed profitably, with full loads of cargo and the smallest possible crew. Significantly, a crew of about a dozen is the optimal size for a self-organizing, self-managing, tightly knit group. Anthropological research has shown that groups larger than this size either have to expend an inordinate amount of time on social grooming activities (politics) to preserve group cohesion, or they have to be structured in a rigid hierarchy and disciplined to instill blind obedience, with vastly lower effectiveness in either case. Such limits appear to be biologically determined: humans have evolved to be most effective in self-organized groups of about a dozen. A smaller crew is problematic, because there would not be enough hands to comfortably man all watches, there being typically two four-hour watches per day per crewman, and two crewmen per watch, for a minimum of six crewmen. Add the captain and the first mate, and that brings it up to eight; a cook (since feeding this large a crew is quite a job) and a bosun (who typically does not stand watches) bring it up to ten. Throw in a mechanic and a steward, and you have a full dozen. And so it turns out that the most efficient vessel is one that can be sailed by a crew of about a dozen men.

High costs of predation were by no means unique to overland transport. At sea, both privateering and piracy abounded, the distinction hinging on the presence of official sanction rather than the manner in which the business was transacted. Privateers carried government-issued letters of marque allowing them to take tribute from citizens of a certain country as reparation for past misdeeds, such as damage caused or non-payment of loans. Pirates lacked such official permission, but the distinction was often an informal one. Additional duties were often imposed at the harbors that were the point of departure and the point of arrival. Since oceangoing vessels are restricted by their deep draft in their options of harbors and port facilities, it is easy for authorities to collect duties and fees from them. Moreover, certain governments went beyond this and designated certain ports as "staple ports"—the only ones through which commercially important products, such as Sicilian wheat, could be shipped, to simplify the process of collecting export duties.

Oceangoing ships were built with economy foremost in mind, cargo capacity second, and crew safety and comfort at sea left as an afterthought. Typically about a third of the expense of a journey was represented by the amortization and maintenance costs of the vessel itself, with the remaining two-thirds going to the crew, as provisions and pay. If the vessel was to be defended against piracy, the additional expense of arming it could as much as triple the costs. Before the development of naval guns, security at sea was largely a matter of having superior numbers in hand-to-hand combat. The advent of naval guns made the contest rather uneven for a time, with large naval ships being able to threaten any smaller vessel with almost total impunity. With the arrival of ubiquitous and powerful small arms, shoulder-fired weapons and a variety of special-purpose missiles and explosives, the odds have been evened, and mutual assured destruction prevails on the high seas. Navy ships have to remain on constant alert against even a small dinghy that might cause them serious damage as happened in Aden in 2000 with the US Navy destroyer USS *Cole*. It is quite a challenge for pirates to gain control of a vessel without getting killed or sunk if the prey vessel is armed and keeps a sharp lookout. Most confrontations with would-be pirates can now be prevented by a simple show of arms.

Although every effort was made to cut costs, the design and construction of ships was mired in conservatism everywhere and sailing technology was slow to diffuse westward from China and the Arab world. Even then, it was absorbed only partially. The pinnacle of Western sailing ship evolution is the unwieldy square-rigged vessel, which required the crew to go aloft in all conditions to handle sail—something that is neither necessary nor desirable, and one of the many problems that the Chinese and the Arabs had solved many centuries previously. And yet these manifestly imperfect vessels were the ones that explored and conquered just about every corner of the globe — a process that had largely run its course by the time the first steam-ship was launched in the 1840s. Countless lives were lost due to poor design, shoddy construction and incompetent command, but so great are the advantages of water transport over land transport that the gains were considered worth the risk.

In the light of this, what transport technologies will be relevant to an energy-scarce, climate-disrupted, socially chaotic future? We can foresee that road traffic will be greatly reduced as paved roads revert to dirt and become eroded and, in places, impassable, as bridges collapse from lack of maintenance, and as predation by both local officials and highwaymen increases both the costs and the dangers. Once again, pedestrian traffic and caravans of pack animals will try to evade official and unofficial predation, opting for the less popular, more circuitous footpaths instead of the direct and open road. Canals and other navigable waterways will once again play a much larger role in inland transport, with barges pulled by draft animals along towpaths and with sailboats carrying freight and passengers along the seacoasts. As the seaports that currently serve container ships, bulk carriers and tankers are submerged under the rising seas, the current hub-and-spoke transport networks will collapse, and smaller coastal communities will once again find ample reason to want to build and provision oceangoing vessels to trade with faraway lands.

Here are some questions we might ask ourselves

- How can we help? What *useful* technological legacy can we bequeath to future generations?
- What if, instead of squandering its remaining resources on lavish parting presents for its aging rentier class, the current profit-and-growth economic paradigm were to be quietly replaced with the idea that society should serve its children and grandchildren, should any be lucky enough to survive?
- What can we *usefully* accomplish in the time remaining before inescapable resource constraints force industrial life-support systems to stop functioning? What technological heirlooms and key pieces of learning could we convey, in the form of a living tradition, to give future generations a chance at surviving the dystopian future we are now working so hard to construct for them?

It is becoming clear that future generations will be faced with a number of new challenges. One is that rapid climate change is very likely to put an end to the last ten thousand years of benign, stable climate. It was this rare episode of climate stability that allowed agriculture to develop and flourish and permitted nomadic tribes to settle down in one place without the risk of starvation. It allowed agrarian societies to produce such large food surpluses that cities and towns could become established, eventually growing to millions of inhabitants, all fed with crops grown elsewhere, at first in the immediate vicinity and now quite far away. As the climate deteriorates, people will be forced to return to a migratory and nomadic existence to minimize the risk of starvation by staying close to the sources of their food and diversifying them across large geographic areas. In other words, they will go to the food rather than having the food brought to them.

Another challenge will be posed by rising sea levels. The latest forecasts indicate that coastal communities will either adapt to life with constant flooding, salt-water inundation and storm erosion, or be abandoned. Ancient ports such as Cádiz, which was built by the Phoenicians and has been in continuous use ever since, will no longer be able to function. Formerly sheltered harbors will become exposed as barrier islands are eroded away by storms. Material from newly eroded shores will form shoals and silt up harbors and navigation channels. Efforts to resist the deterioration such as defending, existing shorelines, building higher jetties and breakwaters, constructing dikes and seawalls and dredging harbors and inlets, will eventually prove futile as sea levels are likely continue to rise for many centuries. Consequently, those who wish to occupy and use the shoreline will have to find ways to cope with constant flooding.

In the parts of the world where people still walk or use pack and draft animals, they will muddle through somehow but it remains a large open question whether or not they will be able to continue to traverse oceans. Throughout history, the ability to sail the oceans has conferred tremendous advantages. Seafaring predates industry, but it does require access to appropriate boatbuilding materials and a seafaring tradition.

Future generations will face three major problems in their attempts to preserve their seafaring abilities:

1. Current, industrial shipbuilding practices, as well as the vessels themselves, will be of no use without both a functioning industrial economy and the widespread availability of transport fuels.

2. Going back to traditional, wood-based shipbuilding techniques will not be possible because logging and deforestation have depleted the supply of the high-quality timber

3. Access to the ocean will be in most places become complicated as the rising seas silt up inlets, navigation channels and harbours and wash away waterfronts. Deep-draft ocean vessels will find land access ob-structed and difficult due to the eroded shoreline.

The vast majority of existing ocean vessels are welded out of steel plate and are propelled by diesel engines that burn bunker fuel, a low-grade petroleum distillate. For their operation, they require industrial facilities such as con-tainer ports (for loading and unloading cargo), bunkering ports (for taking on fuel) and dry docks (for maintenance). A vanishingly small percentage of overall gross tonnage is comprised of sailing vessels, which are built and operated mainly for the purposes of preserving maritime and naval history, luxury and ostentation, recreation and sport — pursuits lacking any practi-cal merit. A truly infinitesimal number of more practical boats is custom-built by professionals or amateurs, and an even smaller number of these is actually sailed extensively on the high seas, but these voyages provide the vast majority of interesting contemporary seafaring narratives ("yarns"). Some of these unusual vessels can provide a glimpse of the future. Although the vast majority of even these vessels rely on industrial materials (marine plywoods and epoxies, fasteners, aluminium extrusions for masts and spars, stainless steel wire rope for the standing rigging and petrochemical-based synthetics such as long-strand polyester for the sails and the running rig-ging) their overall designs are sometimes sufficiently low-tech (which is to say, advanced) to survive the transition to the post-industrial age.

A revival of traditional, wooden shipbuilding is inconceivable in most places, as the required quantities of high-quality timber would be prohibi-tively expensive and its local supply would be quite limited. Most areas of the world, and especially those near seacoasts or navigable rivers, have been extensively logged and largely denuded of old-growth trees — those with dense, clear grain that are useful for building hulls. Forest productivity is also being reduced because rising atmospheric carbon dioxide levels are causing rain to become more acidic. Carbonic acid has a number of nega-tive effects on trees: it dissolves aluminium compounds present in the soil, which plugs up tree roots, starving the trees of nutrients, it dissolves nutrients in the soil, causing them to leach out and drain away, and it harms soil biota that help trees absorb nutrients. Thus even concerted long-term efforts at growing trees suitable for shipbuilding may not yield good results.

Large, deep-draft vessels would not be suitable for the new coastal conditions. Smallish ones, about 60 feet (18 meters) long, with a shoal draft of about 4 feet (120 cm) would be much better. They would have to be sturdily built with flat (rockered but not flared) bottoms to let them settle upright on the bottom at low tide. But it would also have to be a seaworthy, blue water sailing vessel, able to ride out storms up to and including tropical cyclones.

In 2006, I put my findings together in an article, *The New Age of Sail.*[1] At that time I had had very little actual ocean sailing experience, and had to rely almost entirely on secondhand information. I have since purchased a sailboat of the sort I described: a versatile and practical shoal-draft ocean-capable boat. My wife and I sold our apartment and moved aboard the boat. We have since spent close to two years sailing the entire length of the eastern coast of the United States, from Maine to Florida, including rivers, canals and long stretches of the open Atlantic. We have encountered some very lively conditions whipped up by tropical storms and hurricanes. In the process, I was able to learn enough about boatbuilding to improve the design, building a new rudder and making numerous other adjustments and improvements. I also fitted it with solar panels and a wind turbine, a composting toilet and a rainwater collection system.

Dmitry Orlov's shoal-draft boat, *Hogfish*, at anchor in Salem Harbor, Mass.

I am very happy to report that just about everything I wrote in *The New Age of Sail* I have been able to confirm by direct experiment. I am also quite convinced that, in spite of what some sailing traditionalists and fashion-victims might think, shoal-draft seaworthy boats are very much a reality, and that it is quite possible for a dedicated homebuilder to vastly exceed the results of a commercial boatbuilder at a small fraction of the cost. Such boats may not please those people whose minds are fixated on the idea of getting to the finish line just a tiny bit faster than the next competitor, or people who have a fetish for varnished wood and polished bronze, or the various other strange fixations and affectations that affect what little has remained of the sailing world, but it is quite hard to see why they would be relevant.

My boat is decidedly not post-industrial. It is constructed of marine plywood (fir veneers laminated with synthetic adhesive), sheathed in epoxy and fiberglass and painted with polyurethane paints. The masts and spars are aluminium extrusions, the rigging is stainless steel and the sails and lines are of synthetic fiber. It is equipped with advanced electronics, including an autopilot and a GPS chart-plotter. Yet there are many things about the overall design of this boat that are just right. It only draws two feet, it handles very well with the centerboard up (which is only needed when sailing upwind or maneuvering in close quarters) and so it can be sailed over shallows. It can be run aground or beached without risk of damage and it settles upright at low tide. It rides quietly to anchor even in high winds (a surprisingly important but neglected aspect of yacht design). It is fast for its size, and it is so stiff that it is virtually impossible to capsize. Its almost square hull cross section provides far more stowage space than round-bilge boats of much deeper draft. Its motion in a seaway is steady and gentle, allowing us to enjoy a nice cup of tea in conditions where the crews of other boats apparently have had to brace themselves to avoid being tossed about the cabin.

But the choice of materials poses a problem. However, as Arthur Conan Doyle put it, "Once you eliminate the impossible, whatever remains, no matter how improbable, must be the truth." And so, by eliminating all industrial materials and technologies, as well as the pre-industrial materials that are no longer affordable or available in quantity, I have arrived at what must be, in the end, the only viable set of options for building an unlimited number of oceangoing vessels of the sort that would be required. Given the eventual unavailability of steel plate and welding technology, or high-quality hardwood, or petrochemical-based composites and synthetics, the one remaining choice of hull material is…ferrocement. Many such hulls have been built, with mostly good results, the bad ones generally resulting from improper techniques used by overly ambitious beginners enticed by the very low cost of the materials involved. If done correctly, the resulting hull is strong, long-lasting, maintenance-free and fireproof. Cement is a pre-industrial material that was already known to the ancient Romans, who used it, among other things, to surface the spillways of aqueducts. It is currently available as an industrial product and in vast quantities, but in the small quantities needed by artisans for plastering hulls it can be produced using non-industrial techniques, by crushing and baking out limestone and clay in homemade kilns. It could conceivably be made using renewable energy: baking out limestone is potentially a good application for concentrating solar technology, while crushing and grinding can be powered by windmills or waterwheels. Limestone is available in unlimited quantities through manual surface mining in many places throughout the planet. The preferred aggregate used for building ferrocement hulls is river sand — sharp, almost completely indestructible granules of eroded hard rock that have not been weathered by surf or wind — a material that is also ubiquitous.

The steel armature that holds the cement plaster together typically consists of small diameter steel pipe, steel rod and steel mesh. These are industrial materials, but they will remain available for a long time past the end of the industrial age, in the relatively small quantities required for building hulls, because they can easily be reclaimed from abandoned industrial structures and facilities. The armature (called "the basket") is assembled by hand, with simple hand tools, by bending the material into shape and tying it together with short lengths of wire. While the steel armature is a well-understood construction method giving a strong, durable result, it may be possible to replace the mesh and perhaps other parts of the armature with natural fiber. Clearly, thorough testing would be needed before a boatbuilder would commit to such a change but this is not an urgent issue because the quantities of scrap metal that the two centuries of industrial development will have left behind will be sufficient for building a very large number of ferrocement hulls far into the future.

Covering the basket with mortar is usually performed by a gang of expert plasterers in a continuous session that may span several days. To become a first-rate ferrocement plasterer, one would start by becoming a master plasterer and then specifically train for the much more demanding task of plastering hulls. To control porosity, the mortar mix used for hulls has to be quite dry compared to the mixes used for other types of construction, making it more difficult to form it into sheets without any voids and without pulling aggregate to the surface. The skin of mortar has to be fair and smooth and as thin as possible (typically between 12 and 20 mm) but thick enough to prevent any part of the basket from showing through (to prevent corrosion). Tight process control is needed for optimum results, which are achieved by controlling temperature and humidity, keeping all contaminants out of the mortar, using precise mixing and plastering techniques, and keeping to a specific hydration schedule. After plastering, the hull has to be kept moist for about three months, during which it slowly gains strength and plasticity.

Unfortunately, the effects of improper technique often become apparent much later, when the hull leaks, abrades or cracks and the armature rusts, resulting in a shorter service life. However, sudden and catastrophic failures seem to be a rarity, and an older hull that would no longer be used for ocean sailing can still be considered safe for use in sheltered waters. Ferrocement hulls are quite easy to repair, and some that have suffered heavy damage by becoming impaled on rocks and coral-heads were subsequently placed back into service after being quite casually repaired with cement mix and a trowel.

There are likely to be opportunities to perfect the properties of the mortar. Microscopic cracking of the mortar, which is structurally benign but increases porosity, can be prevented by the addition of glass fiber chemically treated to withstand the alkaline environment of the mortar. While glass fiber is composed of minerals that are plentiful, it is currently an industrial product. However, as with cement, it is possible to imagine that a way will be found to produce it using concentrating passive solar in combination with wind or water power. The addition of glass fiber to the aggregate also makes the mortar lighter and more impact-resistant: some recent formulations for architectural use have resulted in quite thin sheets that nevertheless can withstand repeated blows with a pick. Another possible direction of research involves making the mortar self-repairing by inoculating the mortar mix with a culture of calcifying bacteria, along with their favorite food (urea). When a crack starts to form, the bacteria become active and fill the crack with new calcium. It remains to be seen whether increasing ocean acidity resulting from carbon dioxide emissions will interfere with this process.

So the prospects for building quite serviceable sailboat hulls without recourse to industrial materials (with the exception of reused steel) appear to be reasonably good, provided the skills can be established ahead of time and passed on as part of a living tradition. But what about the other essential components of a sailing vessel — the masts, the sails and the rigging? The current, industrial practice is to use extruded aluminium masts, or masts glued up out of precisely fitted planks using high-technology synthetic adhesives. In the past, sailing vessels had "grown" masts, which consisted of a single tree trunk. The smaller vessels could use such a mast in a freestanding fashion, supported only at the deck and shaped to give it a taper toward the top. On larger vessels the masts were supported on all sides by tensioned lines. By the time the age of sail was nearing its end, however, trees of the right size and quality for "grown" masts had become a rarity and shipwrights were forced to switch to "made" masts which consisted of many smaller tree trunks shaped and held together using dowels and hoops.

Although "made" masts could be given arbitrary thickness and taper, eliminating the need for standing rigging, apparently shipwrights could not imagine such a radical departure from the norm. For such radical post-industrial shipbuilding solutions we have to turn to the ancient Chinese, who explored much of the earth in their large sailing junks, which, incidentally, were equipped with freestanding "made" masts of bamboo. The advantages of freestanding masts are numerous: their design is much simpler, they have less wind resistance up high where wind speeds are highest, they can be taken down more easily, to make the vessel less noticeable when navigating inland and so to avoid predation, or to pass under fixed bridges, overhanging trees and other obstructions. It is difficult to design freestanding masts that are particularly tall, but since shoal-draft vessels of the sort being considered here cannot support masts that are much taller than the length of the vessel without making it unstable, equipping them with freestanding, tapered, "made" masts seems the obvious choice.

With regard to sails and control lines, the modern practice is to use low-stretch synthetic fiber such as long-strand polyester. The high strength and low stretch of these materials allowed designs to progress very far in the direction of very large expanses of fabric unsupported by any internal structure, controlled by a few lines, all under very high tension. The pre-industrial practice was to use much weaker and stretchier natural fiber: cotton or linen for sails, and manilla or hemp for rope, limiting the size of each sail. However, the ancient Chinese have done extremely well with gigantic sails made of even weaker materials such as woven grass mat by using an ingenious rig that distributed the loads over many small lines and panels of sailcloth: the Chinese junk rig. Modern adherents of this rig rave about its numerous merits such as the fact that it can be controlled as a unit, and have crossed oceans with sails so threadbare that they could be punctured with a fist, yet they held together through ocean storms because the individual panels were small and braced by stiff battens. At present, the Chinese junk rig is a splendid solution waiting for the problem that is about to present itself: the end of strong, low-stretch synthetic sailcloth. The junk rig is wonderfully versatile, allowing a vessel to be controlled without leaving the pilothouse, tacked up a narrow channel and even sailed backward. Blondie Hasler, who has crossed the Atlantic in his junk-rigged boat *Jester* wrote that the ease of handling was such that he could imagine making the entire crossing in bathrobe and slippers, without once venturing out on deck.

But sometimes an auxiliary form of propulsion is needed — if only to be able to steer when drifting in a tidal or river current while becalmed, or to pass under obstructions with the masts lowered, or to shift berth in close quarters. Luckily, we can once again turn to the Chinese for a post-industrial solution that has already stood the test of time. Oars are not particularly useful on anything but very small sailboats because they would have to be quite long to reach down to the water. This would make them unwieldy and their action awkward and inefficient. Oars are inefficient in any case, because they have to be lifted out of the water and retracted for each stroke, wasting time and energy. The Chinese solution for propelling larger sailing vessels is the *yuloh*: a long, slightly curved sculling oar that extends aft with its blade floating just below the water. To propel the vessel, it is pivoted and moved to and fro by crewmen standing before the mainmast. The resulting motion is vaguely similar to that of a fishtail. With roughly 1 kW peak power output per crewman, and with 2 *yulohs* worked by 4 crewmen each, as much as 8 kW (10 horsepower) can be produced for a duration. On flat, still water this is more than sufficient to move even a fairly large vessel. When not in use, the blades of the *yulohs* are lifted out of the water and lashed to the sides of the hull.

Vessels of the design sketched out in this article would be of immediate practical value to numerous people throughout the world because of the wide variety of purposes to which they can be put. They can be used for transporting passengers and freight over open water and on rivers and canals. They can be used as floating, mobile workshops, schools, clinics, warehouses, offices and residences on coastal land that is increasingly prone to flooding. This would allow people to hold onto their land for as long as possible and to float closer to shore or further inland when the time comes without becoming dispossessed in the process. The boats can be used for seasonal migrations, to gather scarce resources over a wider expanse and to avoid having to spend summers or winters in hot or cold climates. All that is required for building such boats is a bit of coastal land and materials, some of which are free (river sand), some quite inexpensive (cement, recycled metal), and others that can be grown and worked by hand (bamboo, hemp). The largest input is, of course, labor. Much of it can be semi-skilled physical labor that can be contributed by the local community. Some highly experienced, expert labor is also needed but only at certain key stages of the building process to ensure that the results are long-lasting, safe and reliable.

In a world where rising seas are already putting millions of people at risk of losing their homes, their lives or both, a program of building large numbers of inexpensive, practical, utilitarian and versatile sailing craft is a direct way to provide flood-proof, earthquake-proof, fireproof and storm-proof habitation, to build communities, to create local resilience and to provide hope for a survivable future. It is a way to create connections between different parts of the planet that can survive into the post-industrial age. It enables people and goods to be carried in a way that avoids the predation that will be an inevitable element of a disrupted time. It offers us an opportunity to make sure that we remain a seafaring species even as the fossil-fuel era recedes into history, and gives us a way to salvage something very useful out of the wreckage of our industrial past.

Endnote

1. Downloadable from culturechange.org/cms/index.php?option=com_content&task=view&id=67&Itemid=1

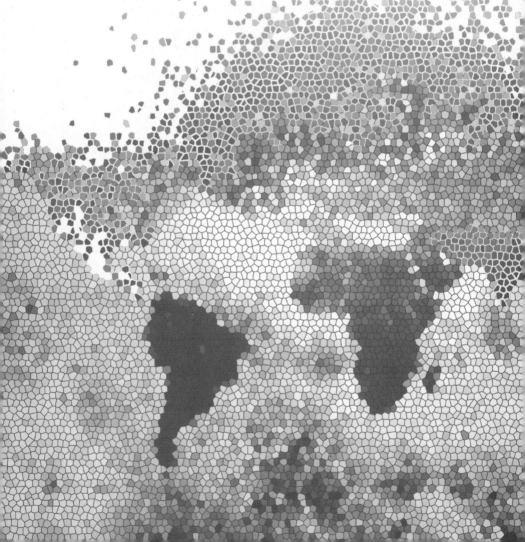

PART VI

CHANGING THE WAY
WE THINK

The Psychological Roots
of Resource Overconsumption

Nate Hagens

Humans have an innate need for status and for novelty in their lives. Unfortunately, the modern world has adopted very energy- and resource-intensive ways of meeting those needs. Other ways are going to have to be found as part of the move to a more sustainable world.

Most people associate the word "sustainability" with changes to the supply side of our modern way of life such as using energy from solar flows rather than fossil fuels, recycling, green tech and greater efficiency. In this essay, however, I will focus on the demand-side drivers that explain why we continue to seek and consume more stuff.

When addressing "demand-side drivers," we must begin at the source: the human brain. The various layers and mechanisms of our brain have been built on top of each other via millions and millions of iterations, keeping intact what "worked" and adding via changes and mutations what helped the pre-human, pre-mammal organism to incrementally advance. Brain structures that functioned poorly in ancient environments are no longer around. Everyone reading this page is descended from the best of the best at both surviving and procreating which, in an environment of privation and danger where most "iterations" of our evolution happened, meant acquiring necessary resources, achieving status and possessing brains finely tuned to natural dangers and opportunities.

This essay outlines two fundamental ways in which the evolutionarily derived reward pathways of our brains are influencing our modern overconsumption. First, financial wealth accumulation and the accompanying conspicuous consumption are generally regarded as the signals of modern success for our species. This gives the rest of us environmental cues to compete for more and more stuff as a proxy of our status and achievement. A second and more subtle driver is that we are easily hijacked by and habituated to novel stimuli. As we shall see, the prevalence of novelty today eventually demands higher and higher levels of neural stimulation, which often need increased consumption to satisfy. Thus it is this combination of pursuit of social status and the plethora of *novel activities* that underlies our large appetite for resource throughput.

Status

Evolution has honed and culled "what worked" by combining the substrate of life with eons' worth of iterations. Modern biological research has focused on the concept of "relative fitness," a term for describing those adaptations that are successful in propelling genes, or suites of genes, into the next generation and that will have out-competed those that were deleterious or did not keep up with environmental change. Though absolute fitness mattered to the individual organisms while they were alive, looking back it was "relative fitness" that shaped the bodies and brains of the creatures on the planet today.

Status, both in humans and other species, has historically been a signaling mechanism that minimized the costs of competition, whether for reproductive opportunities or for material resources. If you place ten chickens in an enclosure there will ensue a series of fights until a pecking order is established. Each bird quickly learns who it can and cannot beat and a status hierarchy is created, thus making future fights (and wastes of energy) less common. Physical competition is costly behavior that requires energy and entails risk of injury. Status is one way to determine who one can profitably challenge and who one cannot. In our ancestral environment, those men (and women) that successfully moved up the social hierarchy improved their mating and resource prospects. Those at the bottom of the status rung did not only possess fewer mating opportunities but many did not mate at all. Status among our ancestors was probably linked to those attributes providing consistent benefits to the tribe: hunting prowess, strength, leadership ability, storytelling skills etc. In modern humans, status is defined by what our modern cultures dictate. As we are living through an era of massive energy gain from fossil fuels, pure physical prowess has been replaced by digital wealth, fast cars, political connections and so on.

It follows that the larger a culture's resource subsidy (natural wealth), the more opportunity there is for "status badges" uncorrelated with basic needs such as strength, intelligence, adaptability and stamina. Though "what" defines status may be culturally derived, status hierarchies themselves are part of our evolved nature. Ancestral hominids at the bottom of the mating pecking order, ceteris paribus, are not our ancestors. Similarly, many of our ancestors had orders of magnitude more descendants than others. For example, scientists recently discovered an odd geographical preponderance for a particular Y chromosome mutation which turns out to be originally descended from Genghis Khan. Given the 16 million odd male descendants alive today with this Y marker, Mr. Khan is theorized to have had 800,000 times the reproductive success than the average male alive on the planet in AD 1200. This does not imply that we are all pillagers and conquerors — only that various phenotypic expressions have had ample opportunity to become hardwired in our evolutionary past.[1]

Mating success is a key driver in the natural world. This is all studied and documented by evolutionary research into the theory of "sexual selection," which Charles Darwin once summarized as the effects of the "struggle between the individuals of one sex, generally the males, for the possession of the other sex."[2] Biologists have shown that a primary way to reliably demonstrate one's "quality" during courtship is to display a high-cost signal — e.g. a heavy and colorful peacock's tail, an energy-expending bird-song concert, or a $100,000 sports car.[3] These costly "handicap" signals are evolutionarily stable indicators of their producer's quality, because cheap signals are too easy for low-quality imitators to fake.[4]

In this sense "waste" was an evolutionary selection! Think of three major drawbacks to a male peacock of growing such a hugely ornate tail:

1. the energy, vitamins and minerals needed to go into the creation of the tail could have been used for other survival/reproductive needs,
2. the tail makes the bird more likely to be spotted by a predator,
3. If spotted, the cumbersome tail makes escape from a predator less likely.

Overall, though, these negative "fitness hits" *must have* been outweighed by the drab female peahen's preference for males with larger, more ornate tails.

With this filter, we can understand the rationale and prevalence of *Veblen* goods (named after the 19th-century economist who coined the term "conspicuous consumption") — a group of commodities that people increasingly prefer to buy as their price gets higher because the greater price confers greater status. This biological precept of signaling theory is alive and well in the human culture.

Novelty

Modern man evolved from earlier hominids under conditions of privation and scarcity at least until about 10,000 years ago. The period since then has been too short a time to make a significant change to millions of years of prior neural sculpture. Nature made the brain's survival systems incredibly efficient. The brain is based on about 40% of all our available genes and consumes over 20% of our calorific intake. Incremental changes in how our brains recognize, process and react to the world around us either contributed to our survival and thus were carried forward, or died out.

Some changes affected *salience*, the ability to notice what is important, different or unusual. Salience recognition is part of what's called the mesolimbic dopamine reward pathway. This pathway is a system of neurons integral to survival efficiency, helping us to instantly decide what in the environment should command our attention. Historically, immediate feedback on what is "new" was critical to both avoiding danger and procuring food. Because most of what happens around us each day is predictable, processing every detail of a familiar habitat wastes brain energy. Such activity would also slow down our mental computer so that what are now minor distractions could prove deadly. Thus our ancestors living on the African savanna paid little attention to the stable mountains on the horizon but were quick to detect any movement in the bush, on the plains or at the riverbank. Those more able to detect and process "novel cues" were more likely to obtain rewards needed to survive and pass on their suites of genes. Indeed, modern experimental removal of the (dopamine) receptor genes in animals causes them to reduce exploratory behavior, a key variable related to inclusive fitness in animal biology.[5]

We are instinctually geared for individual survival — being both reward-driven, and curious. It was these two core traits that the father of economics himself, Adam Smith, predicted in *The Wealth of Nations* would be the drivers of world economic growth. According to Smith, uniting the twin economic engines of self-interest (which he termed self-love) and curiosity was ambition — "the competitive human drive for social betterment." About 70 years later, after reading Adam Smith's *Theory of Moral Sentiments*, Charles Darwin recognized the parallel between the pursuit of wealth in human societies and the competition for resources that occurred among animal species. Our market system of allocating resources and "status" can therefore be seen as the natural social culmination for an intelligent species finding an abundance of resources.

But, as we shall soon see, the revered Scottish philosopher could not have envisioned heli-skiing, Starbucks, slot machines, Facebook, email and many other stimulating and pleasurable objects and activities that people engage in today and to which they so easily become accustomed.

The Mesolimbic Dopaminergic Reward System

Traditional drug abuse happens because natural selection has shaped be-haviour-regulation mechanisms that function via chemical transmitters in our brains.[6] Addicts can become habituated to the feelings they get from cocaine, heroin or alcohol, and they need to increase their consumption over time to get the same neurotransmitter highs. This same neural reward architecture is present in all of us when considering our ecological footprints: we become habituated via a positive feedback loop to the "chemical sensations" we receive from shopping, keeping up with the Joneses (conspicuous consumption), pursuing more stock profits, and myriad other stimulating activities that a surplus of cheap energy has provided.

> Americans find prosperity almost everywhere, but not happiness. For them desire for well-being has become a restless burning passion which increases with satisfaction. To start with emigration was a necessity for them: now it is a sort of gamble, and they enjoy the sensations as much as the profit.
>
> ALEXIS DE TOCQUEVILLE,
> DEMOCRACY IN AMERICA, 1831

An explosion of neuroscience and brain-imaging research tells us that drugs of abuse activate the brain's dopamine reward system that regulates our ability to feel pleasure and be motivated for "more." When we have a great experience — a glance from a pretty girl, a lovemaking romp in the woods, a plate of fresh sushi, hitting 777 on a one-eyed bandit, catching a lunker pike, watching a sunset, hearing a great guitar riff — our brain experiences a surge in the level of the neurotransmitter dopamine. We feel warm, "in the zone" and happy. After a while, the extra dopamine gets flushed out of our system and we return to our baseline level. We go about our lives, looking forward to the next pleasurable experience. But the previous experience has been logged into our brain's limbic system, which, in addition to being a center for pleasure and emotion, holds our memory and motivation circuitry.[7] We now begin to look forward to encores of such heady stimuli and are easily persuaded toward activities that promise such a chemical reprise. These desires have their beginnings outside our conscious awareness. Recent brain-imaging research shows that drug and sexual cues as brief as 33 milliseconds can activate the dopamine circuitry, even if a person is not conscious of the cues. Perhaps there are artistically shaped sexual images hidden in advertisements for whiskey after all....

Historically, this entire system evolved from the biological imperative of survival. Food meant survival, sex meant survival (of genes or suites of genes) and additional stockpiles of both provided success relative to others, both within and between species. There was a discrete payoff to waiting hours for some movement in the brush that signaled "food," or the sound of a particular bird that circled a tree with a beehive full of honey. Our pattern recognition system on the Pleistocene would have been a grabbag of various environmental stimuli that "excited" our brains toward action that correlated with resources (typically food). In sum, the brain's reward pathways record both the actual experience of pleasure as well as ensuring that the behaviors that led to it are remembered and repeated. *Irrespective of whether they are "good" for the organism in the current context — they "feel" good, which is the mechanism our brain has left us as a heritage of natural selection.*

The (Very Important) Mechanism of Habituation

Habituation — getting used to something — and subsequent substance abuse and addiction develops because of the way we learn. Learning depends crucially on the discrepancy between the prediction and occurrence of a reward. A reward that is fully predicted does not contribute to learning.[8] The important implication of this is that learning advances only to the extent to which something is unpredicted and slows progressively as a stimuli becomes more predictable.[9] *As such, unexpected reward is a core driver in how we learn, how we experience life and how we consume resources.*

Dopamine activation has been linked with addictive, impulsive activity in numerous species. Dopamine is released within the brain not only to rewarding stimuli but also to those events that *predict* rewards. It has long been known that two groups of neurons, in the ventral tegmental and the substantia nigra pars compacta areas, and the dopamine they release, are critical for reinforcing certain kinds of behavior. Neuroscientist Wolfram Schultz measured the activity of these dopamine neurons while thirsty monkeys waited for a tone which was followed by a squirt of fruit juice into their mouths. After a series of fixed, steady amounts of juice, the volume of juice was suddenly doubled. The rate of neuron firing went from about 3 per second to 80 per second. But after several trials, after the monkeys had become habituated to this new level of reward, their dopamine firing rate returned to the baseline rate of 3 firings per second after the squirt of juice. The monkeys had become habituated to the coming reward! The opposite happened when the reward was reduced without warning. The firing rate dropped dramatically, but eventually returned to the baseline rate of 3 firings per second.[10]

The first time we experience a drug or alcohol high, the amount of chemical we ingest often exceeds the levels of naturally occurring neurotransmitters in our bodies by an order of magnitude.[11] No matter how brief, that experience is stored in our neural homes for motivation and memory — the amygdala and hippocampus. Getting drunk with your friends, getting high on a skilift, removing the undergarments of a member of the opposite sex for the first time — all initially flood the brain with dopamine alongside a picture memory of the event chemically linked to the body's pleasurable response to it. As such we look forward to doing it again, not so much because we want to repeat the activity, but because we want to recreate that "*feeling*."

But in a modern stimuli-laden culture, this process is easily hijacked. After each upward spike, dopamine levels again recede, eventually to below the baseline. The following spike doesn't go quite as high as the one before it. Over time, the rush becomes smaller, and the crash that follows becomes steeper. The brain has been fooled into thinking that achieving that high is equivalent to survival and therefore the "consume" light remains on all the time. Eventually, the brain is forced to turn on a self-defense mechanism, reducing the production of dopamine altogether — thus weakening the pleasure circuits' intended function. At this point, an "addicted" person is compelled to use the substance not to get high, but just to feel normal —

since one's own body is producing little or no endogenous dopamine response. Such a person has reached a state of "anhedonia", or inability to feel pleasure via normal experiences. Being addicted also raises the risk of having depression; being depressed increases the risk of self-medicating, which then leads to addiction, etc. via positive feedback loops.

In sum, when exposed to novel stimuli, high levels of curiosity (dopamine) are generated, but it is the *unexpected reward* that causes their activation. If I order a fantastic array of sushi and the waiter brings me a toothpick and my check, I am going to have a plunge in dopamine levels which will create an immediate craving for food. It is this interplay between expected reward and reality that underlies much of our behavioral reactions. Ultimately, as it relates to resource consumption, repeated use of any dopamine-generating "activity" eventually results in tolerance. Withdrawal results in lower levels of dopamine and continuous use is required to keep dopamine at normal levels, and even higher doses to get the "high" levels of initial use. Consumers in rich nations are arguably reaching higher and higher levels of consumption tolerance. If there was such a thing as "cultural anhedonia," we might be approaching it.

America and Addiction

It would be pretty hard to be addicted directly to oil; it's toxic, slimy and tastes really bad. But given the above background, we can see how it is possible to become addicted to the energy services that oil provides. Humans are naturally geared for individual survival—curious, reward-driven and self-absorbed—but modern technology has now become a vector for these cravings. Material wealth and the abundant choices available in contemporary US society are unique in human (or animal) experience; never before in the history of our species have so many enjoyed (used?) so much. Within a culture promoting "more," it is no wonder we have so many addicts. High-density energy and human ingenuity have removed the natural constraints on our behavior of distance, time, oceans and mountains. For now, these phenomena are largely confined to developed nations—people living in a hut in Botswana or a yurt in Mongolia cannot as easily be exposed to the "hijacking stimuli" of an average Westerner, especially one living in a big city like London or Los Angeles.

Many activities in an energy-rich society unintentionally target the difference between expected and unexpected reward. Take sportfishing for example. If my brother and I are on a lake fishing and we get a bite, it sends a surge of excitement through our bodies — what kind of fish is it? How big is it? etc. We land an 8-inch perch! Great! A minute later we catch another 8-inch perch — wow, there must be a school! After 45 minutes of catching nothing but 8-inch perch, our brain comes to expect this outcome, and we need something bigger, or a different species, to generate the same level of excitement, so we will likely move to a different part of the lake in search of "bigger" and/or "different" fish. (Though my brother claims he would never tire of catching 8-inch perch I think he's exaggerating.) Recreational fishing is benign (if not to the fish), but one can visualize other more resource-intensive pastimes activating similar circuitry. New shoes, new cars, new vacations, new home improvements, new girlfriends are all present on the modern unexpected reward smorgasbord.

The habituation process explains how some initially benign activities can morph into things more destructive. Weekly church bingo escalates to $50 blackjack tables; the *Sports Illustrated* swimsuit edition results, several years down the road, in the monthly delivery (in unmarked brown packaging) of *Jugs* magazine or webcams locked in on a bedroom in Eastern Europe; youthful rides on a rollercoaster evolve into annual heli-skiing trips, etc. The World Wide Web is especially capable of hijacking our neural reward pathways. The 24/7 ubiquity and nearly unlimited options for distraction on the internet almost seem to be perfectly designed to hone in on our brains' G-spot. Shopping, pornography, gambling, social networking and information searches easily out-compete the non-virtual, more mundane (and necessary) activities of yesteryear. Repetitive internet use can be highly addictive, though psychiatrists in different countries are debating whether it is a true addiction. For better or worse, the first things I do in the morning is a) check what time it is, b) start the coffee machine then c) check my email, to see what "novelty" might be in my inbox. Bills to pay, and emails from people who are not important or interesting, wait until later in the day, or are forgotten altogether.

There are few healthy men on the planet today who do not respond in social settings to the attention of a high-status, attractive 20- to 30-something woman. This is *salient* stimuli, irrespective of the man's marital status. But here is one example of where nature and nurture mesh. Despite the fact that 99+% of our history was polygynous, modern culture precludes men from running around pell-mell chasing women; we have rules, laws and institutions such as marriage. However, habituation to various matrimonial aspects combined with exposure to dozens or even hundreds of alternatives annually in the jet age may at least partially explain the 60%+ divorce rate in modern society.

The entire brain and behavior story is far more complex than just one neurotransmitter but the pursuit of this particular "substance" is clearly correlated with anxiety, obesity and the general increasing of conspicuous consumption in our society. That dopamine is directly involved is pretty clear. Parkinson's disease is a condition where dopamine is lacking in an area of the brain necessary for motor coordination. The drug, Mirapex, increases dopamine levels in that area of the brain, but since pills are not lasers, it also increases dopamine in other areas of the body, including (surprise) the reward pathways. There are numerous lawsuits currently pending by Parkinson's patients who after taking the drug, developed sex, gambling, shopping and overeating compulsions.[12]

Our brain can also be tricked by the food choices prevalent in an abundant-energy society. We evolved in situations where salt and sugar were rare and lacking and signaled nutrition. So now, when we taste Doritos or Ben and Jerry's Chocolate Fudge Brownie ice cream, our reward pathways say "yes yes—this is good for you!!" Our "rational" brain attempts to remind us of the science showing obesity comes from eating too much of the wrong type of foods, but often loses out to the desire of the moment. Fully 30% of Americans are now categorized as obese. And, since we are exporting our culture (via the global market system) to developing countries, it is no surprise that China is following in our footsteps. From 1991 to 2004 the percentage of adults who are overweight or obese in China increased from 12.9% to 27.3%.[13] Furthermore, we can become habituated to repeated presentation of the same food type; we quickly get tired of it and crave something different.[14] We like variety—in food and in other things. Finally, when we overstimulate the brain pleasure centers with highly palatable food, these systems adapt by decreasing their own activity. Many of us now require constant stimulation from palatable (fatty) food to avoid entering a persistent state of negative reward. It is this dynamic that has led scientists to recently declare that fatty foods such as cheesecake and bacon are addictive in the same manner as cocaine.[15] And as we shall see, both what we eat and experience not only alters our own health, but also makes it more difficult to act in environmentally benign ways.

Impulsivity, Discount Rates and Preparing for the Future

Overconsumption fueled by increasing neural high water marks is a problem enough in itself, but such widespread neural habituation also diminishes our ability to think and act about the coming societal transition away from fossil fuels. Economists measure how much we prefer the present over the future via something called a "discount rate." (See Mark Rutledge's essay in this book). A discount rate of 100% means we prefer the present completely and put no value on the future. A discount rate of 0% means we treat the future 1000 years from now equally the same as 5 minutes from now.

Certain types of people have steeper discount rates than others; in general, gamblers, drinkers, drug users, men (vs. women), low IQ scorers, risk-takers, those exhibiting cognitive load, etc. all tend to show more preference for small short-term rewards rather than waiting for larger, long-term ones.[16] On average, heroin addicts' discount rates are over double those of control groups. Furthermore, in tests measuring discount rates and preferences among opium addicts, opioid-dependent participants discounted delayed monetary rewards significantly more than did non-drug using controls. Also, the opioid-dependent participants discounted delayed opium significantly more than delayed money, more evidence that brain chemicals are central to an organism's behavior and that money and other abstractions are secondary.[17] Research has also shown that subjects deprived of addictive substances have an even greater preference for immediate consumption over delayed gratification.[18]

Even if we are not snorting cocaine or binge drinking on a Tuesday night, in a world with so much choice and so many stimulating options vying for our attention, more and more of our time is taken up feeding neural compulsions. In any case, facing large long-term risks like peak oil and climate change requires dedicated long-term thinking—so having neural wiring that, due to cultural stimuli, focuses more and more on the present instead, is a big problem.

The Fallacy of Reversibility aka "The Ratchet Effect"

Though our natural tendency is to want more of culturally condoned pursuits, many such desires do have negative feedbacks. For instance, I can only eat about three cheeseburgers before my stomach sends a signal to my brain that I am full—and at four or five my stomach and esophagus would fill to the level I couldn't physically eat another. However, this is not so with virtual wealth, or many of the "wanting" stimuli promoted in our economic "more equals better" culture. Professor Juliet Schor of Boston University has demonstrated that irrespective of their baseline salary, Americans always say they'd like to make a little more the following year.[19] Similar research by UCLA economist Richard Easterlin (whose "Easterlin Paradox" points out that average happiness has remained constant over time despite sharp rises in GDP per capita) followed a cohort of people over a 16-year period. The participants were asked at the onset to list 10 items that they desired (e.g. sports car, snowmobile, house, private jet). During the 16-year study, all age groups tested did acquire some/many of the things they originally desired. But in each case, their *desires increased more than their acquisitions.*[20] This phenomenon is termed the "Hedonic Treadmill." I believe this behavior is at the heart of the Limits to Growth problem, and gives me less confidence that we are just going to collectively "tighten our belts" when the events accompanying resource depletion get a little tougher. That is, unless we somehow change what it is that we want more of.

The Ratchet Effect is a term for a situation in which, once a certain level is reached, there is no going back, at least not all the way. In evolution the effect means once a suite of genes become ubiquitous in a population, there is no easy way to "unevolve" it. A modern example of this is obesity—as we get fatter the body creates more lipocytes (cells composing adipose tissue). But this system doesn't work in reverse; even though we can lose some of the weight gain, the body can't eliminate these new cells—they are there to stay.

After peak oil/peak credit, the ratchet effect is likely to mean that any rules requiring a more equitable distribution of wealth will not be well received by those who amassed wealth and status when oil was abundant. In biology, we see that animals will expend more energy defending freshly gained territory than they would to gain it if it was unclaimed. In humans, the pain from losing money is greater than the pleasure of gaining it. Economists describe and quantify this phenomenon as the endowment effect and loss aversion. And, as an interesting but disturbing aside, recent research suggests that the dopamine that males receive during acts of aggression rivals that of food or sex.[20, 21] All these different dynamics of "what we have" and "what we are used to" will come into play in a world with less resources available per head.

Old Brain, New Choices

Humans have always lived in the moment but our gradual habituation to substances and activities that hijack our reward system may be forcing us, in aggregate, to live so much for the present that we are ignoring the necessity for urgent societal change. Unwinding this cultural behavior may prove difficult. The sensations we seek in the modern world are not only available and cheap, but most are legal, and the vast majority are actually condoned and promoted by our culture. If the rush we get from an accomplishment is tied to something that society rewards we call it ambition, if it is attached to something a little scary, then we label the individual a "risk taker" and if it is tied to something illegal — only then have we become an "addict" or substance abuser. So it seems culture has voted on which ways of engaging our evolutionarily derived neurotransmitter cocktails are "good" to pursue.

Drug addiction is defined as "*the compulsive seeking and taking of a drug despite adverse consequences.*" If we substitute the word "resource" for "drug," have we meaningfully violated or changed this definition? That depends on the definition of "drug." "*A substance that a person chemically comes to rely upon*" is the standard definition but ultimately it is any activity or substance that generates brain chemicals that we come to require/need. Thus, it is not crude oil's intrinsic qualities we crave but the biochemical sensations to which we have become accustomed arising from the use of its embodied energy.

Take stock trading for example. Neuroscience scans show that stock trading lights up the same brain areas as picking nuts and berries do in other primates.

I think people trade for

1. money/profit (to compete/move up the mating ladder),
2. the feeling of being "right" (whether they ever spend the money or not) and
3. the excitement/dopamine they get from the unexpected nature of the market puzzle.

While these three are not mutually exclusive, it is not clear to me which objective dominates, especially among people who have already attained infinite wealth. (Technically, infinite wealth is their annual expenses divided by the interest rate on Treasury bills. This gives the sum of money that would provide them with an income to buy all they want forever.) When I worked for Lehman Brothers, my billionaire clients seemed less "happy" on average than the $30k-a-year clerks processing their trades. They had more exciting lives perhaps, but they were not happier; that is, their reward baseline reset to zero each morning irrespective of the financial wealth they had amassed in previous days or years. They wanted "more" because they were habituated to getting more—it was how they kept score. Clearly, unless you inherit, you don't get to be a billionaire if you are easily satisfied.

MRI scans show that objects associated with wealth and social dominance activate reward-related brain areas. In one study, people's anterior cingulate (a brain region linked to reward) had more blood and oxygen response to visual cues of sports cars than to limousines or small cars.[22]

If compulsive shopping was a rational process, and our choices were influenced only by need, then brand-name T-shirts would sell no better than less expensive shirts of equal quality. The truth is that many shopping decisions are biased by corporate advertising campaigns or distorted by a desire to satisfy some competitive urge or emotional need. For most of us, the peak "neurotransmitter cocktail" is the moment we decide to buy that new "item." After a brief euphoria and a short respite, the clock starts ticking on the next craving/purchase.

Adaptation Executors

There is a shared mythology in America that we can each enjoy fame and opulence at the top of the social pyramid. 78% of Americans still believe that anybody in America can become rich and live the good life.[23] Although in our economic system, not everyone can be a Warren Buffet or Richard Branson—there are not enough resources—it is the carrot of potential reward that keeps people working 50 hours a week until they retire at 65. All cannot be first. All cannot be wealthy, which makes our current version of capitalism, given the finite resources of the planet, not dissimilar from a Ponzi scheme.

Envy for status is a strong motivator. Increasing evidence in the fields of psychology and economics shows that above a minimum threshold of income/wealth, it's one's relative wealth that matters, not absolute. In an analysis of more than 80,000 observations, the relative rank of an individual's income predicted the individual's general life satisfaction whereas absolute income and reference income had little to no effect.[24] The "aspiration gap" is economic-speak for the relative fitness/status drive toward who/what is at the top of the cultural status hierarchy. For decades (centuries?), China has had a moderate aspiration gap, but since the turbo-capitalist global cues have spread across Asia, hundreds of millions of Chinese have raised their pecuniary wealth targets.

Economist Robert Frank asked people in the US if they would prefer living in a 4,000-square-foot house where all the neighboring houses were 6,000 square feet or a 3,000-square-foot house where the surrounding houses were 2,000 square feet. The majority of people chose the latter — *smaller in absolute terms but bigger in relative size*. A friend of mine says that when he last visited Madagascar, the fifth poorest nation on earth, the villagers huddled around the one TV in the village watching the nation's most popular TV show *Melrose Place*, giving them a window of desire into Hollywood glitz and glamor, and a beacon to dream about and strive for. Recently, a prince in the royal family of UAE paid $14 million for a licence plate with the single numeral "1." "I bought it because I want to be the best in the world," Saeed Abdul Ghafour Khouri explained. What environmental cues do the kids watching TV in the UAE or the US receive?

As a species, we are both cooperative and competitive depending on the circumstances, but it's very important to understand that our neuro-physiological scaffolding was assembled during long mundane periods of privation in the ancestral environment. This is still not integrated into the Standard Social Science Model that forms the basis of most liberal arts educations (and economic theory). A new academic study on relative income as a primary driver of life satisfaction had over 50 references, *none of which* linked to the biological literature on status, sexual selection or relative fitness. Furthermore, increasing cognitive neuroscience and evolutionary psychology research illustrates that we are not the self-interested "utility maximizers" that economists claim, but are highly "other regarding" — we care about other people's welfare as well as our own. Though high-perceived relative fitness is a powerful behavioral carrot, inequality has pernicious effects on societies; it erodes trust, increases anxiety and illness, and leads to excessive consumption.[25] Health steadily worsens as one descends the social ladder, even within the upper and middle classes.[26]

When a child is born, he has all the genetic material he will ever have. All his ancestors until that moment had their neural wiring shaped for fitness maximization — but when he is born, his genes will interact with environment cues showing those ways to compete for status, respect, mating prospects, resources etc. which are socially acceptable. From this point forward, the genes are "fixed" and the infant goes through life as an *"adaptation executor"* NOT a fitness maximizer. What will a child born in the 21st century "learn" to compete for? Historically, we have always pursued social status, though status has been measured in dramatically different ways throughout history. Currently, most people pursue money as a shortcut fitness marker, though some compete in other ways—politics, knowledge, etc. Thus, a large looming problem is that the Chinese and other rapidly developing nations don't just aspire to the wealth of average Americans—they want to go the whole hog to be millionaires.

Conclusions

We are a clever, ambitious species that evolved to live almost entirely off of solar flows. Eventually we worked out how to access stored sunlight in the form of fossil fuels which required very little energy/natural resource input to extract. The population and growth trajectory that ensued eventually oversatisfied the "more is better" mantra of evolution and we've now developed a habit of requiring more fossil fuels and more clever ways to use them every year. There also exists a pervasive belief that human ingenuity will create unlimited substitutes for finite natural resources like oil and water. Put simply, it is likely that our abundant natural resources are not only required, but will be taken for granted until they are gone.

This essay has explored some of the underlying drivers of resource depletion and planetary consumption: more humans competing for more stuff that has more novelty. The self-ambition and curiosity that Adam Smith hailed as the twin engines of economic growth have been quite effective over the past 200 years. But Adam Smith did caution in *Moral Sentiments* that human envy and a tendency toward compulsions, if left unchecked, would undermine the empathic social relationships that would be essential to the successful long-term operation of free markets. Amidst so much novel choice and pressure to create wealth, we are discovering some uncomfortable facts, backed up by modern neurobiology, that confirm his concerns. In an era of material affluence, when wants have not yet been fully constrained by limited resources, the evidence from our ongoing American experiment conclusively shows that humans have trouble setting limits on our instinctual cravings. What's more, our rational brains have quite a hard time acknowledging this uncomfortable but glaring fact.

This essay undoubtedly raises more questions than it answers. If we can be neurally hijacked, what does it suggest about television, advertising, media, etc? The majority of the neuro-economic sources I used in writing this were a *by-product* of studies funded by neuromarketing research! How does "rational utility" function in a society where we are being expertly marketed to pull our evolutionary triggers to funnel the money upwards? How does Pareto optimality—the assumption that all parties to an exchange will be made better off—hold up when considering neuro-economic findings? Recent studies show that American young people (between ages of 8–18) use 7.5 hours of electronic media (internet, iPod, Wii, etc.) per day and, thanks to multitasking, had a total of 11 hours "gadget" exposure per day![27] The children with the highest hours of use had markedly poorer grades and more behavioral problems. How will these stimuli-habituated children adapt to a world of fewer resources?

Not all people pursue money, but our cultural system does. An unbridled pursuit of profits has created huge disparities in digitally amassed monetary wealth both within and between nations, thus holding a perpetually unattainable carrot in front of most of the world's population. So it is not just the amount we consume that is unsustainable, but also the message we send to others, internationally, nationally and in our neighborhoods.

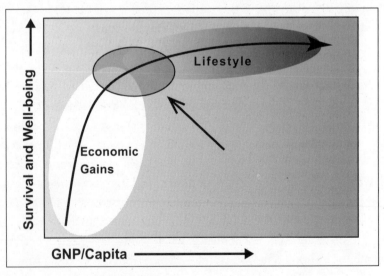

Meeting in the middle? The arrowed circle on this Inglehart Curve represents the highest level of well-being/survival consistent with a low level of resource use. It is therefore a target at which a society should aim. (Source: N. Hagens and R. Inglehart 1997.)

At the same time, traditional land, labor and capital inputs have been subsidized by the ubiquity of cheap energy inputs, and more recently by a large increase in both government and private debt, a spatial and temporal reallocator of resources. These cheap energy/cheap credit drivers will soon be a thing of the past, and this will curtail future global growth aspirations. When this happens, and we face the possibility of currency reform and what it might mean to start afresh with the same resources but a new basket of claims and assumptions, we will need to remember the neural backdrops of competition for relative status, and how people become habituated to high neural stimuli. Perhaps, given the supply-side limits and neural aspirations, some new goals can be attempted at lower absolute levels of consumption by at least partially lowering the amplitude of social rank.

We cannot easily change our penchant to want more. We can only change cultural cues on how we define the "more" and thereby reduce resource use. In the cross-cultural study referenced in the diagram above, we can see that well-being increases only slightly as GNP increases above some minimum threshold. The arrowed circle would be a logical place for international policymakers concerned about planetary resource and sink capacity to aim to reach via taxes, disincentives to conspicuous consumption and subsidies. However, I fear that nations and governments will do little to slow their consumption and will get increasingly locked into defending the status quo instead.

In a society with significant overall surpluses, people who actively lower their own economic and ecological footprint might get by very well because their relative status — which is typically above average — allows them to make such reductions without reaching limits that compromise their well-being. As these people allocate time and resources away from financial marker capital and toward social, human, built and natural capital, they have an opportunity to redefine what sort of "wealth" we compete for and thus potentially lead by example. However, personal experience with people in the lifestyle section of the chart leads me to believe that they will probably continue to pursue more resources and status even if it doesn't improve their well-being.

Put aside peak oil and climate change for the moment. Though it is difficult, we have it in us as individuals and as a culture to make small changes to the way our brains get "hijacked" and, as a result, achieve more benign consequences. For example, we can choose to go for a jog/hike instead of sending ten emails and websurfing, we can choose to have a salad instead of a cheeseburger, we can choose to play a game or read a story with our children instead of making business phone calls. But most of these types of choices require both prior planning and discipline if our brains are not to fall into the neural grooves that modern culture has created. It takes conscious plans to change these behaviors, and for some this will be harder than for others But in choosing to do so, besides slowing and eventually reversing the societal stimulation feedback loop, we are likely to make ourselves healthier and happier. In neuro-speak, many of the answers facing a resource-constrained global society involve the rational neocortex suppressing and overriding the primitive and stronger limbic impulses.

So, ultimately, we must start to address new questions. In addition to asking source/sink questions like "how much do we have" we should begin asking questions like "how much is enough?" Reducing our addictive behaviors collectively will make it easier to face the situations likely to arise during an energy descent. Changing the environmental cues on what we compete for, via taxes or new social values, will slow down resource throughput and give future policymakers time to forge a new economic system consistent with our evolutionary heritage and natural resource balance sheet. We will always seek status and have hierarchies in human society but unless we first understand and then integrate our various demand-side constraints into our policies, culture and institutions, sustainability will be another receding horizon. Though there is probably no blanket policy to solve our resource crisis that would both work and gain social approval, an understanding of the main points of this essay might be a springboard to improve one's own happiness and well-being. Which would be a start....

Endnotes

1. news.nationalgeographic.com/news/2003/02/0214_030214_genghis.html.
2. C. Darwin, *The Descent of Man and Selection in Relation to Sex* (John Murray, 1871).
3. G. F. Miller, "Sexual Selection for Cultural Displays" in *The Evolution of Culture*, eds. R. Dunbar, C. Knight and C. Power (Edinburgh U. Press, 1999), 71–91.
4. A. Zahavi and A. Zahavi, *The Handicap Principle: A Missing Piece of Darwin's Puzzle* (Oxford University Press, 1997).
5. Dulawa et al., "Dopamine D4 Receptor-Knock-Out Mice Exhibit Reduced Exploration of Novel Stimuli," *Journal of NeuroScience*, 19:9550–9556 (1999).
6. M. S. Gerald and J. D. Higley, "Evolutionary Underpinnings of Excessive Alcohol Consumption," *Addiction* 97 (2002): 415–425.
7. Peter Whybrow, *American Mania* (Norton, 2005).

8. P. Waelti, A. Dickinson and W. Schultz, "Dopamine Responses Comply with Basic Assumptions of Formal Learning Theory," *Nature* 412 (2001): 43–48.

9. R. A. Rescorla, A. R. Wagner, "A Theory of Pavlovian Conditioning: Variations in the Effectiveness of Reinforcement and Nonreinforcement," in *Classical Conditioning II: Current Research and Theory,* eds A. H. Black and W. F. Prokasy (Appleton Century Crofts, 1972), 64–99.

10. W. Schultz et al., "A Neural Substrate of Prediction and Reward," *Science,* 275 :1593–1599.

11. R. Dudley, "Fermenting Fruit and the Historical Ecology of Ethanol Ingestion: Is Alcoholism in Modern Humans an Evolutionary Hangover?" *Addiction* 97 (2002): 381–388.

12. Dodd et al., "Pathological Gambling Caused by Drugs Used to Treat Parkinson Disease," *Arch. Neurol.* 62 (2005): 1377–1381.

13. Barry Popkin, "The World Is Fat," *Scientific American* (September, 2007): 94, ISSN 0036-8733.

14. M. Ernst, L. Epstein, "Habituation of Responding for Food in Humans," *Appetite* 38, no. 3 (June 2002): 224–234.

15. P. Johnson, P. Kenny, "Addiction-Like Reward Dysfunction and Compulsive Eating in Obese Rats: Role for Dopamine D2 Receptors," *Nature: Neuroscience* (3/28/2010).

16. Chablis et al., "Intertemporal Choice," *The New Palgrave Dictionary of Economics* (2007).

17. Madden et al., "Impulsive and Self-Control Choices in Opioid-Dependent Patients and Non-Drug Using Control Participants: Drug and Monetary Rewards," *Environmental and Clinical Psychopharmacology* 5, no. 3 (1997): 256–262.

18. L. Giorodano et al., "Mild Opioid Deprivation Increases the Degree that Opioid-Dependent Outpatients Discount Delayed Heroin and Money," *Psychopharmacology* 163 (2002): 174–182.

19. Juliet Schor, *The Overspent American: Why We Want What We Don't Need* (Harper Perennial, 1999).

20. Richard Easterlin, "Explaining Happiness" (September 4, 2003), 10.1073/pnas.1633144100 (especially Table 3).

21. M. Couppis, C. Kennedy, "The Rewarding Effect of Aggression," *Psychopharmacology* 197, no. 3 (April 2008).

22. S. Erket et al.,"Cultural Objects Modulate Reward Circuitry," *Neuroreport* 13, no. 18 (Dec 20 2002): 2499–503 12499856.

23. Robert Samuelson, "Ambition and Its Enemies" *Newsweek* (Aug 23 1999).

24. C. Boyce et al., "Money and Happiness — Rank of Income, Not Income, Affects Life Satisfaction," *Psychological Science* (Feb 2010) pss.sagepub.com/content/early/2010/02/17/0956797610362671.full.

25. Richard Wilkinson and Kate Pickett, *The Spirit Level — Why Greater Equality Makes Societies Stronger* (Bloomsbury Press, 2010).

26. Michael Marmot, *The Status Syndrome: How Social Standing Affects Our Health and Longevity* (Holt Publishing, 2005).

27. *Generation M2 — Media in the Lives of 8–18 Year Olds* (Kaiser Family Foundation, 2010), kff.org/entmedia/upload/8010.pdf.

Busy Doing Nothing:
Seven Reasons for Humanity's Inertia in the Face of Critical Threats and How We Might Remove Them

MARK RUTLEDGE AND BRIAN DAVEY

The addiction to dopamine highs described by Nate Hagens in the previous article is just one reason why humans have failed to curb their excessive resource consumption. Six others are outlined here, some of which are systemic; others the result of the way humanity evolved. Our best chance of counteracting them will come when the crisis pushes us out of our comfortable ruts.

Mark Rutledge writes:

Throughout my 25 years as an environmental activist, I have been struck by the lack of importance other people give to my concerns. For example, the most common response amongst family, friends and classes when I enter into another passionate discourse on the latest climate change science is what I term the "MEGO effect" (My Eyes Glaze Over). It's no better now than it was when I started out, even though the environmental threat has increased and its causes are understood and are rapidly becoming quantified. As Professor David Suzuki put it, the world is on a "blind date with disaster." Yet, rather than this enabling me to move in from the margins and play some useful role in putting matters right, I am beginning to resemble William Blake's "dog starv'd at his Master's gate" which "predicts the ruin of the state."

Well, I'm not happy about this since, without indulging in what Camilla Cavendish of the London *Times* calls "climate porn," we are, as the New Economics Foundation put it in their 2008 publication *The New Green Deal— 100 Months to Save the Planet*, in the final countdown to irreversible climate change. Rather than invite the same glazed looks by writing about the science of climate change and policies to prevent it, however, I'm going to explore some of the reasons for the individual and collective inertia that seems to be the response to the approaching catastrophe.

Reason for Inertia 1: Following the Herd

There is a deeply ingrained human tendency to convince oneself that everything is okay because no one else is worried. Two psychologists, John Darley and Bibby Latané, have demonstrated that the more people who witness an event, the less responsible any one of them feels for doing anything about what they see. They invited students to undertake an exam in an assembly hall. Only one student was in the hall at a time and the rest of the "examinees" were actors. The student and actors were then presented with an exam paper. In the middle of the exam, Darley and Latané started filling the hall with smoke through the ducts and observed the responses. The actors were instructed to continue with their exam but, in each case, the unsuspecting student observed the smoke, looked at the inaction of his or her fellow examinees and continued to write. When the control experiment involved a single student, once the smoke was observed, the individual rapidly made a decision to evacuate the hall. This exercise and others along similar lines demonstrate how, as Camilla Cavendish puts it, "the inaction of other people can make us underestimate threats to our own safety."

Reason for Inertia 2: The Post-Trust Society

We live in what Professor Ragnar Lofstedt calls a *"post-trust society."* The public and thus the electorate no longer trust politicians, regulators or big business. In Ireland, some of the reasons are obvious — infected blood scandals, judicial cover-ups, clerical child abuse and corrupt politicians. The result was demonstrated in the first Lisbon Treaty referendum vote when the mainstream political parties representing 90% of the electorate failed to convince the voters that the treaty should be passed. A motley collection of extremist, single-issue campaigners gained a comprehensive victory over the pro-treaty forces. One of the central planks of their victory was that the voters didn't trust the pro-Europe parties' assurances over corporation tax, abortion and the possibility of conscription to a European army. While these and other issues were cogently disputed and argued, a Millward-Brown survey afterwards showed that a lack of trust was an important factor in the No vote.

Trust levels are falling throughout the OECD as well. For example, in Finland the proportion of people expressing trust in their leaders fell from 65% in the 1980s to 33% in the mid-nineties, and in Germany it dropped from 51% to 29%.

Convincing people to trust, say, Al Gore, John Gormley or Duncan Stewart on climate change is just as hard as the proponents of the Lisbon Treaty (and indeed the Nice Treaty prior to that) experienced. In Autumn 2009, "Climategate" and doubts over the melt-rate of Himalayan glaciers showed the difficulty of communicating "conventional" views in the "post-trust" society. In the public's view, the whole notion of anthropogenic climate change was thrown into doubt and the work of thousands of scientists over the past 20 years was immediately devalued. Bespectacled, bearded scientists have been added to the "post-trust" lists, making it very hard to have science at the forefront of the climate debate. In effect, we are getting a re-play of the smoking debate in the late 1970s and early 1980s when respected scientists like Frederick Seitz were paid by tobacco companies to use the tactic of "uncertainty" to dispute the effects of tobacco on human health.

The emergence of the web has exacerbated the problem. The surfeit of contra-arguments and contra-opinions available on the web makes it hard to trust anything.

Reason for Inertia 3: Distorted Perceptions of Risk

Over the past 20 years, an increasingly aggressive media has used sensationalized headlines to sell papers. In the process, risks have been amplified and benefits played down. *Health in the News, Risk Reporting and Media Influence*, a major report by Roger Harrabin, Anna Coote and Jessica Allen, demonstrated the effects of the sensational face of news reporting in 2003. The report analyzed the news stories on the BBC and in three newspapers and compared the level of coverage of stories on risk with the real likelihood of someone being harmed by the risk in question. It found that scares were usually overplayed in the media. Smoking was killing 120,000 people a year in Britain at the time but it rarely featured in the news. Anyone dying of measles was 34,000 times more likely to have their cause of death mentioned on the news than if they died of smoking.

The BBC News programs surveyed for the research ran one story on smoking for every 8,500 people that died from a smoking-related disease. At the other end of the scale the BBC ran one story per 0.33 people who died of vCJD and one story per 0.25 people who died of measles. The newspapers showed a similar pattern, but their coverage was more proportionate because the news output was balanced by features where public health issues were more likely to figure.

Deaths per BBC News Story	Cause of Death
8,571	Smoking
7,500	Obesity
4,714	Alcohol
19.56	AIDS
2.33	vCJD
0.25	Measles

The sensationalization and amplification of threats like vCJD, SARS and measles versus bigger health risks is shown in the table. Climate change has already entered the risk-attenuated category, helping dampen down our responses individually, collectively and politically. News research organizations have reported that February 2007 was the peak of public interest in climate change; polls since then have shown a decline in public concern on the subject and, by association, in the willingness to act. In Ireland, we have seen simple policy changes around CFL bulbs and a motor-tax regime built around emissions become enmeshed in posturing around extreme scenarios and cheap political point-scoring.

Reason for Inertia 4: The Lack of a Notion of the Future

The collective inertia cannot be attributed exclusively to the "post-trust society" and the way the media portrays risk. There are a number of other factors at play, and these are deeply rooted in the human phenotype. In his Commonwealth Lecture in March 2008, David Suzuki explored the role of evolution in our response to climate change. He starkly outlined some of the worst environmental problems facing us:

• By 2048 marine fish will be commercially extinct.

- The IPCC (Intergovernmental Panel on Climate Change) is now 20 years old but has little to show for its efforts.
- 50,000 species are becoming extinct annually.
- 50% of the world's forests are now gone.
- Global human population, now at 6.6 billion, is expected to rise by 50% by 2050.

Little or no collective responsibility is being taken for these and other worrying projections. Suzuki looked at evolution in an effort to understand why. He pointed out that modern man, *Homo sapiens*, first emerged as a species 150,000 years ago — upright, hairless in what was, in effect, an open-air zoo. The natural attributes that one would expect to have to have to survive in such a situation — strength, speed and sensory development — were not sufficiently well developed to give man a competitive advantage.

That advantage came from intelligence, an intelligence manifest in man's memory, curiosity, inventiveness and ability to think in abstract terms. Even though the reality is the present and our memories are of the past, these attributes combined to *"create a notion of the future."* And, because the brain invented a future, humans recognized that they could affect that future by what they did in the present. Foresight became an important ability that enabled humans survive and flourish.

The ability to look ahead and maneuver to exploit opportunities and avoid threats is just as critical for survival in modern times. For at least the 40 years since the publication of *The Limits to Growth in 1972*, our foresight has warned us that are on an unsustainable path. It is now almost two decades since the 1992 Earth Summit in Rio de Janeiro when scientists warned humanity that "no more than a few decades remain before the chance to avert the threats we now confront will be lost and the prospects for humanity immeasurably diminished." The worldwide response to these messages from those with the resources to bring about change has been almost nil.

The failure of those with the power to allocate resources was graphically portrayed in 2005 by the devastation caused by Hurricane Katrina. Despite warnings about New Orlean's inadequate drainage system and levee height, tax money had not been provided to rectify them. The result was that almost the whole city was flooded and $90 billion in property damage was done over a wide area. More than 1,500 people died in Louisiana alone.

I believe this type of thing happens because while our foresight tells us what needs to be done, we fail to do it because we have evolved into a highly polarized global society where some of the very poor are forced to engage in unsustainable practices such as forest clearance in order to survive while the very rich, those with the resources to make the change, are engaged in a bacchanalian race to excess in which, up to now, no competitor has been seriously penalized for their overconsumption. Indeed, the penalty for underconsuming has been to be left behind. Trapped in this competitive system, our individual and collective ability to guard against threats such as climate change is negligible. We operate in the narrow bandwidth of daily life at the expense of developing a notion of a sustainable future and then actually bringing that future about because that would involve the overconsumers curbing their current consumption.

Reason for Inertia 5: Discount Rates

To understand our attitude to the future, we must look at "human discount rates," their evolutionary origins, and their relevance to the mitigation and adaptation to climate change. The discount rate favors the present over the future: the higher it is, the greater the bias. The term discount rate is commonly associated with the talk of equity analysts and can be defined as *"the interest rate used in determining the present value of future cash flows."* A discount rate approaching 100% means things in the future have no value at all in the present moment. A discount rate of zero means that €1 in 2050 is worth €1 today.

It was always considered that a human discount rate curve (rate/time) was exponential; this meant that we discounted the same period to period. Actual economic experiments have shown that the shape of the discount curve to be hyperbolic; in other words, the early periods have much steeper discount rates than later periods. David Laibson, in his paper "Golden eggs and hyperbolic discounting," indicates that peoples discount rates are 12% during days 0–5 but drop to 4% in days 20–25. We really prefer the present.

Comparisons between the discount rates of animals and humans show differences. Many animals have short lifespans and they have been shaped by evolution to devour food and reproduce quickly before they die. They therefore have a high discount rate. This is not a conscious choice, of course; they are simply behaving in a way that was historically successful since animals that postponed opportunities to eat might come back to find their food had been stolen. As Nate Hagens has put it, "the long arm of selection would have favored organisms that valued immediacy over those who preferred to wait."

A recent study used food rewards to study two monkey species of similar genetic makeup and living in a similar habitat but with different diets. One species was a gummivore; it scratched on trees and waited for the sap to ooze out. The other species was an opportunistic insectivore, grabbing whatever insect it could catch. Not unexpectedly, the monkeys whose feeding behavior required patience had lower discount rates than the other species.

Generally, human discount rates are not as steep as animals. David Laibson reports that in economic games, subjects who choose larger, long-term rewards have their prefrontal cortex activated. This is the part of the brain involved in conscious decision making. Those who chose the smaller, short-term rewards showed neural activity in the limbic system, the emotional mammalian brain. Humans, in effect, have two discount rates: the "thinking" discount rate with a low decline over time and the "emotional" discount rate with a steep decline over a short time. This reinforces the notion that emotions trump reason!

Reason for Inertia 6: Our Brains are Maladapted to Modern Life

In the 1997 book *Evolutionary Psychology: A Primer*, Leda Cosmides and John Tooby set out five core principles. They can be paraphrased as follows:

Principle 1: The brain's circuits are designed to generate behavior that is appropriate to our environmental circumstances.
Principle 2: Our neural circuits were designed by natural selection to solve problems that our ancestors faced during our species' evolutionary history.
Principle 3: Most of what goes on in our minds is hidden from us. As a result, our conscious experience can mislead us into thinking that our circuitry is simpler that it really is. Most problems that we think are easy to solve require very complicated neural circuitry.
Principle 4: Different neural circuits developed specifically to solve different adaptive problems.
Principle 5: Our modern skulls therefore house a Stone Age mind.

In other words, the key to understanding the modern mind is to realize that its circuits were not designed to solve the day-to-day problems of a modern European; they were designed to solve the day-to-day problems of hunter-gatherers. These Stone Age priorities produced a brain far better at solving some problems than others. For example, it is easier for us to learn to fear snakes than electric sockets, even though electric sockets pose a larger threat than snakes do in most modern communities. In many cases, our brains are better at solving the kinds of problems our ancestors faced on the African savannas than they are at solving the more familiar tasks we face in modern life.

Reason for Inertia 7: Our Addiction to a Dopamine Buzz

The neuroscientist and psychiatrist Paul D. MacLean developed his Triune (three brains in one) hypothesis in 1959. He suggests the human brain consists of a "primitive" reptilian brain around the brain stem for controlling basic instinctual survival behavior and thinking. Then there is the mammalian "Limbic" system that handles emotion, memory and feelings associated with unconscious behavioral response patterns. Finally, there is the "neocortex" which developed to enable rational thought and other higher order functions and is unique to humans. But, interestingly, human emotional response patterns depend on the neural pathways that link the right hemisphere of the neocortex to the mammalian brain which in turn links to the reptilian brain. It is these connections, where impulse can override rationality, where humans engage in activity at a societal and personal level that they know to be adverse to our health and well-being but still satiates the reptilian brain in the short term, which continue to dominate our reponse. This scenario can be seen in our relationship with tobacco, alcohol and increasingly food — the rise of obesity, diabetes and heart disease where the short-term primitive needs are met at the expense of our future condition.

Central to this behavior is dopamine. Dopamine, a core neurotransmitter, plays an integral role in our short-term desires. It is the dopamine rush that consumers feel when securing a particular handbag or winning at the bookies. Many of the modern options that engage our neurotransmitters are maladaptive. Pornography and lottery tickets give us feelings identical to those our ancestors were good at pursuing. But now, in the 21st century, they often trick our brains into responding in the way they did which led to evolutionary success.

In his 2008 book *Enough: Breaking Free from the World of More*, John Naish argues that "We are lumbered with 'wanting' brains." We want, want,

want, and are also intrigued by novelty. Our dopamine pleasure centers in our brains are flooded when we acquire and buy. A salesperson talks of "shoe-limics." The dopaminergic system is clearly one of the drivers of our short-term behavior. In essence, more dopamine craving means less concern about climate change.

So Brian, tell me, in view of all these constraints on human behavior, why do you remain optimistic that humanity will be able to change sufficiently to save itself from disaster?

Brian Davey Replies:

I wouldn't describe myself as overly optimistic but I do feel that a lot of people are capable of changing. After all, we all go through major life changes from time to time, and that gives us a collective chance to steer these personal transitions in a more ecological direction. So I think we need to explore what happens when, either intentionally or involuntarily, people move outside of their previous routines and restructure their lives.

It is not really surprising that most people's behavior is difficult to change most of the time. If you want to predict what most people will be doing tomorrow, then the best thing to do is to look at what they were doing yesterday and are doing today. Of course if it is a weekend then what they were doing last weekend would be a better predictor.

Routines make the management of everyday life a lot easier. As the English playwright and author Arnold Bennett put it: "The great advantage of being in a rut is that when one is in a rut, one knows exactly where one is" and "Any change, even a change for the better, is always accompanied by drawbacks and discomforts."

That means that people are usually open to major changes only when they are outside their routines and in transition. More normally they are blinkered and prefer to stay with the familiar. So they may hear the environmental messages of the sort Mark used to deliver but only superficially. Then they ignore them or file them in their minds as "for later action... maybe" and forget them. And if they hear the messages too often, their eyes do glaze over.

Meanwhile their routines, based on an unsustainable use of social and natural commons resources, have a "locked-in" character and are often heavily "context determined." The context includes the interrelated arrangements that arise in the relationships people have, in the places that they live and the equipment and machines that they use, sustained by their incomes and the nature of their jobs — and also by their age, health, experience, education and aspirations (or lack of aspirations).

These different elements fit together in what can be described as a "life-style package." You cannot change most elements of the package very far without having to change the other elements. For example when people become parents they need to find space for their child in their habitat and that, in turn, will affect their day-to-day financial needs. Of course it will affect their time commitments too and their relationships with their partner. A child brings with it the need for a new "package" arrangement.

If You Want to Change You Must
Take Your Relationships With You

If you want to start living differently, in a more environmentally sustainable fashion, you will usually have to take other people along with you; they too will have to change their routines and familiar patterns. Say that you decide to eat less meat for environmental reasons; if you live and eat together with others it isn't easy to do that without them having to change too. Say you want to get involved with an environmental project in your leisure time; again, you can't change how you spend your leisure time without it usually affecting the people with whom you currently spend your leisure.

That is really important because if you cannot bring along the others in your life when you decide to have a more sustainable lifestyle, then your lives with others may start to become desynchronized; partners and children start doing different things. And when people's emotional lives start to become desynchronized it does not augur well for the future of their relationships.[1]

A decision to live a more sustainable life also has knock-on consequences for where you live, your income and/or your savings and your debts. It will probably affect your work — and perhaps how you get to and from work. It may affect joint budgets with your loved ones, which includes time budgets as well as money ones.

A decision to live a more sustainable lifestyle has lots of "knock-on consequences." It takes you into unknown territory and destabilizes your usual relationships with your loved ones. It may require new situations and skills. It may take you out of your comfort zone — or you may fear that it will and decide not to look more closely at it as a result.

De-Routinization

Despite everything, there are also situations where, in the ordinary course of life, routines change or where people seek out a change in the routine because they are frustrated, bored and hemmed in by the life they are living. Every so often people go through lifestyle changes despite the risks. They seek out different things to do, in different places, with different people. As the routine is changed they have a need to review aspects of their lives, to look at options and consider different ways of acting—these are situations that may require new ideas and new skills. They may require help to make the transition too, for there is no guarantee that things will go as they hope or as well. This suggests a different way of looking at mental health crises—as botched transitions when people flounder and are disorientated and distressed by their new lives. This was anticipated by Anthony Storr[2] when he wrote

> Suppose that I become dissatisfied with my habitual self, or feel that there are areas of experience or self understanding which I cannot reach. One way of exploring these is to remove myself from present surroundings and see what emerges. This is not without its dangers. Any form of new organization or integration within the mind has to be preceded by some degree of disorganization. No one can tell, until he has experienced it, whether or not this necessary disruption of former pattern will be succeeded by something better.

There are socially typical transitions and not so typical lifestyle changes. There are voluntary changes that people launch into themselves and changes that they are forced to make, whether they like it or not.

Examples of socially typical transitions are when young adults leave the parental home, get a job and set up relationships of their own. At the other end of life they retire. Pretty much everyone goes through transitions of these kinds; these transitions are socially normal. That is not to say however that everyone makes these transitions easily or successfully. Their previous lives may not have provided the experience, skills, financial and social resources to make the transition successfully. New relationships, activities and places might require resources and skills that people do not have. Stress and distress, disorientation and breakdown are the hallmarks of a botched transition.

Midlife Crises

A slightly less normal, if not unusual, life transition is the midlife crisis where somebody reviews their value system, considers what really matters to them, and decides that the pattern of their life needs fundamental change. They may decide to downshift, accepting a lower income for less paid work and using the extra time for things that matter more to them. Downshifting is not that uncommon and usually means adopting a more sustainable lifestyle. It doesn't fit the argument that people are reluctant to embrace environmental sustainability. In his 2004 book *Growth Fetish*, Clive Hamilton[3] quotes figures from a US survey in which 19% of the adult population declared that they had voluntarily decided to make a change in their lives that resulted in making less money in the previous 5 years. That excluded people taking scheduled retirement. A similar survey in Australia found 23% of 30- to 60-year-olds downshifting.

Life Games

The discussion about midlife crises and the phenomenon of "downshifting" is a useful point from which to explore the important issue of life purposes. The critic of psychiatry Thomas Tsasz developed this idea when he wrote that to be mentally healthy one must have "a game" to play in life. A life game is what one might call a vocational choice, using vocational choice in its widest sense and not just in a narrow career sense. To join an extremist cause or a religious sect, or to become a committed environmentalist are examples of adopted life games. Most people, most of the time, adopt more prosaic life games and the advertising industry tries to structure our life games around shopping, status consumption and holidays — funded out of our work.

It should be noted that there is a distinction between a life game and a lifestyle package. They are not quite the same but there is a subtle interplay between the two of them. Thus, for example, efforts to organize your house and garden in an energy-efficient and self-sufficient manner are not a significant thing in the life game of someone involved in extremist left-wing politics or who lives to promote the truths, as they see it, of a religious sect, although people like this will need to arrange somewhere to live, the same as anyone else. On the other hand, to an environmentalist who is trying to save energy, the organization of their house, with insulation to save energy and a productive vegetable garden, will be very much a part of their lifestyle package on which they concentrate to be consistent with their chosen life game.

Extrinsic and Intrinsic Motivations

In the next few years it is likely that consumption- and status-based life games will become increasingly unviable in manageable lifestyle packages. This is important in the light of the important distinction between people motivated by intrinsic and extrinsic purposes. Psychologists have discovered a great deal of evidence that people motivated by extrinsic goals — like making more money so that they can acquire more of the consumer goods and activities that they want — have more problems maintaining their self-esteem and life satisfaction than those motivated by intrinsic goals. This tells us that there is something very wrong with the assumptions of mainstream economics. In most mainstream economics we get a sense that making money has become the end and chief purpose in and of itself: it is the goal and purpose of life. The life game is to become rich. Full stop. People with this life game will likely be in trouble in a future of expensive energy and wobbly banks.[4]

This is even more important in those circumstances where life transitions are forced on people involuntarily — for example, through redundancy, which at its worst may bring with it the loss of home and the loss of relationships too. Involuntary life transitions may also affect whole communities, as in when a major local employer goes bust. There are serious dangers here, if people cling to unrealistic expectations of returning to a "normality" that is gone forever, and then become bitter and recidivist. In situations where a community in crisis is pervaded by cultural assumptions that favor extrinsic motivations — a high-status, high-consuming lifestyle — there are going to be lots of problems. After the shock of closures, individual community members can only hope to retain aspects of this kind of life if they resort to deviant activity like selling drugs, or acting for loan sharks or resorting to prostitution or pimping, while others dull their disappointment and frustration in other forms of self-destruction.

Seen in this way, help for individuals and communities to adopt more sustainable lifestyles that are socially valued can be seen as crucial to good individual and community mental health. This has been recognized for some time among health promotion and community mental-health professionals. Projects like community gardens, projects that promote cycling and energy efficiency in neighborhoods, are of more than ecological relevance. They suggest that it is possible to organize holistically and try to achieve a number of goals at one time; indeed, that this needs to happen if people are to be able to cope at all.[5]

There have, of course, been many times in history when millions of people come together to adopt common life games in that unite against a common enemy in a war, or adopt a common religion or political ideology. What postmodernist theorists called a "Grand Narrative" may provide the inspiration for a common life game and the social cohesion that makes possible the achievement of far more than can be achieved by individuals or small groups alone. The inspirational power of Grand Narratives can be intoxicating but they may be dangerous too, inspiring a loyalty that leads to conformity, to an inability to see the world any differently from the one portrayed within the conceptual framework of the new ideology and, ultimately, to new forms of tyranny as conformity to the cause is enforced by new leaders.

In current conditions we need something of the intoxicating power of a new Grand Narrative with ideas like the defense of natural and social commons resources as unifying themes, but without the conformity and centralization of a top-down bureaucracy and leadership. There is good reason to hope that we can indeed, this time, have a movement that recognizes the value that comes with preserving diversity. This is because the ecological revolution, if we can call it that, proceeds from the need to resist the homogenizing tendency of the world market—to recognize instead that every field, stream, forest, biotope settlement and building needs a unique management regime to restore ecological health. Nevertheless, the inspirational power and motivational potential of a new movement are already evident, as is clear from the writings and presentations of Paul Hawkens; in his book *Blessed Unrest*, he refers to the civil society movement as "the largest social movement in history" with perhaps as many as one or two million organizations active on the destruction of the environment, against free-market fundamentalism, for social justice and against the loss of indigenous cultures.

Using the Window of Opportunity to Promote More Sustainable Lifestyles

In recent years a number of researchers have investigated whether periods of life transition can be seen as windows of opportunity for promoting more sustainable lifestyles and consumption patterns—albeit in situations less dramatic than those just discussed. The evidence suggests that it is possible alright, but the policy design is not straightforward.

From the point of environmental sustainability, lifestyle and consumption patterns after a significant lifestyle shift may be better, but frequently they are worse. Car use when people move home is an example. Several studies show that "the probability for changes in mobility habits seems to rise with the degree of context variation. Persons who move from a rural area to a city tend to reduce their car use significantly more often than do persons who move from one city to another. These studies also stress, however, that variations in context do not automatically lead to the reduction of car use. While some life events like the transition to retirement, a reduction of income or a relocation to a district with good public transport (PT) may have these effects, there are others which tend to result in higher car use (e.g. birth of a child, relocation to rural areas, increase of income)."[6]

The Importance of Peer Support and Advice

There is never just one thing going on when a lifestyle changes—it is the whole package that is changing. Moreover the person in transition will be taking advice, ideas and information from a variety of sources—from friends, family and peers, and from commercial and other sources. Nevertheless, lifestyle shifts do often provide windows of opportunity for changes in a more sustainable direction. If and when green influences can be brought to bear in these situations, they are then more effective the more they tune into the unique circumstances of the individual—rather than being generic in character. As Schäfer and Bamberg explain:

> The strongest effects seem to result from personal communication that takes the personal circumstances of the addressed person into account. There is also evidence that the behavioral impact is higher if the sender has a similar social background as the addressee.

This points to the need for a movement based in communities—where people giving advice know each other personally—and not on some official program delivered by anonymous bureaucrats. It points to the development of skills by advisers who can really tune in to unique circumstances. It is for reasons like this that we can understand the success of projects like Eco-Teams and the community activities of projects like Transition Towns. In these activities the learning is in the presence of, and between, peers — people who are considering how to organize a household rather like one's own. Indeed, like going to a community garden regularly, this is a way of making new friends — something that one is unlikely to be able to do by accessing all one's needs from the supermarket.

Generic Programs

While this points to the value of peer relationships and support that are more tuned into individual needs there are still occasions when generic policies can be delivered effectively. Thus Schäfer and Bamberg found that the Munich public transport administrations enjoyed considerable success when they specially targeted people newly relocating into Munich.

> Typical elements of these mover-marketing campaigns are the provision of a temporally valid free PT test ticket and PT services-related information as soon as possible after the move. Evaluations of these campaigns indicate a significant impact from these simple measures on new citizens' travel behaviour: New citizens receiving the intervention report a substantive increase of PT use and respective decrease of car use.... Car possession per household is, for example, reduced from 1.5 to 0.9 after relocation and PT is used more often. These effects were significantly higher among the group that was addressed by the campaign in comparison to the control group (increase of 7.6% of the modal split). The results show that the effects were mainly achieved by increasing knowledge about the use of PT. From these results Bamberg (2006) drew the conclusion that linking such campaigns to life events is an effective strategy for increasing behavioural mobility changes.

Obliquity

In a recent book the *Financial Times* columnist and economist John Kay argues that policy, business and life goals are often best achieved not by pursuing them head on, directly, but by an indirect approach. His book is aptly titled *Obliquity*. The complaint of environmentalists, that people are reluctant to change, is often because they are approaching the change process too directly and too generically. Indeed there is always a danger that when one tries to get people to change, and at the wrong times, one is perceived as interfering and moralistic. The implied message that people "should change their ways" is experienced as subtle criticism that can often be rejected — "who are you to tell me how I should live my life?"

An oblique approach is required to deal with the problems that Mark highlights. People change the way they arrange their lives from time to time anyway and/or are forced to do so whether they like it or not. The trick of moving toward more environmentally sustainable lives may be to find ways to intervene in these periods of transition in a way that is experienced as helpful by people who lead by personal example. As far as possible this needs to be tuned into the unique circumstances facing individuals and as far as possible it needs to be in the form of advice and support coming from peer groups. In the difficult times ahead there will certainly be enough people who need this kind of support.

Endnotes

See also my paper "The De-Growth Economy and Lifestyles", produced for the Economic De-Growth for Ecological Sustainability and Social Equity conference, Paris, 18/19th April 2008 events.it-sudparis.eu/degrowthconference/en/themes/.

1. Luigi Boscolo and Paulo Bertrando, *The Times of the Times: A New Perspective in Systemic Therapy and Consultation* (WW Norton, 1993).
2. Anthony Storr, *Solitude* (HarperCollins, 1994), 35.
3. Clive Hamilton, *Growth Fetish* (Pluto Press, 2004), 206.
4. bgmi.us/web/bdavey/Life.htm.
5. B. Davey, "Solving Economic, Social and Environmental Problems Together: An Empowerment Strategy for Losers" in *Alliances and Partnerships in Empowerment*, eds. M. Barnes and L. Warren (Policy Press, 1999).
6. M. Schäfer and S. Bamberg, "Breaking Habits: Linking Sustainable Consumption Campaigns to Sensitive Life Events," *Proceedings: Sustainable Consumption and Production: Framework for Action* (10–11 March 2008), lifeevents.de/media/pdf/publik /Schäfer_Bamberg_SCORE.pdf.

Cultivating Hope
and Managing Despair

JOHN SHARRY

Societies are struggling to come to terms with the nature and extent of the changes facing them both now and in the future. Modern psychological models of motivation and change, and of how people deal with threat and loss, suggest strategies that can be used to help individuals change and to galvanize communities into collective action.

In the last few years there has been a growing public awareness of the twin challenges of climate change and peak oil/resource depletion. The popular awareness has been championed by figures such as Al Gore and many other environmentalists and scientists. In their presentation of the message, many scientists and educators try to delicately balance the prediction of catastrophe with a focus on the positive action that people can take, whether this is recycling, using efficient lightbulbs or more actively lobbying government. Most presenters try to be upbeat, presenting a positive vision of the future with a clear call to action. A common message communicated is the idea that we have "ten years left to act" in order to curtail climate change and save the planet.

Despite this positive focus in public, many scientists are much more gloomy in private. Chris Goodall[1] calls this "the second glass effect." After his hopeful presentations about the different technologies that could save the planet, during the post-lecture wine reception he may begin to share his pessimism as to whether collectively we have left it too late to adopt these technologies or whether the will or political capital exists to introduce them. Indeed, many scientists think the news is far worse than what is publicly broadcast; they believe that we have already bypassed many of the tipping points to avoid dangerous climate change, that catastrophe cannot now be averted and that future generations will suffer on a scale we cannot fully comprehend.

For fear of sending their audience into despair or alienating them and being written off as a "doom and gloom" merchant, many scientists and environmentalists filter the message through a more optimistic lens than reality suggests. If scientists are guilty of this, politicians and government officials are even more so. Focused solely on re-election in a year or two, the last thing a politician wants to do is to talk about the reality of challenges for fear of making people despairing and fearful or, worse, vote not to re-elect them.

Of course the public audience is complicit in this arrangement. Despite the emerging evidence to the contrary, the vast majority of people are happy to live in denial about the severity of problems or imagine that "easy" solutions will be found. The general public belief is that we can more or less continue our current lifestyles as they are. Okay, we might turn down the heating a degree, but the most common belief is that we can continue our current lifestyle and at the same time save the planet. The scale of the impending catastrophe simply hasn't sunk in, nor has the scale of action needed for humanity just to survive. Even with the current economic crisis, most people simply hope that we can "restart the party" and return to the unsustainable economic growth cycle that caused the problems in the first place. To consider radical changes is too scary at the moment and invites just too much despair.

Addiction, Denial and Fear

One way to understand the enduring widespread denial of the consequences of our lifestyles and actions is to consider it in terms of an addiction. We are addicted to the comfortable life that cheap oil has afforded us and are so terrified of being without it that we will deny for as long as possible all evidence of harm. Fear underpins most addictions and causes addicts to refuse to think long term and to keep living day to day, chasing the next fix. This is why advertising campaigns that try to scare the public with the effects of smoking, drinking or drugs rarely work with addicts. The fear that they won't get their drug today is far greater than a vague fear of long-term consequences. As a result, confrontational and fear-based therapeutic approaches to treating addictions have largely been discredited.

More successful therapeutic approaches focus on removing the fear that underpins the addiction and helping the recovering addict envision a positive, drug-free life that is far more attractive and appealing than what the drug has to offer. In a similar way, many of the innovative movements within the environmental field have focused not just on warning about the dangerous consequences of our current trajectory, but also tried to "sell" the benefits of a low-carbon future: closely connected, sustainable communities that are far happier than the disconnected modern world in which we currently live.

While this positive approach has been successful to a degree and led to many people understanding and taking on board these aspirations, sadly it has led to very little actual behavioral change in terms of sustainable lifestyles (even among those who are zealots of the environmental movement) and we are as dependent as we ever were. The reason for this lack of change is the absence of the second important factor necessary to create the conditions for addicts to change: consequences. People with serious addictions are unlikely to change unless they experience directly the negative consequences of their addiction. Given the strength of our enjoyment of and dependency on our Western lifestyle, the threat of consequences somewhere down the line is simply not enough to make us change. It is far easier, in fact, to listen to the many dissenting voices and vested interests that deny that any actual harm is being incurred.

> The only pain that we can avoid in life is the pain caused by trying to avoid pain
>
> R.D. LAING

That resource depletion and climate change remain, for many people, only a vague threat, means that these people will simply not change until they have to. Even though early change or adaptation is far preferable to emergency change and forced adaptation, it's likely that our collective denial will only be punctured when our addicted society is beset by an unending set of crises and catastrophes. Once this happens, it will of course be a very perilous time. People who have been hitherto in comfortable denial will become fearful and desperate and may engage in desperate actions, leading to social unrest, war and societal breakdown. Preparing to manage these social difficulties in the future is likely to be as significant as managing the economy.

Managing Despair

The famous psychologist Kubler Ross[2] proposed a five-stage model of how an individual responds to bereavement or pending loss: denial, anger, bargaining, depression and, finally, acceptance. Once denial is passed, a person may experience great anger at their loss, which is often accompanied by seeking to apportion blame and even seek retribution. This can be followed by bargaining or engaging in wishful thinking or unhelpful strategies to mitigate the loss and then by depression and grief as the impact of the loss finally comes to bear. Kubler Ross argues that once this grief work is done, the person can reach some level of acceptance and integration. Interestingly, many writers in the environmental field describe their own personal journey of awareness in similar terms. They describe a period of denial, before having a "peak oil moment" when they realize that the world on which they depend is unsustainable. This is often followed by a period of despair and, finally, by some acceptance and a commitment to constructive action and hope.

> *The greatest challenge now facing our leaders is to manage the nation's mood as much as it is to manage its economy.*

Such a grief model may also suggest the stages we will collectively go through as the denial about the unsustainability of our current lifestyles is punctured and we are beset by crises and consequences. If the first half of the age of oil has been characterized by exuberance, ever-increasing expansion, and an almost manic consumption of the world's resources, the second half will be characterized by contraction, scarcity and depression. Once the denial falls away and it becomes clear that the decline of our Western industrialization is chronic and long term, collective anger is likely to be widespread. People will seek to blame someone for the situation they are in, and many will look for easy answers or scapegoats. It is at these times that people can choose radical and extreme political views. Just as the economic turmoil and the great depression of the 1930s led to the rise of dictatorships and totalitarian states in Europe, so these times will be fraught by similar dangers. In addition to anger, there is also likely to be widespread depression and despair. This is just as dangerous and has the potential to make people feel helpless in the face of negative forces within society, disabling them from taking action and missing the positive opportunities in their midst.

Just as it's important to prepare for the economic challenges ahead, so it is also important to prepare for the associated psychological, community and societal problems that will emerge. Once the crises occur, community and society leaders will have a particular responsibility to manage the public anger and despair that will emerge in order to avoid the destructive paths of social disorder. The twin challenge will be to help people channel their anger into constructive rather than negative courses of action and to present a vision that inspires hope in the face of widespread difficult circumstances. Such plans will be as crucial as economic and technological ones in helping people survive the transition.

Cultivating Hope

While the Kubler-Ross model provides a useful understanding of the stages of dealing with loss, critics often say that it misses a final step of hopeful and constructive action. Many people who experience loss move beyond acceptance, try to make meaning out of their experience, and channel their energy into constructive action. Many people who have lost a loved one to an illness will put their efforts into supporting others with the same illness, or dedicate themselves to educating others so they can avoid the loss they experienced. In addition, many people report that despite the pain and suffering, the experience of a trauma in the long term can actually have some benefits and help them reorient their life for the better. Many people in the environmental movement describe a similar process after they have been through the initial despair following their "peak oil realization moment." They move beyond acceptance of the facts and commit themselves to constructive action, whether in terms of educating others or building sustainable communities. Many report their life as being better, more integrated and even more hopeful once they became aware of the coming crises.

> *It is in the deepest despair that is born the greatest hope.*
>
> MIGUEL DE UNAMUNO

A second criticism of the five-stage grief model is that it is too simple and linear and that, in fact, people dealing with the prospect of a serious loss oscillate between positive and negative emotions. At times people can be in denial and at other times feel acceptance; they can alternate between anger and despair at their predicament and other times feel hope about what will come to pass. The family therapist Carmel Flaskis[3] talks about the coexistence of hope and hopelessness in working with people dealing with trauma and loss. People can move from great sadness, pain, despair and injustice to, at other times, great hope, courage, forgiveness and resilience. The key is to achieve some sort of balance between the two and to learn to cultivate hope in the face of despair. Helping people cope with trauma is about helping them express, understand and manage their despair, as well as helping them cultivate hope and new meaning beyond the original experience. Good therapeutic work is characterized by compassion (accepting the person whatever feelings they have and wherever they are on the grief process) reflection (highlighting to the person that they have choices in how they respond to the trauma that is affecting them) and empowerment (helping the person channel their energy into constructive courses of action).

Such approaches can be applied to whole communities dealing with actual or potential trauma. The Buddhist Joanna Macy[4] leads "despair and empowerment" workshops designed to help groups express and process the feelings of grief at the destruction of the people and the planet, with a view to helping them overcome helplessness and hopelessness and reach a more empowered, constructive position. Such work may prove to be more important in the future when the consequences of climate change and resource depletion begin to bite and community despair is more widespread.

Building Resilience

In my work as a mental-health professional I have been struck at how differently various people cope with adversity or challenging life events. Some people become traumatized and damaged by what has happened to them and can become embittered or angry even for years after the original events. Other people are able to move on from the trauma and not let it damage them in the same way; in some cases they're able to learn from it and even turn it into a positive force in their life. Modern psychologists are very interested in the concept of resilience; they want to understand what qualities and protective factors allow an individual to cope with trauma and adversity. Many different things seem to make a difference, but the ability to be flexible in challenging circumstances is crucial. Whether a person can think constructively (making the best of the situation as it is) or take an active rather than a passive coping stance (such as taking action to make life better or combat the negative effects), and whether they have access to good-quality support at the time of the trauma and afterwards, can all contribute to better coping and survival.

> *Anything that does not kill me makes me stronger.*
>
> FREDERICH NIETZSCHE

In his great work *Man's Search for Meaning*, the psychologist Victor Frankl[5] describes his experience as a prisoner in a Nazi concentration camp and shares his observations of how differently people coped there. Some were overwhelmed and descended into despair; others were better able to survive, depending on how they responded to circumstances imposed upon them. For Frankl, the crucial factor was finding meaning in the experience and making positive choices no matter how much the person's freedom was curtailed. After the war, he went on to develop his therapeutic method on finding meaning in all forms of existence, no matter how traumatic or difficult. It is this meaning that provides the person with a positive reason to continue living. In the future, how we cope with the new conditions of contracting resources and curtailed freedom will depend not only on our collective resilience and adaptability but also on our ability to make sense of and find meaning in our new circumstances.

A Community of Hope

Recent psychological research has highlighted the importance of hope as an essential precondition to human happiness, particularly in the face of difficult change and adversity. Charles Snyder,[6] one of the leading researchers in the field, has defined hope as born out of having a clear goal/vision and the sense of the means to make progress toward it. While hope is often considered an individual human trait or feeling, Kaethe Weingarten[7] has conceived it as a shared creation between people. When people are overwhelmed by adversity and feel hopelessness or despair, it is their contact with other caring people that lifts them or creates the conditions for renewed hope. For this reason she argues that people

> *Hope is something you create together.*
>
> KAETHE WEINGARTEN

in despair should resist isolation and seek connection, and people who possess some hope should resist indifference and reach out and support others. This is the basis of a resourceful, and resilient, community.

One of the most innovative movements that is meeting the challenge of the coming crises is the Transition Towns movement.[8] By bringing people together around shared concerns, building collective vision and common meaning, and focusing people on constructive action, the movement does much to create hope in individuals and communities in the face of despair. Furthermore, the movement not only builds resilience in local economies by reducing dependence on fossil fuels etc., but it also builds resilience in communities that will be havens for the many people who will feel despair and loss as the future crises deepen. Critics of the movement who argue that many of the local actions are not sufficient for dealing with what are global problems miss the point completely. While the current actions may not be the ones to solve the problems (indeed no one knows exactly the correct actions needed), over time the movement creates a resourceful community that will be best placed to adapt to future challenges and thus preserve hope for future generations.

Conclusion

We are facing very uncertain and difficult times. In addition to the twin challenges of peak oil and climate change and the resultant economic and societal problems, we face very deep challenges to our collective psyche and spirit as people. When we consider the scale of the problems we face, it is easy to retreat into denial or wishful thinking or feel despair, helpless or hopeless about change.

> *Hope is definitely not the same thing as optimism. It is not the conviction that something will turn out well, but the certainty that something makes sense regardless of how it turns out.*
>
> VÁCLAV HAVEL

How we cope will depend largely on how resourceful we are and whether we can build communities that nurture hope rather than despair, keep people together rather than apart and cultivate creative adaptation in the face of adversity rather than destructive action. This is the best chance for our children.

> *Hope is the process of arriving at a goal — no matter how much it has shifted — and making sense of the journey there.*
>
> KAETHE WEINGARTEN

When despair threatens to overwhelm us, rather than being lured towards anger or hatred, we can remember the words of Kaethe Weingarten, who said "you can do hope without feeling hope." Creating hope is largely a choice about taking constructive action and you don't have to wait until you feel hopeful to take this action. I think this is what Shaun Chamberlain[9] means when he speaks of the "pessimism of the intellect and the optimism of the will."

While we may doubt that our actions may work, we still act in the best faith we can. Furthermore, when we take collective, concrete and constructive action, in the process we generate hope and a sense of movement and possibility. We also counterbalance the cynicism, despair and inaction that could hobble the next generation. In this way, we can give them the freedom and encouragement to embrace their future. Now that is something to be hopeful about.

Endnotes

1. Chris Goddall, *Ten Technologies to Save the Planet* (Green Profile, 2008).
2. Elizabeth Kubler-Ross, *On Grief and Grieving* (Simon and Schuster, 2005).
3. Carmel Flaskas, "The Balance of Hope and Hopelessness," in *Hope and Despair in Narrative and Family Therapy*, eds. C. Flaskas, I. McCarthy and J. Sheehan (Routledge, 2007).
4. As cited in Richard Heinberg, *Peak Everything* (Clairview, 2007).
5. Victor Frankl, *Man's Search for Meaning* (Simon and Schuster, 1959).
6. C. R. Snyder, *Handbook of Hope: Theory, Measures, and Applications* (Academic Press, 2000).
7. Kaethe Weingarten, "Hope in a Time of Global Despair," in *Hope and Despair in Narrative and Family Therapy*, ed. C. Flaskas, I. McCarthy and J. Sheehan, (Routledge, 2007).
8. Rob Hopkins, *The Transition Handbook: From Oil Dependency to Local Resilience* (Green Books, 2008).
9. Shaun Chamberlin, *The Transition Timeline* (Green Books, 2009).

Collapse or No Collapse:
We Need to Respect to Survive

Lucy McAndrew

*Respect for ourselves, for others and for nature is fundamental to survival
because it is what gives us a sense of our place in the world and, when we
lose that, we float free of the very network of relationships that sustains us.*

Aretha Franklin famously sang about it, and the concept has been widely
discussed in arenas as diverse as politics and psychotherapy, but what does
respect really mean in the 21st century? I believe that in this time of increasing volatility and uncertainty, it has new resonance and a deeper meaning:
that we can acknowledge and consider the needs of others, without losing
sight of our own. In short, as I explain below, it means choosing to take
responsibility for our actions and for their consequences, wherever and by
whomever they are felt. And if we are to have a stable future, it means doing
this now, irrespective of whether or not we are poised for collapse.

As a skeptic I find it particularly hard to read all the predictions of imminent global financial[1] and, possibly, ecological[2] collapse without wanting to question the grounds on which they're made. After all, if one cliché
could be used to sum up our experience to date, it's that "the future is hard
to predict."[3]

But rather than predicting what we might do if the world we know dissolves, I want to explore what we might do regardless of what the future
holds. What might the key be to a transition to a better place — personally,
socially, politically, ecologically and economically? I believe that the key is
respect. Respect is fundamental to survival because it gives us a sense of our
place in the world, and when we lose that, we float free of the very network

of relationships that sustain us. And since we are not islands, as John Donne so memorably reminded us, free-floating doesn't work for us: we die. Only by respecting what we are and taking responsibility for how we interact with one another and the world can we hope to manage a collapse or gradual subsidence of society, or even a stable transition to a civilized future.

There is no doubt that today we exist in an uncomfortably and unnecessarily parasitic relationship with one another and, critically, with the natural world. Buying cheap electronic goods at the price of someone else's childhood is possible only because the children in question live elsewhere, out of sight. Faced with the horror of their daily reality, few of us could stomach the end product, just as few who watched *Fast Food Nation*[4] found eating McDonald's thereafter anything other than a queasy experience.

This lack of focused reflection on the basic laws of cause and effect allows us to tolerate the intolerable. It's like any other behavior that is damaging to the self. Because we cannot see what is happening to our insides when we eat junk food, binge drink, smoke or snort drugs, we are able to put the impact to one side. And in doing so, we can choose not to reflect on the abusive relationship we've created with ourselves; to do so would demand that we take much more responsibility.

So, even though we have the capacity to reflect, we're able to compartmentalize our thinking because often there's no immediately visible effect that we have to face as a result of our behavior. This compartmentalization means, however, that we can wilfully ignore exploitation and abuse.

What has brought us to this state? I believe that it is our extravagance, which, when combined with willful ignorance, frequently overrides the one ability that, more than any other, has ensured our survival as a species: our ability to think.

This ability to think, including our ability to imagine, analyze and digest, is a highly sophisticated and versatile tool. To maximize this versatility, we need to change the way(s) we think to become more flexible in our responses and gear our skills more toward enhancing our survival than to parasitism or exploitation.

We are capable of broadening our understanding of our place and our responsibilities — we have to if we are to survive — providing we feel positive about the potential impact of any action we take.[5] This demands that we become extravagant in a new way — in our thinking. Integrated thinking that takes into account all systems, animate and inanimate, is essential because it embraces and accommodates the whole complex web of interests in the world.

Some people claim, however, that exploitation is fundamental to the nature of life.[6] I would counter that the "nature red in tooth and claw" view is outmoded as a way of seeing relationships in the biotic community.[7] Frank Ryan's book *Virolution* makes clear that even humans and viruses can interact to the benefit of both, albeit in an aggressive symbiosis. And I believe that it is symbiosis, not parasitism, that will enable our species to ride out the consequences of our past and present detrimental acts. In fact, it is far more "natural" for us to be conscious of our attachment to, and responsibilities toward, the world than it is for than it is for us ravenously to consume to the point of fracture and explosion.

More than anything else, it is our ability to empathize, to imagine ourselves in someone else's position, which has enhanced our survivability as a species.[8] This ability probably evolved from having to spend so long looking after dependent young. We then extended it and found that it worked in groups. We now know that it works in whole nations and even internationally. It works to our benefit. And we must now use it in our approach to nature as a whole.

But could a shift of mindset actually mitigate some of the worst potential effects of our present blindness? I believe strongly that it could. Our relationship with nature to date has been one of attempted domination and control over what has often threatened to annihilate us: "we shall overcome." We have attempted to submerge the natural beneath a layer of urban dust, to subjugate the "beast" to meet our needs (and wants). The world's current difficulties — ecological, social and economic — show us that this relationship is no longer useful. Nature, and society at large, is in dire need of our capacity to think critically and to solve problems. And without a crucial shift from this old attitude of "we will overcome" to one of "we have to take responsibility," we face the horror of fragmentation which, when it comes to problem-solving, will leave us high and dry.

To bring about a change of attitude from willful ignorance of exploitation to one of respectful and responsible engagement requires huge courage. Violent panic can come from the fear induced by having to take control of something we haven't taken control of before. And if fear is allowed to overrun the required transition to a more stable world, we are likely to see scenes of extreme aggression. So we need courage to overcome the fear.

If we survive such conflict, what remains of us? The risk is that the aftermath of this kind of madness and aggression can bring with it a broken mind, one that seeks further avoidance or dies. If we are, as many in this book argue, poised for collapse, or even if what we are witnessing in the world is a slow disintegration, we must understand that our current direction, with our wilful refusal to see what we are doing, can only end in internal disintegrity. Disintegration is not conducive to people pulling together to imagine and create a better relationship, to repairing the damage, to reconstructing society with positive aims in mind. It's possible that disintegration will create a spiral of destructive behaviors for humans which could repeat itself until either the species wipes itself out, or we learn to open our eyes.[9] This is anti-evolution, and it's not a direction we can afford to take.

The alternative is that we remain calm. We examine ourselves in the context of what we know: that we are evolved living systems, along with every other organism and biotic system on the planet. And we fit in to that system not at the top, but as one piece in the puzzle.

For respect to mean anything, there must be a rationale on which we can base our attitude. Traditionally, this has involved reference to an external power: we respect our fellows, for example, because they, too, are made in the image of God. I want to suggest that there is a far simpler, more rational argument on which we can base our attitude of respect.

At the heart of this argument is the idea that all evolved living systems have something fundamental in common: certain goals and conditions that can be termed their "good," which they pursue, sometimes consciously, more often inherently. This is what inherent worth is: a "good" pursued. In many cases, the conditions for a life in pursuit of that good are simple: unpolluted water and air, space and a source of energy.

By why respect a "good," especially if it is in conflict with my own? The answer is based on our inherent ability to recognize this qualitative aspect of life, this "good." The American author and psychiatrist Mark Goulston has argued, convincingly, that humans are physiologically hardwired to empathize with other human beings, once we see what their experience is. And precisely because we can empathize — because we think, see, understand this common ground — means we have an obligation to acknowledge it. That we are thinking entities, to use Descartes' phrase,[10] thus puts us in a unique position in relation to any knowledge we have: we have the capacity to act on that information consciously, with deliberation. In other words, we understand that we have a choice about any action we take. And that the process of making that choice begins with the idea that, knowing what we do, we owe it to the world to respect it and to respect the systems and people within it. We cannot recognize something and then ignore it. Integrating our knowledge and our actions becomes imperative. We have to act on what we know.

Some would argue that this is not viable. For a start, it's too time-consuming to consider each individual organism when making a decision about what to do. But this is fear talking — fear, perhaps, of being over-whelmed. We cannot avoid our impact on the world; we have to take re-sponsibility for it, to respond collectively and individually to what we are doing. Respect requires that we think about it, not ignore it or see it as some-one else's problem. Cutting off knowledge is, then, wilful self- and species-destruction.

Very simply, respect, coming from a latinate root, "to look back at," im-plies the sweeping of one's mental eye over something. Respect means we have to look back at what we are and at what we have done, and identify what has worked and what has failed. This doesn't require profound intel-lectual talent. It requires only a little thought. And because thinking is what humans do, it is perfectly natural to reflect in this way.

Respect is not neutral. It is, in fact, many things at once: an evaluation and a recognition of the worth of something; an acknowledgment of less-than-perfect knowledge, and a willingness to learn more; self-recognition and acknowledgment, but without prioritization of the self; realization of the needs of others, but without prioritizing those over the needs of the self; and, finally, and most importantly, because most often neglected, it is an awareness of the needs of the natural community of living organisms, from complex to simple, on the basis that the good of life in them is owed ac-knowledgment by the good of life in us.[11]

And first in line for such acknowledgment is nature itself, which is now at our mercy. We need to respond responsibly, respectfully, if our control of our situation is not to continue to come at the expense of so much of the rest of the living world. This realization is also an awareness of payback time: our existence as creatures of culture and technology has been at the price of reduced value overall.[12] We owe a debt of restitution to the rest of the living world. But even if we didn't, we cannot afford to continue to cost this much, for our own sakes, though this is a weaker argument for changing our at-titude.[13]

Say, however, that we are now facing a situation of hardship, a situation where our ability to maintain an attitude of respect is challenged by, for instance, a failure to meet basic needs like food, and a lack of infrastructure, jobs, money or security. How, under these circumstances, might an attitude of respect prove beneficial?

It is empirically evident that respectful engagement during crises is more effective as a strategy for enabling a successful distribution of goods to survivors, than fear- or profit-driven engagement, providing (and this is important) that the dice are not weighted in favor of profit-driven engagement benefitting more participants, or benefitting them to a degree that outweighs respectful engagement.[14] All other things being equal, respectful engagement allows people to distribute goods equitably, to maintain the natural environment to the common good, to create or maintain a sense of control amongst those involved and to develop resistance to aggressive exploitation by outsiders.

In contrast, engagement that relies on imposition of rules, or on fragmentation, results in lowered immune responses to disease, fragmentation within groups in response to community requirements (less help given to rape victims, for instance), "learned helplessness" and less self-reliance in the context of basic survival responses (less initiative in terms of crop growing or developing community-building projects) and less interest in the environment, resulting in fewer attempts to protect or preserve the ecology or habitats in which human populations subsist.

And so, where are we now? Our current position in Ireland is complex. On the one hand, our debt far outstrips our assets, which has knock-on effects in terms of social and personal respect (drug and alcohol abuse, suicide and depression, marital breakdown and community fragmentation associated with job loss). On the other hand, the "learned helplessness" associated with an overly controlling, institutionally and politically powerful religious community (one that perpetrated sexual, psychological and physical abuse), and the added problems associated with poverty and deprivation, have to a large degree been tackled.

Even traditionally marginalized groups (asylum seekers, travelers) have been more or less accommodated. Unfortunately, the possibility of economic and environmental crisis also threatens the stability of this new-found tolerance. Unfortunately, too, while an overt attempt to address treatment of land and biota has been made through EU-funded programs (the designation of areas as Special Areas of Conservation, for instance) the covert understanding has remained that, if and when necessary, human interests will always trump those of the natural world. But fragmented thinking like this will not enable us to deal with the problems we face now, or those we might or are likely to face in the future. As I explained above, now is the time for truly integrated thinking, extravagant thinking, which accommodates the whole complex web of interests.

"You can't eat the scenery," one local politician once lectured me. And it's true: considering all interests is time-consuming. In a collapse situation, it is hard to imagine individuals or even communities thinking beyond their own immediate needs. Yet humans have reacted throughout history to emergencies in a variety of ways, and every time, it is the reactions that involve more forethought, and take a broader view of the situation, which most benefit the individuals involved.

There are many examples in human history that support the contention that living with respect for one's surroundings, however extreme the conditions, is a survival asset. From the Himalayas to Nazi Germany, from the Andes plane crash described in *Alive* to the stories of children surviving in refugee camps, living with respect for where one is, who one is with, and what one is, is the most profoundly life-protecting principle one can learn.[15]

Respectful engagement thus protects us in times of crisis, but, more importantly, I would argue that it also enhances our chances of survival even when we're not in crisis. Whether in the personal or the political sphere, the ecological or the economic, relationships can be shattered by disparagement, distrust and fear.

An example of what happens when respect disappears is found in Colin Turnbull's book *The Mountain People*,[16] in which he reflects (albeit controversially) on the experience of the Ik tribe after their lands were drastically reduced when the government decided to section off part of their former ranging ground as a national park. The result, tragically but inevitably, was that the Ik suffered dreadful privation as a result of this reduction in space. They starved. According to Turnbull, so complete was the fragmentation caused by the move, that individuals displayed no empathy toward one another. Turnbull presented evidence that respect had disappeared entirely by the time he wrote of his own attempts to intervene, and highlighted the derision with which such attempts were met.

Can you learn to respect? There is strong evidence to suggest that, yes, people can. First, they can be taught the rationale behind respect—who to respect, and why—and then they can practise it between one another and the world. It is a cumulative effect; the more people who do it, the more authority it has. This is obviously useful during emergencies. However, even if no emergency occurs, developing such an attitude toward not only other people but also toward the rest of the living world is something worth pursuing for its own sake.

If nothing changed about how our society operated, but we centered ourselves on the notion of respect, we would no longer be able to justify buying cheap clothing from factories that employ children in India, or plastic games made by a labor force of indentured slaves in China. We would fundamentally change our relationship with other countries, our trade agreements, our toleration for war or forced migration. This would not necessarily weaken our economic position. In fact, if we acted strongly on this, the likelihood is that our international reputation would benefit.

If we took seriously the notion of respect for nature, even if nothing else altered, we would put aside land specifically for other creatures' use, ensure there were migration routes between fields and consider the impact of water use not just on human communities but on all the organisms, fish to foul, bacteria to blue-green algae, for whom water is a "good." We could even consider "reparation" for the abuse of ecosystems and species in the past. Rather than decreasing our yield, however, this alteration in land use could actually increase the output, since a more balanced agriculture will rely on advanced technologies, or none. The exploitative and abusive tools we've used will be obsolete.

This would, obviously, dramatically alter our society, even if the economy limped on. It would, of course, dramatically alter the economy too. Would it make us weaker, or more vulnerable to aggressive moves by other societies that did not center on respect? No. Balancing interests does not mean subsuming our own interests for the interests of others, so self-defense (personal as well as military) would be encouraged, but in balance with other interests rather than to their exclusion. If communities strengthened, our resilience to aggression would increase, not decrease. If our economy operated differently from those of our neighbors, this would not necessarily put us at a disadvantage but might even increase our ability to trade successfully. Respect tends to breed respect.

Now, what of the crash? If the current prevailing attitude which fails to center on respect does not change and economic and then social breakdown

ensues, we face an exponential increase in violence, fear, suspicion, the closing of borders, panic, mental-health problems and environmental degradation.[17] If the predominant attitude is one of fear or contempt, there will be
huge obstacles to overcome. And if we pay only lip service to the idea of
respect and how it might be disseminated, there will be little incentive to believe in "good" as common ground. Bringing respect to the fore will require
extraordinary extravagance of thought, which will, in turn, require bravery
and courage.

Better for all, then, to envisage a scenario where respect has taken hold
as the prevailing point of view. If we begin to center our attitudes and actions on respect, then we will be able to focus on what we can do together,
for the common good. In such a scenario, what benefits us individually can
be balanced with what benefits the wider community and the non-human
environment. And while it is hard to imagine a human society that is in
perfect harmony with its landscape, it is still possible to imagine a society
that has such harmony as an underlying goal, in recognition of the fact that
drawing ourselves into a respectful relationship with our environment—
people, biota, place—is to our benefit. Such a strategy allows us to survive,
even thrive, in better balance than the strategy we have pushed ourselves
toward to date: short-term thrill at long-term cost.

The state of the world is potentially perilous but predicting an apoca-
lypse is risky. We could be wrong. However, one thing is certain: we exist in
an unsustainable relationship with nature, with one another and, to a large
degree, with ourselves. We can argue that this is a time to retreat, or we
can do what we do best: increase our sense of responsibility, intervene, act,
care. Exploitation will exhaust us and the planet. We need something more
regenerative if we are to develop resilience. Respect provides that regeneration. All it takes is the effort to look back.

Endnotes

1. M. Chossudovsky and A. G. Marshall, *The Global Economic Crisis: The Great Depression of the Twenty-First Century* (Global Research Press, 2010).
2. J. M. Hollander, *The Real Environmental Crisis: Why Poverty Not Affluence is the
   World's Number One Enemy* (University of California Press, 2003).
3. S. Pilorz, a NASA physicist and personal friend who was involved in cosmological
   programs, reflecting on his experience at the cosmological level.
4. Eric Linklater, *Fast Food Nation*, (Director, 2005).
5. Self-respect and a sense of control are integral to one another. Without a sense of being able to influence the situation, self-respect in regard to that situation is absent.

C. Peterson, S. Maier and M. Seligman, *Learned Helplessness: A Theory for the Age of Personal Control* (Oxford University Press, 1995).

6. Exploitation is fundamental to the nature of life: this notion comes to us from Darwin and even before, when the understanding of natural selection as the process by which evolution occurred was seen as one purely of competition. In the years since the theory of evolution first became widely known, the mechanisms of evolution have been studied in more depth and it has become increasingly evident that competition for survival is only one element of energy output. Strategies to allow cooperation or, at the very least, some balance between species survival, have become evident as a far more successful and predominant mode of evolution. See Margulis. L, *Symbiotic Planet: A New Look at Evolution* (Basic Books, 1998).

7. F. Ryan, *Virolution* (Harper Collins, 2009).

8. R. Joyce, *The Evolution of Morality* (Massachusetts Institute of Technology Press, 2007).

9. The notion that we repeat destructive patterns of behaviors even though they have brought us no benefits is written about extensively, but one interesting take has been S. Sutherland in *Irrationality* (Constable & Co., 1992), where he talks of the tendency to ignore or contort evidence and to become entrenched in a position, regardless of what happens next. As a psychologist, he recommends that we practise open-mindedness (tolerance) and acting with kindness toward one another as the only viable antidote to the irrational tendencies that are particularly prevalent in emergencies.

10. R. Descartes in *Meditations 6* proposed "res cogitans," the thinking thing, as a means of our conceiving of our mental processes. While he was undoubtedly mistaken to think of the world as dualistically divided into mind and body, his ideas have been enormously influential in how we see ourselves and our relationship with the world.

11. For a full discussion of respect for nature, and in particular, for the idea of "good" as a basis on which to found inherent worth, P. Taylor's book, *Respect for Nature: A Theory of Environmental Ethics* (Princeton University Press, 1986), is essential reading.

12. R. Elliot, *Faking Nature: The Ethics of Environmental Restoration* (Routledge, 1997), discusses our impact in detail.

13. Instrumental value is contrasted with inherent value: the former is value only for something else; the latter is the perception of value in something which exists because that thing exists. A hamburger has instrumental value to me if I only need to eat to live. A place has inherent value if it is perceived as worthwhile regardless of what good it can do anyone else.

14. The Great Famine in Ireland resulted in land-grabbing by some individuals at the cost of their weaker neighbors. Undoubtedly, the fragmentation of the community and the imposition of rules by external forces whose policies were felt to have caused the famine in the first place allowed people to justify illegitimate behavior in their own lives.

15. P. Paul Reid, *Alive: The Story of the Andes Survivors* (Lippincott, 1974).

16. C. Turnbull, *The Mountain People* (Touchstone, 1987).

17. H. Rolston, "Why Study Environmental Ethics?" in *Environmental Ethics: The Big Questions*, ed. D. R. Keller (Wiley-Blackwell, 2010).

Enough: A Worldview
for Positive Futures

*While the adoption of new technologies is crucial, so too is the need for
a new, self-limiting worldview recognizing that "enough is plenty." This
philosophy of "enough" is about the optimum—having exactly the right
amount and using it gracefully. Adopting such a worldview would nourish
a culture of adapted human behavior in which social justice could prevail
and at least some of the Earth's ecosystems would have the chance to renew
themselves.*

It seems that at no time in recent history have people had as many questions
as they do today. Here are just a few:
- How can we live in harmony with nature? How do we stop global
  warming, associated climate change and the destruction of ecosystems?
- How can we eliminate poverty, provide security and create sufficiency
  for all?
- How do we restore an ethic of care for people and for the Earth?

In short, how can we put human and planetary well-being at the heart of
all our decision-making? In this paper I propose a philosophy and practice
with the potential to answer these questions. It is in essence a worldview,
and I call it Enough. This worldview applies insights from flourishing ecosystems and from moral thinking to the big philosophical questions about
how we should live.

Given the crises of ecology and social justice now facing us, the need
for a new worldview is as crucial as new technology. We're all born with the

capacity for *enough*; everybody has a part to play in the creation of a culture of enough, as a way to understand the world and live in it. It is not a new idea, but I believe it has new resonance and value in today's world and that it should be revisited and revived as a way to deal with life and the challenges it will bring.

In the modern world, we tend to equate happiness with success, and in turn we define success as material possessions and external achievement. We emphasize constant activity and visible, measurable wealth over experience and reflection. Even our notions of what is beautiful are limited: we're not sensitive to the inherent elegance of restraint and limits. However, many languages have proverbs or sayings that reflect the insight that enough is as good as a feast. In Irish, for example, the same phrase — *go leor* — means both "enough" and "plenty." *Enough* is about optimum, having exactly the right amount and using it gracefully. It is about being economical with what we have, without waste of resources or effort, but without being stingy either.

Ideas concerning the beauty and value of *enough* are not alien or distasteful, although embracing them fully is not a well-developed option either, because they are so countercultural.[1] Many of us recognize the value of *enough* at the same time as we receive strong messages to keep growing. In the contradiction between two different messages there lies the potential for wisdom. Striving for *enough* in the midst of a world of more is a way to cope with the demands of the modern world. It can help us to balance the different roles we occupy and the worlds we inhabit, and to make sound decisions and choices.

Modernist culture currently values untrammelled economic growth above all other types of growth. At this time, as many countries experience recession, most people are fixated on getting growth started again. Such growth "works" in the sense that it brings short-term material wealth to small groups in countries where it's practised. But we know that many of its activities create the greenhouse gases that cause global warming. We also know that the industrialized agriculture favored by a growth culture creates food insecurity, puts small farmers out of business and uses cruel practices in "growing" animals. The emphasis on economic growth at all costs has encouraged us to deny the consequences of always using resources from communities and ecosystems, but never giving to those same communities and systems.

This culture also affects our understanding of the term "development." Development comes to mean increasing levels of consumption. It implies that the ideal state for all is to live some version of a suburban lifestyle, commuting to work, with salaries, pensions, cars and various other possessions seen as essential to a modern lifestyle, along with speedy foreign travel. This ideal state is available to anybody who complies with the work-earn-spend system and is willing to be productive and to compete with others. We are required to use our creativity and imagination in the service of profit and "growing" our economies in this narrow sense. But our imaginations have been constrained by this worldview, so that we have largely lost any understanding that progress and advancement for the human race can take many other forms. Throughout the minority world, there is a reluctance to ask hard questions about the nature of progress; as a collective, we're unwilling to question the very system that is causing our problems.

Within a worldview of *enough*, it would be more appropriate to say that all societies (the so-called underdeveloped as well as the "developed") require transformation. In other words, all societies on earth today need a fundamental shift in values and worldview: they need to converge around the idea of deep security. And this security has to be based on equity and justice: sufficiency for all, without excess for some and misery for others. It is not simply "security of the fittest" while the weak die off.

In the past, we did not need to make a big deal of *enough*; it was built into our lives in many ways. Our language recognized it in phrases like "*enough* is as good as a feast," and "waste not, want not." But in modern life the sense of *enough* is badly underdeveloped; in affluent societies we have largely forgotten the wisdom captured in the old sayings. *Enough* is radically different from our current affluent Western obsession with expansion and accumulation. We would benefit from exploring its value for us in the future. It is knowledge recognized by earlier generations; its value has become obscured in the world of more, but it has the potential to be very useful to us at this time. Knowledge takes many forms, including practical skills, interpersonal skills and critical thinking. All forms are essential and of equal importance.

Thinking About Progress

This is a time in history when we need to make collective plans in ways we didn't have to do in the past. Some very serious planning for us as a global, connected species is required, because developments have for the most part gone beyond the optimum. We need to make choices that will ensure all aspects of human security, including climate, food, water and peace.

One of the most important choices we have to make is to stop denying or ignoring the consequences of economic growth. Never has so much information been available to us about the effects of our actions. We know that we need to reduce demand and slow consumption, in order to stop global warming and climate change, and to nurture forms of economic activity that would be more life-enhancing than relentless growth. A second choice is even more important: to apply wisdom and passion in acting on the information we have. We need to examine our situation honestly, profoundly and self-reflectively. This is not about inducing a guilt trip or causing a paralysis of blame, but about acting responsibly.

Part of acting responsibly is to look within and ask how we can promote other ways of knowing the world and acting in it. The philosophy of "more" has channeled human development through a very narrow gate, where the focus is always on outer action and material accumulation. In this channel, the stream gets very fast and turbulent. Survival is difficult and this has resulted in the development of our worst human capacities: indifference, cruelty, denial, a narrow materialism and short-term thinking in an effort to compete with others. In this channel, the claims of ecology, morality, aesthetics and spirituality get lost. We need to reclaim the inner life, where we can reflect on other possibilities for human development, other ways of being in the world, including living according to a philosophy of enough.

It would be easy to dismiss *enough* as a form of stopping progress or even as a naïve attempt to reclaim the past. But it's really about creating many different kinds of human growth and expansion. A culture of *enough* would judge human progress in diverse ways and not just in the quantitative, measurable sense of increasing GDP. Such a culture would always attempt to balance our considerable scientific achievements with an increase in our moral, ecological, spiritual and emotional development. Humane and ecologically sound cultures would be a mark of progress and human advancement.

Enough and Ecology

The words "ecology" and "economics" have the same root; "eco" means "home" or "household." *Enough* returns economics to the scale of the household, makes it focus on the needs of the systems that sustain us and insists that economics recognize how everything is connected in "the wider household of being."[2] *Enough* treats markets, money, trade, science, technology, competition and profit — all the elements of modern growth economies — as good, creative activities that can be harnessed for the good of people and the planet if they are kept within moral and ecological boundaries. It distinguishes vibrant economic activity from unregulated economic growth.

Ecology differs from environmentalism, which is a modern way of trying to manage and limit the destructive effects of growth-related activities on the natural world. Ecology is a way of looking at the big picture, including the whole person and the place of humans in the systems of the earth. We need to know more about our planet in order to overcome the ways the modern world can cut us off from ecosystems and from diversity. An ecological outlook encourages a sense of belonging, which helps us to create meaning. And for many, meaning is lacking in the cultures that grow up in tandem with growth economies.[3]

Scientific insights into the natural world have made the marvels of healthy ecological systems available to us. They do not waste; they are economical in the original sense of the word; they elegantly and spontaneously[4] observe limits. They are, in other words, truly sustainable. We could take our cues from these organic systems and encourage human, social and economic systems modeled on them.

We should not idealize nature, however, as it can just as easily be co-opted for fascist ends as for justice. Everyone wants their ideas to be seen as "natural;" it is a very powerful concept, because it suggests that what is natural is right and unstoppable — it provides a moral justification of sorts. For instance, nature can be employed to suggest that there is a natural hierarchical order of relationships in human society, among different races or ethnic groups, or between the sexes. Proponents of unrestrained global markets and growth economies say that such systems are a natural progression for humans and that there is no alternative to them, even if they sometimes have considerable downsides.

We can use insights from the study of nature as a way to examine the kinds of systems that support life. We know that healthy ecosystems are rich in diversity and that they can provide more for their "inhabitants" (human, plant or animal) than impoverished systems, even if both kinds of system have the same nutrient resources to start with. For example, an ecologically run garden has a closed nutrient cycle; nothing leaves it in the form of waste, and it uses everything it produces to provide nourishment for the soil and the plants. We also know that healthy systems accommodate growth, but of a cyclical rather than an unlimited kind. Nature favors cycles because they come to an organic end after a suitable period of growth.[5] They do not go on growing because in nature, that is a cancer.

Humans today need to consciously self-regulate. Other species and systems, those which have not developed cultures that devalue limits, know spontaneously when enough is enough, but humans have to choose it. For economic development to be beneficial, it has to conform to very strict ecological and moral limits. Of course, we will never reach perfect agreement on the question of what the limits should be. But rather than try to set absolute rules for them, the important thing is that we start and strive to maintain a wide-ranging conversation about limits. The full potential of *enough* cannot be seen from where we currently stand in affluent countries. It becomes clear only as we travel along its path and put it into practice.

Enough and Aesthetics

To appreciate *enough*, we need an aesthetic sense that recognizes the elegance of sufficiency. *Enough* has a beauty that is completely appropriate for our time. What if the cutting edge came to mean, rather than the never-ending expansion of boundaries, the art of walking that edge between less and more, sometimes balancing, sometimes slipping? It would be beautiful and challenging at the same time.[6] Wealth could come from achieving balance and wholeness, and would include humor, fun, laughter and creativity.

However, if we consider them to be about mediocrity or deprivation, it will be difficult to embrace *enough* and its recognition of limits. The notion of limits has come to assume certain negative connotations. *Enough* can put us back in touch with the parts of ourselves that respond positively to the beauty of scale and sufficiency, the parts that empathize with the rest of creation. The arts — the record in music, painting, writing or dancing of what we have found beautiful or meaningful[7] — also work with a notion of limits. The artist has to prevent the work from exceeding itself, from becoming unwieldy or going on for too long. Otherwise the finished product becomes meaningless.

Enough and Morality

Cultural and personal appreciations of the beauty of *enough* also constitute the beginnings of a moral practice. A conversation about morality — the principles and values that underpin our actions — is essential for a different kind of long-term public culture, one that does not rest on the idea that we are fundamentally economic beings. Morality, like ecology, examines how all things can flourish in relation to each other. Both are concerned with connection and the effect that different parts of a system have on each other.

A moral quest asks us to consider things we would often rather ignore. It asks us to reflect on our place in this world, the extent of the damage that humans have done in the world and the responsibility each of us has for creating a just world: what, in short, are our obligations to other people and to the earth itself? We often don't do enough of this, so *enough* requires that we do more of what we neglect to do right now. And it requires more than asking what is wrong; it involves going on to ask, "how can we behave in ways that are right?" Morality and ethics require that we examine the consequences of our beliefs and actions in areas beyond ourselves and our immediate environment, and in the long term.

A lack of moral development is distinct from a breakdown in organized religion. Institutional religions have traditionally held a monopoly on moral pronouncements, and indeed have tended to emphasize the guilt and shame aspects of our private lives. Progressive religious leaders are thankfully now recognizing the need to broaden moral understanding, and that is to be welcomed. But we must not leave morality to religions; it is something we all need to concern ourselves with, whether we take a religious view of the world or not. Morality can be thought of as another way of naming politics, since politics too is concerned with human and planetary well-being.[8]

World economics needs to be subjected to moral and ecological scrutiny. There is a moral dilemma involved in the way that economics, narrowly understood, has taken away our capacity to live good lives. We produce and consume to "keep the economy going" but in the process, we also destroy many of the less tangible features of life that support and sustain us. "Maximum individual choice" is the big mantra within growth economics: we are promised enormous numbers of choices, which are supposed to make us happy. We often talk about equality as if it means having the right to shop on an equal footing with other people. But many of the choices available are meaningless and cause unwanted and unnecessary complexity in our lives; they are not actually available to all and they often come at a price: ecological destruction and social injustice.

Enough recasts choice as moral decisions that strive for the common good. That means taking into account all other humans, community systems, the earth, and ourselves as individuals or small family groups. This may mean setting limits on certain kinds of expansion and accumulation, because of the ways they close off decent choices for others. Taking a moral stance forces us to inquire into what is really going on in the world around us, not just in our own private or family sphere. So the moral dimension of *enough* is also concerned with justice and fairness.

Enough and Spirituality

Spirituality involves full and constant attention to and awareness of what is happening, even if this is painful. Full attention is spiritual in a sense that has nothing to do with institutional religion. If we truly pay attention to the present, then we cannot ignore what is going on around us, the social and environmental realities that we are part of. And if we stop denying and ignoring, then we will no longer be prepared to live with some of the things we see.[9]

Securing peace of mind is one part of spirituality, and to this end, many contemporary interpretations of spirituality would have us simply acknowledge and accept what we see. But merely to acknowledge the world's wrongs is more likely to bring despair, when we realize the extent of the wrongs. The only way to find peace is to resist what is wrong[10] and attempt to do right. The public side of the spiritual path — attention to social and economic systems — cannot be ignored in favor of the personal. Spiritual searching today must be infused with a political flavor if it is to be relevant to the contemporary scene.

Many people are already searching for peace of mind in the private realm with activities like yoga, tai chi, reiki, meditation, psychotherapy and poetry. Unfortunately, many spiritual activities, as taught or practised in the West, emphasize the pleasant and the personal and do not refer to a broader social or cultural search, or offer a sense of the bigger picture. It is not enough to embrace spirituality, if it is only to escape one's own pain. For example, a spiritual celebration of nature, uplifting and healing as it is, is not complete if it ignores the ways that nature is being violated by economic growth, or if the spirituality fails to defend nature. In any case, ecology teaches us that one part of a system cannot be truly healthy if other parts are in trouble. Spirituality can all too easily become the pursuit of the pleasant, a sort of tranquilizer. It can be used as an excuse for ignoring or denying what is going on in the world.[11]

Morality and spirituality appropriate to our times bridge the gap between public and private. They are political matters, because both are relevant to the world around us and to our inner lives. An ecological outlook enables us to look at context, that is, the bigger picture or web, in which our private lives are lived. The search for *enough* enables us to broaden our horizons and critique the systems that set the scene for our lives. It brings together resistance to what is wrong in the public domain as well as in the personal; it helps us to see the need for life-giving systems and gives us a desire to work toward them. Spirituality, like morality and ecology, is a recognition of deeper levels within ourselves and between ourselves and the world.[12] All three are concerned with being conscious of how everything in the world functions in relation to everything else.

We cannot know all the aspects of *enough* without actually doing it. It is a way of being in the world, not a simple set of rules for living. It is like a path whose end point we cannot see before we start out. This is part of its spiritual dimension: although we can understand it cognitively in minutes, it can take a lifetime of practice to come to truly know it. But the beauty of it is that, the more we walk on the road, or practise the philosophy, the more we become aware of the nuances and value of the practice. So *enough* can be a slow realization along the way, and in the process bring with it dramatic insights or transformations. It can also take the form of new knowledge that nobody has yet envisaged. There are difficult sides to any spiritual way, such as doubt, fear, failure, uncertainty and struggle. These are to be accepted for what we can learn from them; pushing them aside is another form of denial.

Enough has a good history; it is rooted in past generations and has been valued and practised by several great wisdom traditions, including religions, especially those traditions that have an ecological outlook and view humans as part of the great natural systems. Buddhism, Taoism, Jainism, Hinduism, Christianity and the Ancient Greeks have for thousands of years promoted the virtues of moderation. Although *enough* does not rely on religious doctrine, neither is it rigidly secular; its spiritual and ecological dimensions take it beyond any view of life and the world that values only the strictly rational, observable and material. Spirituality is about who we are when all inessential trappings are stripped away; it also concerns the most important connections we have in the world.

Enough has an immediate value for individuals in our current culture; it can help us cope with the personal and social effects of what can sometimes seem like a runaway world. Working out what is enough in one's life is a way to get some peace of mind and capacity to deal with hectic daily activities. It is a way to be content, not in the sense of tolerating poor quality, but in the sense of knowing what is valuable and what is not, and relishing the good things we have already. It provides security in times of boom and recession.

Public Policies Based on the Concept of *Enough*

Enough is at the heart of many concrete proposals and frameworks for making the changes we need in order to live well in the future. Such proposals include Contraction and Convergence and Cap and Share,[13] both based on the idea of a fair distribution of carbon-emissions quotas to all citizens of the globe. Another framework concerns basic financial security for everybody, which can in turn contribute to general security and a global retreat from growth, while also encouraging local development. This has developed into the idea of a universal basic income, which provides sufficient cash for every citizen to have the basics for a decent life.[14] *Enough* also underpins a growing worldwide food movement, based on intelligent local agricultural practices and the renewal of a food culture in places where it has died out. The basic premise of intelligent agriculture is that food production and food consumption should take place as close together as possible.[15]

In an ideal world, governments make laws based on such frameworks, creating structures for sustainability. With key structures in place, citizens would see an improvement in the quality of life. In turn, this would give a new culture of *enough* a chance to flourish; its full potential could emerge, co-created by government and citizens. It is important, therefore, that activists continue to push for such frameworks to be formally introduced. In the meantime, though, we live in a gap between what is and what might be, and in the absence of formal public policies based on *enough*, citizens need to take up the role of leaders and promote a culture of *enough*.

Citizen-Leadership for *Enough*

We cannot all be official, designated leaders, but if leadership is about taking risks and bringing other people along in a new vision, then we can all do it. We need to rid ourselves of the idea that only experts can lead us. A leader is anyone who wants to help[16] and leadership is an everyday thing, not something apart from day-to-day living. It's not confined to those who have decision-making power in institutions or states. We can all, irrespective of age, occupation or role, regularly ask questions about how we should live, what is good, how we can achieve well-being for everybody, how we can respect the earth and how we can take the long-term view and try to see the whole picture. We can engage in conversation with others about these issues. A society that does not cultivate the art of asking questions cannot count on finding answers to its most pressing issues.[17]

As citizen-leaders, we have to find ways to amplify the attractive identity of *enough* and related concepts. We have to get them into public awareness and get people talking about them and seeking others who are interested.[18] This includes providing information, but crucially, it is also about building influence for those ideas. We need the world to pick up on the message of *enough* in a thousand different ways, in all its different expressions, whether in personal or public life. We can draw on key attitudes such as stability, creativity, equity and participation. We can lead a movement for quality, wholeness, sufficiency, well-being, morality, ecology and full human potential. At the same time this movement resists injustice, quantification, monetarism, denial, isolation, cruelty and the deskilling of human beings.

The choice to live by a key attitude like *enough* is political in the broadest sense of the word. Politics is about public, collective choices and is closely connected to morality. Political and moral concerns include the values, culture and mindset that underpin the overt laws or rules that govern society. Party politics and parliamentary democracy are only a tiny part of politics.

Conclusion

Enough is a concept that is intrinsically moral, intrinsically ecological and intrinsically healthy. Practising it allows us to get what is needed from the world to sustain human flourishing, but without taking too much from individuals or from social and natural systems. It is also about how to give adequately to the world around us. So it is about the relationship between humans and the world, how we get and how we give. In our modern worldview, we have limited our understanding of how everything is connected to everything else.

The problems are all connected with each other. But just as importantly, the solutions are also interconnected. A sense of *enough* creates the conditions that will allow a critique of growth. It can also nourish a culture of adapted human behavior which will give at least some of the earth's ecosystems a chance to renew themselves and at the same time allow social justice to emerge.

Enough is neither cynical nor utopian, but hopeful. It is based on our potential for good. Simple but not simplistic,[19] it is a principled way of understanding and being that requires us to get the balance right between the inner world of contemplation and the outer world of observable action. We can think about the future in a hopeful way, grounded in the belief that humans can live up to their potential for good and for moral action. The problems facing us are very serious, but if we look only at the extremely hard realities and avoid the language of possibility, then the realities seem just too much, and we risk slipping into cynicism, denial or despair. We need to lay claim to the notion that human beings have the capacity to intervene in, influence and shape the forces that structure our lives.

There is no perfect worldview; anything taken to an extreme will show its shadow side or become dogma. But a reflexive attitude can prevent the way of *enough* from becoming rigid. This means sticking with the questions and not flinching from the challenges inherent in them. *Enough* is a key concept for the future. Living, adaptive and dynamic, it encourages creativity and diversity for groups and individuals around the world. It can help us to forge connections and discover common ground. And right now, as a positive first step toward an increasingly precarious future, it might just be *enough* to bring us real hope.

Endnotes

1. Bill McKibben, *Enough: Genetic Engineering and Human Nature*, (Bloomsbury, 2004), 227.
2. Ursula K Le Guin, "Life in the Wider Household of Being," an interview with Ursula K le Guin by Erika Milo for *North by Northwest* (Nov 2003), northbynorthwest.org.
3. Edmund V O'Sullivan, *Transformative Learning: Educational Vision for the 21st Century* (University of Toronto Press, 1999), 231.
4. Bill McKibben, *Enough: Genetic Engineering and Human Nature* (Bloomsbury, 2004), 214.
5. Barbara Brandt, *Whole Life Economics: Revaluing Daily Life* (New Society Publishers, 1995).
6. Bill McKibben, *Enough: Genetic Engineering and Human Nature* (Bloomsbury, 2004), 217.
7. Ibid., p. 218.
8. Terry Eagleton, *After Theory* (Basic Chapters, 2003).
9. Roger S. Gottlieb, *A Spirituality of Resistance: Finding a Peaceful Heart and Protecting the Earth* (Rowman and Littlefield, 2003), 32.
10. Roger S. Gottlieb, *A Spirituality of Resistance: Finding a Peaceful Heart and Protecting the Earth* (Rowman and Littlefield, 2003).
11. Roger S. Gottlieb, *A Spirituality of Resistance: Finding a Peaceful Heart and Protecting the Earth* (Rowman and Littlefield, 2003), 13–18.

12. David Selby, "The signature of the Whole: Radical Interconnectedness and its Implications for Global and Environmental Education," pp. 87, 88, in *Expanding the Boundaries of Transformative Learning*, eds. Edmund V. O'Sullivan, Amish Morell and Mary Ann O'Connor (Palgrave Macmillan, 2002), 77–93.

13. Aubrey Meyer, *Contraction and Convergence: The Global Solution to Climate Change*, Schumacher Briefing, no. 5. (Green Books, 2005).

14. Clive Lord, *A Citizens' Income: A Foundation for a Sustainable World* (Jon Carpenter, 2003). Also see citizensincome.org.

15. Colin Tudge, *So Shall We Reap: What's Gone Wrong with the World's Food — and How to Fix It*. (Penguin, 2004). Also Colin Tudge, *Feeding People is Easy* (Paripublishing, 2007).

16. cf Cornelius Castoriadis, cited in Henry A Giroux, *Public Spaces, Private Lives: Beyond the Culture of Cynicism* (Rowman and Littlefield, 2001), 81.

17. Meg Wheatley calls this getting the idea into the relational or communication networks, in her chapter *Leadership and the New Science: Discovering Order in a Chaotic World* (Berrett-Koehler Publications, 2006), 87.

18. Distinctions made in Anne Goodman, *Now What? Developing our Future: Understanding our Place in the Unfolding Universe* (Peter Lang, 2003), 303–4.

19. Ibid.

PART VII

IDEAS FOR ACTION

Escape Routes:
Fleeing Vesuvius—Which Way
Should We Go?

COMPILED BY CAROLINE WHYTE

The editors and I asked this books' contributors to send us their recommendations for things that could be done on a personal, community, national and international level to help prepare for the future. Naturally enough, our request was interpreted differently by different people: some contributors focused exclusively on the subject of their articles in the book, such as the need to curtail greenhouse gas emissions or undertake financial reforms, whereas others took the opportunity to provide much more general advice.

Additionally, not everyone was convinced that it's helpful to think in terms of escape routes at all. Lucy McAndrew wrote in this regard that "the bottom line is that there is no escape route. If we have created an unstoppable economic domino effect, we've also created, with more devastating consequences, an unstoppable environmental effect—in terms of climate change and in terms of biodiversity collapse." As we'll see though, she doesn't think we should just despair over this situation; she has some ideas for concrete action which I've included further down.

Emer O'Siochru also believes that "there is nowhere to escape to," but her reasoning is somewhat different. She goes on:

We are already reasonably well placed here in Ireland compared to anywhere else in the developed world. We should instead stand our ground [...] There is no single cataclysmic [event] to escape from. The events we fear are in the now, happening daily and weekly, all the time. These events will build, breach a threshold, cause major disruption followed by a re-adjustment and form a new baseline from which events will build again. Whether we allow the disruption/s to be so complete that substantive recovery is not possible is entirely in our own hands. The future is ours to create out of this process; nothing is predetermined.

On that note, let's start looking at recommendations for the different levels of action.

Personal Action

Re-Skilling and Staying Healthy

Most of the contributors share a belief in the importance of developing skills that would make us less reliant on the industrialized economy. David Korowicz suggests that "an investment in knowledge and skills is the wisest and cheapest of investments". Brian Davey describes how most people in low-energy civilizations are skilled in basic food growing and preparation, making and repairing clothes and maintaining their shelter: "Activities and training that prefigure these basics are most useful — and many people [in industrialized countries] don't have these skills, which are not valued."

In a similar vein, Nate Hagens believes that "novelty activities" that are plentiful in the oil age will die out and be replaced by "activities more aligned with human time scales — like gardening, or art, or sports," and he too believes that it's a good idea to get involved with such activities sooner rather than later. He adds that "human capital — one's health, skills and talents — will start to replace the security of being able to buy anything with enough digits in the bank — indeed getting back to top physical health is one of the best investments of time and resources one can make, irrespective of future resource availability."

Oscar Kjellberg suggests that we should "take an interest in basic food growing and preparation and shelter maintenance," while Lucy McAndrew says we need to "practise basic husbandry." Anne Ryan comments that "with gardening, transport, technology, recycling, cooking and growing, you can pass on what you know and learn from others." More detailed ideas for developing food security can be found in Bruce Darrell's panel on page 418.

Wise Spending

Dan Sullivan thinks we should consider whether we are reinforcing existing power structures with our spending, or helping to change them: "Regardless of the environmental consequences, money spent on land and natural resources is money given to privileged title holders, while money spent on labor products is money given to your fellow producers. Although all products involve both labor and natural resources, the proportions vary widely."

Patrick Andrews emphasizes the effects of our decisions as individual consumers on the economy and environment. He writes "I recommend you really reflect on who you are supporting when you spend money. What is the nature of the businesses you are engaging with? What's their purpose and what is your relationship to them? What impact do they have in your community? Can you influence them? We tend to underestimate what impact we can have as customers — by being more conscious of all the choices we make each day when we spend our money, we can have a positive influence on the businesses we engage with."

Corinna Byrne has a specific suggestion along those lines: "if consumers insist on detailed food-labeling based on the carbon footprint of products, this would help to drive agriculture to reduce emissions."

Material Investments: Choosing Frugality
and Reducing Greenhouse Gas Emissions

Dmitry Orlov, among others, discusses spending more in terms of its personal effects than its effects on the economy as a whole. This fits with his general analysis, which suggests that the larger economic system will probably collapse so there's little point in large-scale consumer activism. He thinks you should "make arrangements to lose your money slowly over time rather than all at once in a single financial confidence hiccup. Withdraw your money from circulation by tying it down in durable objects that are guaranteed to have residual use value in a non-industrial context."

Dan Sullivan shares this emphasis on frugality: "Personally, use as little land and natural resources as you can without unduly hampering yourself. Repair rather than replace, and look for products whose value reflect labor costs rather than resource costs."

John Sharry believes you should "remember to make the most of the wealth and resources you currently have, as these will be much more scarce in the future." Oscar Kjellberg advises you to "get rid of your unsustainable assets and make yourself debt free. Involve yourself and your money in a community with natural resources to fall back on in case something happens." Richard Douthwaite also believes that we need to cultivate frugality and build community bonds: "Each family should try to reduce its outgoings as far as possible because it will not be able to rely on an outside income in future. It should therefore link with its neighbors to meet common needs." As we shall see, this theme of building community is a very popular one.

David Korowicz comments that "we will never be materially richer than now, what we have is a precious resource to be used wisely." He describes what he calls "resilient investments," the aim of which, he says, "is not to give a conventional return-on-investment. It is to preserve your welfare in an uncertain future by providing something that is likely to be useful and important in that future. It does not have to make financial sense now." He believes that "now is the time to liquidate assets held abroad (property, investments); and non-resilient ones at home." He also thinks that "real assets, production and skills" will hold more value in relative terms than "cash, equities, bonds and much property."

He has some suggestions for specific things to invest in: "Just because energy and food have the most direct impact on the collapse of systems does not mean that we should just think only in terms of investing directly in renewable energy and food. We might also think of workhorses, trailers and harnesses; containers and demi-johns; barges and sail boats; shovels and hoes; basic chemicals; waste recycling; curing and preserving; bottling and canning; forestry and hydro-saws; reserve communications systems; storage facilities; and so on."

Corinna Byrne stresses the need for personal investments that reduce greenhouse gas emissions: "Switching from the use of peat for home heating to renewable technologies such as solar and geothermal power is recommended. The installation of small wind turbines to power one's home will also help. When it comes to food, much of what we eat is produced under emissions-intense conditions. Growing your own and purchasing locally may contribute to reducing emissions."

With regard to energy use, it may be better to keep things as simple as possible, even if that means losing some efficiency. David Korowicz writes "Don't be seduced by the most efficient technology. It is far better to have something simple and locally repairable, even if inefficient, than something highly dependent upon globalized systems for upgrades, components and repairs."

Dmitry Orlov thinks we should "consider what's coming in the context of emergency preparedness — except that this emergency is not expected to end. Stockpile supplies and learn skills to maintain and repair your most

Should Money Be
Abandoned Altogether?

Dmitry Orlov suggests that you should "gradually shift from using money to using barter and payments in kind for all of your necessities." In his first article for this book he elaborated on this idea, arguing that barter is generally misrepresented and its potential played down by economics textbooks, and suggesting that "when we use money, we cede power to those who create money (by creating debt) and who destroy money (by canceling debt)." For this reason he thinks it's misleading to suggest that any kind of money, including local or community currencies, can be helpful. His view contrasts with that of some of the other contributors who believe that local currencies are useful and that larger-scale currencies, if well-designed and issued by the users could be useful too.

With regard to local currency, I think that much of the disagreement is semantic. If we created a barter system of the type that Orlov describes in his paper, where people "barter whatever they can offer for any of a number of the things they want", and if there were more than two people involved, then we'd presumably make a list of all the things being offered and pass it around so that everyone involved could take a look. And if there was a big variety of things being offered, as one would hope would be the case, we could perhaps make it easier to figure out how much of one thing could be exchanged for another by creating a unit of account, in which case we would (hey presto) have created a local currency.

It so happens that that's the way that the local currency in the area where I live was set up. It's been quite helpful to me for making personal connections, which, as we'll see, is one of the things that Orlov and many of this book's other contributors recommends doing to prepare for the future. Of course it's entirely possible that I would have made those same connections anyway by some other means, but the currency is a relatively quick and unfussy way to do so.[1]

This isn't to say that it's perfect, though. It's a LETS-type system, so it doesn't have any mechanism to encourage people to spend their money if they have a lot of it, or to pay off debt if they are indebted. So far that hasn't been very problematic, perhaps because of the small scale of the currency—there are fewer than one hundred people involved. However, as Richard Douthwaite discusses in his article on money, other new currencies are being designed in such a way as to try and avoid these flaws altogether.

The Liquidity Network is one of them. Its sophistication comes at a price, though; as Graham Barnes writes, "one side-theme of LQN has been whether its dependence on electronic trading (and therefore inability to cope in a meltdown scenario with no telecoms) should be addressed. The issue has been set to one side in the hope that if and when that scenario comes to pass the LQN will already have played a valuable role in cementing local cohesion." The question of whether or not to invest time and energy in such a system therefore forms a part of the larger question of how we should allocate our precious remaining fossil fuel.

What about larger-scale money systems? We could see a reversion to gold coin or something equally durable and unreliant on the grid. If so, small rural communities would probably hardly ever use such money but would have a pot of coins buried somewhere for occasional use, as Orlov suggests in his article.

It may also be possible, though, to use the financial crisis as an opportunity to take a more imaginative approach to our larger-scale money. After all, the specifics of how such money is created and how it functions have changed greatly over the centuries. Glyn Davis points out in his history of money that "money is not an inert object, but a creature responsive to society's demands."[2] Niall Ferguson, the economic historian cited by David Korowicz in his article, writes in his book *The Ascent of Money* that "it seems possible that wholly new forms of financial institution will spring up in the wake of the [present financial] crisis." He goes on:

> This might be the perfect opportunity to set up an old-fashioned kind of merchant bank, focused on relationships rather than transactions, and aiming to build the trust that so many established banks have forfeited.[3]

Ferguson's mention of trust brings to mind Orlovs' comment in his article that "finance is about the promises we make to each other, and to ourselves." It follows that if we change the nature of those promises then we get a different kind of finance. Oscar Kjellberg writes in this regard:

"All actions to prepare for a sustainable society with less energy and complexity require the investment of time and resources and these investments need to be financed. Ordinary banks will not provide this finance because of degrowth and high risks. In order to make best use of limited resources and reduce investment risks we need a new organization that brings savers and entrepreneurs into communities where there is a lot of knowledge about those involved and their proposal, a lot of feedback and where the risk is shared among—preferably—everyone in the community."

We'll take a further look at contributors' suggestions for money systems on the national and international levels below.

important possessions and equipment for as long as possible after new products and replacement parts and supplies are no longer manufactured. Devise alternatives for heating, cooking and transportation that do not rely on fossil fuels. Find alternatives to inhabiting the landscape that do not rely on current built-up infrastructure and provide you with direct access to food (plants and animals)."

Avoiding a Bunker Mentality

A number of the contributors believe that there is a danger of overemphasizing the role that self-sufficiency should play. Graham Barnes is one of them. He writes that "despite a personal predilection for living in the moment, I would place 'taking an interest in the future' as #1 on a personal action level — above the other contender — reskilling/self-sufficiency — which I support and admire but can be part of a bunker mentality."

Lucy McAndrew makes a moral argument for building community: "[…] we must, for the sake of all that is valuable in the human, resist the urge to shrink our moral circle. We must overcome the tendency that fear will imbue us with to fortify our own 'castles' at the expense of community."

She goes on to suggest: "Instead, and against every fear-mongering product and media-call, we must create links within villages and towns and recognize that even those who think they are against us are actually for us, since they, too, are for survival." Some readers might question whether being for survival means being for everyone's survival, or for the survival of one's own community, or even just one's own self.

But in any case, there are other practical reasons to avoid a bunker mentality, some of which David Korowicz identifies: "Your wealth will not provide you with a separate peace. Firstly, because most of what is regarded as wealth will vanish. Secondly, we are all dependent on the globalized economy, if it fails, if fails us all. Thirdly, you are unlikely to survive without the skills and networks of others. Finally, sitting upon your hoard surrounded by the anxious and destitute is not safe."

Emer O'Siochru describes the negative effects of a bunker mentality on the larger community: "Attempting to recreate self-sufficiency at family level in basic food, energy and shelter is not a realistic strategy if generally adopted. Others have pointed out its flaws if adopted unilaterally. Its widespread adoption would certainly accelerate knowledge destruction and social breakdown. It is exactly the same failed strategy adopted by the Congested District Board and the later Land Commission that so undermined the village communities on the Western seaboard, caused centuries of emigration and destroyed the Irish language."

The Role of Specialization

Emer O'Siochru writes that "specialization fostered by the growth of settlements is still the same powerful wealth and well-being building tool it was when it pulled Europe out of the Dark Ages. Increasing local life-support system integration requires more and better specialist technical knowledge, not less."

In apparent contrast, Brian Davey believes that "most of us are too specialized for our own good. The chief danger is to think that we are special and that our unique information and skills, which currently fit a high-energy, highly specialized economy, will remain indispensable."

It seems likely that in the future almost all of us will spend more of our time on activities that are geared to basic day-to-day survival, such as growing food, chopping wood, making and mending clothes, maintaining shelters and looking after livestock. However, specialization will have an important role to play as well; it just won't be dependent on high-energy inputs anymore.

Davey is probably right in suggesting that people who spend a great deal of their time in front of a computer screen, such as myself, will experience some big changes in their lives. Instead we'll need people like coopers, a profession that's not very much in demand at the moment but that used to be quite important (my great-grandfather was one). Another profession likely to experience a resurgence in popularity is blacksmithing. And some existing professions will remain too, of course: we'll need expert plasterers to build the kind of ship hulls that Dmitry Orlov describes in his second article, midwives, potters, architects who know how to use local building materials, vets, bakers — the list goes on.

An Uncluttered Mental Landscape

Anne Ryan emphasizes simplicity, both in material and in psychological terms: "it is always easier to cultivate hope if one is coping well with present circumstances. We can all use *enough* to create personal stability. Avoid being too busy, or having a surfeit of possessions; cut down on unnecessary decisions. It is true liberation to know how to live well with just the right amount of material accumulation. Talk to friends and family members about these issues."

Lucy McAndrew discusses the need for imaginative thinking: "Remember that empathy is reaching out with your imagination, it is a stretch, an extravagance, and therefore it is characteristic, essential to what we are as animals. What extravagant humanity has done is to reach out into the material realm and ensure its comfort, at the cost of the future. Now we have to use our imaginations extravagantly to square the circle of how we can maintain our own comfort in the face of increasingly discomforting environmental realities, and in the face of an increasing knowledge of the effects of our actions."

Graham Barnes, as already mentioned, believes it is important to try to think clearly about the future. He points out that "most of us lead busy lives. Much has been written about the work/life balance and there has been a tempering of the American Dream 'work for success' ethic with a search for 'quality time.' But the zeitgeist is changing more fundamentally than that now. Work and quality of life are two legs of the stool; the third is future. Securing a sensible work/life balance on its own is a self-centered agenda and only an unstable equilibrium is possible without the third leg."

Nate Hagens also emphasizes the need to take an accurate view of the future: "Ultimately, we have been living beyond our aggregate means for sometime and are presently in a society-wide 'Wile E. Coyote' moment. Given the prevalence of 'unexpected reward' as a driver of our behavior, to lower our expectations of the future, and redefine for ourselves and our family what we consider 'success' will be a psychological robust strategy that will serve us well in many ways. Who knows, if enough people get healthy, make new friends, redefine wealth and change their skill sets to something useful for when the fossil pixie dust starts to disappear, we will have not only improved our individual futures but in doing so made a more resilient, sustainable culture as well." As we've seen in Davie Philip's article, movements such as the Transition Towns one are built on the premise that the future need not be uniformly worse than the present, but rather, as Hagens implies, that progress will be measured in more accurate ways than the present practice of conflating it with an increase in GDP and personal spending.

John Sharry comments that "being aware of the coming peak oil/climate crises can take its personal toll on an individual's mental health. Seriously contemplating the consequences can cause you to feel anxiety, depression and at times despair. Further, because your awareness will take you outside the large-scale denial in mainstream society, you are likely to feel an 'outsider' or marginalized. Certainly if you talk publicly about the problems you can be perceived as a bit of 'crank' or even a 'killjoy' socially. Preserving your own mental health and well-being is as important as taking action and there are many things that can help."

He advises us to "seek support from like-minded people who share your concerns and who don't belong to the mainstream denial. Joining an environmentally aware organization such as Transition Towns, Cultivate or Feasta will bring you into contact with a support community." He believes we have to "accept that the majority of people will not accept the problems and be largely in denial until a major crisis hits. See your job as building an 'oasis' of awareness and preparedness with a small group of like-minded people."

He continues: "Many people who face a 'fatal diagnosis' report that after an initial period of grief or despair, the news can make their daily life more precious as they learn to appreciate what they have. Learn to enjoy the moment and to prioritize the things that matter the most to you in your daily life such as connection with family and friends etc."

David Korowicz also emphasizes the importance of friendship, in particular its psychological benefits: "you will have to stand up and put your neck on the line [since the longer you wait to take action the more options will be lost]. It can be lonely. Find some fellow travelers to share in the trials and triumphs; and the hilarious predicament in which you find yourselves."

Nate Hagens adds that "for many reasons if there is less stuff to go around, and higher possibility of certain stuff not being available, having more friends, (and a variety of them) will help both individual and community trajectories." Let's go on then to investigate how some of those community trajectories might play out.

Local/Community Action

Almost all contributors place particular emphasis on community-level action. Emer O'Siochru writes that "the most effective scale to intervene is the local or community scale so I will disregard the others to give it its due prominence. A resilient local community can act as a circuit breaker to halt or slow a cascading collapse of the larger systems and provide absolutely essential support for individuals and families while they adjust to the new reality. My recommendations are both practical and political [...] Get thee to a village or small rural town. A ghost estate house might be got very cheap. If you can afford to, hold on to your rural house as a summer dacha and/or your city house as the best place to be in a sudden or single emergency event."

Dan Sullivan thinks that when you're deciding where to live you should "vote with your feet but vote intelligently. The municipalities, states and countries that get the biggest shares of their revenue from taxes on land, natural resources and pollution will have more stable economies and more affordable lifestyles for productive citizens than those which tax productivity." He believes we need to "show local governments how they can prosper from untaxing productivity and up-taxing land, pollution, and resource extraction to the degree that those things happen in their neighborhoods."

Building Community

Dmitry Orlov suggests you "make connections with people around you and work to identify ways to gain access to what you need to survive in absence of an official economy. Convert virtual communities to face-to-face interaction. Make enough personal connections so that you can go 'electronically dark' if the network fails or take yourself off the map if the political climate turns predatory."

Brian Davey also takes a pragmatic approach: "the issue is not: what can I (or I and my family) do to survive the coming crunch?"—it is what can the communities and networks that I belong to do to survive? And what is my contribution to the collective process? As a rule of thumb, if you play a role looking after the community in these basic activities, it is likely that the community will look after you. Important in this respect is to provide support for those members of communities that are vulnerable—the elderly, disabled, sick."

He believes that at present we tend to neglect our ties with neighbors in favor of more geographically distant relationships: "[...] many of us are members of very widely dispersed communities who keep in touch via electronic and digital communications and we may have very limited near contact with people who live in close geographical proximity. In a crunch situation distant relationships may remain important but, for the provision of essential supplies, it is obviously closer communities, and what they are doing collectively, that are important. Many of us don't really belong to local communities, so the first step may be getting to know neighbors. People eating together is a good start — the word companion comes from the Latin 'com pani' — with bread." Neighborhood street parties and potlucks, where everyone contributes something, have a role to play here.

Davey continues: "This may seem very banal and we may see ourselves as having a more important leadership role, becoming a hero or heroine of local, national or international enviromental politics. In fact, it is not the leading lights who make fine speeches and internet videos that are the most important when things start to get difficult — but the ones who can train others how to bake bread, and how to grow the grain to make it with...."

"Anyone reading this book is unlikely to be a complete social isolate and without any practical skills at all — but if you are — then just join something. A community garden is ideal. If you look you will find a few odd people out there who have also seen the chaos coming...like those in the Transition Initiatives. Far more than worrying about how you are going to invest your remaining money, though that's important — get involved!"

Similar approaches to building community are suggested by Anne Ryan: "Join any of the existing movements: for local food, a local credit union, a local exchange system, swap club or transition-town group. Or join a group campaigning for carbon quotas or citizens' income. You can also bring your knowledge and your questions into groups to which you already belong, such as church, trade union, sports club, study group or workplace."

How Big Should a Community Be?

The answer to this depends on what the community is trying to do. Graham Barnes comments that "actions appropriate for a 'precinct' of maybe 150 people are rather different from those appropriate for a 'demos' of 30,000. Feasta is arguably a precinct; a Liquidity Network [for developing a local currency] probably needs a catchment area of 30,000 or so for critical mass and substantial self-sufficiency. Community currencies are an important part of the emerging localist agenda, but only a part of it."

Community size can make a difference in the ease of spreading information. Barnes explains that "in a precinct you may be preaching to the converted. In the process the precinct becomes better informed but can create more distance between the group and the man in the street. In a demos, you have to spread the word with more accessible and less 'technical' messages, and [the Liquidity Network] must become expert at this type of dialogue."

Developing a Food Security Strategy

Bruce Darrell

Start by assuming that the land producing your food is deficient in essential minerals and has an imbalance of major nutrients. Assume that the food produced will be deficient in key minerals and will be of minimal nutritional value. Assume that this food may prevent you from starving, but will not sustain or improve your health. Your key task is to correct mineral deficiencies and balance soil fertility.

Educate yourself about the relationship between:

- the availability and balance of the minerals in the soil
- the productivity and health of plants grown in that soil
- the nutritional quality of the food produced
- the health of the animals and humans that consume that food
- the amount of resources expended on healthcare
- the extent of nutrient cycling used
- the overall resilience of your family/community/society

Develop a Food Security Strategy. Determine what food security would look like for your family and community in two, five and ten years' time. Develop a map or plan on how to achieve these goals which would answer the following questions:

- How much food will be produced and what type of diet is most appropriate?
- Who will be producing food and how are they going to get the necessary skills?
- Where will the food be produced and what facilities and transformations are needed?
- How will knowledge and information be obtained, recorded and shared?
- How will access be secured to the land, facilities and seeds needed to produce food?
- How will the water, minerals and fertility be sourced and cycled?
- How will supplies of food be stored, processed and distributed?
- How will surpluses and deficiencies be exchanged within the community and with other communities?

Map your land and the surrounding landscape to determine which areas are needed for ecological services and biodiversity, which areas can be best used for intensive food production, and which areas can be mined for nutrients, material and soil to improve the first two. This ecological triage will see the long-term degradation of parts of the landscape but the significant improvement in the quality and productivity of other areas.

Test the soil to determine the fertility availability and balance, the deficiencies of trace minerals and potential toxicity caused by excessive amounts of heavy metals and pollutants. Develop strategies for dealing with both the deficiencies and toxicity, including changing the location and method of food production if necessary.

Concentrate efforts on smaller areas of land rather than having a diffuse effect over a larger area. It is better to produce smaller amounts of higher-quality food than to try to produce large amounts of low-quality food with increased risk of losing everything.

Use remaining access to money and affordable energy to import fertility and trace minerals, to make major structural changes to the landscape, to build necessary infrastructure and to purchase tools and equipment that will assist in future food production.

Import the broad spectrum of trace elements in the form found in seaweed or other plant materials, ground rock dust or sea salt. Import concentrated forms of specific nutrients that you know are deficient in your soil and carefully incorporate them, ideally through the composting process. Do not let a strict adherence to organic principles or beliefs in natural gardening methods prevent you from quickly fixing what is deficient.

Increase the nutrient-retention capability and biological activity of your soil by increasing the organic content of the soil, incorporate biochar if appropriate, and change the land-management practices to reduce soil erosion and leaching of minerals.

Capture the fertility and carbon that currently flows through your community. This can be done through composting, sheet mulching, anaerobic digestion, production of biochar, and through fungal decomposition. Incorporate this material into the land designated to produce your food, or store it until this land becomes available.

Restrict exports of fertility from your land and community, unless you have an abundant and sustainable supply of fresh minerals and fertility to replace what is exported. If minerals are difficult or expensive to obtain, do not sell or trade food as a means of obtaining cash or other materials and goods.

Develop sustainable and robust nutrient cycling systems so that all of the minerals and fertility that are harvested is returned to the land. This includes human wastes.

Test the nutritional density of your food by using a simple refractometer to determine the amount of sugars, vitamins, minerals and other solids that are dissolved in the juice of vegetables, fruit and plant sap. The nutritional density should increase as mineral deficiencies are corrected, fertility is balanced and production methods are changed to increase the biological health of your soil. If it doesn't, you are doing something wrong. Food with high nutritional density will improve your health, and is a sign of a healthy and abundant ecosystem.

Community Activities

Laurence Matthews thinks communities need to engage in meaningful debate about climate change: "The need at local level is [...] to change public opinion: for people to argue in the pubs, in the shops, in the churches, and not least to their local political representatives, for the need to take climate change seriously; to counter the complacent feeling that recycling and cutting down on plastic bags are in some way an adequate response to climate change. Profligate use of carbon, e.g. frequent air travel, has to be seen as irresponsible and socially unacceptable, in the same way that drink-driving has become. This will take courage, persistence and diplomacy."

In order to discuss important issues effectively, we sometimes need to take a step back and discuss the discussion itself. In this vein, Patrick Andrews reminds us to reflect on the manner in which communities function, and to try and ensure that everyone is getting a say: "At community level, I suggest you pay attention to the ways that individuals interact when they get together in your community. Are the discussions dominated by a few people, or is everyone's voice heard. Do the structures encourage proper conversations? Are the voices of both men and women able to be heard? What about young and old?"

Lucy McAndrew also focuses on the emotional health of communities: "we must practise trust and empathy, not at the expense of ourselves (we must learn self-defense, too!) but so that we can create a meme, a mental virus which will infect and inspire the people around us and allow us to deal with any forthcoming crisis in the most dignified, the most respectful and, in the highest sense, the most human way imaginable."

In addition to these ideas, what tangible actions should communities take? Richard Douthwaite believes they should strive to become as economically independent as possible: "Every community should try to meet its basic needs from its own resources and any necessities brought in from outside should be largely to increase choice and balance by similar goods going the other way — exchanging apples for oranges, for example." One can imagine a scenario such as that described in Orlov's second article, where apples and oranges are transported by small sailing boats, along with spices and other goods that travel relatively easily and are in high demand.

Several contributors discuss the topic of community finance. David Korowicz suggests that "investing within your community makes you safer by making the community stronger." He thinks we should "invest to avoid stranded assets. At some stage in an investment cycle there may be a major disruption that will halt the project. Ensure that useful assets will be left behind. For example, don't front-load grid infrastructure investment; develop localized energy generation first."

Richard Douthwaite elaborates on the idea of investing within one's community: "Every community should have its own investment organization to allow its residents to invest in activities in their own community. This will enable them to take a holistic view of possible investments. They will be able to assess their social and environmental return as well as the income they are likely to generate."

Oscar Kjellberg has a similar proposal for developing local investment unions: "Stimulate people to reflect on who they are supporting when they are saving money. Find ways to attract savings from investors who want to save with your community and its assets rather than paper assets at stock exchanges or in equity funds that will lose even more of their value as the oil crunch worsens. Develop local enterprises through a community investment bank which should be a place where savers and entrepreneurs can socialize and discuss the development of the community. Create a local business alliance around it." Community-supportive investment tools such as the equity partnerships and local energy bonds described in this book would fit in neatly with this approach.

To these suggestions we can add the many that Davie Philip makes in his article on the Transition Towns movement. One that particularly struck me is that "as a community [you need to] identify and strengthen your physical, social and human assets. Value the tangible and the intangible, especially the skills and talents of local people." As mentioned above, setting up a local currency could help with this.

Limits to Community Action

For certain issues, however, it seems clear that action on a local or community level is insufficient; one of these is climate change. This cannot be tackled by local initiatives alone as one community's good work could very easily be undone by another's negligence. Laurence Matthews writes, with regard to this, that "developing local resilience etc. is all very well in itself and as an awareness-raising exercise, but the urgent need is for serious national and global action." So now let's look at those types of action in more detail.

National Action

The differences in contributors' approaches become more pronounced at this level. Anne Ryan writes that "if you find you are having success with a local movement, you could go a bit further afield, into national civil society, international civil society, even into government. That is not to say that we should all try to get elected; it is also important to maintain civil society — all those groupings and activities that exist outside the state and the free-trade market — so that government is always reminded of its responsibilities."

This approach assumes that the current political system, with its emphasis on the roles played by different stakeholders such as governments and business, will be viable in the future. However, Graham Barnes believes that it cannot deal adequately with the problems we are facing. He writes: "It is impossible to know whether politicians are dim, lazy or think they perceive a self-interest in the dysfunctional status quo. And pointless trying to find out. It seems likely that the nation state will be more of an obstacle than a progressive partner for the changes needed. It is in any case relatively powerless compared to international business. So I wouldn't exactly say 'don't bother' with national action agendas, but I would demand proof of seriousness from any national politicians before spending any time with them."

In contrast, Dan Sullivan thinks we need to avoid demonizing those in power: "[we should] focus on *what* is right or wrong rather than *who* is right or wrong. Some of the great changes of history were triggered by people from among the privileged elite realizing that their privileges were wrong and doing something about it."

Emer O'Siochru, for her part, believes that "politics really do matter. The Nation State is not dead nor should we wish its demise. Political power is useful, at the very least to remove bureaucratic obstacles, and at best to undertake the fiscal and monetary reforms that could really help us. People who are aware of the crisis should not be too proud nor too clever to march in the streets."

Anne Ryan agrees with O'Siochru that large-scale collective action is worthwhile: "Efforts for change are most successful when people work together. Solidarity can amplify the voice of the movement of *enough*; and when your voice has a better chance of being heard, your hope is maintained."

When one remembers that, just prior to the current war in Iraq, record numbers of people marched in the streets all over the world to oppose it but that they were nonetheless ignored by most of the politicians involved, it's tempting to conclude that this kind of action is a waste of time. However, the historical record provides plenty of examples where popular pressure did produce political results.

Of course, popular pressure is a double-edged sword: sometimes it brings about results that are highly undesirable, as Brian Davey points out in the article he coauthored with Mark Rutledge. But in my view this should not be taken as a reason to refrain from political activism — rather the opposite. People will need to have accurate information and to know their options in order to avoid mass panic.

John Sharry writes in this regard that "while the general population is largely in denial about the nature and scale of the problems we face, this will change very quickly once a series of major crises hit. At this point people will become devastated, angry and very volatile. It is crucial at this point to have a worked-out and well-communicated understanding of what is happening that provides a pathway forward that brings people together. We need to prepare to provide leadership to a devastated population so as to avoid large scale social unrest and a dangerous social vacuum, and instead inspire people toward constructive action." In this context, Davie Philip's definition of leadership as "the ability to inspire initiative and new thinking with those around us" seems appropriate.

Although Sharry provides a strong practical argument for political involvement, we might well wonder whether we have enough time for this kind of strategy. Dmitry Orlov doesn't think so. He writes that we should "stop wasting time and energy on conventional activism or political involvement. It is more efficient to simply wait for people to come round than to actively try to persuade them. Take "Believe me now, or believe me later!" as your motto. Time is on your side, not on the side of those who insist that they be persuaded."

While it's certainly clear that time and energy are scarce, we've already seen how the nature of some of our problems — climate change in particular — is such that the need for large-scale action appears to be inescapable. Specifically, there need to be enforceable global caps on greenhouse gas emissions, plus a global framework to encourage carbon sequestration and the preservation of existing carbon stocks.

That's the stick that forces us to engage in political action, but there are carrots as well. Anne Ryan comments in her article that "politics is about public, collective choices and is closely connected to morality." Seen in that light, the implications of some of the international programs that are suggested in this book are quite stunning. What if we combined the curtailing of greenhouse gas emissions with ending the Third World debt crisis and providing billions of people around the world with a nest egg for investing in renewable energy, healthcare and education? The world would likely become a considerably more stable place in political terms, which is an obvious improvement, but it would also be a better one in that we would have taken a step toward redressing many historic injustices. Personally I think that that would be quite a worthwhile thing to try and do, well worth a stab anyway.

The question of political strategy remains, though. Haranguing politicians to try and get them to adopt certain policies might well backfire, particularly if the general public isn't convinced of them either. As Brian Davey says in his second article, sometimes a more oblique approach works better.

It's also worth remembering that there isn't always a clear cutoff between active attempts at persuasion and the simple relating of facts: often both things happen in the same conversation. What if a curious but not-entirely-convinced person asks questions about the decisions one has made about one's life? How much time, if any, should one devote to answering such questions?

So What Should Governments Do?

Well, let's assume that governments are willing to act as we wish. What should they actually do? John Sharry is most concerned with the short- and medium-term challenge of dealing with system collapse:

"Whereas many people within the environmental movement are envisioning what a sustainable society might look like, the most dangerous time will [be] the transition time which will be experienced as societal and economic collapse. Preparing for managing this transition time is crucial to survival. [...] In small informed groups, prepare a series of national emergency or 'disaster' plans that will attempt to anticipate the exact nature of the many near future crises that will occur so that a range of adaptive responses can be strategized and prepared. This can include plans for dealing with energy and food scarcity, mass unemployment, population migration, currency and financial collapse etc. Both community, national and international responses need to be considered [...] so that informed community and national leaders as well as plans and policies can be available once the major crises hit."

In order to deal with future problems we'll obviously need to have competent people around, and so Emer O'Siochru argues that we need to "campaign politically to hold our young and well educated in Ireland. We will need all our various engineers, scientists, mechanics, medical professionals and even generalists like architects, planners and system engineers. It is very important for the middle-aged amongst readers to note that a youthful population is the only real insurance of a modicum of comfort for our old age."

On a more general level, Laurence Matthews emphasizes the responsibility governments have to be honest. He writes that we need to "induce governments to speak out plainly to their populations, to tell them the truth in plain language, as in wartime. Can they not pay their people the compliment of treating them as adults rather than fickle children who must be shielded from the truth? We need some leadership, in fact."

Of course, it is possible that many politicians are simply unable to comprehend the depth of the predicament we are in. One certainly gets that impression when one looks at the investments that governments are currently making. David Korowicz points out that we need to avoid unwise investments at the national level as well as the individual one: "Don't dig a deeper hole — buying a new car, or building more airports, motorways and incinerators is just…stupid."

Dan Sullivan draws also draws our attention to the ways that governments allocate taxpayer money: "Avoid supporting subsidies for greener technology, for greener technology merely pollutes less, and subsidies for technology increase dependence on technology. Paying someone to pollute less is still paying someone to pollute. Those who have arranged their lives so they can travel mostly by walking and bicycling should not have to support those who drive cars with their tax money, even if they are supporting those who drive electric cars."

He thinks national governments need to delegate more responsibility: "Politically, ask national governments to do less, and to allow local governments greater flexibility. Consider that an ordinary citizen can easily talk to all of his municipal officials, but has an increasingly […] difficult time reaching county, state and national officials. In contrast, the lobbyists for Exxon, which has gasoline stations in tens of thousands of municipalities across the United States, have influenced every US Senator and Congressman. Yet they have never spoken to the people who run most of the municipalities where their gas stations are located."

Money and Business

Richard Douthwaite focuses on the role played by a nation's currency. He thinks that there needs to be at least two types of currency, one for saving and the other for spending. Moreover, countries should keep their income and capital flows apart, as was done in the Sterling Area in the past: "International capital flows should not be mixed up with income flows. Each country or region should ensure that its import/export account for consumption purposes is always in balance. Imbalances may be permitted in capital flows but only for the purchase of capital goods."

He believes that we need to move away from debt-based money, and that the area which a currency serves needs to be smaller, for the most part, than at present: "Apart from short-term personal loans, debt-based lending should be phased out in favor of income- or output-sharing participation. Debt-free money systems should be introduced at regional level."

Patrick Andrews also discusses finance, in particular changes to banking: "My biggest dream at the national level is to turn a bank into a social enterprise, one that is owned by the community (not by the government—it is very different!) and where the voice of customers, staff, the community and the environment are heard in the boardroom. We should all push for that. This is not an easy thing to set up and implement, there will be lots of resistance at all levels. But to have a bank truly focused on serving the community as a whole would be worth pushing for."

This fits in closely with Oscar Kjellberg's idea, described above in the section on community and in more detail in his article, of developing community investment banks where savers and entrepreneurs would make decisions about the development of their community together. As mentioned above, Kjellberg thinks that local business alliances should be built around these types of community banks. On a national level, he suggests that the local business alliances should be joined into a national network.

Land, Energy and Climate Change

As described in Emer O'Siochru's article, a basic change in the taxation system could help to address climate change and future energy shortages. Here are her recommendations for national-level action: "Campaign politically for a site value tax on all developed and potential development land that will create the economic incentives to develop local integrated energy, food and waste systems in our rural settlements." Dan Sullivan's article explains how such a tax would also shelter communities from economic storms by discouraging speculation on property.

O'Siochru continues: "Campaign politically for a land value tax on the remaining agricultural, forest, bog land and scrubland that will create the economic incentives for preserving healthy ecosystem services i.e. carbon capture and storage and biodiversity while maximizing food production for local and export consumption. If we do not use our large area of fertile land productively, others in dire need will see that it is used, but perhaps in a way that might suit us less." Of course it's also possible that such land would be commandeered by people who aren't in particularly dire need — i.e. rich people — to meet their energy demands, which adds to the urgency of the situation.

Richard Douthwaite suggests that "a Community Energy Agency should be established to provide advisory and management services to communities wishing to develop their local renewable energy resources. The Agency would also guarantee the bonds issued by communities to raise the necessary finance for as long as it was providing management services." In his article he describes in more detail how the relationship between energy and money could play out in such a scenario.

Douthwaite also thinks that "each country should strive to become renewable energy self-reliant as rapidly as possible because the cost in terms of the share of national output that will need to be given up to make the switch later on will be much higher." In this regard it's important to take energy returns on investments into account. Tom Konrad, in his article, points out that demand-side technologies such as smart electric meters and well-designed public transport have a very high energy return on investment, and their adoption could therefore help us to overcome the difficulties caused by moving away from fossil-fuel use.

Corinna Byrne makes a number of specific recommendations for addressing climate change. She believes we need to "refocus the value of peatlands from energy to carbon storage and sequestration and utilize alternative renewable technologies such as wind and bio-refining to provide for energy needs."

She also describes a mechanism for dealing with livestock numbers in different countries: "Ireland, working through the EU, should seek to have global livestock numbers capped at their current level and to have the animal units allowed under the cap allocated to governments according to the number of animals kept in each country at present."

These recommendations would obviously apply on an international level as well. Let's move on to that now.

International Action

Patrick Andrews writes: "Internationally, support 'treeshaverightstoo' and push for the voice of the environment to be heard at the highest level of international decision-making."

One of the reasons why the environment has so quiet a voice at present is that it is not recognized as a legal entity. To some readers, it may seem absurd to suggest that something that is not human, and not even a discrete object, could have legal rights. However, there is a precedent for this, albeit a rather notorious one: the corporation.

The treeshaverightstoo website was set up by Polly Higgins, an international environmental lawyer who addressed the UN in late 2008 on her proposal for a Universal Declaration of Planetary Rights. As she points out on her website, there has been a gradual evolution in the recognition of legal rights. Initially, they applied only to educated males with property, but over the centuries they were gradually extended to include all humans. The most recent extension was to include children.

Children can be represented legally by an advocate if they are not old enough to represent themselves, and Higgins believes that the same approach could be taken to represent the rights of species other than humans, and the planet as a whole. In late 2008, Ecuador became the first country to adopt a constitution that includes enforceable Rights of Nature. Many of the ideas described in this book, such as Cap and Share, land value tax, the Carbon Maintenance Fee and changes in the nature of legal tender, will need legal enforcement, and their cases would probably be considerably strengthened by such a measure.

However, other changes are necessary too. Another reason that the environment has such a quiet voice is that it can't afford a big loudspeaker, unlike the CEOs of large companies and the politicians whose campaigns they fund. So many economists argue that environmental resources need to be priced more accurately. With the correct price signals, they believe consumers would make spending decisions that are much more in line with reality.

Laurence Matthews uses this reasoning in his suggestions for global action on climate change:

- we must get a price put on carbon — most of the other policies and technologies needed will then take care of themselves;
- this price must rise quickly until it curtails emissions and promotes "sinks," enough to start reducing [carbon dioxide] concentrations;
- such a price will only be politically sustainable if it is not seen as a "tax" and if it is seen to be equitable;
- Cap and Share is one of the simplest schemes to do all this, bypassing much of the Kyoto-style deadlocks and rendering superfluous much of the time-consuming and distracting Clean Development Mechanism/carbon-trading complexities.

While the price of the carbon dioxide emissions under Cap and Share would certainly give people pause about spending money on fossil fuels, Matthews makes it clear in his article that Cap and Share would also set an absolute limit on emissions — the cap — which would remain in place regardless of their price. The fossil-fuel producers would have to buy emissions permits in order to sell their product, and there would only be a certain number of these permits available.

Thus, even if there was a recession that caused a slump in demand for fossil fuels, and the price of fossil fuels then went down accordingly, we couldn't have a repeat performance of what has tended to happen in the past with such recessions — namely, the low prices of fossil fuels triggering a resurgence in demand for them which then undermines renewable energy development. The cap would remain in place no matter what the economic circumstances were, and so there would always be a constraint on the absolute quantity of emissions that could be produced. As the cap was tightened year by year, fewer and fewer permits would be issued and the amount of overall emissions would decrease accordingly. This would enable policymakers and developers of renewable energy to make realistic long-term plans and investments.

So, while price would play an important role in Cap and Share, it wouldn't have to handle the task of reducing emissions all by itself. This approach seems sound because it reflects the general role that price plays in the economy: pricing things accurately can be useful but it can't solve all our environmental and social problems, and you have to be careful with it.

Another shortcoming of pricing is that in the absence of additional measures it can't reduce the instability of an economy that is dependent on debt. Richard Douthwaite writes in this regard: "The scarcity rents which fossil energy and other commodity producers enjoy must be limited to the amount they can spend with their customers on consumption goods and services. A system needs to be put in place to prevent this level being exceeded. With fossil fuels, this could be by Cap and Share, which would capture the rents and spread them as income around the world. Alternatively, the consuming countries could set up an energy-buyers' cartel which would serve the same purpose."

As Douthwaite says, the introduction either of an energy-buyers' cartel or of Cap and Share would help to stabilize the world's financial system by preventing capital from surging around the world, and by relieving debt. Cap and Share has other advantages as well: it would reduce greenhouse gas emissions, as we've already seen, and it could significantly reduce global poverty and income inequality, at least in the short term while the price of emissions was high.

Dan Sullivan would probably disagree with this analysis, though. He writes: "The poor nations of the world do not merely happen to be poor. Rather, they are poor because they are plundered by international financiers and by absentee landlords. End the plunder, and you end the poverty. Even the people of resource-poor nations need to establish systems of freedom and justice before compensation [for resource use] will do them any good. Otherwise, compensation will follow the pattern that US foreign aid has always followed, taxing poor people in rich countries to subsidize rich people in poor countries."

Indeed, at present much foreign aid also has the effect of subsidizing the companies in rich countries that provide the aid. However, the commons-based philosophy behind the per-capita distribution of emissions permits dovetails rather neatly with current development theory, which emphasizes individual agency, and there does seem to be good evidence that cash transfer programs are an effective way to reduce poverty.[4] Moreover, the equitable nature of Cap and Share is a point in its favor in ethical terms as well as practical ones.

A scheme such as Cap and Share isn't without risks, though. Douthwaite goes on to describe one of them: the possibility that "the higher prices for fossil fuels [triggered by a cap on emissions] will lead to increased deforestation and the release of carbon from soils as land is converted to bioenergy production." He suggests a solution: "The introduction of a Carbon Maintenance Fee [would] preserve and increase the stock of carbon held in soils and the biomass growing on them."

Corinna Byrne, similarly, emphasizes the need to preserve current carbon stocks: she writes that we should "push for tropical deforestation to be reduced and for the global forest cover loss to be halted," and she, too, suggests that "governments could introduce the Carbon Maintenance Fee as a reward for holding and sequestering carbon in soils and biomass and to penalize for carbon releases."

In order for such a scheme to be effective it would be necessary to measure carbon stocks accurately, so she thinks we need to "advocate the development of remote sensing techniques to map carbon stocks with the aim of improving estimates of the standing stock of carbon in biomass and changes in those stocks through time."

Byrne also draws our attention to the fact that carbon dioxide is not the only greenhouse gas. There are other gases whose emissions need to be curtailed: "Nitrous oxide [emissions reduction] needs to be prioritized because an increased nitrous oxide concentration is likely to lead to an increased methane concentration and thus a greater total warming effect than from the nitrous oxide alone (as nitrous oxide destroys ozone which destroys methane). Policy should be focused on reducing nitrous oxide releases, taking in reductions in methane emissions whenever these are compatible, such as in the use of anaerobic digesters." Such digesters could be used to produced energy for communities.

Along with several of the other contributors, she also believes that biochar production has important potential: "The use of biochar is one of the few strategies that gives any basis for optimism that the excess CO_2 in the atmosphere can actually be removed." If the claims that have been made for the benefits of biochar have any foundation, it could prove to be an enormous help in addressing climate change, and also as a fuel source. As Emer O'Siochru mentions in her chapter, it could help to revive local economies as well.

Byrne has some specific suggestions about REDD, the international system for offsetting emissions by allowing countries which emit beyond their allowances to compensate for this by paying for other countries to emit less. This system has significant flaws, which Byrne describes in her article. She recommends that we "reject offsetting via REDD altogether or tighten the limits on how much can be done with a view to phasing it out completely by 2020. Funding for whole-country REDD schemes should come from the proceeds of auctioning EU emissions trading system permits (EUAs) after 2012 until a global system can be put in place."

Dan Sullivan writes that "it is not necessary to support elaborate international schemes to make resource-consuming nations compensate nations from which the resources have been taken. It is only necessary for resource-exporting nations to levy substantial royalty charges on their own land and resources, to tax pollution, to untax labor and to get control of their own money." REDD would probably qualify as one of the "elaborate international schemes" that he criticizes.

A New International Currency

As mentioned above, Richard Douthwaite believes that the scarcity rents for commodities should not be allowed to expand infinitely, but rather should be curtailed and then recycled back to the people and countries who are buying the commodities, preferably by means of trade rather than as loans. A system such as Cap and Share would not only guarantee this recycling of rents, but it would also divide them among the whole population.

However, this measure would not be sufficient for achieving greater financial stability, as we would still be using debt-based money for all of our transactions, and, as we have seen in the many articles in this book that discuss the financial system, that type of money is highly volatile and dependent on unsustainable economic growth.

So Douthwaite also believes that "a new international trading currency should be established to replace currencies like the dollar, the euro and sterling. It would be given into circulation according to the amount of trading a country was doing and its first use should be to discharge foreign debt. In times of disaster such as the Pakistan floods, additional money could be created to finance the relief effort, thus spreading the cost fairly around the world." A change of this kind is not as radical as you might think. The world already has a non-debt quasi-currency which is given into circulation by the IMF. It is called Special Drawing Rights (SDRs) or more popularly "paper gold." The IMF insists that SDRs are not a currency but an "international reserve asset" which can be sold for currencies such as the dollar and the euro. They were first issued in 1969 to supplement IMF member countries' official foreign exchange reserves. Only two issues have been made since, the most recent on August 28, 2009 in response to the global financial crisis. This was because, after the previous distribution in 1979–81, the United States vetoed futher issues so that its dollars were used as reserves instead. Unfortunately, SDRs are not shared out on the basis of population but according the maximum amount of financial resources that each member state is obliged to contribute to the IMF. This means that the bigger, richer countries get most.

A New Life in Old Places?: A Personal Comment

There's been much discussion in this book of the possibility of sudden collapses in civilizations, with whole ways of life being brought to an abrupt end. However, it's also true that in certain circumstances, ways of life can fizzle away slowly rather than going out with a bang.

That's been the case in the area where I live, in southern Burgundy in central France. The interesting thing about this area is that, like Pompeii, you can get an unusually clear idea of what life was like in the past. Hereabouts, the high point was the Middle Ages, specifically the eleventh and twelfth centuries, when the great Benedictine abbey at Cluny was enormously wealthy and politically influential. At that time, the villages of the area almost all rebuilt their churches with the help of Italian masons who used hand tools and knotted ropes to measure the stones they worked with, and who left behind a rich legacy of intricate carvings. Such carvings appear not only on the churches but on people's houses, and frequently depict scenes from everyday life.

The historian Edwin Mullins speculates that the reason for this sudden flowering of artistic expression was that everyone was relieved that the world hadn't come to an end in AD 1000, contrary to much dire prediction at the time.[5] But whatever the cause, the artistic frenzy wasn't to be repeated. The power of Cluny began to wane from the thirteenth century on, and there were no more audacious building projects.

Village life continued, however, and the area remained modestly prosperous until well into the twentieth century. Recently I took a stroll around the village where my husband and I live, Lys, with a neighbor who is in his seventies and who still lives in the house that he was born in. He pointed out various buildings in the center of the village and told me "that was a café, that was a grocery, that was a smithy, that was another café, that was a carpenter's workshop."

Even though they're eerily quiet now, the buildings left behind from the businesses are mostly in rather good shape. In fact, the villages as a whole have a bit of an unreal, fairytale look to them, almost too picture-perfect.

The cause of the businesses' disappearance will probably be obvious to most readers. But just for the sake of thoroughness, I asked my neighbor why they had closed. He smiled wryly at me and said "the supermarkets" — which was of course a shorthand way of saying "the fossil-fuel-based economy." Just as in many parts of rural Ireland, the arrival of private cars and the economies of scale used by supermarkets had undercut small local enterprises.

However, the dreamy quality of the villages remained unexplained. Eventually though it occurred to me that just as the volcanic ash which flooded Pompeii had a preservative effect on its buildings, these villages too had been flooded and preserved. But in their case it's capital from elsewhere — money conjured up by the use of fossil pixie dust, to use Nate Hagens' phrase — which has done the flooding. People from Paris and Lyon, and foreigners from Switzerland, Belgium, Germany, Britain, the United States and even New Zealand, have bought second homes here, most of them medieval dwellings that they've lovingly restored. They generally fly into Paris or Lyon or drive down and spend a few weeks of the year here, usually during the summer as the winters are fairly intense.

I don't mean to vilify those people who have second homes in the area — they've helped to support the local economy by hiring local masons and roofers to work on their restorations. Their interest in the local culture and history is genuine, and some of them are our friends.

But the uncomfortable fact remains that, as with all communities that don't have much year-round occupancy, it's not possible to keep services such as shops going. Additionally, locals have been priced out of many of the more comfortable homes. And of course, there's also the niggling matter of the whole setup being wildly unsustainable.

I asked my neighbor how long ago all of those small businesses closed down and, much to my surprise, he told me that some of them — even the blacksmith — lasted into the 1980s. He also explained that the land around our house had been a farm which served some of the villagers. He himself had worked with draft horses on farms in the area until the mid-1960s. The communally owned woods on the hillside above were, and still are, a source of game for hunters. In the not-so-distant past, the hunters would hike over the hills to Tournus, a town on the easily navigable river Saone, to sell furs.

All of this conjures up an image of a kind of rural paradise, overflowing with abundance, which I'm sure wasn't entirely the case. But then again, it's important not to over-romanticize the modern industrial system either.

Aptly enough, the other day I was in a local supermarket with my toddler daughter. It was busy and there were long queues at the checkouts. We'd been waiting for a few minutes in a queue that had barely moved when my daughter told me that nature was calling.

The aisles were completely blocked with loaded shopping trolleys, so I pushed our trolley aside and went to ask a couple of the staff, who were stacking shelves, if she could use the toilet in the back of the supermarket. They told me that I'd have to get a key from the welcome desk, so we made our way over to it. But there was nobody there; everyone was helping at the checkouts. It occurred to me then that we could just go out the automatic entrance door, which was nearby, and my daughter could fertilize a tree outside, but when we went over to the door it wouldn't open.

There was an electronics stand laden with gleaming gadgets right next to the door, and I asked the young woman who was behind it if she could open the door for us. She looked up distractedly from her mobile phone and told me that she was sorry, but it wasn't possible. I assumed she meant that it was against some kind of shop rule to open the door, so I explained why we needed to go out. She apologized again and told me that if she had been able to, she would have opened the door, but it only opened from the outside and the staff had no control over it.

Thankfully my daughter and I did manage to get out eventually by running the gauntlet of the shopping trollies in a checkout aisle. But the whole little episode got me thinking about escape routes, and unnecessarily complex labyrinths designed to suck people so that they consume more resources, and the relative powerlessness of the people working in the labyrinth.

This was just a minor incident, of course, but the contrast between our experience at the supermarket and at our local farmer's market, which takes place once a week, could hardly be greater. There, many of the vendors know my daughter by name, and if you end up waiting a long time in a queue it's likely to be because the vendor is having a chat with someone, rather than because some unfortunate customer didn't have quite enough cash on them to pay for everything in their trolley and the cashier is having to call up the supermarket manager in order to get permission to cancel part of the sale transaction.

The emptiness of material abundance without enough human connection is made very clear when we consider the things that small children really need, as opposed to the things that advertisers say they need. And there's another group besides children that is particularly badly served at present. Those houses in the villages around here that aren't second homes are generally occupied by people like my neighbor — people in their seventies and eighties who have witnessed the slow death of their communities. It would be wonderful if they could see life in the villages again; children playing, adults working and socializing.

Of course I don't mean to imply that I think everything should revert to the way it was before the era of fossil fuels. There's plenty of room for anaerobic digestors and solar water heaters here and elsewhere, and even if there wasn't, we've seen in this book that going back to the past is not an option. But there are a great many rural places in the world waiting to be occupied again, in a somewhat different manner from before, and there's still time — just about — to learn valuable skills from the older generation.

It's interesting to note that most of the inhabitants of Pompeii did realize in time that they were experiencing a true emergency. They managed to flee to safety, escaping the volcano's ashes. So let's hope that this parallel with our present situation also holds.

Endnotes

1. In the course of preparing this conclusion I asked the person who administers the transactions in our local currency, Mathilde Béguier, if it's overly time-consuming, and she said that she doesn't find it a problem. I asked what she would do if there was a big increase in transactions. She said that she would divide the work up with others, but that if membership increased as well, the best solution would be to start up more local currencies in order to deal with the overflow.
2. Glyn Davies, *A History of Money from Ancient Times to the Present Day* (University of Wales Press, 2002), 642.
3. Niall Ferguson, *The Ascent of Money* (Penguin, 2008), 358.
4. See for example "The Social Protection Floor: A Joint Crisis Initiative of the UN Chief Executives Board for Co-ordination on the Social Protection Floor," UNDP/ILO (2009) and Joseph Hanlon, Armando Barrientos and David Hulme, *Just Give Money to the Poor: The Development Revolution from the South*, (Kumerian Press, 2010).
5. Edwin Mullins, *In Search of Cluny: God's Lost Empire* (Signal, 2006).

Should the United States
Try to Avoid a Financial Meltdown?

*Many Americans believe that the US cannot avoid hyperinflation or a catastrophic financial crash. **Tom Konrad**'s position is slightly different. He thinks that while a crash is possible, the system is more likely to end with a whimper rather than a bang and that any progress towards building a more sustainable society will be undermined unless the country undergoes significant cultural change. With the confidence that comes from living on the other side of the Atlantic, however, **Richard Douthwaite** thinks he's wrong and that, in Fleeing Vesuvius terms, what he's saying amounts to "let's allow this flow of lava to pass over us. Some of our institutions will be burned up and lots of people will have a bad time but, after it's over, we can rebuild in a more sustainable way". Here's how the debate between them went:*

Richard: I think we agree, Tom, that the United States is trapped in a downward spiral, blocked on one side of its balance sheet by insupportable debts and on the other by unsustainable asset values. When the spiral was running upwards, almost everyone was delighted because the value of their houses and other assets was increasing and enabling them to live well by borrowing more. The increased borrowings injected additional purchasing power into the economy. This increased the price people were able to pay for assets — which, of course, they bought with borrowed money. It was a wonderful flight from reality while it lasted

But in 2007 and 2008, when the high energy and commodity prices generated by a global boom pushed up the cost of necessities and left the weakest borrowers with too little money to service their debts, many of those flying on borrowed wings came crashed to. down. The sub-prime mortgage crisis set the spiral turning in the other direction, pulling everything down rather than pushing it up.

In this new environment, no-one wishes to borrow to buy assets since their prices are still falling. People are fearful about their financial future and have cut their spending, increased their saving and are trying hard to pay back their loans. This has given the downward spiral an extra twist as the lack of demand has cut national income and increased unemployment, sucking even more families into the debt trap.

The imbalance between asset values and incomes has widened the gap between rich and poor. The US is one of the most unequal countries in the world and the richest 1% of the population enjoy almost 24% of the nation's income, up from only 9% in 1976. This was the reason for the death of the American Dream. More than 80% of the increase in national income generated by economic growth between 1980 and 2005 went to this group. The heads of companies did particularly well. They earned an average of 42 times as much as the average worker in 1980, but 531 times as much in 2001.

This imbalance is closely linked to the imbalance between asset values and GDP. Whenever the top 1% get a further increase in income, they spend very little of it on American-made goods and services — in other words, in ways which create many jobs for other people. Most is invested in assets and has the effect of driving their prices up or at least limiting further falls.

If conventional policies continue to be followed, the gap between rich and poor makes it very difficult to see how the US economy can avoid a continuing decline, still less how it can ever "recover". Any pick-up in the economy can only come from a pick-up in demand for US goods and services but the rich aren't going to consume any more, the poor can't afford to and the various levels of government are overborrowed as it is. The federal government's deficit in 2010 was expected to be over 10% and many local governments have had to make extremely painful cuts. The only possible conventional source of extra demand is an increase in exports but that's going to be difficult to achieve as the manufacturing base has been badly eroded by free trade policies and there is huge competition from the rest of the world.

What all this says to me is that an unconventional policy is needed that gets money into ordinary people's hands without asking anyone to take on any more debt. Would you agree?

Tom Konrad: While I agree with your assessment of the situation, I disagree about the proper goal for a long term shift to a sustainable economy. A sustainable economy operates at a much lower level of economic activity and its primary driver of economic activity is not consumer spending. America's problem is cultural as well as economic. We have an unsustainable culture, where status is equated with material wealth. The race to acquire more material wealth is in its essence unsustainable. The death of the American Dream of universal home ownership is not just a product of inequality: Universal home ownership leads to sprawl, and is incompatible with a sustainable society.

Our most important task is to bring our culture back to one much more like that of our founding fathers, where industry and hard work are the source of status, instead of the possession of material wealth. Benjamin Franklin used to fetch the paper for his printing shop in a wheelbarrow with an intentionally squeeky wheel. His intent was to call attention to the fact that he did this manual labor for himself, raising his reputation as an hard worker. Today, such manual labor is more likely to be seen as a badge of shame, and fit only for immigrants. Our debt-fueled society has led Americans to believe that we are entitled to everything we want, including the luxury of not working for it.

Putting money into people's hands without requiring anything in return will simply reinforce America's unsustainable culture. Instead, current debts should only be absolved through the arduous process of bankruptcy. Social inequity should be addressed through high taxes on inheritance and programs such as the Earned Income Tax credit, while the income tax and Social Security payments (which reduce the rewards of work) should be replaced with a large and meaningful carbon tax on energy, including the embodied carbon of imported goods.

These tax changes should help reward sustainable industry, and reduce the incentives to live the lavish, unsustainable lifestyles to which Americans have come to believe we are entitled.

Richard Douthwaite: What you are saying, Tom, is that before the people of the United States can rediscover the virtues of thrift and hard work, they need to pass through the fires of Vesuvius in order to be cleansed of their false consumerist values. My view is that there is a better, surer way to achieve this result. The hundreds of thousands of corporate and personal bankruptcies you envisage would destroy incomes, savings, pensions and asset values. People would become fearful, bitter and possibly violent as a result. They would look around for scapegoats (the Jews, perhaps?) or turn to crime.

Consequently, I just can't see a period of financial turmoil creating a good basis for building a better society. A worse one seems much more probable as extremist leaders are likely to emerge in response to mass un-employment and the rich could well use force to protect themselves and their lifestyle. The positive things you want like a carbon tax would be much harder to introduce ("What, you want to tax the energy that makes me so productive?") and Dan Sullivan's land-value tax ideas was would be rejected outright because people would realise that such a tax would prevent their property values from ever recovering to whatever they were at their peak.

The choice before the US is either to increase incomes by enough to sup-port the current level of debts and asset values, or to write down debts and asset values until they correspond with current income levels. In essence, I'm proposing increasing incomes by enabling more people to work while you, although not exactly wanting a massive deflation, think that one is nec-essary and would ultimately prove beneficial.

The main reason you seem to reject my job creation route is that it would involve giving everyone some money "for nothing" for a few years while enough jobs were being created to raise the national income by enough to enable it to support the country's massive public and private sector debts. Let's go through my proposal carefully to see if your objections really hold.

In November 2010 the Federal Reserve said that the recovery was "dis-appointingly slow" and it would inject money it had created out of nothing into the economy by buying $600bn-worth of long-term Treasury bonds from their holders before July 2011. As it had already announced it would buy $250bn to $300bn worth of bonds over that period, the announcement meant that between December 2010 and June 2011, the Fed will be handing over about $3,000 for every person resident in the United State to investors in exchange for their bonds. It hopes that the investors will spend the money in ways which boost the economy but it seems unlikely that they will.

Instead of the $3,000 per head being passed to investors, I would like to see some of it being given as a gift to state and county governments so that they can restore local services and rehire the folk they have sacked. I would like the remainder to go on an equal per capita basis to every US resident in a form which prevented them from using it in any other way than to pay down their loans. This would strengthen the banking system, People with no debt would be required to invest it in, say, community facilities or the transition to renewable energy.

It would not be necessary to give this money away for nothing. It could be part of a package involving, say, the introduction of a carbon tax although Peter Barnes' Cap and Dividend, the US equivalent of Feasta's Cap and Share, would be much better. This puts up the price of fossil fuel according to its carbon content but returns every cent to the public. Everyone gets the same amount, so those people who use less than the average amount of fuel come out better off. What do you think? Would enabling people to clear their debts for three or four years while jobs were being re-created and the financial system was being restored to balance really be demoralizing?

Tom Konrad: Bankruptcy replaces unsupportable debt with debt which is (barely) supportable. The losses are borne by the lenders foolish enough to extend unsupportable credit. Inflation destroys incomes and asset values by cheapening them, and the losses are borne by savers who have tried to do all the right things to prepare for their futures.

I certainly see your "solution" would feel much better in the short term but I don't see how it will do anything to help with the cultural problems I think are the root cause of our current and future crises. Americans are not going to scale back their lifestyles (a must in a sustainable world) without some pain. As long as we pursue strategies that avoid pain, no lessons will be learned and we will simply be setting the stage for the next crisis.

I agree my solutions are not politically feasible, while yours are fairly close to the current policies of deficit spending and quantitative easing (printing money.) Americans are not ready for the necessary painful adjustments, and they would no doubt look around for someone to blame besides themselves. Just because we're not ready for it does not mean it's not the right thing to do.

Richard Douthwaite: I don't think we can avoid pain whatever we do. As Chris Vernon's article shows, fossil energy supplies are likely to contract very rapidly over the next 40 years. The economy will contract with them, turning everyone's lives upside down. That will be very painful. My proposal is an attempt to minimise the pain by ensuring that we have a functioning monetary system to help us through a wrenching transition to a low-carbon economy. What's your alternative strategy to get families and communities through the next forty years? Can you protect savers whose money has been invested in activities which are based on cheap energy from taking hefty losses? I can't, but an inflation would mean their losses were gradual rather than near-total and overnight.

Tom Konrad: I believe that your course is a well-intentioned attempt to treat symptoms but may actually worsen the disease, and you believe that my course may kill the patient.

I agree the proper goal is to minimize the pain of the transition to a low carbon economy, but I believe much of that pain is necessary to avoid future bubbles caused by excess stimulus in the face of declining energy supplies. A root cause of the last (housing and debt) bubble was the Fed's stimulus in response to the dot-com crash, with the money driving up asset values to unsustainable levels. Too much stimulus now, whether it takes the form of giving money directly to households or the Federal Reserve buying Treasury bonds will simply lead to new bubbles and new crises.

In order to reduce the pain today, we should focus on enabling debt renegotiation in the place of bankruptcies. Yet the remaining debt not only needs to be supportable on the reduced incomes that come with lower economic activity, it needs to be large enough that Americans do not just learn the lesson that we can borrow as much as we want and there will be no consequences.

Savers who invested in cheap-energy supporting businesses, like heavy debtors, should take losses. They also have a lesson to learn, and that lesson is that investments in sustainable businesses are sustainable assets, while investments in unsustainable businesses will decline. Investors who invested in sustainable businesses such as energy efficiency, resource conservation, alternative transportation, and sustainable agriculture, are already doing their part to shift our economy in a more sustainable direction, and the fruits of their wise investing should not be appropriated through inflation.

Investors have ways to protect themselves from inflation (by buying commodities or inflaion-indexed bonds, for instance) or from declining energy supplies (by buying the securities that are aiding the transition.) If investors must protect themselves against inflation as well, they will have fewer resources (both financial and mental) to dedicate to the transition to a sustainable economy.

Just as the attitudes of ordinary households are important in helping them adjust to a sustainable economy which is not based on debt-fueled consumerism, the attitudes of investors are important in deploying the capital we need for the transition. Cultural attitudes are not changed by pretty speeches; cultural attitudes are formed by real world experiences.

The only way I see to change the American culture to one that is compatible with a sustainable economy is to make both households and investors who have lived and invested unsustainably bear much of the consequences of their actions.

Yes, we must let the lava of Vesuvius wash over us, because it will wash over the most unsustainable parts of our economy and culture. We should not build dams in a vain attempt to stop the lava, especially when those dams are piled on the foundations of a sustainable future economy.

EPILOGUE
FLEEING VESUVIUS

There were frequent rumblings, some of them subterranean, that resembled thunder, and some on the surface, that sounded like bellowings; the sea also joined in the roar and the sky re-echoed it. Then suddenly a portentous crash was heard, as if the mountains were tumbling in ruins; and first huge stones were hurled aloft, rising as high as the very summits, then came a great quantity of fire and endless smoke, so that the whole atmosphere was obscured and the sun was entirely hidden, as if eclipsed. Thus day was turned into night and light into darkness. Some thought that the Giants were rising again in revolt (for at this time also many of their forms could be discerned in the smoke and, moreover, a sound as of trumpets was heard), while others believed that the whole universe was being resolved into chaos or fire.

Therefore they fled, some from the houses into the streets, others from outside into the houses, now from the sea to the land and now from the land to the sea; for in their excitement they regarded any place where they were not as safer than where they were.

While this was going on, an inconceivable quantity of ashes was blown out, which covered both sea and land and filled all the air. It wrought much injury of various kinds, as chance befell, to men and farms and cattle, and in particular it destroyed all fish and birds. Furthermore, it buried two entire cities, Herculaneum and Pompeii, the latter place while its populace was seated in the theater. Indeed, the amount of dust, taken all together, was so great that some of it reached Africa and Syria and Egypt, and it also reached Rome, filling the air overhead and darkening the sun. There, too, no little fear was occasioned, that lasted for several days, since the people did not know and could not imagine what had happened, but, like those close at hand, believed that the whole world was being turned upside down, that the sun was disappearing into the Earth and that the Earth was being lifted to the sky.

— From *Roman History* by Cassius Dio (164–c.235), a Roman senator of Greek descent

Contributors

 PATRICK ANDREWS qualified as a solicitor in 1988 and spent many years working in the UK and abroad for large corporations, specializing in cross-border transactions. In 2002 he left the corporate world, driven by a concern about its impact on society and the planet. He now teaches and writes about alternatives to conventional ownership and governance structures, and works with business leaders devising new ways of organizing. He helped develop a radical financial and governance structure for Riversimple LLP. He lives in the New Forest in England with his wife and son, and a big vegetable patch.

 GRAHAM BARNES has been part of Feasta's Liquidity Network team since November 2008 and became a Senior Policy Advisor in December 2009. As a neophyte economist (his doctorate is in Computer Science), he has been getting to grips with what he calls "the strange concept of money". He splits his time between Kildare and Dorset, where he co-owns a converted Edwardian department store and runs a consulting business bridging online technology and the travel and tourism industry.

 CORINNA BYRNE is a Fulbright scholar and is currently completing her PhD in soil carbon in the Carbolea Research Group at the University of Limerick. She is a member of the Feasta Executive Committee and coordinator of the Feasta-led Carbon Cycles and Sinks Project which began work in late 2008. She lives near Ardrahan, Co. Galway.

 CHRIS COOK has been involved in the regulation and development of markets and enterprises for 25 years, including six years as a director of a global energy exchange. He is currently working in the area where the internet and markets converge, mainly in Scotland with Nordic Enterprise Trust (NET) and seed funding from Innovation Norway. His aim is to develop new partnership-based enterprise models and related financial products and services. He lives in Scotland.

JULIAN DARLEY is the founder of both Global Public Media and Post Carbon Institute, pioneer organizations which work to provide education about and demonstrate solutions for problems of energy depletion, climate change and ecosystem decline. He is also the author of *High Noon For Natural Gas: The New Energy Crisis*. He holds an MA in journalism from the University of Texas and an MSc in social research and the environment from the University of Surrey. He is now an academic researcher, a consultant and dramatic writer. His current work focuses on the intersection of business, government and civil society in pursuit of decision-making and power distribution in a world of fast-changing energy and environmental parameters. He lives near London.

BRUCE DARRELL grew up in Canada where he was educated as an architect. Since moving to Ireland he has been actively involved in developing sustainable communities with Dublin Co-housing and more recently with Ireland's first eco-village in Cloughjordan, Tipperary, where he is active in the areas of education, food and land use. He has a keen interest in developing urban and small-scale agriculture systems and in exploring the many possibilities and benefits of reintegrating human habitation with food production. He runs several courses on how to grow food and is working to establish a series of research and educational gardens. He is currently nearing the completion of a home for his family in Cloughjordan which he self-built with his neighbor.

BRIAN DAVEY trained as an economist but, aside for a brief spell working in eastern Germany showing how to do community development work, has spent most of his life working in the community and voluntary sector in Nottingham particularly in the health promotion, mental health and environmental fields. He helped develop Ecoworks, a community garden and environmental project for people with mental health problems. He is a member of the Feasta Energy and Climate Working Group and the Coordinator of Cap and Share UK. His life-long interest is why and how people and systems break down. He lives in Nottingham.

RICHARD DOUTHWAITE is an economist, journalist and author specializing in energy, climate and sustainability issues. He is a cofounder of Feasta and serves on its executive committee. His books include *The Growth Illusion* (1992), *Short Circuit* (1996) and *The Ecology of Money* (1999). He lives near Westport, Co. Mayo.

ALEX EVANS is a Non-Resident Fellow at the Center on International Cooperation (CIC) at New York University, where he runs CIC's work on climate change resource scarcity and global public goods and works with organizations including the UN, the World Bank and the Brookings Institution. He completed a joint CIC–Chatham House project on the international implications of rising food prices in 2009. From 2003 to 2006 he was Special Adviser to Hilary Benn, then the UK Secretary of State for International Development. He lives in London.

GILLIAN FALLON studied French and psychology at university before going to work as a cook, eventually opening a restaurant with a friend. She then re-trained in publishing and has worked as a writer, journalist and editor for 15 years, most recently in academic publishing. She has a particular interest in food security and in the challenges involved in communicating the many complex messages derived from systems thinking to a non-specialist audience. She has been a member of Feasta's Executive Committee since 2006 and currently divides her time between Dublin and Co. Kerry.

NATE HAGENS recently completed his PhD in Natural Resources from the University of Vermont, studying issues surrounding the end of the growth-based global society. On the supply side, he studied biophysical analyses on measuring our natural resources in natural resource terms (as opposed to dollars). On the demand side, he researched how our evolved neural algorithms created both opportunities and constraints in dealing with resource limits. Ultimately a new more sustainable economic system would better match our demand drivers with our natural resource balance sheet. He is a director of the Post Carbon Institute, the Institute for Integrative Economic Research (IIER) and the Institute for the Study of Energy and Our Future, the parent of online energy analysis site theoildrum.com. In earlier years he worked on the dark side as a hedge fund manager on Wall Street and as an investment manager at the firms Salomon Brothers and Lehman Brothers.

TIM HELWEG-LARSEN has been Director of the Public Interest Research Centre since 2006. He trained as an engineer in renewable energy at Warwick University, before going on to project manage small-scale renewable projects in the Indian Himalayas. Tim has an extensive history of climate change research and advocacy. He has worked on climate policy with the Global Commons Institute, representing it at the UN climate change negotiations between 2002 and 2006. He has lectured at University of East London on climate, energy and economic issues, and led the Zero Carbon Britain report published by the Centre for Alternative Technology in 2007. In 2009–10 he chaired The Offshore Valuation Group, a consortium of government and industry bodies seeking to place a value on the UK's full offshore renewable energy resource, resulting in a report, "The Offshore Valuation." In 2011 he will be starting a new social enterprise to enable energy users to become investors in the renewable energy projects that supply their needs.

 OSCAR KJELLBERG is an economist, agronomist and, after helping to develop the Swedish interest-free JAK Bank for 17 years, a banker. He is now engaged as a consultant in the development of the new debt-free and risk-sharing forms of savings and finance that are needed to enable entrepreneurs to assemble suitable mixes of equity and loan capital during the risky transition to sustainability. He lives on an old tugboat in Stockholm harbor during the summer months and in an apartment ashore during the winter.

 TOM KONRAD is a financial analyst, freelance writer and policy wonk specializing in renewable energy and energy efficiency. He manages green stock market portfolios and promotes clean energy by testifying before legislators and regulators on energy policy. He writes articles about investing in clean energy for AltEnergyStocks.com and about energy policy and economics on "Clean Energy Wonk." He is a Chartered Financial Analyst (CFA) charterholder, and has a Ph.D. in mathematics from Purdue University, where he wrote his thesis on complex dynamics, a branch of chaos theory. His study of chaos theory led to his conviction that knowing the limits of our ability to predict is much more important than predictions themselves, a lesson he applies to both climate science and the financial markets.

 DAVID KOROWICZ is a physicist and human systems ecologist. He is a member of Feasta's executive committee and works as an independent consultant. He is on the board of Comhar, Ireland's Sustainable Development Council. He circulated *Tipping Point: Near-Term Systemic Implications of a Peak in Global Oil Production* in early 2010. His interests include systemic risk, risk management and emergency planning. He owns an English-language bookshop in Kyrgyzstan but lives in Dublin.

 LAURENCE MATTHEWS is a mathematician who has worked as a university lecturer and in the transport industry where he carried out consultancy work on five continents. For several years he has lectured and campaigned on the psychology of climate change, and has given evidence to the Environment Select Committee of the House of Commons. He is currently Chair of Cap and Share UK, an NGO promoting Cap & Share in Britain. He lives on the English-Welsh border near Hay-on-Wye.

 LUCY MCANDREW is a doctoral research student at NUI Galway. Her area of interest is environmental ethics and particularly the notion of respect as a concept around which a broad ethic, which would include an environmental ethic, could be built. She worked as a Voluntary Service Overseas volunteer in Sudan, Indonesia and Kenya and as a research assistant to Professor Barbara Harrell-Bond, founder of Oxford University's Refugee Studies Programme. She lives with her husband and children in Erris, Co. Mayo.

 KENNETH MULDER is Farm Manager and Research Associate at Green Mountain College in Poultney, Vermont. He has a PhD in ecological economics from the Gund Institute for Ecological Economics at the University of Vermont and has published several articles on establishing metrics for energy harvesting technologies. His current work is focused on the energy efficiency of human- and oxen-powered agriculture systems.

 DMITRY ORLOV is the author of the award-winning book *Reinventing Collapse: The Soviet Example and American Prospects*. Born in Russia, he moved to the US while a teenager, and traveled back repeatedly to observe the Soviet collapse during the late eighties and mid-nineties. He is an engineer who has worked in many fields, including high-energy physics research, e-commerce and internet security. He has recently been experimenting with off-grid living and renewable energy by giving up his house and car. Instead, he has been living on a sailboat, sailing it up and down the Eastern Seaboard, and commuting by bicycle. He believes that, given appropriate technology, we can greatly reduce personal resource consumption while remaining perfectly civilized.

EMER O'SIOCHRU is a qualified architect and valuation surveyor. She was a founder of Feasta and serves on its executive committee. She is director of EOS Future Design which designs and develops sustainable systems and settlements. She also manages the Feasta-led Smart Tax Network which is funded by the Irish Department of the Environment, Heritage and Local Government to develop tax policies in areas related to the environment. She lives in Dublin.

DAVIE PHILIP has over 12 years' experience managing events and projects in the "sustainability" sector in Ireland. He was a founding member of both Feasta and Sustainable Projects Ireland Ltd., the company behind the eco-village project in Cloughjordan, Co. Tipperary, where he now lives. In 2000 he set up the Sustainable Ireland Cooperative with Ben Whelan, which trades as Cultivate. With Cultivate he organizes networking and learning events including the annual Convergence sustainable living festival. He has produced a number of educational programs including *Tipping the Balance*, a CD-ROM learning resource exploring the UN Millennium Development Goals; and *The Little Earth Show*, a four-part radio drama for Feasta. He directed *The Powerdown Show*, a 10-part TV show, and has developed "Community Powerdown: Training for Leadership, Livelihoods and Local Resilience," a course designed to help communities respond to oil depletion and climate change. He is currently the coordinator of Transition Ireland and Northern Ireland and sits on the board of SEAI, the Sustainable Energy Authority of Ireland.

JAMES PIKE is an architect and was a founder partner in Delany Mac Veigh and Pike, which was set up in 1964. This practice evolved into O'Mahony Pike in 1992. He has played a continuing role in the Royal Institute of the Architects of Ireland since the 1960s and was its president in 2006–7. He is currently Chairman of the Irish Architecture Foundation and a founding member of the Urban Forum. He contributes to many urban design projects in his practice and has promoted research projects on sustainability issues with the Dublin Institute of Technology and University College Dublin. He has played a major role in several publications including *Dublin City in Crisis: New Housing and New Housing in Context*. He lives in Dublin.

Mark Rutledge has spent 20 years working with a number of global healthcare companies and is currently European Supply Chain Director with a major healthcare company. He has a BSc from the National University of Ireland, Maynooth, and gained a MSc in environmental science from University College Dublin in 2007. His final thesis is centered on aspects of the carbon cycle, central to any discussion on climate change. He has been Country Director of The Ecology Foundation and a consultant to the Dáil parliamentary committee on Climate Change and Energy Security. He has served on the Feasta executive committee and with a number of other NGOs involved in environment and climate change. He currently works in Galway during the week and returns home to Dublin at weekends.

 Anne B. Ryan is currently a lecturer at the Department of Adult and Community Education, at the National University of Ireland, Maynooth. Her research and teaching interests include deep security, citizen-leadership, morality and identity. She has been researching, writing and conducting workshops about the philosophy of "enough" for many years. Her books include *Enough is Plenty: Public and Private Policies for the 21st Century* (2009), *Feminist Ways of Knowing* (2001) and *Balancing Your Life* (2002). She is a Feasta Trustee and lives in Celbridge, Co. Kildare.

 Eamon Ryan holds a commerce degree from University College Dublin. Before entering politics, he set up and ran two businesses, Irish Cycling Safaris and Belfield Bike shop. He first became involved in politics in 1998 when he was co-opted to Dublin City Council. Before his election to the Dáil in 2002 he was an active member and chairman of the Dublin Cycling Campaign and served on the Advisory Committee of the Dublin Transport Office. Prior to his appointment as Minister for Communications, Energy and Natural Resources when the coalition government was formed in 2007 he was the Green Party spokesperson for Transport and Enterprise, Trade and Employment and opposition convenor on the Joint Oireachtas Committee for Communication, Marine and Natural Resources. He is married to the writer Victoria White and they have four young children.

JOHN SHARRY trained as a scientist, social worker and psychotherapist. He is Director of the Parents Plus Charity and a weekly columnist for *The Irish Times*. He is the author of ten books in counseling and mental health including three best-selling positive psychology books and seven popular self-help books for parents and families. His writing has been translated into eight languages including Spanish, Japanese, Chinese and Arabic. He is particular interested in how a psychological perspective is crucial in understanding how people will respond to the current peak oil/climate change crises. His website is solutiontalk.ie. He lives in Dublin.

DAN SULLIVAN has focused on reconciling the views of left and right since he was ten and says he has arrived at a perspective remarkably similar to that of classical liberals and early progressives. He has been researching ramifications of land value tax since 1978 and has led successful efforts to get shifts to land value tax in Pittsburgh, where he lives, and in other Pennsylvania cities. He is currently the director of education of Saving Communities, a Pittsburgh-based NGO, and is an adviser to the Council of Georgist Organizations, an umbrella group for land value tax educators and advocates.

CHRIS VERNON holds masters degrees in computational physics and earth system science, has studied energy systems and environmental decision making and is currently working toward a PhD in glaciology focusing on the Greenland ice sheet. He has a decade's engineering experience in the field of cellular telecoms, specializing in radio network architecture and off-grid power systems in emerging markets. He is also a Trustee at the Centre for Sustainable Energy and a European editor of The Oil Drum, a popular weblog studying energy security and policy and regularly speaks on energy security. To get away from the computer he competes in triathlon events. He lives in Bristol.

CAROLINE WHYTE grew up in Belfast and Dublin and studied philosophy at Trinity College Dublin. Her involvement with Feasta began in 2002 while she was living in the western United States. She collaborated with Richard Douthwaite on an online update of his book *Short Circuit: Strengthening Local Economies in an Unstable World*, and she has been managing the Feasta website since 2003. She studied ecological economics at Mälardalen University in Sweden in 2005–6, writing a master's thesis on the relationship between central banking and sustainability. She lives in a disused quarry in central France.

Index

If you have enjoyed *Fleeing Vesuvius,*
you might also enjoy other

BOOKS TO BUILD A NEW SOCIETY

Our books provide positive solutions for people who want to
make a difference. We specialize in:

**Sustainable Living • Green Building • Peak Oil
Renewable Energy • Environment & Economy
Natural Building & Appropriate Technology
Progressive Leadership • Resistance and Community
Educational & Parenting Resources**

New Society Publishers

ENVIRONMENTAL BENEFITS STATEMENT

New Society Publishers has chosen to produce this book on recycled paper made
with **100% post consumer waste,** processed chlorine free, and old growth free.
For every 5,000 books printed, New Society saves the following resources:[1]

24	Trees
2,141	Pounds of Solid Waste
2,356	Gallons of Water
3,073	Kilowatt Hours of Electricity
3,893	Pounds of Greenhouse Gases
17	Pounds of HAPs, VOCs, and AOX Combined
6	Cubic Yards of Landfill Space

[1]Environmental benefits are calculated based on research done by the Environmental Defense
Fund and other members of the Paper Task Force who study the environmental impacts of the
paper industry.

For a full list of NSP's titles, please call 1-800-567-6772 *or check out our website* at:
www.newsociety.com

NEW SOCIETY PUBLISHERS